THE EXPRESSION OF THE EMOTIONS
IN MAN AND ANIMALS

CHARLES DARWIN was born in Shrewsbury in 1809, the son of a doctor, and grandson of both Erasmus Darwin and of the industrialist Josiah Wedgwood. He entered Edinburgh University in 1825, where he studied medicine before transferring, in 1827, to Christ's College Cambridge. In 1831, Darwin embarked on the *Beagle*, bound for South America. He returned in 1836, and in 1839 published his *Journal of Researches into the Geology and Natural History of the various countries visited by H.M.S. Beagle*. His great work, *On the Origin of Species by Means of Natural Selection*, was published on 24 November 1859. It was an immediate success: the first edition of 1,250 copies sold out the same day. In *The Descent of Man, and Selection in Relation to Sex* (1871) Darwin laid out his theory of sexual selection arguing that human beings had evolved from higher primates. A year later, *The Expression of the Emotions in Man and Animals* was published. Then there followed *The Effects of Cross and Self Fertilization of Vegetable Mould Through the Action of Worms* (1881). He died in 1882 from a heart attack and was buried in Westminster Abbey.

PAUL EKMAN is Professor of Psychology at the University of California at San Francisco. He is editor of *Darwin and Facial Expression* and *The Nature of Emotion* and author of *Telling Lies: Clues to Deceit in the Marketplace, Politics and Marriage*.

More from the reviews:

'Interesting and compulsive... For long enough, he was the only scientist to ask why expressions occur in a particular form, surely because it related to his larger evolutionary theories. This is also why he had no hesitation in writing what he regarded as an emotional life of animals in an enchanting and wonderfully readable style. This publication of a forgotten masterpiece is provocatively relevant, surprising and fresh.'

CARL MACDOUGALL, *Scotland on Sunday*

This is a newly discovered portrait of Darwin by the London photographer Herbert Rose Barraud. It was taken in 1881, nine years after *Expression* was published, just a year before Darwin died, and is believed to be his last portrait. The original photograph is now in the Huntington Library in San Marino, California. A copy was published in *Scientific American*, November 1995 issue.

Charles Darwin

THE EXPRESSION
OF THE
EMOTIONS IN
MAN AND ANIMALS

THIRD EDITION

*With an Introduction, Afterword
and Commentaries by*
PAUL EKMAN

ESSAY ON THE HISTORY OF
THE ILLUSTRATIONS BY PHILIP PRODGER

OXFORD
UNIVERSITY PRESS

OXFORD
UNIVERSITY PRESS

Oxford   New York
Auckland   Bangkok   Buenos Aires
Cape Town   Chennai   Dar es Salaam   Delhi   Hong Kong   Istanbul
Karachi   Kolkata   Kuala Lumpur   Madrid   Melbourne   Mexico City   Mumbai
Nairobi   São Paulo   Shanghai   Singapore   Taipei   Tokyo   Toronto

First published in Great Britian in 1872 by John Murray
Second Edition published in 1889

Third Edition published by Oxford University Press 1998

Introduction, Afterword, and Commentaries Copyright © Paul Ekman 1998
Appendix Three, Four, and Five Copyright © Philip Prodger 1998

Published by Oxford University Press, Inc.
198 Madison Avenue, New York, New York, 10016
http://www.oup-usa.org

Oxford is a registered trademark of Oxford University Press

Library of Congress Cataloging-in-Publication Data

Darwin, Charles, 1809-1882.
The expression of the emotions in man and animals / Charles Darwin
With an introduction, afterword, and commentaries by Paul Erkman.
3rd ed.
p. cm.
Includes bibliographical references and index.
ISBN 0-19-515806-7
1. Emotions. 2. Expression. 3. Facial expression.
4. Psychology, Comparative.
I. Erkman, Paul.
II. Title.

QP401.D3 1996 97-36434
152.4--dc21

1 3 5 7 9 8 6 4 2

TABLE OF CONTENTS

In the first edition the following note appeared beneath the listing of Plates:

N.B. Several of the figures in these seven Heliotype Plates have been reproduced from photographs, instead of from the original negatives; and they are in consequence somewhat indistinct. Nevertheless they are faithful copies, and are much superior for my purpose to any drawing, however carefully executed.

Appendix V, Concordance of Illustrations, provides information about where each illustration appeared in the First Edition, as well as information about the orientation of the illustrations, the maker of each one and the medium employed.

ACKNOWLEDGMENTS

I am grateful to my editor at HarperCollins, Philip Gwyn Jones, for suggesting that I write an introduction for a new edition of this book, and for his continued enthusiasm when the undertaking grew far beyond what he originally had in mind. I am grateful also to Toby Mundy, my other editor at HarperCollins, for his patience and extraordinary commitment to this project. I am deeply indebted to Helena Cronin, at the London School of Economics, who provided encouragement, challenges, help, introductions to Darwin scholars, and many other kind offices when I began work during the spring of 1995 while on sabbatical in London. I thank the University of California for providing me with that sabbatical, and the [US] National Institute of Mental Health, whose support for nearly forty years has been a *sine qua non* [Research Scientist Award, MH06092].

I had help from many people working in the manuscript room of Cambridge University Library. Especially helpful and patient were Godfrey Waller, the superintendent, and Joy Harvey from the Darwin Papers Project. Jon Topham, the former Director of that project, gave me some useful leads. I had the good fortune to meet Phillip Prodger, when I discovered that most of the Darwin archival material I wanted had been checked out to him. I was amazed that anyone else was examining the illustrations relevant to *Expression*. Phillip has been a great help on many issues; his scholarship can be seen in the Appendices he wrote for this book. I thank Robert Hinde for being my host at St John's College during one of my stays in Cambridge, and for stimulating conversation about the nature of expression. Thanks also to John Maynard Smith, W. John Smith, and Don Symons for encouragement on this project.

A number of Darwin scholars kindly agreed to read the introduction, afterword and commentaries: Janet Browne, Michael Ghiselin, and Richard Burkhardt. William Irwin, Harriet Oster, Karl Heider and Paul Kaufman offered many suggestions about clarifying my meaning. Nancy Etcoff and Helena Cronin had the interest and forbearance to read my manuscripts twice, and were willing to read selected portions another time! My wife, Mary Ann Mason, also read what I wrote more than once and encouraged me to tell more of the story in the Afterword. I thank also Joan Bossert, my editor at Oxford, for her very many helpful suggestions which improved my writing.

Wanda Matsubayashi, who has been providing me with secretarial help for twenty years, was once again crucial in bringing my work to completion: the editing of the Darwin text, inserting new material, moving illustrations and footnotes, was a formidable task.

I thank Harriet Oster and Véronique Haynal for providing translations from French, and Father Moses M. Nagy from Latin.

PAUL EKMAN
San Francisco
October 1996

LIST OF ILLUSTRATIONS

FIGURES

xi

PREFACE TO
THE THIRD EDITION

PAUL EKMAN

This is the most complete edition of *The Expression of the Emotions in Man and Animals* ever published. The first edition was originally published in 1872. The second edition of *Expression* (like Darwin, I shall use just this one word to refer to the book), was edited by his son Francis. It included revisions and new material which Charles had expected to see in a second edition, but his publisher, John Murray, would not bring out a second edition until all the copies of the first were sold. After an amazingly large initial sale – 9,000 in the first four months – sales slackened and correspondence shows that neither Darwin nor his publisher could understand why. My hunch is that everyone in England who wanted a copy bought one in those initial months, for it was a well-publicized book about a popular topic, written by a famous author, appearing just one year after *Descent of Man*.*[1]

The second edition appeared in 1889, seven years after Charles Darwin died. There have been many subsequent reprints of *Expression*, in English and in other languages, but these were of the first not the second edition, even though Francis Darwin made clear in his Preface that the second edition contained changes his father had wanted.† As far as I can tell, the second edition is virtually unknown, although it is listed in a compendium of

---

* Footnotes which are technical or which simply provide the source for the text are at the end of the book, and are indicated by number. Footnotes which readers may find interesting as they are reading the book are provided at the bottom of the page, as is this one.

† The only edition generally available in English today was published by the University of Chicago in 1965. It is a facsimile, but not of the original printing

xiii

Darwin's publications.[2] (A copy of the second edition is available in the Pickering and Chatto edition of the *Works of Darwin*, edited by Barrett and Freeman, although it is very expensive.) Some of the reprints of the first edition have included material chosen by the editor, not by Darwin.

This third book can be considered definitive because it contains the changes that Charles Darwin had wanted but which his son did not include in the second edition. It has more of Darwin's text and more of his illustrations than any prior edition. Based on Darwin's correspondence with his publisher, his letters to others, and his notes in his own copy of *Expression* in the archives at the Cambridge University Library manuscript room, I believe this edition is as Darwin would have wanted it to be. He had revised a few passages in response to some critical reviews, and wanted to include further evidence from many people who wrote to him telling him of other examples of what he had written about. Checking Charles Darwin's own copy of *Expression*, in which he had noted all the changes he wanted to make in a second edition, against the second edition that Francis Darwin produced, I found that Francis left out a few of the changes his father wanted. I have restored them. Although they are minor, I can see no reason to disregard what appear to be Charles Darwin's instructions. (Appendix II lists the differences in the body of the text between the first and second editions.)

In the second edition Francis Darwin published the new material as footnotes, enclosed in brackets to distinguish them from the footnotes for the first edition. For the most part, these are additions his father had indicated he wanted, but Francis also added a few bits of information on his own initiative and did not distinguish these from what his father had wanted. The only way I could tell them apart is by the date that was sometimes inserted with these notes. Those after Charles Darwin's death in 1882 were presumably written by Francis.

---

of the first edition. D. Appleton and Company, Darwin's original American publisher, reset the first edition, and it is a facsimile of the second printing of the 1897 Appleton version.[3]

In the second edition the bottoms of the pages are quite cluttered, since they contain both the first and second edition footnotes. Many of these only contain references to literature now more than a hundred years old, which most readers will not want to check as they read what Darwin wrote. I have moved the reference material from both editions to the end of the book; second edition references can be distinguished because they are in brackets. A number of typographical errors were detected in the second edition, some repeating errors in the first edition and some new mistakes. I hope they have now been corrected.[4]

I have also taken the liberty of including other information relevant to the book. For example, in Chapter XI Darwin mentions that the expression of guilt on the face of his son, then two years and seven months . . . led to the detection of his little crime [p. 261]. Darwin did not tell us what the 'crime' was, or even the sex of his child. I thought it would be not only interesting but important to find out. Readers who knew more about the incident would be better able to judge what emotion that child may have been feeling. I had good luck. Darwin kept a notebook recording his observations of his children. Looking up his notes on his first child, William, for that time period I found a complete and charming description of the crime which I included in Chapter XI (see pp. 261–2).[5]

There are many observations and explanations in *Expression* that current scientific knowledge confirms were correct; others we now know were completely wrong; and a few about which scientists continue to argue! In the *Afterword* I discuss current thinking about one of the most important issues raised by Darwin – the universality of facial expression. There are some matters more specifically tied to Darwin's text which I thought the reader should not wait until the end to know about, for these I have written *Commentaries* within *Expression*, clearly marked off to distinguish them from Darwin's words. Following Darwin's example, I sought to have included in these commentaries the ideas of many other scientists working on these issues which Darwin raised: Linda Camras, Suzanne Chevalier-Skolnikoff, Roger Crumley, R. Andrew Cuthbertson, Richard Davidson,

Daniel G. Freedman, David Heiden, Jerome Kagan, Dacher Keltner, Eric Klinghammer, Robert Levenson, William Mason, Harriet Oster, Sue Parker, Stephen Porges, Phillip Prodger, Willibald Ruch, Klaus Scherer, Amotz Zahavi, and Philip Zimbardo. Sometimes I have quoted directly from what they wrote to me; at others, I have paraphrased them. I also include at the end of *Expression* an extraordinary obituary of Charles Darwin written by Thomas Huxley for the journal *Nature* (Appendix 1).

Darwin was one of the first scientists to publish a book with photographic illustrations, and there is a fascinating essay at the end of the book, written by the English art historian Phillip Prodger, about Darwin's use of illustrations (Appendix III).[6] This edition is also more complete in the illustrations than previous ones. While there were many photographs in the first and second editions of *Expression*, there were three instances when engravings made from a photograph were included rather than the photograph itself. I found out why in Darwin's correspondence.

On 10 May 1871 Darwin wrote to his publisher: 'I am very much perplexed what to decide about printed photographs and woodcuts. I believe the former would certainly be the best.' A few weeks later he wrote, '. . . some of my friends tell me that they think photos will be better than even facsimile engravings, in as much as the former are a guarantee of absolute accuracy.' But in August his publisher wrote back declaring that woodcuts or engravings would have to be used because the photographs were too expensive.[7] I found the original photographs in the Cambridge University Library archival material, and I have included two of them, which differ from the engravings in what they reveal.

In one of the engravings, Fig. 26, expressive lines in the forehead were added which do not appear in the original photograph. Fig. 27 shows the photograph from which the engraving was made, and the forehead is quite inexpressive. In another engraving, Fig. 28, some of the details apparent in the photograph (which I have added as Fig. 29) were eliminated in the engraving. Where those illustrations appear I comment on why Darwin may have made those changes. He occasionally discussed pictures which did not appear in the first or second editions, apparently to reduce costs. I have found and included them. Figures 19, 20 and Fig. 2 on Plate IV are photographs Darwin obtained from Duchenne, which he discussed on pages 151 and 228. Figure 21 is probably the Hogarth engraving which Darwin described on p. 238. For the first time the reader can see these four illustrations.

The left–right orientation of the photographs changed over the course of different printings of the first edition. The 1965 reprint edition published by the University of Chicago Press has the orientation correct, with just a few exceptions. In Appendix IV, Prodger and I explain how we determined what Darwin intended the left–right orientation should be.

It is easier for the reader, but more expensive for the publisher, if the photographs appear near or next to the paragraphs that describe them. This was not done in the first and second editions, nor in the reprinted editions I have seen. Instead many photographs were collected onto a single page. The reader is sometimes required to go back and forth from the text to the illustrations, often many pages apart. In this edition the photographs appear near the words to which they belong. Because of this I have had to renumber some of the figures and plates, and this is indicated on the listing of illustrations at the beginning of the book.

Appendix V is a Concordance of Illustrations, which compares those that appeared in the most commonly printed prior edition with how and where the illustrations appear in this edition. Appendix VI simply lists the words that appeared in the Index to the First Edition.

P. E.
San Francisco, 1996

'I have no great quickness of apprehension or wit . . . my power to follow a long and purely abstract train of thought is very limited . . . [but] I am superior to the common run of men in noticing things which easily escape attention, and in observing them carefully.'

CHARLES DARWIN

PREFACE TO
THE SECOND EDITION

The first edition not having been exhausted during the lifetime of my father, he had no opportunity of publishing the material collected with a view to a second edition. This material, consisting of a mass of letters, extracts from and references to books, pamphlets and reviews, I have attempted to utilise in the present volume. I have also made some use of what has been written since the publication of the first edition, but my reading has been very far from complete.

A few corrections of the text have been made, in which I have followed the pencilled remarks in my father's copy of the book. The other additions are given as footnotes and are distinguished by being enclosed in square brackets.

FRANCIS DARWIN

Cambridge,
2 September, 1889

Unfortunately, Francis Darwin did not distinguish in the text which material was added on his own initiative, and which his father had indicated he wanted added for a new edition. Both are contained in bracketed footnotes at the bottom of the relevant pages. As far as I can tell from checking Charles Darwin's copy of *Expression* (which contains notes for changes he wanted) and other sources, most of the bracketed material was written or selected by Charles Darwin.

INTRODUCTION
TO THE THIRD EDITION

PAUL EKMAN

In its wealth of fascinating observations about human and animal expressions this extraordinary book is unparalleled even today, more than one hundred years after it was written. Darwin illuminates not only our expressions, but those of cats, dogs, horses and many other animals. He noticed how we often purse our lips when we are concentrating on doing or remembering something; how in anger we tighten the muscle around our eyes and expose our canine teeth; and how we open our mouths when we listen intently. We want to touch with our faces those we love; we can bite affectionately – not only humans do this; so do dogs and cats. Pleasure is demonstrated in quite different ways in our domesticated animals, Darwin reminds us: cats purr and rub against us, while dogs lick us and wag their tails. In anger that tail acts quite differently in dogs, cats and horses. These are just a small sample of the fascinating observations Darwin describes in each chapter.

Darwin was more than just a close and careful observer, he was an explainer. For each and every expression, Darwin asks and answers the question of why a particular movement, rather than some other, occurs with a particular emotion. Why do we purse rather than press our lips when we concentrate? Why do we bite rather than lick when we feel affectionate? He tells us why just the inner corners of our brows, rather than the entire brow, are pulled up when we feel sorrow. He tells us why we blush with embarrassment instead of our skin becoming pale. For this emotion – embarrassment – Darwin provides more than an explanation for how it is expressed, he gives us a penetrating analysis of the emotion itself. Can we become embarrassed when we are totally alone or is this a uniquely social emotion? Are all emotions social or can we feel anger, fear, sadness, and enjoyment when we are alone as well as when we are with others?

We find in this book Darwin's answers not only to these intriguing questions but to much grander ones as well. A fundamental question is whether we *learn* which expressions to make when we are angry, sad or happy, or whether such 'knowledge' is innate. Are expressions, like the words we speak, different in every language, or are they the same for all people, no matter who those people are, where they live, the culture they grow up in or the language they speak? What about the head nods and shakes we use to say 'yes' and 'no', and the shrug for 'I don't know'? Are they also universal, or are they body language, different in each dialect group? Darwin argues that our expressions of emotion are universal (that is, innate not learned) and the product of our evolution. Neither our expressions nor our emotions are unique to human beings; other animals have some of the same emotions, and some of the expressions shown by animals resemble our own.

The distinction between emotional expressions and gestures has been incorporated in current work on non-verbal communication. While gestures can refer to nearly anything – thoughts, plans, actions, wishes, fantasies, and so forth – the expressions pertain simply to the emotions. Expressions typically involve the face and the voice and, to a much lesser extent, body movement or posture. Darwin focused most on facial expressions, although he gave some attention to other expressions.* Gestures typically are shown in hand movements, although a few involve facial movement. Darwin recognized that gestures are not universal, but are socially learned conventions, varying as language does from one locale to another. But he noted a few exceptions: the

---

* Most research on expression since Darwin has also focused on the face, not the voice. Recently scientists have made progress in identifying the vocal expressions of emotion. See especially the work of the German psychologist Klaus Scherer.[1]

shrug, for example. While it does not occur in every culture, it is used in so many places that it is hard not to think it is the product of our evolution. Darwin offers an explanation for these nearly universal gestures.

For most of the century after Darwin wrote about expression, his views were rejected or simply ignored. The intellectual and scientific world was dominated by those who saw culture as determining every important aspect of our behaviour. As influential an anthropologist as Margaret Mead[2] claimed that facial expressions differ from culture to culture as much as language, customs, attitudes and values. We may all have the same facial muscles, but they combine to form different expressions of emotion in each culture. Cultural relativists, such as Mead, claimed that the same expression signifies different emotions in different cultures and some expressions, which might be unique to one culture, might never be shown in any other. So a smile could signify anger in one culture, joy in another, sadness in yet another, and there might be no smile in still another. Just as there are different words for happiness in each language, there would be a different expression for happiness. A few scientists went so far as to claim that the very idea of emotions was an invention of Western culture. Emotions are a fiction (they said) – an explanatory device used in some cultures to explain what they do; emotions have no biological or psychological reality.

Nearly all those who opposed Darwin's view of emotional expression (the 'nurture-not-nature' advocates) argued from the examples or reports of an outside observer in a strange culture. It is easy to be misled in such a situation, to become the victim of preconceptions. In the Afterword I explain more about the problems encountered when a scientist works in a foreign culture, and of my experience working in Papua New Guinea.

Although much of the time Darwin, too, relied upon anecdotal examples, he did attempt to obtain more systematic evidence on the question of universality. He wrote to people, primarily British colonialists, who had travelled or lived in different cultures, asking if they had seen a particular expression when someone felt a particular emotion. In Britain he showed photographs of expressions to people to find out if they agreed about the emotion shown in each expression. Darwin included some of those pictures in his book, allowing readers to participate in the experiment. We can see whether the message we get from each expression fits with the results Darwin got from his informants. In this same spirit I have included in the Afterword a few of the pictures I took of an isolated, stone-age people in Papua New Guinea thirty years ago. Readers can judge for themselves whether or not they can understand the expressions of a people from a culture enormously different from their own.

It is only in the last thirty years that systematic research using quantitative methods has tested Darwin's ideas about universality. I was one of the first to do such research, and I expected I would prove Darwin wrong. My findings caused me and many other social and behavioral scientists to change their mind. While most now accept the evidence for universality, there are still a few vocal critics who argue that emotional expressions are culture-specific, like language, or don't exist at all. In the Afterword I describe the history of this argument, the reasons why it became so impassioned, and the evidence, showing that the issues Darwin raised are alive and relevant today.

Darwin asked a question about emotional expression that few other scientists asked in his own time or since. Most scientists studying emotion and expression address the 'what', 'how' or 'when' question. *What* expressions are shown for each emotion? *How* are they produced? *When* do they occur? Darwin also deals with these, but he was one of the first, and for a long time the only scientist, to ask the 'why' question: *Why* do expressions occur in a particular form?

There is still argument about the validity of the three principles Darwin proposed to answer the *Why* question; that is, why particular expressions are made for particular emotions. He called the first principle 'serviceable habits', by which he meant that some expressions originated in movements useful to our progenitors, similar to what ethologists today call 'intention movements'. His second principle of 'antithesis' claimed that some expressions were selected because they look different from expressions of opposite emotions. We shrug our shoulders when we feel helpless because it is the opposite of the movements of the arms, shoulders and hands made when we are asserting ourselves aggressively. No one knows if Darwin was right, but it is an ingenious explanation, and better than any other offered for why we shrug when we feel helpless.

His third principle, 'the direct action of the nervous system', was vague, but little was then known about brain activity relevant to emotion. In a letter to a reviewer who had criticized him for not being clear about this principle, Darwin acknowledged the criticism 'was perfectly just' (see commentary, p. 87). Chapter III, about this principle, it is full of fascinating observations about emotion, expression and human nature. For example, Darwin notes how limits on our conscious attention can distract us from feeling pain; how some facial muscles are less subject to our control and betray our true feelings despite our efforts to conceal them; and he provides an amazingly lucid and accurate description of the stages of grief.

Darwin focused his attention on the 'why' question because of its relevance to a much larger issue central to his evolutionary theory: the continuity of species. His purpose was to show, through the study of expression, that humans are not a separate divinely created species. In 1806, one of the leading authorities on expression of the time, Sir Charles Bell, had written an influential book arguing precisely the opposite.* Janet Browne,[4] an English historian and the most recent biographer of Darwin, wrote that Bell '. . . had insisted there were muscles in the human face without analog in the animal kingdom, designed by the Creator for the display of specifically human emotions'. Darwin's book would prove that neither our expressions nor our facial musculature are unique; they are as much the product of our evolution as internal physiology.[5] 'The same principles he

---

* Bell wrote, '. . . the most remarkable muscle in the human face is the corrugator supercilii which knits the eyebrows with an enigmatic effect which *unaccountably, but irresistibly conveys the idea of mind*' [p. 139]. In his copy of Bell's book, Darwin underlined that line and wrote the note, 'monkey here? . . . I have seen well developed in monkeys . . . I suspect he never dissected monkey.'[3]

expounded to explain the origin of human expression – why we make one expression and not another on our face for a given emotion – explain facial expressions, vocalizations, and body movements in other animals. If he convinces us that the same principles explain all primate expressions, we would have to accept the continuity of species, a cornerstone of his evolutionary explanation of the origin of our species. American historian Sandra Herbert put it this way: 'If he could show that man and at least some other animals possessed a similar system of emotional expression, he could substantiate his claim that there existed a gradation among mental phenomena between man and animal.'[6]

The continuity of species is today taken for granted by biologists and nearly all social scientists – but not the general public. A recent public opinion poll in the United States posed this question:

> After I read off three statements, please tell me which one comes closest to describing your views about the origin and development of man:
> * God created man pretty much in his present form at one time within the last 10,000 years. [46 *percent endorsed this view*]
> * Man has developed over millions of years from less advanced forms of life. God had no part in the process. [9 *percent endorsed this view*]
> * Man has developed over millions of years from less advanced forms of life, but God guided this process, including man's creation. [40 *percent endorsed this view*]
> [5 *percent were not certain which view to endorse*][7]

More than one hundred years after Darwin, nearly half those questioned reject evolution totally, which is accepted as the sole explanation of our origin by only nine percent of the people polled. In his time, not only did the general populace believe in Creation, so did nearly all scientists. Darwin was keenly aware that his *Origin of Species*, published thirteen years before *Expression* in 1859, was a direct challenge to prevailing views. It caused great controversy, was rejected by orthodox theologians, accepted enthusiastically by many general readers and to Darwin's disappointment, attacked by many in the scientific community.[8]

The last grand issue *Expression* addressed was whether human beings descended from common progenitors (monogenist), or whether the groups in different geographical locales might have descended from different animal progenitors (polygenist). Racists who considered Africans inferior to Europeans had proposed that they were descended from different ancestors, one less developed than the other. Darwin argued for a single ancestor; that we are one species that came from common progenitors. If expressions were indeed universal, if they could be explained by the same principles for all people, that would add further evidence of common descent. While Darwin regarded his evidence of universality as support for his evolutionary explanation of the origin of our species, a creationist could argue otherwise. If we are all descended from Adam, we would indeed all have the same expressions of emotion. The relevance of expressions to the argument against the creationists rests not on their universality but on showing that these expressions are not unique to man, that the principles which explain why expressions are made apply to species other than humans.

Darwin wrote *Expression* in a very short time, starting two days after he corrected the page proofs of *Descent of Man* (published in 1871) and completing it in four months, before he compiled the sixth and last edition of *Origin of Species*. But he began developing his ideas about expression many years before *Origin* was first published. 'My first child was born on December 27th, 1839, and I at once commenced to make notes on the first dawn of the various expressions which he exhibited, for I felt convinced, even at this early period, that the most complex and fine shades of expression must all have had gradual and natural origin.'[9]

Darwin may have not been entirely candid in describing how he developed his three principles for explaining expressions. American psychologist Howard Gruber wrote that Darwin '. . . described himself as having conformed to the accepted canons of inductive science, withholding larger judgments until justified by a fullness of observation: [Darwin wrote] "I arrived, however, at these three Principles only at the close of my observations." (*Expression*, Chapter 1, p. 33.) Actually, they all occur in the M and N notebooks, written in 1838–39. [Darwin defended] his unpopular views by suggesting that he had been driven to them by a mass of unassailable evidence, rather than the less acceptable reality that much of his evidence had been indeed patiently assembled, but only after his views were quite well developed.'[10] Herbert gives a similar account: '. . . the accepted scientific posture in the 1830s was not that of the theorist. Thus the theoretical Darwin of the late 1830s was forced to mask his own interest under the guise of being a more ordinary practitioner of science than he indeed was.'[11]

Before Darwin, facial expression had been chiefly the concern of physiognomists, who maintained that character or personality was revealed by the static appearance of the face, the size and shape of the features, and their proportions.[12]* Darwin made extensive use of the writings of three physicians of his century, who were concerned with the anatomy of expression, and focused on emotion, although these men did not rule out the possibility of reading personality from physiognomy.

Duchenne de Boulogne, a French neurologist, published his pioneering research in 1862,[15] ten years before *Expression*. In it, he reported which muscles act to form some of the facial expressions. Darwin reprinted in *Expression* some of Duchenne's photographs, which he also showed to people, asking for their interpretation of them. The French anatomist Gratiolet's lectures on expression were published in 1865, and Bell's analysis of the musculature involved in expression had been published in 1806. Although, as I explained earlier, Darwin differed from Bell on the origin of facial expressions, he made use of Bell's descriptions of expression and praised many of his observations.

No one today pays much attention to Gratiolet, Bell, or even Duchenne; almost everyone now studying the facial expressions

---

* Such ideas are still found today in recent popular books.[13] I believe they persist because they contain a grain of truth. We do derive some correct impression about personality from facial expressions, but not from the static features. Seeing repeated expressions of sadness or elation or anger, we can, for example, infer that someone is melancholic, euphoric or hostile. We derive incorrect information as well; for example, the lips narrow in anger, so people with thin lips are often thought to be unfriendly, cruel or hostile.[14]

of emotion acknowledges that the field began with Darwin's *Expression*. But there is a puzzle to explain. *Expression* was not always so recognized; in fact until very recently the book had been studiously ignored. Yet it was a bestseller when it was published in England in 1872. Nine thousand copies were sold in the first four months. By the turn of the century it had also been published in the United States, the Netherlands, France, Germany, Italy and Russia. In Darwin's day every educated person knew of his work and revolutionary theory. By the time *Expression* was published, '. . . hardly a qualified biologist was left who had not become an evolutionist'.[16] Today scientist and layman alike know who Darwin is, but not his book on expression. Many biologists do not even know that Darwin wrote such a book; in psychology, sociology, and anthropology there were few references to *Expression* for a hundred years after it was published.

The puzzle is how a bestselling book, by a world-famous author, became virtually forgotten for ninety years. Why was it lost? How was it rediscovered? How could this happen to such an illustrious author, writing on an intriguing topic with such an enticing title – *The Expression of the Emotions in Man and Animals*? I think there are five factors that can explain this puzzle.*

Expression was criticized by many scientists because, in their view, Darwin was guilty of the sin of anthropomorphism – ascribing to animals what we humans feel and think. He did not simply describe the expressions shown by other animals, he wrote about their emotions. For example, he said that monkeys experienced pleasure, grief, vexation, jealousy, and so on. The American zoologist Michael Ghiselin believes that Darwin wrote about animals having emotions as a stylistic device, in part to make his points more readily understood.[17] But it was more than that; Darwin was convinced and tried to convince his readers that emotions and their expressions were not unique to humans.

---

* Phillip Prodger, the English art historian who has written appendices on Darwin's use of illustrations which appear at the end of the book, suggests a sixth factor. He thinks the book may have lost popularity because the illustrations were dated. He may be right, but I think readers today will find these illustrations interesting precisely because they are not modern.

Some students of animal behavior in this century were, until very recently, loath to describe what animals did in terms of emotions. It wasn't scientific. Instead they described only the animal's behavior, remaining silent on whether it represented or expressed an emotion. This is part of the same thinking that produced the behaviorist movement in psychology, which held that true scientists did not make inferences about things they did not directly observe. Thinking, planning and feeling were all banned from scientific study. Ghiselin described a scientist who thought that Darwin should not have written that a cat was 'in an affectionate mind' when rubbing against someone's leg; Darwin should have said the cat was engaging in 'cutaneous stimulation'.[18] Such behaviorism is now in steep decline. Thinking is once again a legitimate topic for scientific inquiry, and research on emotion is now one of the most active areas of psychological research.

There is disagreement today among those who study animal behavior about whether expressions should be considered signs of emotion, related to internal physiological changes. Some maintain that it is more useful to consider the expressions as simply communicative signals, and many studies have done that, describing only what animals do. (In the Afterword I explain why this is a false dichotomy. We don't have to choose whether an expression is part of an emotion or a communicative signal. In reality, it is both.) Other scientists have concluded that the evidence of signaling shows Darwin was correct to consider them signs of emotion. The American primatologist Suzanne Chevalier-Skolnikoff wrote: 'Through the examination of behavioral sequences and the interpretation of how the behavior functions, primatologists are fairly confident that the interpretation of the emotional nature of facial behavior in nonhuman primates is correct.'[19]

Those who maintain that animals have emotions do not agree about exactly how many different emotions they show; for that matter, those studying humans do not agree on the subject either. Most agree that humans manifest at least five distinct emotions: anger, fear, sadness, disgust and enjoyment; the argument is about how many more there might be. Many who study animal behavior describe fear in species ranging from rats to monkeys; play (enjoyment?) and aggression (anger?) are also commonly described in many animals. Just how many more some animals might experience, and how the experience, expression and physiology of an emotion, such as fear, might differ from one species to another, has yet to be clarified.

Among those who grant that animals have emotions, there is still uncertainty about whether animals can feel those emotions. Are animals – other than humans – actually aware of what they feel? Can they think about or anticipate the emotions they are likely to feel? Are words required for such an awareness and consideration of emotional feelings?[20]

This is not just an abstract or academic question. It has direct implications for one of the most heated moral debates in today's world. Darwin's argument for the continuity of species, and in particular his claim that animals have emotions, have provided fuel for the animal rights movement. If we grant that animals feel terror about impending pain, and distress and sadness when separated from their offspring or mates, if they not only feel these emotions but are aware of these feelings, it may become difficult to justify experiments on animals, caging them in zoos, using at least some of the present slaughter methods, and for some to decide whether or not animals should be eaten.

The second reason why *Expression* did not have the influence it deserved was Darwin's reliance on anecdotal rather than systematic data. While one can argue about the justification for Darwin's anthropomorphism, there is no disputing the fallibility of anecdotal information. It is dubious at best, good for illustrating, but not for rigorously testing an observation. The amount of behavior observed is too small, reported without much information about the full context in which it occurred, and without checks for the possible bias of the person who is making the observation.

Darwin was aware of the problems inherent in anecdotal data, and did place more confidence in a report which described the full circumstances in which behavior occurred. But he was limited primarily to information provided by others, since he was confined to his home by illness for most of the last forty-two years of his life, when he wrote all of his major books. He received information from many people with whom he corresponded, commissioned some photographs and obtained others, which he studied. (Janet Browne wrote to me: 'I think he would have used this "collecting" technique even if he was fit and well. This was his favored research method.') While he often dealt with faulty data, his unique strength was his use of so many different kinds of data to test his theory. He gathered observations from others about people in different cultures, infants, children, the insane, the blind, and a variety of animals. No one writing about emotional expression today has used such diverse sources.

A third possible reason why the book has been neglected is that Darwin explained the origin of some expressions by relying on an idea common in his day but now known to be false – that characteristics acquired in a person's lifetime can be inherited. The best known proponent of the theory of the inheritance of acquired characteristics was the French scientist Jean Baptiste de Lamarck, who was the first to use the word 'biology'. Lamarck maintained that evolutionary change occurred as a result of an animal's attempt to improve its situation. In his book *Zoological Philosophy* (1809) he described two 'laws' to explain how this happened. Organs, he said, are improved with repeated use, and deteriorate with disuse, and those improvements or deteriorations are incorporated into the hereditary material and passed on to the next generation. This came to be known as the inheritance of acquired characteristics, or use-inheritance.

Darwin scholars have argued about the extent to which Darwin accepted the inheritance of acquired characteristics,[21] but there is no doubt that he did rely upon it to explain the origin of many expressions. For example, he wrote: '. . . from what we know of inheritance, there is nothing improbable in the transmission of a habit to the offspring at an earlier age than that at which it was first acquired by the parents.' (p. 45). And again: 'Such habitual movements are often, or generally inherited.' (p. 54). Darwin did not understand how inheritance works. The American historian Carl Degler wrote: 'Like the great majority of natural scientists of the late nineteenth century, Darwin was ignorant of the principles of Mendelian genetics, even though Gregor Mendel's pathbreaking work had been published soon after the appearance of *The Origin of Species*. (Darwin's own copy of Mendel's paper on the basic principles of genetics was found in his library after his death with its pages still uncut.)* The scientific disproof of use-inheritance first appeared in the work of the German embryologist and committed Darwinian, August Weisman. Seven years after Darwin's death, Weisman showed that 'changes in an animal's body or behavior in its lifetime . . . [did not appear] in its offspring.'[23]

The fourth reason why *Expression* was ignored was that Darwin did not explain the origin of emotional expressions in terms of their communicative value. Today the focus is on what and how expressions communicate. Because Darwin did not deal with communication, his ideas seemed irrelevant to current thought, and many missed the wealth of information he provides that is actually directly relevant to communication. He could easily have described how expressions develop and are preserved because, over the course of evolution, one member of a species has been able to derive information about another from the expression observed, and perhaps also for inter-species communication. But Darwin did not do this. He avoided any discussion of how expressions communicate information until the very end of his book. In the last chapter he wrote one paragraph acknowledging that expressions have communicative value, but did not mention that this was relevant to their evolution.

Why did Darwin so conspicuously avoid dealing with the communicative value of these expressions? He must have considered this and decided not to take that course. We can only speculate

---

* When I visited Darwin's home I noted that after page 90 the pages were uncut in Darwin's copy of Karl Marx's *Das Kapital*, personally inscribed by Marx to Darwin. It is amusing to note that Marx did not think much of Darwin's writing style. Marx wrote in a letter: 'Darwin's book is very important and it suits me well that it supports the class struggle in history from the point of view of natural science. One has, of course, to put up with the crude English method of discourse.'[22]

that Darwin might have thought that if he dealt with communication he would weaken his challenge to the creationists. Remember that Sir Charles Bell had said expressions had been given to man by his Creator to communicate intimate feelings. Darwin may well have thought he could more effectively assault Bell by not dealing with communication at all. The American historian Richard Burkhardt Jr. wrote: '. . . in constructing his argument against the idea that special structures in man had been designed by the Creator for the purpose of non-verbal communication, Darwin appears to have overreacted . . .'[24]

The last reason why *Expression* has so long been ignored is probably the most important of all, and most central to its continuing importance, and neglect. This was Darwin's evidence that expressions are innate, that these signs of our emotions are the product of our evolution and are therefore part of our biology. This was completely incompatible with the reigning dogmas. Watson, the founder of behaviorism, rejected the notion that inheritance played any part in explaining our social behavior. He claimed that we need only consider what is learned to understand man. Learning, he said, is the only proper focus for psychology. The popularity of Watson's view may reflect the fact that it was harmonious with the democratic *Zeitgeist* – the hope that all men could be equal if their environments were equally benevolent. Equal opportunity would create men and women who were the same in all respects. Ghiselin wrote: 'Although it is easy to sympathize with such democratic zeal, its concealment of the truth has not been without its deleterious effects . . . Rejecting inheritance for metaphysical reasons served only to hinder the progress of psychology. And it is sobering to observe that democratic societies are every bit as prone to the kind of dogmatism that caused the Soviet Union to reject Mendelian inheritance and to embrace Lysenkoism because the latter, like the Watsonian notion, fitted in better with the prevailing creed.'*[25]

* Trofim Denisovich Lysenko (1898–1976) was a Ukrainian biologist and plant physiologist who rose to power in the Stalin era. He declared that the Mendelian theory of genetics, widely accepted outside the Soviet Union, was erroneous, and scientists who did not agree with him were discredited. In its place Lysenko

Anthropology had its own parallel to behaviorism: an insistence that culture completely determines social life, with amazing accounts of how even the most basic elements of how we mate, procreate, and bring up our children are totally constructed by culture and differ from one place to another. Relativism not universality was, and to a large extent still is, central to much of anthropology.[26] A number of anthropologists claimed there was no innate contribution to expression, no constants across cultures in any aspect of human facial expression.

Today most scientists reject such absolute relativism: nature and nurture both play a role in all human behavior. Emotions are both the product of our evolution, particularly their physiology and expression, and of what we have learned, especially our attempts to manage our emotions, our attitudes about our emotions and our representations of them verbally. There are still some who disagree – cultural relativists or social constructionists – but they no longer dominate scientific thinking. The intellectual climate has changed; it is now much more hospitable to Darwin's *Expression*.

Many, nearly simultaneous, factors combined to effect this change. It came about partly as a result of strong evidence, published in the late 1960s and early 1970s, that expressions do show universality. There was also an increasing disillusionment with the narrow confines of behaviorism and the emergence of cognitive science in psychology, which re-established the legitimacy of studying thoughts and ideas. If it was respectable to study scientifically phenomena which cannot be directly observed, it was not much of a further step for the study of emotions to become once again respectable. The rapid growth of behavioral genetics, and findings from studies of temperament, helped to

---

proposed that changes brought about in one generation could be inherited by the next generation. This use-inheritance, neo-Lamarckian theory was thought to be congenial to the Soviet dream that the society could completely construct the person, without genetic constraints. It was not until the end of the Khrushchev era in 1964 that the USSR rejoined the rest of the world in subscribing to Mendelian genetics, which does not agree that learned behavior can be passed on genetically.

bring nature back as a partner in the enterprise. The burst of knowledge about the brain, and the discoveries, one after another, of the embodiment of so many psychological characteristics was another factor. The Human Genome Project, and the continual unfolding of how many individual differences have a genetic basis, have changed the intellectual and scientific climate. Nurture is not being thrown out, but it is no longer the only determinant of human behavior.

In the past five years there has been a renaissance of interest in Darwin. Three biographies have been published, dozens of books for the layman about evolutionary theory have appeared, and the new field of evolutionary psychology, which embraces Darwinian thinking, has emerged. It is time to read *Expression* and benefit from its many insights to further understand the emotions in man and animals. It is time to learn from Darwin about the most intimate and private part of our lives – our emotions and their public display, our expressions.

Charles Darwin

THE EXPRESSION
OF THE
EMOTIONS IN
MAN AND ANIMALS

CONTENTS

3

INTRODUCTION
TO THE FIRST EDITION

BY CHARLES DARWIN

Many works have been written on expression,[1] but a greater number on physiognomy – that is, on the recognition of a character through the study of the permanent form of the features. With this latter subject I am not here concerned. The older treatises,[2] which I have consulted, have been of little or no service to me. The famous *Conférences*[3] of the painter Le Brun, published in 1667, is the best known ancient work, and contains some good remarks. Another somewhat old essay, namely, the *Discours*, delivered 1774–82, by the well-known Dutch anatomist Camper,[4] can hardly be considered as having made any marked advance in the subject. The following works, on the contrary, deserve the fullest consideration.

Sir Charles Bell, so illustrious for his discoveries in physiology, published in 1806 the first edition, and in 1844 the third edition of his *Anatomy and Philosophy of Expression*.[5] He may with justice be said, not only to have laid the foundations of the subject as a branch of science, but to have built up a noble structure. His work is in every way deeply interesting; it includes graphic description of the various emotions, and is admirably illustrated. It is generally admitted that his service consists chiefly in having shown the intimate relation which exists between the movements of expression and those of respiration. One of the most important points, small as it may at first appear, is that the muscles round the eyes are involuntarily contracted during violent expiratory efforts, in order to protect these delicate organs from the pressure of the blood. This fact, which has been fully investigated for me with the greatest kindness by Professor Donders of Utrecht, throws, as we shall hereafter see, a flood of light on several of the most important expressions of the human countenance. The merits of Sir C. Bell's work have been undervalued or quite ignored by several foreign writers, but have been fully admitted by some, for instance by M. Lemoine, who with great justice says: 'Le livre de Ch. Bell devrait être médité par quiconque essaye de faire parler le visage de l'homme, par les philosophes aussi bien que par les artistes, car, sous une apparence plus légère et sous le prétexte de l'esthétique, c'est un des plus beaux monuments de la science des rapports du physique et du moral.'[6] ['Charles Bell's book should be studied by all those – philosophers as well as artists – who are trying to give voice to the face of man, for beneath its superficial appearance and the pretext of aesthetics, this book is one of the most impressive monuments to scientific work on the relations between the physical and moral realms.']

Darwin does not tell us that he wrote this book to challenge Bell's claim that some of our facial muscles were given by God to express human emotions. In a letter to Alfred Russel Wallace in March 1867 Darwin wrote: 'I want, anyhow, to upset Sir C. Bell's view . . . that certain muscles have been given to man solely that he may reveal to other men his feelings.'[C1] Darwin chose his words more carefully in writing in his autobiography, 'During the summer of the following year, 1840, I read Sir C. Bell's admirable work on Expression, and this greatly increased the interest which I felt in the subject, though I could not at all agree with his belief that various muscles had been specially created for the sake of expression.'[C1b] Commenting on this matter Janet Browne wrote, 'If Darwin could demonstrate another, more practical purpose for such facial muscles, a purpose that clearly linked us to the rest of nature he would weaken Bell's and all other natural theologians' arguments and strengthen the case for expression as a product of evolution.'[C2] (I have discussed this in my Introduction.) Later in *Expression* Darwin describes his disagreement with some of Bell's more specific claims: that animals have more limited expressions than humans (p. 144), about which muscles are under voluntary control (p. 217), and that the frowning muscle (corrugator) is unique to humans (p. 219).

From reasons which will presently be assigned, Sir C. Bell did not attempt to follow out his views as far as they might have been carried. He does not try to explain why different muscles are brought into action under different emotions; why, for instance, the inner ends of the eyebrows are raised, and the corners of the mouth depressed, by a person suffering from grief or anxiety.

Darwin could make the same criticism of nearly all current studies of facial expression, which, like Bell, have not addressed this question. Darwin is one of the only scientists to ask the *why* question – why this particular facial expression for this emotion, rather than some other expression.

In 1807 M. Moreau edited an edition of Lavater on physiognomy,* in which he incorporated several of his own essays, containing excellent descriptions of the movement of the facial

* *L'Art de connaître les Hommes*, etc., by J. C. Lavater. The earliest edition of this work, referred to in the preface to the edition of 1820 in ten volumes, as containing the observations of M. Moreau, is said to have been published in 1807; and I have no doubt that this is correct, because the 'Notice sur Lavater' at the commencement of volume i is dated 13 April, 1806. In some bibliographical works, however, the date of 1805–9 is given; but it seems impossible that 1805 can be correct. Dr Duchenne remarks (*Mécanisme de la Physionomie Humaine*, 8vo edit., 1862, p. 5 and *Archives Générales de Médecine, Jan. et Fév.*, 1862 that M. Moreau '*a composé pour son ouvrage un article important*', etc., in the year 1805, and I find in volume i of the edition of 1820 passages bearing the dates of 12 December, 1805, and another, 5 January, 1806, besides that of 13 April, 1806, above referred to. In consequence of some of these passages having thus been *composed* in 1805, Dr Duchenne assigns to M. Moreau the priority over Sir C. Bell, whose work, as we have seen, was published in 1806. This is a very unusual manner of determining the priority of scienctic works; but such questions are of extremely little importance in comparison with their relative merits. The passages above quoted from M. Moreau and from Le Brun are taken in this and all other cases from the edition of 1820 of Lavater, vol. iv, p. 228, and vol. ix, p. 279.

muscles, together with many valuable remarks. He throws, however, very little light on the philosophy of the subject. For instance, M. Moreau, in speaking of the act of frowning, that is, of the contraction of the muscle called by French writers the *sourcilier* (*Corrugator supercilii*), remarks with truth: 'Cette action des sourciliers est un des symptômes les plus tranchés de l'expression des affections pénibles ou concentrées.' ['This action of the eyebrows is one of the most distinctive signs of painful or intense feelings.'] He then adds that these muscles, from their attachment and position are fitted 'à resserrer, à concentrer les principaux traits de la *face*, comme il convient dans toutes ces passions vraiment oppressives ou profondes, dans ces affections dont le sentiment semble porter l'organisation à revenir sur elle-même, à se contracter et à *s'amoindrir*, comme pour offrir moins de prise et de surface à des impressions redoubtables ou importunes'. ['To tighten up and focus the principal features of the *face*, as is characteristic of all passions truly oppressive or profound, of all feelings which seem to make the organism turn inward on itself, to contract and to *shrink*, as if to offer less grip, less surface to frightful or disturbing impressions.'] He who thinks that remarks of this kind throw any light on the meaning or origin of the different expressions, takes a very different view of the subject to what I do.

Lavater's claim that personality could be read from the size and shape of the facial features was very popular for fifty years or more before Darwin's time, and it almost aborted Darwin's career. He nearly missed the opportunity to join the voyage of the *Beagle* because the ship's captain, Robert Fitz-Roy, applying Lavater's ideas to Darwin's face, thought Darwin was not fit for a long sea voyage. Darwin mentioned this in his *Autobiography*: '. . . on becoming very intimate with Fitz-Roy, I heard that I had run a very narrow risk of being rejected, on account of the shape of my nose! He was an ardent disciple of Lavater, and was convinced that he could judge a man's character by the outline of his features; and he doubted whether anyone with my nose could possess sufficient energy and determination for the voyage. I think he was afterwards well-satisfied that my nose had spoken falsely.'[C3]

It is hard to conceive of what might have happened if Fitz-Roy had refused to allow the young Darwin to accompany him. In the introduction to Darwin's account of the voyage, Leonard Engel wrote, 'In its influence on modern man's outlook upon the world, no voyage since Columbus matches the voyage described in this book . . . It was the vast and changing panorama of life, both living and extinct, observed by Darwin during the *Beagle*'s cruise that set him on the road to *The Origin of Species*.'[C4]

In the above passage there is but a slight, if any, advance in the philosophy of the subject, beyond that reached by the painter Le Brun, who, in 1667, in describing the expression of fright, says: 'Le sourcilier qui est abaissé d'un côté et élevé de l'autre, fait voir que la partie élevée semble le vouloir joindre au cerveau pour le garantir du mal que l'âme aperçoit, et le côté qui est abaissé et qui paraît enflé, nous fait trouver dans cet état par les esprits qui viennent du cerveau en abondance, comme pour couvrir l'âme et la défendre du mal qu'elle craint; la bouche fort ouverte fait voir le saisissement du coeur, par le sang qui se retire vers lui, ce qui l'oblige, voulant respirer, à faire un effort qui est cause que la bouche s'ouvre extrêmement, et qui, lorsqu'il passe par les organes de la voix, forme un son qui n'est point articulé; que si les muscles et les veines paraissent enflés, ce n'est que par les esprits que le cerveau envoie en ces parties-là.' ['The eyebrow, which is lowered on one side and raised on the other, gives the impression that the raised part wants to attach itself to the brain, to protect it from the evil the soul perceives; and the side that is lowered, and which looks swollen, seems to be placed in that position by the phantoms that pour forth from the brain, as though to shield the soul and protect it from the evil it fears; the wide-open mouth manifests the shock to the heart caused by the blood flowing back to it, which forces it to work harder to draw a breath, which is why the mouth gapes widely open and why, when the breath passes through the larynx and speech organs, it emits an inarticulate sound; for if the muscles and the veins seem swollen, it is only through the actions of the phantoms the brain sends forth.'] I have thought the foregoing sentences worth quoting, as specimens of the surprising nonsense which has been written on the subject.^{C5}

The Physiology or Mechanism of Blushing, by Dr Burgess, appeared in 1839, and to this work I shall frequently refer in my thirteenth chapter.

In 1862 Dr Duchenne published two editions, in folio and octavo, of his *Mécanisme de la Physionomie Humaine*, in which he analyses by means of electricity, and illustrates by magnificent photographs, the movements of the facial muscles. He has generously permitted me to copy as many of his photographs as I desired. His works have been spoken lightly of, or quite passed over, by some of his countrymen. It is possible that Dr Duchenne may have exaggerated the importance of the contraction of single muscles in giving expression; for, owing to the intimate manner in which the muscles are connected, as may be seen in Henle's anatomical drawings[7] – the best I believe ever published – it is difficult to believe in their separate action. Nevertheless, it is manifest that Dr Duchenne clearly apprehended this and other sources of error, and as it is known that he was eminently successful in elucidating the physiology of the muscles of the hand by the aid of electricity, it is probable that he is generally in the right about the muscles of the face. In my opinion, Dr Duchenne has greatly advanced the subject by his treatment of it. No one has more carefully studied the contraction of each separate muscle, and the consequent furrows produced on the skin. He has also, and this is a very important service, shown which muscles are least under the separate control of the will. He enters very little into theoretical considerations, and seldom attempts to explain why certain muscles and not others contract under the influence of certain emotions.

Despite the credit Darwin gave to Duchenne here and later in this book, Duchenne's book soon went out of print; it was not translated into English, and his pioneering discoveries about facial expressions were ignored by nearly all scientists until 1982.[C6] Now there is an English language translation of Duchenne's book, with additional chapters describing its importance to current work on emotion, art, and facial plastic surgery.[C7] My work with Friesen[C8] has built upon Duchenne's observations to provide a comprehensive tool for describing and measuring the movement of the facial muscles, and more than a dozen recent studies have supported Duchenne's ideas about how to distinguish voluntary from involuntary smiling. They show, for example, that it is possible to distinguish whether people are genuinely enjoying themselves or feigning enjoyment.[C9] See also my commentary in chapter 8, pages 201 and 203, about Duchenne and smiling.

A distinguished French anatomist, Pierre Gratiolet, gave a course of lectures on expression at the Sorbonne, and his notes were published (1865) after his death, under the title of *De La Physionomie et des Mouvements d'Expression*. This is a very interesting work, full of valuable observations. His theory is rather complex, and, as far as it can be given in a single sentence (p. 65), is as follows: 'Il résulte, de tous les faits que j'ai rappelés, que les sens, l'imagination et la pensée elle-même, si élevée, si abstraite qu'on la suppose, ne peuvent s'exercer sans éveiller un sentiment corrélatif, et que ce sentiment se traduit directement, sympathiquement, symboliquement ou métaphoriquement, dans toutes les sphères des organes extérieurs, qui le racontent tous, suivant leur mode d'action propre, comme si chacun d'eux avait *été directement affecté*.' ['The result of all of the facts I have mentioned is that the senses, the imagination, and thought itself – elevated and abstract as we assume it to be – cannot function without evoking associated feeling; and that feeling is transmitted directly, symbolically, sympathetically, or metaphorically to all parts of the peripheral organs, which all react each in its own way, as though they have *been directly affected*.']

Gratiolet appears to overlook inherited habit, and even to some extent habit in the individual; and therefore he fails, as it seems to me, to give the right explanation, or any explanation at all, of many gestures and expressions. As an illustration of what he calls symbolic movements, I will quote his remarks (p. 37), taken from M. Chevreul, on a man playing at billiards: 'Si une bille dévie légèrement de la direction que je joueur prétend lui imprimer, ne l'avez-vous pas vu cent fois la pousser du regard, de la tête et même des épaules, comme si ces mouvements, purement symboliques, pouvaient rectifier son trajet? Des mouvements non moins significatifs se produisent quand la bille manque d'une impulsion suffisante. Et, chez les joueurs novices, ils sont quelquefois accusés au point d'éveiller le sourire sur les lèvres des spectateurs.' ['If a billiard-ball deviates slightly from the direction the player intended to give it, have you not seen him push it with a look, with his head and even his shoulders, as if these purely symbolic movements could correct its path? Not less significant movements follow when the billiard-ball lacks sufficient impulse. And, with inexperienced players these movements are sometimes so pronounced that they provoke a smile on the lips of spectators.'] Such movements, as it appears to me, may be attributed simply to habit. As often as a man has wished to move an object to one side, he has always pushed it to that side; when forwards, he has pushed it forwards; and if he has wished to arrest it, he has pulled backwards. Therefore, when a man sees his ball travelling in a wrong direction, and he intensely wishes it to go in another direction, he cannot avoid, from long habit, unconsciously performing movements which in other cases he has found effectual.

As an instance of sympathetic movements Gratiolet gives (p. 212) the following case: 'Un jeune chien à oreilles droites, auquel son maître présente de loin quelque viande appétissante, fixe avec ardeur ses yeux sur cet objet dont il suit tous les mouvements, et pendant que les yeux regardent, les deux oreilles se portent en avant comme si cet objet pouvait être entendu.' ['A young dog with straight ears, whose master, from a distance, shows him an appetizing piece of meat, follows avidly with his eyes every movement of that object, and while the eyes look, the two ears bend forward as though the object could be heard.'] Here, instead of speaking of sympathy between the ears and eyes, it appears to me more simple to believe, that as dogs during many generations have, whilst intently looking at any object, pricked their ears in order to perceive any sound; and conversely have looked intently in the direction of a sound to which they may have listened, the movements of these organs have become firmly associated together through long-continued habit.

Dr Piderit published in 1859 an essay on expression, which I have not seen, but in which, as he states, he forestalled Gratiolet in many of his views. In 1867 he published his *Wissenschaftliches System der Mimik und Physiognomik.* It is hardly possible to give in a few sentences a fair notion of his views; perhaps the two following sentences will tell as much as can be briefly told: 'The muscular movements of expression are in part related to imaginary objects, and in part to imaginary sensorial impressions. In this proposition lies the key to the comprehension of all expressive muscular movements.' (p. 25) Again: 'Expressive movements manifest themselves chiefly in the numerous and mobile muscles of the face, partly because the nerves by which they are set into motion originate in the most immediate vicinity of the mind-organ, but partly also because these muscles serve to support the organs of sense.' (p. 26) If Dr Piderit had studied Sir C. Bell's work, he would probably not have said (p. 101) that violent laughter causes a frown from partaking of the nature of pain; or that with infants (p. 103) the tears irritate the eyes, and thus excite the contraction of the surrounding muscles. Many good remarks are scattered throughout this volume, to which I shall hereafter refer.

Short discussions on expression may be found in various works, which need not here be particularized. Mr Bain,* however, in

* [In Mr Bain's review of Darwin on expression: being a postscript to the *Senses and the Intellect,* 1873, p. 698, the author writes: 'Mr Darwin quotes the statement I have given of the law' (of diffusion), 'and remarks that it "seems too general to throw much light upon special expressions"; which is quite true; nevertheless,

two of his works has treated the subject at some length. He says,[8] 'I look upon the expression so-called as part and parcel of the feeling. I believe it to be a general law of the mind that, along with the fact of inward feeling, or consciousness, there is a diffusive action or excitement over the bodily members.' In another place he adds, 'A very considerable number of the facts may be brought under the following principle: namely, that states of pleasure are connected with an increase, and states of pain with an abatement, of some, or all, of the vital functions.' But the above law of the diffusive action of feelings seems too general to throw much light on special expressions.

Mr Herbert Spencer, in treating of the feelings in his *Principles of Psychology* (1855), makes the following remarks: 'Fear, when strong, expresses itself in cries, in efforts to hide or escape, in palpitations and tremblings; and these are just the manifestations that would accompany an actual experience of the evil feared. The destructive passions are shown in a general tension of the muscular system, in gnashing of the teeth and protrusion of the claws, in dilated eyes and nostrils, in growls; and these are weaker forms of the actions that accompany the killing of prey.' Here we have, as I believe, the true theory of a large number of expressions; but the chief interest and difficulty of the subject lies in following out the wonderfully complex results. I infer that some one (but who he is I have not been able to ascertain) formerly advanced a nearly similar view, for Sir C. Bell says,[9] 'It has been maintained that what are called the external signs of passion, are only the concomitants of those voluntary movements which the structure renders necessary.' Mr Spencer has also published a valuable essay on the physiology of laughter,* in which he insists on 'the general law that feeling passing a certain pitch, habitually vents itself in bodily action'; and that 'an overflow of

---

he himself employs, for that very purpose, a mode of stating it that I believe to be still more vague.' Charles Darwin seems to have felt the justice of Mr Bain's criticism, as I judge by pencilled notes on his copy of the postscript.]

* *Essays, Scientific, Political, and Speculative*, second series, 1863, p. 111. There is a discussion on laughter in the first series of essays, which discussion seems to me of very inferior value.

nerve-force undirected by any motive, will manifestly take first the most habitual routes; and if these do not suffice, will next overflow into the less habitual ones.' This law I believe to be of the highest importance in throwing light on our subject.*

All the authors who have written on expression, with the exception of Mr Spencer – the great expounder of the principle of evolution – appear to have been firmly convinced that species, man of course included, came into existence in their present condition. Sir C. Bell, being thus convinced, maintains that many of our facial muscles are 'purely instrumental in expression'; or are 'a special provision' for this sole object.[10] But the simple fact that the anthropoid apes possess the same facial muscles as we do,[†] renders it very improbable that these muscles in our case serve exclusively for expression; for no one, I presume, would be inclined to admit that monkeys have been endowed with special muscles solely for exhibiting their grimaces.[‡] Distinct uses, independently of expression, can indeed be assigned with much probability for almost all the facial muscles.

Sir C. Bell evidently wished to draw as broad a distinction as possible between man and the lower animals; and he consequently asserts that with 'the lower creatures there is no expression but

---

* Since the publication of the essay just referred to, Mr Spencer has written another, on 'Morals and Moral Sentiments', in the *Fortnightly Review*, 1 April 1871, p. 426. He has, also, now published his final conclusions in vol. ii of the second edit. of the *Principles of Psychology*, 1872, p. 539. I may state, in order that I may not be accused of trespassing on Mr Spencer's domain, that I announced in my *Descent of Man*, that I had then written a part of the present volume: my first MS. notes on the subject of expression bear the date of the year 1838.

† Professor Owen expressly states (*Proc. Zoolog. Soc.*, 1830, p. 28) that this is the case with respect to the orang, and specifies all the more important muscles which are well known to serve with man for the expression of his feelings. See, also, a description of several of the facial muscles in the chimpanzee, by Professor Macalister, in *Annals and Magazine of Natural History*, vol. vii, May, 1871, p. 342.

‡ [In the first edition the grimaces were described as 'hideous'. The author struck out the adjective in deference to a critic in the *Athenaeum*, 9 November, 1872, p. 591, who does 'not see what the hideousness of the grimaces has to do with a question that has no connexion with beauty'.]

what may referred, more or less plainly, to their acts of volition or necessary instincts'. He further maintains that their faces 'seem chiefly capable of expressing rage and fear'.[11] But man himself cannot express love and humility by external signs so plainly as does a dog, when with drooping ears, hanging lips, flexuous body, and wagging tail, he meets his beloved master. Nor can these movements in the dog be explained by acts of volition or necessary instincts, any more than the beaming eyes and smiling cheeks of a man when he meets an old friend. If Sir C. Bell had been questioned about the expression of affection in the dog, he would no doubt have answered that this animal had been created with special instincts, adapting him for association with man, and that all further enquiry on the subject was superfluous.

Although Gratiolet emphatically denies[12] that any muscle has been developed solely for the sake of expression, he seems never to have reflected on the principle of evolution. He apparently looks at each species as a separate creation. So it is with the other writers on expression. For instance, Dr Duchenne, after speaking of the movements of the limbs, refers to those which give expression to the face, and remarks:[13] 'Le créateur n'a donc pas eu à se préoccuper ici des besoins de la mécanique; il a pu, selon sa sagesse, ou – que l'on me pardonne cette manière de parler – par une divine fantaisie, mettre en action tel ou tel muscle, un seul ou plusieurs muscles à la fois, lorsqu'il a voulu que les signes caractéristiques des passions, même les plus fugaces, fussent écrits passagèrement sur la face de l'homme. Ce langage de la physionomie une fois créé, il lui a suffi, pour le rendre universel et immuable, de donner à tout être humain la faculté instinctive d'exprimer toujours ses sentiments par la contraction des mêmes muscles.' ['The creator has not had to concern himself here with mechanical requirements; he has been able, in his wisdom, or – if you will forgive the expression – by divine whim, to move one muscle or another, one or many muscles at a time, when he has wanted the characteristic evidence of emotions, however fleeting, to be written in passing on the face of man. Once this pattern of physiognomy was created, it was enough for him, in order to make it universal and immutable, to give to every human being the instinctive faculty to express his feelings by always contracting the same muscles.']

Many writers consider the whole subject of expression as inexplicable. Thus the illustrious physiologist Müller says,[14] 'The completely different expression of the features in different passions shows that, according to the kind of feeling excited, entirely different groups of the fibres of the facial nerve are acted on. Of the cause of this we are quite ignorant.'

No doubt as long as man and all other animals are viewed as independent creations, an effectual stop is put to our natural desire to investigate as far as possible the causes of expression. By this doctrine, anything and everything can be equally well explained; and it has proved as pernicious with respect to expression, as to every other branch of natural history. With mankind some expressions, such as bristling of the hair under the influence of extreme terror, or the uncovering of the teeth under that of furious rage, can hardly be understood, except on the belief that man once existed in a much lower and animal-like condition. The community of certain expressions in distinct though allied species, as in the movements of the same facial muscles during laughter by man and by various monkeys, is rendered somewhat more intelligible if we believe in their descent from a common progenitor. He who admits on general grounds that the structure and habits of all animals have been gradually evolved, will look at the whole subject of expression in a new and interesting light.

The study of expression is difficult, owing to the movements being often extremely slight, and of a fleeting nature. A difference may be clearly perceived, and yet it may be impossible, at least I have found it so, to state in what the difference consists. When we witness any deep emotion, our sympathy is so strongly excited, that close observation is forgotten or rendered almost impossible; of which fact I have had many curious proofs. Our imagination is another and still more serious source of error; for if from the nature of the circumstances we expect to see any expression, we readily imagine its presence. Notwithstanding Dr Duchenne's great experience, he for a long time fancied, as he states, that several muscles contracted under certain emotions, whereas he ultimately convinced himself that the movement was confined to a single muscle.

In order to acquire as good a foundation as possible, and to ascertain, independently of common opinion, how far particular movements of the features and gestures are really expressive of certain states of the mind, I have found the following means the most serviceable. In the first place, to observe infants; for they exhibit many emotions, as Sir C. Bell remarks, 'with extraordinary force'; whereas, in after life, some of our expressions 'cease to have the pure and simple source from which they spring in infancy'.[15]

Although Darwin here relied upon a generally accepted belief – that infants show pure expressions, because they have not yet learned to control display of their emotions – there is a complication he did not foresee. In early infancy facial expressions of emotion may not be as differentiated as they are later in life, and, if that is true, infancy was not as useful a period for observing pure expressions as Darwin thought. Indeed, it could even be misleading. Scientists today disagree whether or not adult-like facial expressions are present in infancy, or whether they emerge only in late infancy and early childhood.[C10]

In the second place, it occurred to me that the insane ought to be studied, as they are liable to the strongest passions, and give uncontrolled vent to them. I had, myself, no opportunity of doing this, so I applied to Dr Maudsley, and received from him an introduction to Dr J. Crichton Browne, who has charge of an immense asylum near Wakefield, and who, as I found, had already attended to the subject. This excellent observer has, with unwearied kindness sent me copious notes and descriptions, with valuable suggestions on many points; and I can hardly overestimate the value of his assistance. I owe also, to the kindness of Mr Patrick Nicol, of the Sussex Lunatic Asylum, interesting statements on two or three points.

Thirdly, Dr Duchenne galvanized, as we have already seen, certain muscles in the face of an old man, whose skin was little sensitive, and thus produced various expressions which were photographed on a large scale. It fortunately occurred to me to show several of the best plates, without a word of explanation, to above twenty educated persons of various ages and both sexes, asking them, in each case, by what emotion or feeling the old man was supposed to be agitated; and I recorded their answers in the words which they used. Several of the expressions were instantly recognized by almost every one, though described in not exactly the same terms; and these may, I think, be relied on as truthful, and will hereafter be specified. On the other hand, the most widely different judgements were pronounced in regard to some of them. This exhibition was of use in another way, by convincing me how easily we may be misguided by our imagination; for when I first looked through Dr Duchenne's photographs, reading at the same time the text, and thus learning what was intended, I was struck with admiration at the truthfulness of all, with only a few exceptions. Nevertheless, if I had examined them without any explanation, no doubt I should have been as much perplexed, in some cases, as other persons have been.

Darwin describes here his use of a method to find out what information is conveyed by an expression: asking people to judge the emotion shown in a photograph without any information about the situation in which the expression occurred, and determining whether or not they agree. This has become the most commonly used method for studying facial expression, although Darwin is rarely cited as the first to use it.

Fourthly, I had hoped to derive much aid from the great masters in painting and sculpture, who are such close observers. Accordingly, I have looked at photographs and engravings of many well-known works; but, with a few exceptions, have not thus profited. The reason no doubt is, that in works of art, beauty is the chief object; and strongly[16] contracted facial muscles destroy beauty. The story of the composition is generally told with wonderful force and truth by skilfully given accessories.

Fifthly, it seemed to me highly important to ascertain whether the same expressions and gestures prevail, as has often been asserted without much evidence, with all the races of mankind, especially those who have associated but little with Europeans. Whenever the same movements of the features or body express the same emotions in several distinct races of man, we may infer, with much probability, that such expressions are true ones – that is, are innate or instinctive. Conventional expressions or gestures, acquired by the individual during early life, would probably have differed in the different races, in the same manner as do their languages. Accordingly I circulated, early in the year 1867, the following printed queries with a request, which has been fully responded to, that actual observations, and not memory, might be trusted. These queries were written after a considerable interval of time, during which my attention had been otherwise directed, and I can now see that they might have been greatly improved. To some of the later copies, I appended, in manuscript, a few additional remarks:

(1) Is astonishment expressed by the eyes and mouth being opened wide, and by the eyebrows being raised?

(2) Does shame excite a blush when the colour of the skin allows it to be visible? and especially how low down the body does the blush extend?

(3) When a man is indignant or defiant does he frown, hold his body and head erect, square his shoulders and clench his fists?

(4) When considering deeply on any subject, or trying to understand any puzzle, does he frown, or wrinkle the skin beneath the lower eyelids?

(5) When in low spirits, are the corners of the mouth depressed, and the inner corner of the eyebrows raised by that muscle which the French call the 'grief muscle'? The eyebrow in this state becomes slightly oblique, with a little swelling at the inner end; and the forehead is transversely wrinkled in the middle part, but not across the whole breadth, as when the eyebrows are raised in surprise.

(6) When in good spirits do the eyes sparkle, with the skin a little

wrinkled round and under them, and with the mouth a little drawn back at the corners?

(7) When a man sneers or snarls at another, is the corner of the upper lip over the canine or eye tooth raised on the side facing the man whom he addresses?

(8) Can a dogged or obstinate expression be recognized, which is chiefly shown by the mouth being firmly closed, a lowering brow and a slight frown?

(9) Is contempt expressed by a slight protrusion of the lips and by turning up the nose, with a slight expiration?

(10) Is disgust shown by the lower lip being turned down, the upper lip slightly raised, with a sudden expiration, something like incipient vomiting, or like something spit out of the mouth?

(11) Is extreme fear expressed in the same general manner as with Europeans?

(12) Is laughter ever carried to such an extreme as to bring tears into the eyes?

(13) When a man wishes to show that he cannot prevent something being done, or cannot himself do something, does he shrug his shoulders, turn inwards his elbows, extend outwards his hands and open the palms; with the eyebrows raised?

(14) Do the children when sulky, pout or greatly protrude the lips?

(15) Can guilty, or sly, or jealous expressions be recognized? though I know not how these can be defined.

(16) Is the head nodded vertically in affirmation, and shaken laterally in negation?

Observations on natives who have had little communication with Europeans would be of course the most valuable, though those made on any natives would be of much interest to me. General remarks on expression are of comparatively little value; and memory is so deceptive that I earnestly beg it may not be trusted. A definite description of the countenance under any emotion or frame of mind, with a statement of the circumstances under which it occurred, would possess much value.

There was one more sentence at the end of the instructions which Darwin sent to his informants: 'An answer within six or eight months, or even a year, to any *single* one of the foregoing questions would be gratefully accepted.' There was also another question on the original list: 'As a sign to keep silent, is a gentle hiss uttered?' Darwin may have left this off in some of the lists he sent, but it is on the original printed list in the archives at Cambridge University. Darwin never discussed this question, perhaps because unlike the others it does not deal with expression or gesture.[C11]

To these queries I have received thirty-six answers from different observers, several of them missionaries or protectors of the aborigines, to all of whom I am deeply indebted for the great trouble which they have taken, and for the valuable aid thus received. I will specify their names, etc., towards the close of this chapter, so as not to interrupt my present remarks. The answers relate to several of the most distinct and savage races of man. In many instances, the circumstances have been recorded under which each expression was observed, and the expression itself described. In such cases, much confidence may be placed in the answers. When the answers have been simply yes or no, I have always received them with caution. It follows, from the information thus acquired, that the same state of mind is expressed throughout the world with remarkable uniformity; and this fact is in itself interesting, as evidence of the close similarity in bodily structure and mental disposition of all the races of mankind.

Sixthly, and lastly, I have attended, as closely as I could, to the expression of the several passions in some of the commoner animals; and this I believe to be of paramount importance, not of course for deciding how far in man certain expressions are characteristic of certain states of mind, but as affording the safest basis for generalization on the causes, or origin, of the various movements of expression. In observing animals, we are not likely to be biased by our imagination; and we may feel safe that their expressions are not conventional. From the reasons above assigned, namely, the fleeting nature of some expressions (the changes in the features being often extremely slight); our sympathy being easily aroused when we behold any strong emotion, and our attention thus distracted; our imagination deceiving us, from knowing in a vague manner what to expect, though certainly few of us know what the exact changes in the countenance are and lastly, even our long familiarity with the subject – from all these causes combined, the observation of expression is by no means easy, as many persons, whom I have asked to observe certain points, have soon discovered. Hence it is difficult to determine, with certainty, what are the movements of the features and of the body, which commonly characterize certain states of the mind. Nevertheless, some of the doubts and difficulties have, as I hope, been cleared away by the observation of infants – of the insane – of the different races of man – of works of art, and lastly, of the facial muscles under the action of galvanism, as effected by Dr Duchenne.

But there remains the much greater difficulty of understanding the cause or origin of the several expressions, and of judging whether any theoretical explanation is trustworthy. Besides, judging as well as we can by our reason, without the aid of any rules, which of two or more explanations is the most satisfactory, or are quite unsatisfactory, I see only one way of testing our conclusions. This is to observe whether the same principle by which one expression can, as it appears, be explained, is applicable in other allied cases; and especially, whether the same general principles can be applied with satisfactory results, both to man and the lower animals. This latter method, I am inclined to think, is the most serviceable of all. The difficulty of judging of the truth of any theoretical explanation, and of testing it by some distinct line of investigation, is the great drawback to that interest which the study seems well fitted to excite.

Finally, with respect to my own observations, I may state that they were commenced in the year 1838; and, from that time to the present day, I have occasionally attended to the subject. At the above date, I was already inclined to believe in the principle of evolution, or of the derivation of species from other and lower forms. Consequently, when I read Sir C. Bell's great work, his view, that man had been created with certain muscles specially adapted for the expression of his feelings, struck me as unsatisfactory. It seemed probable that the habit of expressing our feelings by certain movements, though now rendered innate, had been in some manner gradually acquired. But to discover how such habits had been acquired was perplexing in no small degree. The whole subject had to be viewed under a new aspect, and each expression demanded a rational explanation. This belief led me to attempt the present work, however imperfectly it may have been executed.

I will now give the names of the gentlemen to whom, as I have said, I am deeply indebted for the information in regard to the expressions exhibited by various races of man, and I will specify some of the circumstances under which the observations were in each case made. Owing to the great kindness and powerful influence of Mr Wilson, of Hayes Place, Kent, I have received from Australia no less than thirteen sets of answers to my queries. This has been particularly fortunate, as the Australian aborigines rank among the most distinct of all the races of man. It will be seen that the observations have been chiefly made in the south, in the outlying parts of the colony of Victoria; but some excellent answers have been received from the north.

Mr Dyson Lacey has given me in detail, some valuable observations, made several hundred miles in the interior of Queensland. To Mr R. Brough Smyth, of Melbourne, I am much indebted for observations made by himself, and for sending me several of the following letters, namely: From the Rev. Mr Hagenauer, of Lake Wellington, a missionary in Gippsland, Victoria, who has had much experience with the natives. From Mr Samuel Wilson, a landowner, residing at Langerenong, Wimmera, Victoria. From the Rev. George Taplin, superintendent of the native industrial settlement at Port Macleay. From Mr Archibald G. Lang, of Coranderik, Victoria, a teacher at a school where aborigines, old and young, are collected from all parts of the colony. From Mr H. B. Lane, of Belfast, Victoria, a police magistrate and warden, whose observations, as I am assured, are highly trustworthy. From Mr Templeton Bunnett, of Echuca, whose station is on the borders of the colony of Victoria, and who has thus been able to observe many aborigines who have had little intercourse with white men. He compared his observations with those made by two other gentlemen long resident in the neighbourhood. Also from Mr J. Bulmer, a missionary in a remote part of Gippsland, Victoria.

I am also indebted to the distinguished botanist, Dr Ferdinand Müller, of Victoria, for some observations made by himself, and for sending me others made by Mrs Green, as well as for some of the foregoing letters.

In regard to the Maoris of New Zealand, the Rev. J. W. Stack has answered only a few of my queries; but the answers have been remarkably full, clear, and distinct, with the circumstances recorded under which the observations were made.

The Rajah Brooke has given me some information with respect to the Dyaks of Borneo.

Repecting the Malays, I have been highly successful; for Mr F. Geach (to whom I was introduced by Mr Wallace), during his residence as a mining engineer in the interior of Malacca, observed many natives, who had never before associated with white men. He wrote me two long letters with admirable and detailed observations on their expression. He likewise observed the Chinese immigrants in the Malay archipelago.

The well-known naturalist, H. M. Consul, Mr Swinhoe, also observed for me the Chinese in their native country; and he made enquiries from others whom he could trust.

In India, Mr H. Erskine, whilst residing in his official capacity in the Ahmednugur District in the Bombay Presidency, attended to the expression of the inhabitants, but found much difficulty in arriving at any safe conclusions, owing to their habitual conceal-ment of all emotions in the presence of Europeans. He also obtained information for me from Mr West, the judge in Canara, and he consulted some intelligent native gentlemen on certain points. In Calcutta, Mr J. Scott, curator of the Botanic Gardens, carefully observed the various tribes of men therein employed during a considerable period, and no one has sent me such full and valuable details. The habit of accurate observation, gained by his botanical studies, has been brought to bear on our present subject. For Ceylon I am much indebted to the Rev. S. O. Glenie for answers to some of my queries.

Turning to Africa, I have been unfortunate with respect to the negroes, though Mr Winwood Reade aided me as far as lay in his power. It would have been comparatively easy to have obtained information in regard to the negro slaves in America; but as they have long associated with white men, such observations would have possessed little value. In the southern parts of the continent Mrs Barber observed the Kafirs and Fingoes, and sent me many distinct answers. Mr J. P. Mansel Weale also made some observations on the natives, and procured for me a curious document, namely, the opinion, written in English, of Christian Gaika, brother of the Chief Sandilli, on the expressions of his fellow-countrymen. In the northern regions of Africa Captain Speedy, who long resided with the Abyssinians, answered my queries partly from memory and partly from observations made on the son of King Theodore, who was then under his charge. Professor and Mrs Asa Gray attended to some points in the expressions of the natives, as observed by them whilst ascending the Nile.

On the great American continent, Mr Bridges, a catechist residing with the Fuegians, answered some few questions about their expression, addressed to him many years ago. In the northern half of the continent Dr Rothrock attended to the expressions of the wild Atnah and Espyox tribes on the Nasse River, in North-Western America. Mr Washington Matthews, Assistant-Surgeon in the United States Army, also observed with special care (after having seen my queries, as printed in the *Smithsonian Report*) some of the wildest tribes in the Western parts of the United States, namely, the Tetons, Grosventres, Mandans, and Assinaboines; and his answers have proved of the highest value.

Lastly, besides these special sources of information, I have collected some few facts incidentally given in books of travels.

As I shall often have to refer, more especially in the latter part of this volume, to the muscles of the human face, I have had a diagram (Fig. 1) copied and reduced from Sir C. Bell's work, and two others, with more accurate details (Figs 2 and 3), from Henle's well-known *Handbuch der systematischen Anatomie des Menschen*. The same letters refer to the same muscles in all three

Fig. 1. Diagram of
the muscles of the face,
from Sir C. Bell.

Fig. 2. Diagram from Henle

Fig. 3. Diagram from Henle

A Occipito-frontalis, or frontal muscle.
B Corrugator supercilii, or corrugator
   muscle.
C Orbicularis palpebrarum, or
   orbicular muscles of the eyes.
D Pyramidalis nasi, or pyramidal
   muscle of the nose.
E Levator labii superioris alaeque nasi.
F Levator labii proprius.

G Zygomatic.
H Malaris.
I Little zygomatic.
K Triangularis oris, or depressor
   anguli oris.
L Quadratus menti.
M Risorius, part of the Platysma
   myoides.

figures, but the names are given only of the more important ones
to which I shall have to allude. The facial muscles blend much
together, and, as I am informed, hardly appear on a dissected
face so distinct as they are here represented. Some writers consider that these muscles consist of nineteen pairs, with one
unpaired;[17] but others make the number much larger, amounting
even to fifty-five, according to Moreau. They are, as is admitted

by everyone who has written on the subject, very variable in structure; and Moreau remarks that they are hardly alike in half-a-dozen subjects.[18] They are also variable in function. Thus the power of uncovering the canine tooth on one side differs much in different persons. The power of raising the wings of the nostrils is also, according to Dr Pinderit,[19] variable in a remarkable degree; and other such cases could be given.

Anatomical dissections have found variability in the size of the facial muscles and even questioned whether a few of the muscles are present at all. However, I believe that the differences in people's ability to make certain facial movements voluntarily is not usually due to the absence of the muscle, for I have often observed that people who cannot make a muscle movement deliberately will show that movement when it is brought forth spontaneously by an emotion. Also, nearly everyone who has spent enough time trying to make some of the more difficult movements (for example, raising one eyebrow at a time), eventually succeeds.

Finally, I must have the pleasure of expressing my obligations to Mr Rejlander for the trouble which he has taken in photographing for me various expressions and gestures. I am also indebted to Herr Kindermann, of Hamburg, for the loan of some excellent negatives of crying infants; and to Dr Wallich for a charming one of a smiling girl. I have already expressed my obligations to Dr Duchenne for generously permitting me to have some of his large photographs copied and reduced. All these photographs have been printed by the Heliotype process, and the accuracy of the copy is thus guaranteed. These plates are referred to by roman numerals.

I am also greatly indebted to Mr T. W. Wood for the extreme pains which he has taken in drawing from life the expressions of various animals. A distinguished artist, Mr Riviere, has had the kindness to give me two drawings of dogs – one in a hostile and the other in a humble and caressing frame of mind. Mr A. May has also given me two similar sketches of dogs. Mr Cooper has taken much care in cutting the blocks. Some of the photographs and drawings, namely, those by Mr May, and those by Mr Wolf of the Cynopithecus were first reproduced by Mr Cooper on wood by means of photography, and then engraved: by this means almost complete fidelity is ensured.

CHAPTER I

General Principles of Expression

The three chief principles stated – The first principle – Serviceable actions become habitual in association with certain states of the mind, and are performed whether or not of service in each particular case – The force of habit – Inheritance – Associated habitual movements in man – Reflex actions – Passage of habits into reflex actions – Associated habitual movements in the lower animals – Concluding remarks.

I will begin by giving the three principles, which appear to me to account for most of the expressions and gestures involuntarily used by man and the lower animals, under the influence of various emotions and sensations.* I arrived, however, at these three principles only at the close of my observations. They will be discussed in the present and two following chapters in a general manner. Facts observed both with man and the lower animals will here be made use of; but the latter facts are preferable, as less likely to deceive us. In the fourth and fifth chapters, I will describe the special expressions of some of the lower animals; and in the succeeding chapters those of man. Everyone will thus be able to judge for himself, how far my three principles throw light on the theory of the subject. It appears to me that so many expressions are thus explained in a fairly satisfactory manner, that probably all will hereafter be found to come under the same or closely analogous heads. I need hardly premise that movements or changes in any part of the body – as the wagging of a dog's tail,

---

* Mr Herbert Spencer (*Essays*, second series, 1863, p. 138) has drawn a clear distinction between emotions and sensations, the latter being 'generated in our corporeal framework'. He classes as feelings both emotions and sensations.

the drawing back of a horse's ears, the shrugging of a man's shoulders, or the dilatation of the capillary vessels of the skin – may all equally well serve for expression. The three principles are as follows:

I. *The principle of serviceable associated habits.* Certain complex actions are of direct or indirect service under certain states of the mind, in order to relieve or gratify certain sensations, desires, etc.; and whenever the same state of mind is induced, however feebly, there is a tendency through the force of habit and association for the same movements to be performed, though they may not then be of the least use. Some actions ordinarily associated through habit with certain states of the mind may be partially repressed through the will, and in such cases the muscles which are least under the separate control of the will are the most liable still to act, causing movements which we recognize as expressive. In certain other cases the checking of one habitual movement requires other slight movements; and these are likewise expressive.

II. *The principle of antithesis.* Certain states of the mind lead to certain habitual actions, which are of service, as under our first principle. Now when a directly opposite state of mind is induced, there is a strong and involuntary tendency to the performance of movements of a directly opposite nature, though these are of no use; and such movements are in some cases highly expressive.

III. *The principle of actions due to the constitution of the nervous system, independently from the first of the will, and independently to a certain extent of habit.* When the sensorium is strongly excited, nerveforce is generated in excess, and is transmitted in certain definite directions, depending on the connection of the nerve-cells, and partly on habit: or the supply of nerve-force may, as it appears, be interrupted. Effects are thus produced which we recognize as expressive. This third principle may, for the sake of brevity, be called that of the direct action of the nervous system.

With respect to our *first principle*, it is notorious how powerful is the force of habit. The most complex and difficult movements can in time be performed without the least effort or consciousness. It is not positively known how it comes that habit is so efficient in facilitating complex movements; but physiologists admit[1] 'that the conducting power of the nervous fibres increases with the frequency of their excitement'. This applies to the nerves of motion and sensation, as well as to those connected with the act of thinking. That some physical change is produced in the nerve-cells or nerves which are habitually used can hardly be doubted, for otherwise it is impossible to understand how the tendency to certain acquired movements is inherited. That they are inherited we see with horses in certain transmitted paces, such as cantering and ambling, which are not natural to them – in the pointing of young pointers and the setting of young setters – in the peculiar manner of flight of certain breeds of pigeon, etc. We have analogous cases with mankind in the inheritance of tricks or unusual gestures, to which we shall presently recur. To those who admit the gradual evolution of species, a most striking instance of the perfection with which the most difficult consensual movements can be transmitted is afforded by the humming-bird Sphinx-moth (*Macroglossa*); for this moth, shortly after its emergence from the cocoon, as shown by the bloom on its unruffled scales, may be seen poised stationary in the air, with its long hair-like proboscis uncurled and inserted into the minute orifices of flowers; and no one, I believe, has ever seen this moth learning to perform its difficult task, which requires such unerring aim.

Darwin's observation – that a physical change is produced in nerve cells that are habitually used – has proved correct. Merzenich[C12] has shown that the acquisition of a motor skill changes the representation of different fingers in the motor cortex. Karni and associates[C13] found increased flow to the motor cortex when skill in the use of fingers was acquired. Darwin's further suggestion that such brain changes are then inherited is an example of use-inheritance, which we know now is incorrect. This evidence for such inheritance (e.g., the pointing of young pointers) is due not to inheritance of a learned trait but to selectively breeding animals who show a propensity to acquire readily a particular skill.

When there exists an inherited or instinctive tendency to the performance of an action, or an inherited taste for certain kinds of food, some degree of habit in the individual is often or generally requisite. We find this in the paces of the horse, and to a certain extent in the pointing of dogs; although some young dogs point excellently the first time they are taken out, yet they often associate the proper inherited attitude with a wrong odour, and even with eyesight. I have heard it asserted that if a calf be allowed to suck its mother only once, it is much more difficult afterwards to rear it by hand.* Caterpillars which have been fed on the leaves of one kind of tree, have been known to perish from hunger rather than to eat the leaves of another tree, although this afforded them their proper food, under a state of nature;[2] and so it is in many other cases.

The power of association is admitted by everyone. Mr Bain remarks, that 'actions, sensations, and states of feeling, occurring together or in close succession, tend to grow together, or cohere, in such a way that when any one of them is afterward presented to the mind, the others are apt to be brought up in idea'.[†] It is so important for our purpose fully to recognize that actions readily become associated with other actions and with various states of

---

* A remark to much the same effect was made long ago by Hippocrates and by the illustrious Harvey; for both assert that a young animal forgets in the course of a few days the art of sucking, and cannot without some difficulty again acquire it. I give these assertions on the authority of Dr Darwin, *Zoonomia*, 1794, vol. i, p. 140. [Confirmed by Dr Stanley Haynes, in a letter to the author.]

† *The Senses and the Intellect*, 2nd edit., 1864, p. 332. Professor Huxley remarks (*Elementary Lessons in Physiology*, 54th edit., 1872, p. 306), 'It may be laid down as a rule, that, if any two mental states be called up together, or in succession, with due frequency and vividness, the subsequent production of the one of them will suffice to call up the other, and that whether we desire it or not.'

mind, that I will give a good many instances, in the first place relating to man, and afterwards to the lower animals. Some of the instances are of a very trifling nature, but they are as good for our purpose as more important habits. It is known to everyone how difficult, or even impossible it is, without repeated trials, to move the limbs in certain opposed directions which have never been practised. Analogous cases occur with sensations, as in the common experiment of rolling a marble beneath the tips of two crossed fingers, when it feels exactly like two marbles. Everyone protects himself when falling to the ground by extending his arms, and as Professor Alison has remarked, few can resist acting thus, when voluntarily falling on a soft bed. A man when going out of doors puts on his gloves quite unconsciously; and this may seem an extremely simple operation, but he who has taught a child to put on gloves, knows that this is by no means the case.

When our minds are much affected, so are the movements of our bodies; but here another principle besides habit, namely the undirected overflow of nerve-force, partially comes into play. Norfolk, in speaking of Cardinal Wolsey, says:

'Some strange commotion
Is in his brain: he bites his lips and starts;
Stops on a sudden, looks upon the ground,
Then, lays his finger on his temple; straight,
Springs out into fast gait; then, stops again,
Strikes his breast hard; and anon, he casts
His eye against the moon: in most strange postures
We have seen him set himself.'

Hen. VIII, iii, 2.

A vulgar man often scratches his head when perplexed in mind; and I believe that he acts thus from habit, as if he experienced a slightly uncomfortable bodily sensation, namely, the itching of his head, to which he is particularly liable, and which he thus relieves. Another man rubs his eyes when perplexed, or gives a little cough when embarrassed, acting in either case as if he felt a slightly uncomfortable sensation in his eyes or windpipe.*

From the continued use of the eyes, these organs are especially liable to be acted on through association under various states of the mind, although there is manifestly nothing to be seen. A man, as Gratiolet remarks, who vehemently rejects a proposition, will almost certainly shut his eyes or turn away his face, but if he accepts the proposition, he will nod his head in affirmation and open his eyes widely. The man acts in this latter case as if he clearly saw the thing, and in the former case as if he did not or would not see it. I have noticed that persons in describing a horrid sight often shut their eyes momentarily and firmly, or shake their heads, as if not to see or to drive away something disagreeable; and I have caught myself, when thinking in the dark of a horrid spectacle, closing my eyes firmly. In looking suddenly at any object, or in looking all around, everyone raises his eyebrows, so that the eyes may be quickly and widely opened; and Duchenne remarks[3] that a person in trying to remember something often raises his eyebrows, as if to see it. A Hindoo gentleman made exactly the same remark to Mr Erskine in regard to his countrymen. I noticed a young lady earnestly trying to recollect a painter's name, and she first looked to one corner of the ceiling and then to the opposite corner, arching the one eyebrow on that side; although, of course, there was nothing to be seen there.

Consistent with Darwin's observation, there is evidence[C14] that people in Western cultures avert their gaze and turn their faces away when feeling shame, as if hiding from observation. I also noted this in the preliterate people I studied in New Guinea, which suggests this is a universal.[C15] I asked them to show me different emotions, and when I asked them to show shame, they all averted their gaze and turned their faces away. When I did this work in 1967–8, most of the people I studied would not have had the opportunity to learn this from

* Gratiolet (*De la Physionomie*, p. 324), in his discussion on this subject, gives many analogous instances. See p. 42, on the opening and shutting of the eyes. Engel is quoted (p. 323) on the changed paces of a man, as his thoughts change.

Western culture: they had little or no contact with out-siders and no exposure to film, television or photographs. Clinical observations also support Darwin. For example, when a psychiatric patient was repressing a strongly felt emotion, I saw a long eye closure, suggesting that she did not want to see something. Darwin's idea, that the biological function of a sensory mechanism such as sight can metaphorically become associated with a wider set of meanings related to the physical function of the sensory mechanism, should apply not just to sight but more generally to other sensory mechanisms, such as hearing and tasting.

In most of the foregoing cases, we can understand how the associated movements were acquired through habit; but with some individuals, certain strange gestures or tricks have arisen in association with certain states of the mind, owing to wholly inexplicable causes, and are undoubtedly inherited. I have else-where given one instance from my own observation of an extra-ordinary and complex gesture, associated with pleasurable feelings, which was transmitted from a father to his daughter, as well as some other analogous faets.* Another curious instance of

* *The Variation of Animals and Plants under Domestication*, vol. ii, p. 6. The inherit-ance of habitual gestures is so important for us, that I gladly avail myself of Mr F. Galton's permission to give in his own words the following remarkable case: 'The following account of a habit occurring in individuals of three consecutive generations is of peculiar interest, because it occurs only during sound sleep, and therefore cannot be due to imitation, but must be altogether natural. The particu-lars are perfectly trustworthy, for I have enquired fully into them, and speak from abundant and independent evidence. A gentleman of considerable position was found by his wife to have the curious trick, when he lay fast asleep on his back in bed, of raising his right arm slowly in front of his face, up to his forehead, and then dropping it with a jerk, so that the wrist fell heavily on the bridge of his nose. The trick did not occur every night, but occasionally, and was indepen-dent of any ascertained cause. Sometimes it was repeated incessantly for an hour or more. The gentleman's nose was prominent, and its bridge often became sore from the blows which it received. At one time an awkward sore was produced, that was long in healing, on account of the recurrence, night after night, of the blows which first caused it. His wife had to remove the button from the wrist

an odd inherited movement, associated with the wish to obtain an object, will be given in the course of this volume.

There are other actions which are commonly performed under certain circumstances, independently of habit, and which seem to be due to imitation or some sort of sympathy. Thus persons cutting anything with a pair of scissors may be seen to move their jaws simultaneously with the blades of the scissors. Children learning to write often twist about their tongues as their fingers move, in a ridiculous fashion. When a public singer suddenly becomes a little hoarse, many of those present may be heard, as I have been assured by a gentleman upon whom I can rely, to clear their throats; but here habit probably comes into play, as we clear our own throats under similar circumstances. I have also been told that at leaping matches, as the performer makes his

---

of his night-gown as it made severe scratches, and some means were attempted of tying his arm.

'Many years after his death, his son married a lady who had never heard of the family incident. She, however, observed precisely the same peculiarity in her husband; but his nose, from not being particularly prominent, has never yet suffered from the blows. [Since this was first written, the event has occurred. He was fast asleep in his arm-chair after a very fatiguing day, when he awoke by finding that he had considerably lacerated his nose with his nail.] The trick does not occur when he is half-asleep, as, for example, when dozing in his arm-chair, but the moment he is fast asleep it is apt to begin. It is, as with his father, intermittent; sometimes ceasing for many nights, and sometimes almost incessant during a part of every night. It is performed, as it was by his father, with his right hand.

'One of his children, a girl, has inherited the same trick. She performs it, likewise with the right hand, but in a slightly modified form; for, after raising the arm, she does not allow the wrist to drop upon the bridge of the nose, but the palm of the half-closed hand falls over and down the nose, stroking it rather rapidly. It is also very intermittent with this child, not occurring for periods of some months, but sometimes occurring almost incessantly.'

[Mr R. Lydekker (letter n. d.) communicates a remarkable instance of an inherited peculiarity producing a characteristic drooping of the eyelids. The peculiarity is the paralysis, or more probably, the absence, of the *levator palpebrae*. It first showed itself in a woman, Mrs A.; she had three children, one of whom, B., inherited the peculiarity. B. had four children, all of whom were affected with the hereditary droop; one of these, a daughter, married, and had two children, of whom the second showed the peculiarity, but on one side only.]

spring, many of the spectators, generally men and boys, move their feet; but here again habit* probably comes into play, for it is very doubtful whether women would thus act.

Reflex actions. Reflex actions, in the strict sense of the term, are due to the excitement of a peripheral nerve, which transmits its influence to certain nerve-cells, and these in their turn excite certain muscles or glands into action; and all this may take place without any sensation or consciousness on our part, though often thus accompanied. As many reflex actions are highly expressive, the subject must here be noticed at some little length. We shall also see that some of them graduate into, and can hardly be distinguished from actions which have arisen through habit.† Coughing and sneezing are familiar instances of reflex actions. With infants the first act of respiration is often a sneeze, although this requires the co-ordinated movement of numerous muscles.

---

* [An American physician states, in a letter to the author, that while attending women in labour he sometimes finds himself imitating the muscular efforts of the patient. This case is of interest because habit is necessarily excluded.]

† Professor Huxley remarks (*Elementary Physiology*, 5th edit., p. 305) that reflex actions proper to the spinal cord are *natural*; but, by the help of the brain, that is through habit, an infinity of *artificial* reflex actions may be acquired. Virchow admits ('Sammlung wissenschaft. Vorträge', etc., *Ueber das Rückenmark*, 1871, pp. 24, 31) that some reflex actions can hardly be distinguished from instincts; and, of the latter, it may be added, some cannot be distinguished from inherited habits. [With regard to this experiment, a critic remarks that, if correctly recorded, it demonstrates volition and not reflex action, while another gets rid of the difficulty by impugning the authenticity of the experiment. Dr Michael Foster (*Text Book of Physiology*, edit. 2, 1878, p. 473), speaking of the action of the frog, says that it 'looks at first like an intelligent choice. A choice it undoubtedly is; and were there many instances of similar choice, and were there any evidence of a variable automatism, like that of a conscious volition, being manifested by the spinal cord of the frog, we should be justified in supposing that the choice was determined by an intelligence. It is, however, on the other hand, quite possible to suppose that the lines of resistance in the spinal protoplasm are so arranged as to admit of an alternative action; and seeing how few and simple are the apparent instances of choice witnessed in a brainless frog, and how absolutely devoid of spontaneity or irregular automatism is the spinal cord of a frog, this seems to be the more probable view.']

Respiration is partly voluntary, but mainly reflex, and is performed in the most natural and best manner without the interference of the will. A vast number of complex movements are reflex. As good an instance as can be given is the often-quoted one of a decapitated frog, which cannot of course feel, and cannot consciously perform, any movement. Yet if a drop of acid be placed in the lower surface of the thigh of a frog in this state, it will rub off the drop with the upper surface of the foot of the same leg. If this foot be cut off, it cannot thus act. After some fruitless efforts, therefore, it gives up trying in that way, seems restless, as though, says Pflüger, it was seeking some other way, and at last it makes use of the foot of the other leg and succeeds in rubbing off the acid. Notably we have not here merely contraction of the muscles, but combined and harmonized contractions in due sequence for a special purpose. These are actions that have all the appearance of being guided by intelligence and instigated by will in an animal, the recognized organ of whose intelligence and will has been removed.[4]

We see the difference between reflex and voluntary movements in very young children not being able to perform, as I am informed by Sir Henry Holland, certain acts somewhat analogous to those of sneezing and coughing, namely, in their not being able to blow their noses (i.e. to compress the nose and blow violently through the passage), and in their not being able to clear their throats of phlegm. They have to learn to perform these acts, yet they are performed by us, when a little older, almost as easily as reflex actions. Sneezing and coughing, however, can be controlled by the will only partially or not at all; whilst the clearing the throat and blowing the nose are completely under our command.

When we are conscious of an irritating particle in our nostrils or windpipe – that is, when the same sensory nerve cells are excited, as in the case of sneezing and coughing – we can involuntarily expel the particle by forcibly driving air through these passages; but we cannot do this with nearly the same force, rapidity, and precision, as by a reflex action. In this latter case the sensory nerve-cells apparently excite the motor nerve-cells without any waste of power by first communicating with the cerebral hemispheres – the seat of our consciousness and volition. In all cases there seems to exist a profound antagonism between the same movements, as directed by the will and by a reflex stimulant, in the force with which they are performed and in the facility with which they are excited. As Claude Bernard asserts, 'L'influence du cerveau tend donc à entraver les mouvements réflexes, à limiter leur force et leur étendue'. ['The influence of the brain thus tends to hinder reflex movements, to limit their strength and extent.'][5]

The conscious wish to perform a reflex action sometimes stops or interrupts its performance, though the proper sensory nerves may be stimulated. For instance, many years ago I laid a small wager with a dozen young men that they would not sneeze if they took snuff, although they all declared that they invariably did so; accordingly they all took a pinch, but from wishing much to succeed, not one sneezed, though their eyes watered, and all, without exception, had to pay me the wager. Sir H. Holland remarks[6] that attention paid to the act of swallowing interferes with the proper movements; from which it probably follows, at least in part, that some persons find it so difficult to swallow a pill.

Another familiar instance of a reflex action is the involuntary closing of the eyelids when the surface of the eyes is touched. A similar winking movement is caused when a blow is directed towards the face; but this is an habitual and not a strictly reflex action, as the stimulus is conveyed through the mind and not by the excitement of a peripheral nerve. The whole body and head are generally at the same time drawn suddenly backwards. These latter movements, however, can be prevented, if the danger does not appear to the imagination imminent; but our reason telling us that there is no danger does not suffice. I may mention a trifling fact, illustrating this point, and which at the time amused me. I put my face close to the thick glass-plate in front of a puff-adder in the Zoological Gardens, with the firm determination of not starting back if the snake struck at me; but, as soon as the blow was struck, my resolution went for nothing, and I jumped a yard or two backwards with astonishing rapidity. My will and reason were powerless against the imagination of a danger which had never been experienced.

> The American psychologist Susan Mineka[C16] has found that humans are biologically prepared to respond in a fearful way to snake-like shapes. Perhaps Darwin would have been more successful in not 'starting back' if the organism striking towards him was not a snake.

The violence of a start seems to depend partly on the vividness of the imagination, and partly on the condition, either habitual or temporary, of the nervous system. He who will attend to the starting of his horse, when tired and fresh, will perceive how perfect is the gradation from a mere glance at some unexpected object, with a momentary doubt whether it is dangerous, to a jump so rapid and violent, that the animal probably could not voluntarily whirl round in so rapid a manner. The nervous system of a fresh and highly-fed horse sends its order to the motor system so quickly, that no time is allowed for him to consider whether or not the danger is real. After one violent start, when he is excited and the blood flows freely through his brain, he is very apt to start again; and so it is, as I have noticed, with young infants.

> In the paragraph that follows, Darwin was correct about the eye blink as an essential part of what is called the 'startle reaction'. There are a few other facial movements that also occur during a startle reaction.[C17] I don't know of any research on whether Darwin was correct in his observation that the eye blink is absent in the young infant's startle reaction. It would be interesting to know if the other parts of the startle response are also absent.

A start from a sudden noise, when the stimulus is conveyed through the auditory nerves, is always accompanied in grown-up persons by the winking of the eyelids.* I observed, however,

---

* Müller remarks (*Elements of Physiology*, Eng. tr., vol. ii, p. 1311) on starting always being accompanied by the closure of the eyelids.

that though my infants started at sudden sounds, when under a fortnight old, they certainly did not always wink their eyes, and I believe never did so. The start of an older infant apparently represents a vague catching hold of something to prevent falling. I shook a pasteboard box close before the eyes of one of my infants, when 114 days old, and it did not in the least wink; but when I put a few comfits into the box, holding it in the same position as before, and rattled them, the child blinked its eyes violently every time, and started a little. It was obviously impossible that a carefully-guarded infant could have learnt by experience that a rattling sound near its eyes indicated danger to them. But such experience will have been slowly gained at a later age during a long series of generations; and from what we know of inheritance, there is nothing improbable in the transmission of a habit to the offspring at an earlier age than that at which it was first acquired by the parents.

This is an especially blatant example of how completely Darwin accepted the now discredited idea of the inheritance of acquired characteristics. Habits learned by the parents *cannot* be inherited by their offspring.

From the foregoing remarks it seems probable that some actions, which were at first performed consciously, have become through habit and association converted into reflex actions, and are now so firmly fixed and inherited, that they are performed, even when not of the least use,* as often as the same causes arise, which originally excited them in us through the volition.

In contemporary terms we would speak of over-learned habits, or behavior which has become automatic.

---

* Dr Maudsley remarks (*Body and Mind*, p. 10) that 'reflex movements which commonly effect a useful end may, under the changed circumstances of disease, do great mischief, becoming even the occasion of violent suffering and of a most painful death.'

In such cases the sensory nerve-cells excite the motor cells, without first communicating with those cells on which our consciousness and volition depend. It is probable that sneezing and coughing were originally acquired by the habit of expelling, as violently as possible, any irritating particle from the sensitive air-passages. As far as time is concerned, there has been more than enough for these habits to have become innate or converted into reflex actions; for they are common to most or all of the higher quadrupeds, and must therefore have been first acquired at a very remote period. Why the act of clearing the throat is not a reflex action, and has to be learnt by our children, I cannot pretend to say; but we can see why blowing the nose on a handkerchief has to be learnt.

It is scarcely credible that the movements of a headless frog, when it wipes off a drop of acid or other object from its thigh, and which movements are so well co-ordinated for a special purpose, were not at first performed voluntarily, being afterwards rendered easy through long-continued habit so as at last to be performed unconsciously, or independently, of the cerebral hemispheres.

So again it appears probable that starting was originally acquired by the habit of jumping away as quickly as possible from danger, whenever any of our senses gave us warning. Starting, as we have seen, is accompanied by the blinking of the eyelids so as to protect the eyes, the most tender and sensitive organs of the body; and it is, I believe, always accompanied by a sudden and forcible inspiration, which is the natural preparation for any violent effort. But when a man or horse starts, his heart beats wildly against his ribs, and here it may be truly said we have an organ which has never been under the control of the will, partaking in the general reflex movements of the body. To this point, however, I shall return in a future chapter.

The contraction of the iris, when the retina is stimulated by a bright light, is another instance of a movement which it appears cannot possibly have been at first voluntarily performed and then fixed by habit; for the iris is not known to be under the conscious control of the will in any animal.* In such cases some explanation, quite distinct from habit, will have to be discovered. The radiation of nerve-force from strongly-excited nerve-cells to other connected cells, as in the case of a bright light on the retina causing a sneeze, may perhaps aid us in understanding how some reflex actions originated. A radiation of nerve-force of this kind, if it caused a movement tending to lessen the primary irritation, as in the case of the contraction of the iris preventing too much light from falling on the retina, might afterwards have been taken advantage of and modified for this special purpose.

It further deserves notice that reflex actions are in all probability liable to slight variations, as are all corporeal structures and instincts; and any variations which were beneficial and of sufficient importance would tend to be preserved and inherited. Thus reflex actions, when once gained for one purpose, might afterwards be modified independently of the will or habit, so as to serve for some distinct purpose. Such cases would be parallel with those which, as we have every reason to believe, have occurred with many instincts; for although some instincts have been developed simply through long-continued and inherited habit, other highly complex ones have been developed through the preservation of variations of pre-existing instincts – that is, through Natural Selection.

Darwin here shows how readily he can explain expressions by natural selection rather than relying, as he often does in this chapter, on the inheritance of acquired characteristics.

I have discussed at some little length, though as I am well aware, in a very imperfect manner, the acquirement of reflex actions, because they are often brought into play in connection with move-

---

* [Dr Baxter (letter, 8 July, 1874) calls attention to a statement in Virchow's *Gedächtnissrede über Johannes Müller*, to the effect that Müller had command over the iris. Professor Beer, of Bonn, is said by Lewes (*Physical Basis of Mind*, 1877, p. 377) to have had the power of contracting or dilating the pupils at will. 'Here ideas act as motors. When he thinks of a very dark space the pupil dilates, when of a very bright spot the pupil contracts.']

ments expressive of our emotions; and it was necessary to show that at least some of them might have been first acquired through the will in order to satisfy a desire, or to relieve a disagreeable sensation.

Associated habitual movements in the lower animals. I have already given in the case of man several instances of movements, associated with various states of the mind or body, which are now purposeless, but which were originally of use, and are still of use under certain circumstances. As this subject is very important for us, I will here give a considerable number of analogous facts, with reference to animals; although many of them are of a very trifling nature. My object is to show that certain movements were originally performed for a definite end, and that, under nearly the same circumstances, they are still pertinaciously performed through habit when not of the least use. That the tendency in most of the following cases is inherited, we may infer from such actions being performed in the same manner by all the individuals, young and old, of the same species. We shall also see that they are excited by the most diversified, often circuitous, and sometimes mistaken associations.

Dogs, when they wish to go to sleep on a carpet or other hard

Fig. 4 Small dog watching a cat on a table.
From a photograph taken by Mr Rejlander

surface, generally turn round and round and scratch the ground with their fore-paws in a senseless manner, as if they intended to trample down the grass and scoop out a hollow, as no doubt their wild parents did, when they lived on open grassy plains or in the woods.* Jackals, fennecs, and other allied animals in the Zoological Gardens, treat their straw in this manner; but it is a rather odd circumstance that the keepers, after observing for some months, have never seen the wolves thus behave. A semi-idiotic dog – and an animal in this condition would be particularly liable to follow a senseless habit – was observed by a friend to turn completely round on a carpet thirteen times before going to sleep.

Many carnivorous animals, as they crawl towards their prey and prepare to rush or spring on it, lower their heads and crouch, partly, as it would appear, to hide themselves, and partly to get ready for their rush; and this habit in an exaggerated form has become hereditary in our pointers and setters. Now I have noticed scores of times that when two strange dogs meet on an open road, the one which first sees the other, though at the distance of one or two hundred yards, after the first glance always lowers its head, generally crouches a little, or even lies down; that is, he takes the proper attitude for concealing himself and for making a rush or spring, although the road is quite open and the distance great. Again, dogs of all kinds when intently watching and slowly approaching their prey, frequently keep one of their fore-legs doubled up for a long time, ready for the next cautious step; and this is eminently characteristic of the pointer. But from habit they behave in exactly the same manner whenever their attention is aroused (Fig. 4). I have seen a dog at the foot of a high wall, listening attentively to a sound on the opposite side, with one leg doubled up; and in this case there could have been no intention of making a cautious approach.

* [From a review (*Nature*, 1881, p. 196) by H. N. Moseley of Bessel's account of the *Polaris* expedition, it appears that the Esquimaux dogs never turn round before lying down, and this fact is in harmony with the above explanation, for the Esquimaux dogs cannot, for countless generations, have had an opportunity of trampling for themselves a sleeping place in grass.]

Dogs after voiding their excrement often make with all four feet a few scratches backwards, even on a bare stone pavement, as if for the purpose of covering up their excrement with earth, in nearly the same manner as do cats. Wolves and jackals behave in the Zoological Gardens in exactly the same manner, yet, as I am assured by the keepers, neither wolves, jackals, nor foxes, when they have the means of doing so, ever cover up their excrement, any more than do dogs.* Hence, if we rightly understand the meaning of the above cat-like habit, of which there can be little doubt, we have a purposeless remnant of an habitual movement, which was originally followed by some remote progenitor of the dog-genus for a definite purpose, and which has been retained for a prodigious length of time. The burying of superfluous food is a very different habit.†

Dogs and jackals[7] take much pleasure in rolling and rubbing their necks and backs on carrion. The odour seems delightful to them, though dogs (at least well-fed dogs) do not eat carrion. Mr Bartlett has observed wolves for me, and has given them carrion, but has never seen them roll on it. I have heard it remarked, and I believe it to be true, that the larger dogs, which are probably descended from wolves, do not so often roll in carrion as do smaller dogs, which are probably descended from jackals. When a piece of brown biscuit is offered to a terrier of mine and she is not hungry (and I have heard of similar instances), she first tosses it about and worries it, as if it were a rat or other prey; she then repeatedly rolls on it precisely as if it were a piece of carrion, and at last eats it. It would appear that an imaginary relish has to be given to the distasteful morsel; and to effect this the dog acts in his habitual manner, as if the biscuit was a live animal or smelt like carrion, though he knows better than we do that this is not the case. I have seen this same terrier act in the same manner after killing a little bird or mouse.

Dogs scratch themselves by a rapid movement of one of their

---

* This sentence was added in the second edition.
[See Appendix 2 for explanations of differences between first and second editions.]
† See p. 397 for a sentence eliminated here from the first edition.

hind feet; and when their backs are rubbed with a stick, so strong is the habit, that they cannot help rapidly scratching the air or the ground in a useless and ludicrous manner. The terrier just alluded to, when thus scratched with a stick, will sometimes show her delight by another habitual movement, namely, by licking the air as if it were my hand.*

Horses scratch themselves by nibbling those parts of their bodies which they can reach with their teeth; but more commonly one horse shows another where he wants to be scratched, and they then nibble each other. A friend whose attention I had called to the subject, observed that when he rubbed his horse's neck, the animal protruded his head, uncovered his teeth, and moved his jaws, exactly as if nibbling another horse's neck, for he could never have nibbled his own neck. If a horse is much tickled, as when curry-combed, his wish to bite something becomes so intolerably strong, that he will clatter his teeth together, and though not vicious, bite his groom. At the same time from habit he closely depresses his ears, so as to protect them from being bitten, as if he were fighting with another horse.

A horse when eager to start on a journey makes the nearest approach which he can to the habitual movement of progression by pawing the ground.† Now when horses in their stalls are about to be fed and are eager for their corn, they paw the pavement or the straw. Two of my horses thus behave when they see or hear the corn given to their neighbours. But here we have what may almost be called a true expression, as pawing the ground is universally recognized as a sign of eagerness.

Cats cover up their excrements of both kinds with earth; and

---

* [Mr Turner, of Farnborough, Kent, states (letter, 2 October, 1875) that when the tails of horned cattle are rubbed, 'just below the root', they invariably twist their bodies, stretch their necks, and begin to lick their lips.

It would seem from this that the dog licking the air need have nothing to do with licking his master's hand – for the above explanation is hardly applicable in the case of cattle.]

† [The Hon. Hugh Elliott (letter n. d.) describes a dog going through the pantomime of swimming as it was being carried over a river.]

my grandfather* saw a kitten scraping ashes over a spoonful of pure water spilt on the hearth; so that here an habitual or instinctive action was falsely excited, not by a previous act or by odour, but by eyesight. It is well known that cats dislike wetting their feet, owing, it is probable, to their having aboriginally inhabited the dry country of Egypt; and when they wet their feet they shake them violently. My daughter poured some water into a glass close to the head of a kitten; and it immediately shook its feet in the usual manner; so that here we have an habitual movement falsely excited by an associated sound instead of by the sense of touch.

Kittens, puppies, young pigs and probably many other animals, alternately push their fore-feet against the mammary glands of their mothers, to excite a freer secretion of milk, or to make it flow. Now it is very common with young cats, and not at all rare with old cats of the common and Persian breeds (believed by some naturalists to be specifically distinct), when comfortably lying on a warm shawl or other soft substance, to pound it quietly and alternately with their fore-feet; their toes being spread out and claws slightly protruded, precisely as when sucking their mother. That it is the same movement is clearly shown by their often at the same time taking a bit of the shawl into their mouths and sucking it; generally closing their eyes and purring from delight. This curious movement is commonly excited only in association with the sensation of a warm soft surface; but I have seen an old cat, when pleased by having its back scratched, pounding the air with its feet in the same manner; so that this action has almost become the expression of a pleasurable sensation.

Having referred to the act of sucking, I may add that this complex movement, as well as the alternate protrusion of the fore-feet, are reflex actions; for they are performed if a finger moistened with milk is placed in the mouth of a puppy, the front part of whose brain has been removed.[8] It has recently been stated in France, that the action of sucking is excited solely through the

---

* Dr Darwin, *Zoonomia*, 1794, vol. i, p. 160. I find that the fact of cats protruding their feet when pleased is also noticed in the same volume of *Zoonomia*, at p. 151.

sense of smell, so that if the olfactory nerves of a puppy are destroyed, it never sucks. In like manner the wonderful power which a chicken possesses only a few hours after being hatched, of picking up small particles of food, seems to be started into action through the sense of hearing; for with chickens hatched by artificial heat, a good observer found that 'making a noise with the finger-nail against a board, in imitation of the hen-mother, first taught them to peck at their meat'.[9]

I will give only one other instance of an habitual and purpose-less movement. The sheldrake (*Tadorna*) feeds on the sands left uncovered by the tide, and when a worm-cast is discovered, 'it begins patting the ground with its feet, dancing as it were, over the hole', and this makes the worm come to the surface. Now Mr St John says, that when his tame sheldrakes 'came to ask for food, they patted the ground in an impatient and rapid manner'.[10] This therefore may almost be considered as their expression of hunger. Mr Bartlett informs me that the flamingo and the kagu (*Rhinochetus jubatus*) when anxious to be fed, beat the ground with their feet in the same odd manner. So again kingfishers, when they catch a fish, always* beat it until it is killed; and in the Zoological Gardens they always beat the raw meat, with which they are sometimes fed, before devouring it.

Darwin conspicuously ignores the possibility that these expressions have been preserved and modified through natural selection because of their adaptive value in providing information to other members of the species. Burkhardt has offered two explanations of why Darwin did not use this 'Darwinian' explanation: he wanted to show that not everything can or should be explained in terms of its adaptive value; and, in opposing the creationists, he would avoid the topic of communication since the creationists had claimed God had given man these expressions to communicate.[C18]

---

* [It is not correct to say that kingfishers always act in this manner. See Mr C. C. Abbott, *Nature*, 13 March, 1873, and 21 January, 1875.]

We have now, I think, sufficiently shown the truth of our first principle, namely, that when any sensation, desire, dislike, etc., has led during a long series of generations to some voluntary movement, then a tendency to the performance of a similar movement will almost certainly be excited, whenever the same, or any analogous or associated sensation, etc., although very weak, is experienced; notwithstanding that the movement in this case may not be of the least use. Such habitual movements are often, or generally inherited; and they then differ but little from reflex actions. When we treat of the special expressions of man, the latter part of our first principle, as given at the commencement of this chapter, will be seen to hold good; namely, that when movements, associated through habit with certain states of the mind, are partially repressed by the will, the strictly involuntary muscles, as well as those which are least under the separate control of the will, are liable still to act; and their action is often highly expressive. Conversely, when the will is temporarily or permanently weakened, the voluntary muscles fail before the involuntary. It is a fact familiar to pathologists, as Sir C. Bell remarks,[11] 'that when debility arises from affection of the brain, the influence is greatest on those muscles which are, in their natural condition, most under the command of the will'. We shall also, in our future chapters, consider another proposition included in our first principle; namely, that the checking of one habitual movement sometimes requires other slight movements; these latter serving as a means of expression.

Darwin's principle of serviceable habits, stripped of its Lamarckian interpretation, is quite consistent with ethological interpretations of how signals evolved from what are called intention movements, and provides the foundation for current concepts of how signals become ritualized or formalized.[C19]

CHAPTER II

General Principles of Expression – continued

The principle of antithesis – Instances in the dog and cat – Origin of the principle – Conventional signs – The principle of antithesis has not arisen from opposite actions being consciously performed under opposite impulses.

We will now consider our second principle, that of antithesis.* Certain states of the mind lead, as we have seen in the last chapter, to certain habitual movements which were primarily, or may still be, of service; and we shall find that when a directly opposite state of mind is induced, there is a strong and involuntary tendency to the performance of movements of a directly opposite nature, though these have never been of any service. A few striking instances of antithesis will be given, when we treat of the special expressions of man; but as, in these cases, we are particularly liable to confound conventional or artificial gestures and expressions with those which are innate or universal, and which alone deserve to rank as true expressions, I will in the present chapter almost confine myself to the lower animals.

When a dog approaches a strange dog or man in a savage or hostile frame of mind he walks upright and very stiffly; his head is slightly raised, or not much lowered; the tail is held erect and quite rigid; the hairs bristle, especially along the neck and back;

* [For criticisms of the principle of antithesis (which has not met with much acceptance), see Wundt, *Essays*, 1885, p. 230; also his *Physiologische Psychologie*, 3rd edit.; also Sully, *Sensation and Intuition*, 1874, p. 29. Mantegazza (*La Physiono-mie*, 1885, p. 76) and L. Dumont (*Théorie Scientifique de la Sensibilité*, 2nd edit., 1877, p. 236) are also opposed to the principle.]

the pricked ears are directed forwards, and the eyes have a fixed stare (see Figs 5 and 7). These actions, as will hereafter be explained, follow from the dog's intention to attack his enemy, and are thus to a large extent intelligible. As he prepares to spring with a savage growl on his enemy, the canine teeth are uncovered, and the ears are pressed close backwards on the head; but with these latter actions, we are not here concerned. Let us now suppose that the dog suddenly discovers that the man whom he is approaching is not a stranger, but his master; and let it be observed how completely and instantaneously his whole bearing is reversed. Instead of walking upright, the body sinks downwards or even crouches, and is thrown into flexuous movements; his tail, instead of being held stiff and upright, is lowered and wagged from side to side; his hair instantly becomes smooth; his ears are depressed and drawn backwards, but not closely to the head; and his lips hang loosely. From the drawing back of the ears, the eyelids become elongated, and the eyes no longer appear round and staring. It should be added that the animal is at such times in an excited condition from joy; and nerve-force will be generated in excess, which naturally leads to action of some kind. Not one of the above movements, so clearly expressive of affection, is of the least direct service to the animal. They are explicable, as far as I can see, solely from being in complete opposition or antithesis to the attitude and movements which, from intelligible causes, are assumed when a dog intends to fight, and which consequently are expressive of anger. I request the reader to look at the four accompanying sketches, which have been given in order to recall vividly the appearance of a dog under these two states of mind. It is, however, not a little difficult to represent affection in a dog, whilst caressing his master and wagging his tail, as the essence of the expression lies in the continuous flexuous movements.

The American ethologist Erich Klinghammer commented on Darwin's description of the dog: 'While Darwin's description of the dog's behavior is excellent, it does not always lead to attack, it depends on the

Fig. 5. Dog approaching another dog with hostile intentions.
By Mr Riviere

Fig. 6. The same in a humble and affectionate frame of mind.
By Mr Riviere

circumstances, i.e., are the dogs on neutral ground, or on the home ground of one of the dogs? I would call this threat behavior, and it is usually not followed by an attack.'

Klinghammer also noted that Darwin discusses the dog's behavior *vis à vis* another person, rather than another dog. He disagrees with Darwin's statement that submissive or threatening behavior is of no service to the animal: 'Saying that the friendly behavior is merely the antithesis of the threat behaviors is not a sufficient explanation; because this friendly behavior has an immediate effect on the owner or another dog.'

The American ethologist and behavior geneticist Daniel G. Freedman commented on Darwin's discussion of the dog: 'Darwin is aware of submissiveness, but the naturalistic notion of, say, wolves forming an hierarchical pack is missing. Social hierarchies is a major concept in animal observation today, and many of Darwin's examples of antithesis would be now seen in terms of hierarchy.'

Fig. 7. Half-bred shepherd dog in the same state as in Fig. 5.
By Mr A. May

Fig. 8. The same caressing his master.
By Mr A. May

We will now turn to the cat. When this animal is threatened by a dog, it arches its back in a surprising manner, erects its hair, opens its mouth and spits. But we are not here concerned with this well-known attitude, expressive of terror combined with anger; we are concerned only with that of rage or anger. This is not often seen, but may be observed when two cats are fighting together; and I have seen it well exhibited by a savage cat whilst plagued by a boy. The attitude is almost exactly the same as that of a tiger disturbed and growling over its food, which every one must have beheld in menageries. The animal assumes a crouching position, with the body extended; and the whole tail, or the tip alone, is lashed or curled from side to side. The hair is not in the least erect. Thus far, the attitude and movements are nearly the same as when the animal is prepared to spring on its prey, and when, no doubt, it feels savage. But when preparing to fight, there is this difference, that the ears are closely pressed backwards;

the mouth is partially opened, showing the teeth; the fore-feet are occasionally stuck out with protruded claws; and the animal occasionally utters a fierce growl. (See Figs 9 and 10.) All, or almost all, these actions naturally follow (as hereafter to be explained), from the cat's manner and intention of attacking its enemy.

Let us now look at a cat in a directly opposite frame of mind, whilst feeling affectionate and caressing her master; and mark how opposite is her attitude in almost every respect. She now stands upright with her back slightly arched, which makes the hair appear rather rough, but it does not bristle; her tail, instead of being extended and lashed from side to side, is held quite stiff and perpendicularly upwards; her ears are erect and pointed; her mouth is closed; and she rubs against her master with a purr instead of a growl. Let it further be observed how widely different is the whole bearing of an affectionate cat from that of a dog, when with his body crouching and flexuous, his tail lowered and wagging, and ears depressed, he caresses his master. This contrast in the attitudes and movements of these two carnivorous animals, under the same pleased and affectionate frame of mind, can be explained, as it appears to me, solely by their movements standing in complete antithesis to those which are naturally assumed when these animals feel savage and are prepared either to fight or to seize their prey.

Freedman commented, 'Another concept not available to Darwin was territoriality, e.g., as exemplified by dog's spreading urine markings and male cat spraying. Dogs are used around the world to warn of strangers who are transgressing their territory. Cats are loners in their territory and challenge only other cats, whereas dogs pack-up easily and as we know bark at human strangers as well.'

In these cases of the dog and cat, there is every reason to believe that the gestures both of hostility and affection are innate or inherited; for they are almost identically the same in the

Fig. 9 Cat, savage, and prepared to fight. Drawn from life by Mr Wood

Fig. 10 Cat in an
affectionate frame of
mind. By Mr Wood

different races of the species, and in all the individuals of the same race, both young and old.

I will here give one other instance of antithesis in expression. I formerly possessed a large dog, who, like every other dog, was much pleased to go out walking. He showed his pleasure by trotting gravely before me with high steps, head much raised, moderately erected ears, and tail carried aloft but not stiffly. Not far from my house a path branches off to the right, leading to the hot-house, which I used often to visit for a few moments, to look at my experimental plants. This was always a great disappointment to the dog, as he did not know whether I should continue my walk; and the instantaneous and complete change of expression which came over him, as soon as my body swerved in the least towards the path (and I sometimes tried this as an experiment) was laughable. His look of dejection was known to every member of the family, and was called his *hot-house face*. This consisted in the head drooping much, the whole body sinking a little and remaining motionless; the ears and tail falling suddenly down, but the tail was by no means wagged. With the falling of the ears and his great chaps, the eyes became much changed in appearance, and I fancied that they looked less bright. His aspect was that of piteous, hopeless dejection; and it was, as I have said, laughable, as the cause was so slight. Every detail in his attitude was in complete opposition to his former joyful yet dignified bearing; and can be explained, as it appears to me, in no other way, except through the principle of antithesis. Had not the change been so instantaneous, I should have attributed it to his lowered spirits affecting, as in the case of man, the nervous system and circulation, and consequently the tone of his whole muscular frame; and this may have been in part the cause.

I am less convinced that this is an instance of antithesis. Instead, it seems better explained as dejection or what Darwin called 'lowered spirits'. He apparently did not accept this as the full explanation because it happened so quickly and the occasion, from his point of view, was so slight.

We will now consider how the principle of antithesis in expression has arisen. With social animals, the power of intercommunication between the members of the same community – and with other species, between the opposite sexes, as well as between the young and the old – is of the highest importance to them. This is generally effected by means of the voice, but it is certain that gestures and expressions are to a certain extent mutually intelligible. Man not only uses inarticulate cries, gestures, and expressions, but has invented articulate language; if, indeed, the word *invented* can be applied to a process, completed by innumerable steps, half-consciously made. Any one who has watched monkeys will not doubt that they perfectly understand each other's gestures and expression, and to a large extent, as Rengger asserts,[1] those of man. An animal when going to attack another, or when afraid of another, often makes itself appear terrible, by erecting its hair, thus increasing the apparent bulk of its body, by showing its teeth, or brandishing its horns, or by uttering fierce sounds.

As the power of intercommunication is certainly of high service to many animals, there is no *a priori* improbability in the supposition that gestures manifestly of an opposite nature to those by which certain feelings are already expressed, should at first have been voluntarily employed under the influence of an opposite state of feeling. The fact of the gestures being now innate, would be no valid objection to the belief that they were at first intentional; for if practised during many generations, they would probably at last be inherited. Nevertheless it is more than doubtful, as we shall immediately see, whether any of the cases which come under our present head of antithesis, have thus originated.

Darwin here grants the importance of intercommunication. If he had followed that line of reasoning, it would have been logical to suppose that opposite movements would be selected for their signal value. He would then have explained the smile, for example, as being selected for communication over the course of evolution, because it is a movement different from all the negative facial expressions of emotion – anger, fear, disgust or sadness. As the antithetical emotion, one would expect the smile to stand out in marked contrast to the other expressions and indeed that is what we have found. It is the only positive facial expression, contrasting with five negative expressions (fear, anger, disgust, sadness and contempt). One can recognize that someone is smiling from a further distance (100 metres) than any of the negative facial expressions.[C20] And when expressions are presented for only a fraction of a second, the smile is recognized more accurately than the negative emotional expressions.

The British philosopher Helena Cronin has raised the possibility that the ease of recognizing the smile may not be due to its being the antithetical expression, but because our brains might be primed to recognize smiles. If that is so, the scientists working on how single cells in the brain respond to faces should find there are smile-specific cells. To my knowledge no one has yet studied this possibility.

With conventional signs which are not innate, such as those used by the deaf and dumb and by savages, the principle of opposition or antithesis has been partially brought into play. The Cistercian monks thought it sinful to speak, and as they could not avoid holding some communication, they invented a gesture language, in which the principle of opposition seems to have been employed.[2] Dr Scott, of the Exeter Deaf and Dumb Institution, writes to me that 'opposites are greatly used in teaching the deaf and dumb, who have a lively sense of them'. Nevertheless I have been surprised how few unequivocal instances can be adduced. This depends partly on all the signs having commonly had some natural origin; and partly on the practice of the deaf and dumb and of savages to contract their signs as much as possible for the sake of rapidity.* Hence their natural source or origin often

---

* See on this subject Dr W. R. Scott's interesting work, *The Deaf and Dumb*, 2nd edit., 1870, p. 12. He says, 'This contracting of natural gestures into much shorter gestures than the natural expression requires, is very common among the

becomes doubtful or is completely lost; as is likewise the case with articulate language.

Many signs, moreover, which plainly stand in opposition to each other, appear to have had on both sides a significant origin. This seems to hold good with the signs used by the deaf and dumb for light and darkness, for strength and weakness, etc. In a future chapter I shall endeavour to show that the opposite gestures of affirmation and negation, namely, vertically nodding or laterally shaking the head, have both probably had a natural beginning. The waving of the hand from right to left, which is used as a negative by some savages, may have been invented in imitation of shaking the head; but whether the opposite movement of waving the hand in a straight line from the face, which is used in affirmation, has arisen through antithesis or in some quite distinct manner, is doubtful.

If we now turn to the gestures which are innate or common to all the individuals of the same species, and which come under the present head of antithesis, it is extremely doubtful whether any of them were at first deliberately invented and consciously performed. With mankind the best instance of a gesture standing in direct opposition to other movements, naturally assumed under an opposite frame of mind, is that of shrugging the shoulders. This expresses impotence or an apology – something which cannot be done, or cannot be avoided. The gesture is sometimes used consciously and voluntarily, but it is extremely improbable that it was at first deliberately invented, and afterwards fixed by habit; for not only do young children sometimes shrug their shoulders under the above states of mind, but the movement is accompanied, as will be shown in a future chapter, by various subordinate movements, which not one man in a thousand is aware of, unless he has specially attended to the subject.

Dogs, when approaching a strange dog, may find it useful to show by their movements that they are friendly, and do not wish

---

deaf and dumb. This contracted gesture is frequently so shortened as nearly to lose all semblance of the natural one, but to the deaf and dumb who use it, it still has the force of the original expression.'

to fight. When two young dogs in play are growling and biting each other's faces and legs, it is obvious that they mutually understand each other's gestures and manners. There seems, indeed, some degree of instinctive knowledge in puppies and kittens, that they must not use their sharp little teeth or claws too freely in their play, though this sometimes happens and a squeal is the result; otherwise they would often injure each other's eyes. When my terrier bites my hand in play, often snarling at the same time, if he bites too hard and I say *gently, gently*, he goes on biting, but answers me by a few wags of the tail, which seems to say 'Never mind, it is all fun'. Although dogs do thus express, and may wish to express, to other dogs and to man, that they are in a friendly state of mind, it is incredible that they could ever have deliberately thought of drawing back and depressing their ears, instead of holding them erect – of lowering and wagging their tails, instead of keeping them stiff and upright, etc., because they knew that these movements stood in direct opposition to those assumed under an opposite and savage frame of mind.

Again, when a cat, or rather when some early progenitor of the species, from feeling affectionate first arched its back, held its tail perpendicularly upwards and pricked its ears, can it be believed that the animal consciously wished thus to show that its frame of mind was directly the reverse of that, when from being ready to fight or spring on its prey, it assumed a crouching attitude, curled its tail from side to side and depressed its ears? Even still less can I believe that my dog voluntarily put on his dejected attitude and *hot-house face*, which formed so complete a contrast to his previous cheerful attitude and whole bearing. It cannot be supposed that he knew that I should understand his expression, and that he could thus soften my heart and make me give up visiting the hot-house.

Hence for the development of the movements which come under the present head, some other principle, distinct from the will and consciousness, must have intervened. This principle appears to be that every movement which we have voluntarily performed throughout our lives has required the action of certain muscles; and when we have performed a directly opposite movement, an opposite set of muscles has been habitually brought into play – as in turning to the right or to the left, in pushing away or pulling an object towards us, and in lifting or lowering a weight. So strongly are our intentions and movements associated together, that if we eagerly wish an object to move in any direction, we can hardly avoid moving our bodies in the same direction, although we may be perfectly aware that this can have no influence. A good illustration of this fact has already been given in the Introduction, namely, in the grotesque movements of a young and eager billiard-player, whilst watching the course of his ball. A man or child in a passion, if he tells anyone in a loud voice to begone, generally moves his arm as if to push him away, although the offender may not be standing near, and although there may not be the least need to explain by a gesture what is meant. On the other hand, if we eagerly desire some one to approach us closely, we act as if pulling him towards us; and so in innumerable other instances.

As the performance of ordinary movements of an opposite kind, under opposite impulses of the will, has become habitual in us and in the lower animals, so when actions of one kind have become firmly associated with any sensation or emotion, it appears natural that actions of a directly opposite kind, though of no use, should be unconsciously performed through habit and association, under the influence of a directly opposite sensation or emotion. On this principle alone I can understand how the gestures and expressions which come under the present head of antithesis have originated. If indeed they are serviceable to man or to any other animal, in aid of articulate cries or language, they will likewise be voluntarily employed, and the habit will thus be strengthened. But whether or not of service as a means of communication, the tendency to perform opposite movements under opposite sensations or emotions would, if we may judge by analogy, become hereditary through long practice; and there cannot be a doubt that several expressive movements due to the principle of antithesis are inherited.

Klinghammer commented, 'Lorenz and Tinbergen later pointed out that intention movements provide the raw material from which signals are sharpened through natural selection. It is not surprising that Darwin anticipated this. The thought that the first intentions would be practiced for many generations, and at last would be inherited is a Lamarckian interpretation that is not his usual way of looking at the evolution of behavior and morphological characteristics.'

CHAPTER III

General Principles of Expression – concluded

The principle of the direct action of the excited nervous system on the body, independently of the will and in part of habit – Change of colour in the hair – Trembling of the muscles – Modified secretions – Perspiration – Expression of extreme pain – Of rage, great joy, and terror – Contrast between the emotions which cause and do not cause expressive movements – Exciting and depressing states of the mind – Summary.

We now come to our third principle, namely, that certain actions, which we recognize as expressive of certain states of mind, are the direct result of the constitution of the nervous system, and have been from the first independent of the will, and, to a large extent, of habit. When the sensorium is strongly excited nerve-force is generated in excess, and is transmitted in certain directions, dependent on the connection of the nerve-cells, and, as far as the muscular system is concerned, on the nature of the movements which have been habitually practised. Or the supply of nerve-force may, as it appears, be interrupted. Of course every movement which we make is determined by the constitution of the nervous system; but actions performed in obedience to the will, or through habit, or through the principle of antithesis, are here as far as possible excluded. Our present subject is very obscure, but, from its importance, must be discussed at some length; and it is always advisable to perceive clearly our ignorance.

The most striking case, though a rare and abnormal one, which can be adduced to the direct influence of the nervous system, when strongly affected, on the body, is the loss of colour in the hair, which has occasionally been observed after extreme terror or grief. One authentic instance has been recorded, in the case of a man brought out for execution in India, in which the change of colour was so rapid that it was perceptible to the eye.*

American psychophysiologist Stephen Porges has commented: 'Darwin emphasized the nervous system as a causal mechanism that limits the range of emotional expression and experience. By noting the relation between the nervous system and habit, he provided an antecedent to the contemporary concept of species or developmental preparedness not only to express specific affect states, but also to learn specific associations.'

Another good case is that of the trembling of the muscles, which is common to man and to many, or most, of the lower animals. Trembling is of no service, often of much disservice, and cannot have been at first acquired through the will, and then rendered habitual in association with any emotion. I am assured by an eminent authority that young children do not tremble, but go into convulsions under the circumstances which would induce excessive trembling in adults. Trembling is excited in different individuals in very different degrees, and by the most diversified causes – by cold to the surface, before fever-fits, although the temperature of the body is then above the normal standard; in blood-poisoning, delirium tremens, and other diseases; by general failure of power in old age; by exhaustion after excessive fatigue; locally from severe injuries, such as burns; and, in an especial manner, by the passage of a catheter. Of all emotions, fear notoriously is the most apt to induce trembling; but so do occasionally

* See the interesting cases collected by M. G. Pouchet in the *Revue des Deux Mondes*, 1 January, 1872, p. 79. An instance was also brought some years ago before the British Association at Belfast. [Lange (*Über Gemüthsbewegungen*, translated from the Danish by Kuralla. Leipzig: 1887, p. 85) quotes from Mantegazza the account of a lion-tamer, whose hair fell off in a night after a life-and-death struggle in a lion's cage. A similar case is quoted of a girl who lost every hair on her body, even to her eyelashes, in a few days after suffering great terror during the fall of a house.]

great anger and joy. I remember once seeing a boy who had just shot his first snipe on the wing, and his hands trembled to such a degree from delight, that he could not for some time reload his gun;* and I have heard of an exactly similar case with an Australian savage, to whom a gun had been lent. Fine music, from the vague emotions thus excited, causes a shiver to run down the backs of some persons. There seems to be very little in common in the above several physical causes and emotions to account for trembling; and Sir J. Paget, to whom I am indebted for several of the above statements, informs me that the subject is a very obscure one. As trembling is sometimes caused by rage, long before exhaustion can have set in, and as it sometimes accompanies great joy, it would appear that any strong excitement of the nervous system interrupts the steady flow of nerve-force to the muscles.†

The manner in which the secretions of the alimentary canal and of certain glands — as the liver, kidneys, or mammae — are affected by strong emotions, is another excellent instance of the direct action of the sensorium on these organs, independently of the will or of any serviceable associated habit. There is the greatest difference in different persons in the parts which are thus affected, and in the degree of their affection.

The heart, which goes on uninterruptedly beating night and day in so wonderful a manner, is extremely sensitive to external stimulants. The great physiologist, Claude Bernard,[1] has shown how the least excitement of a sensitive nerve reacts on the heart; even when a nerve is touched so slightly that no pain can possibly be felt by the animal under experiment. Hence when the mind is strongly excited, we might expect that it would instantly affect in a direct manner the heart; and this is universally acknowledged and felt to be the case. Claude Bernard also repeatedly insists, and this deserves especial notice, that when the heart is affected it reacts on the brain; and the state of the brain again reacts

* [The boy in question was actually Darwin himself. See *Life and Letters of Charles Darwin*, vol. i, p. 34.]
† Müller remarks (*Elements of Physiology*, Eng. translat. vol. ii, p. 934) that when the feelings are very intense, 'all the spinal nerves become affected to the extent of imperfect paralysis, or the excitement of trembling of the whole body'.

through the pneumo-gastric nerve on the heart; so that under any excitement there will be much mutual action and reaction between these, the two most important organs of the body.*

The vaso-motor system, which regulates the diameter of the small arteries, is directly acted on by the sensorium, as we see when a man blushes from shame; but in this latter case the checked transmission of nerve-force to the vessels of the face can, I think, be partly explained in a curious manner through habit. We shall also be able to throw some light, though very little, on the involuntary erection of the hair under the emotions of terror and rage. The secretion of tears depends, no doubt, on the connection of certain nerve-cells; but here again we can trace some few of the steps by which the flow of nerve-force through the requisite channels has become habitual under certain emotions.

Porges has commented: 'Darwin acknowledged the importance of the dynamic bi-directional relationship between visceral organs and the brain via the autonomic nervous system. His emphasis on bi-directional communication via the pneumogastric nerve (i.e., vagus) although minimized by physiologists and psychologists

---

* See Mosso (*La Peur*, p. 46), on the effect of emotion on the circulation in the brain. He gives an interesting account of cases in which, owing to injuries to the skull, the pulsation of the brain could be observed. In the same work of Mosso's are a number of interesting observations on the influence of the emotions on the circulation. He has demonstrated, by means of his plethysmograph, the effect of emotion in causing a diminution in the volume of the arm, etc.; and, by means of his balance, has shown the flow of blood to the brain under very small stimuli – for instance, when a slight noise, not sufficient to wake the patient, is made in the room in which he is asleep. Mosso considers the action of emotion on the vaso-motor system as adaptive. The violent action of the heart in terror, is supposed to be of use as preparing the body generally for great exertion. In a similar manner he explains the pallor of terror (ibid. p. 73): 'Quand nous somme menacés d'un péril, quand nous ressentons une frayeur, une émotion, et que l'organisme doit rassembler ses forces, une contraction des vaisseaux sanguins se produit automatiquement, et cette contraction rend plus actif le mouvement du sang vers les centres nerveux.' ['When a risk threatens, when we feel the emotion of fear, and the organism has to gather its strength, a contraction of the blood vessels occurs automatically and this contraction speeds up the flow of blood to the nerve centres.']

for over one hundred years, is now the focus of contemporary research and theory on both emotion and health. Darwin's views of the contribution of the autonomic nervous system to emotional regulation predate Cannon and James and provide a more realistic model of the dynamic feedback between peripheral and central structures. Darwin's statement is important because it emphasizes afferent feedback from the heart to the brain, independent of the spinal cord and the sympathetic nervous system, as well as the regulatory role of the vagus in the expression of emotions.'

A brief consideration of the outward signs of some of the stronger sensations and emotions will best serve to show us, although vaguely, in how complex a manner the principle under consideration of the direct action of the excited nervous system on the body, is combined with the principle of habitually associated, serviceable movements.

When animals suffer from an agony of pain, they generally writhe about with frightful contortions; and those which habitually use their voices utter piercing cries or groans. Almost every muscle of the body is brought into strong action. With man the mouth may be closely compressed, or more commonly the lips are retracted, with the teeth clenched or ground together. There is said to be 'gnashing of teeth' in hell; and I have plainly heard the grinding of the molar teeth of a cow which was suffering acutely from inflammation of the bowels. The female hippopotamus in the Zoological Gardens, when she produced her young, suffered greatly; she incessantly walked about, or rolled on her sides, opening and closing her jaws, and chattering her teeth together.[2] With man the eyes stare wildly as in horrified astonishment, or the brows are heavily contracted. Perspiration bathes the body, and drops trickle down the face. The circulation* and

---

* [According to Mantegazza, *Azione del Dolore sulla Calorificazione*, Milan, 1866, slight and transitory pains produce in the rabbit a rise in the pulse-rate; but this he considers to be due to the muscular contractions which accompany the pain, rather than to the pain itself. Severe and prolonged pain cause enormous diminution of the rate of the pulse, and this slowing lasts for some considerable time.]

respiration* are much affected. Hence the nostrils are generally dilated and often quiver; or the breath may be held until the blood stagnates in the purple face. If the agony be severe and prolonged, these signs all change; utter prostration follows, with fainting or convulsions.

A sensitive nerve when irritated transmits some influence to the nerve-cell, whence it proceeds; and this transmits its influence, first to the corresponding nerve-cell on the opposite side of the body, and then upwards and downwards along the cerebro-spinal column to other nerve-cells, to a greater or less extent, according to the strength of the excitement; so that, ultimately, the whole nervous system may be affected.[3] This involuntary transmission of nerve-force may or may not be accompanied by consciousness. Why the irritation of a nerve-cell should generate or liberate nerve-force is not known; but that this is the case seems to be the conclusion arrived at by all the greatest physiologists, such as Müller, Virchow, Bernard, etc.[†] As Mr Herbert Spencer remarks, it may be received as an 'unquestionable truth that, at any moment, the existing quantity of liberated nerve-force, which in an inscrutable way produces in us the state we call feeling, *must* expend itself in some direction – must generate an equivalent manifestation of force somewhere'; so that, when the cerebro-spinal system is highly excited and nerve-force is liberated in excess, it may be expended in intense sensations, active thought, violent movements, or increased activity of the glands.[4] Mr Spencer further maintains that an 'overflow of nerve-force, undirected by any motive, will manifestly take the most habitual routes; and, if these do not suffice, will next overflow into the less habitual ones'. Consequently the facial and respiratory muscles, which are the most used, will be apt to be first brought into

* [In the case of the higher animals, pain, according to Mantegazza, causes the respiration to become hurried and irregular, and may afterwards cause it to become slower. See his paper in the *Gazzetta medica Italiana Lombardia*, vol. 5, Milan, 1866.]

† Müller (*Elements of Physiology*, Eng. trans. vol. ii, p. 932) in speaking of the nerves, says, 'any sudden change of condition of whatever kind sets the nervous principle into action'. See Virchow and Bernard on the same subject in passages in the two works referred to in my last footnote.

action; then those of the upper extremities, next those of the lower,[5] and finally those of the whole body.*

An emotion may be very strong, but it will have little tendency to induce movements of any kind, if it has not commonly led to voluntary action for its relief or gratification; and when movements are excited, their nature is, to a large extent, determined by those which have often and voluntarily been performed for some definite end under the same emotion. Great pain urges all animals, and has urged them during endless generations, to make the most violent and diversified efforts to escape from the cause of suffering. Even when a limb or other separate part of the body is hurt, we often see a tendency to shake it, as if to shake off the cause, though this may obviously be impossible. Thus a habit of exerting with the utmost force all the muscles will have been established, whenever great suffering is experienced. As the muscles of the chest and vocal organs are habitually used, these will be particularly liable to be acted on, and loud, harsh screams or cries will be uttered. But the advantage derived from outcries has here probably come into play in an important manner; for the young of most animals, when in distress or danger, call loudly to their parents for aid, as do the members of the same community for mutual aid.

What Darwin describes in the first few sentences of this paragraph is quite consistent with the thinking of a current emotion theorist, the Dutch psychologist Nico Frijda,[C21] who emphasizes the role of action plans for each emotion. Later, Darwin says that not every emotion has any specific action regularly associated with it, and those emotions that don't, have no facial expression (see commentary, p. 83).

---

* Sir H. Holland, in speaking (*Medical Notes and Reflexions*, 1839, p. 328) of that curious state of the body called the *fidgets*, remarks that it seems due to 'an accumulation of some cause of irritation which requires muscular action for its relief'.

Another principle, namely, the internal consciousness that the power or capacity of the nervous system is limited, will have strengthened, though in a subordinate degree, the tendency to violent action under extreme suffering. A man cannot think deeply and exert his utmost muscular force. As Hippocrates long ago observed, if two pains are felt at the same time, the severer one dulls the other. Martyrs, in the ecstasy of their religious fervour have often, as it would appear, been insensible to the most horrid tortures. Sailors who are going to be flogged sometimes take a piece of lead into their mouths, in order to bite it with their utmost force, and thus to bear the pain. Parturient women prepare to exert their muscles to the utmost in order to relieve their sufferings.

We thus see that the undirected radiation of nerve-force from the nerve-cells which are first affected – the long-continued habit of attempting by struggling to escape from the cause of suffering – and the consciousness that voluntary muscular exertion relieves pain, have all probably concurred in giving a tendency to the most violent, almost convulsive, movements under extreme suffering; and such movements, including those of the vocal organs, are universally recognized as highly expressive of this condition.

These are both interesting explanations, but I don't understand why Darwin considered them instances of his third principle: the direct action of the nervous system. The violent struggle during pain to escape from the cause of suffering is an instance of engaging in actions which serve to reduce an unpleasant feeling; these actions also signal to others that this is being felt. Blocking out one unpleasant sensation by deliberately generating a stronger sensation – the flogged sailor biting on a piece of lead – is another instance of specific movements that cope with an unpleasant feeling state, in this case by blocking sensations. But here the movement is, as Darwin indicates, deliberate, while squirming in pain is an automatic attempt to withdraw from the source of pain, even when it will not serve to accomplish relief.

As the mere touching of a sensitive nerve reacts in a direct manner on the heart, severe pain will obviously react on it in like manner, but far more energetically. Nevertheless, even in this case, we must not overlook the indirect effects of habit on the heart, as we shall see when we consider the signs of rage.

When a man suffers from an agony of pain, the perspiration often trickles down his face; and I have been assured by a veterinary surgeon that he has frequently seen drops falling from the belly and running down the inside of the thighs of horses, and from the bodies of cattle, when thus suffering. He has observed this, when there has been no struggling which would account for the perspiration. The whole body of the female hippopotamus, before alluded to, was covered with red-coloured perspiration whilst giving birth to her young. So it is with extreme fear; the same veterinary has often seen horses sweating from this cause; as has Mr Bartlett with the rhinoceros; and with man it is a well-known symptom. The cause of perspiration bursting forth in these cases is quite obscure; but it is thought by some physiologists to be connected with the failing power of the capillary circulation; and we know that the vaso-motor system, which regulates the capillary circulation, is much influenced by the mind. With respect to the movements of certain muscles of the face under great suffering, as well as from other emotions, these will be best considered when we treat of the special expressions of man and of the lower animals.

One of the most commonly used measures of emotion is sweating in the hands. Heart rate, which Darwin describes below, is another widely used measure of the physiological changes which occur with emotion.

We will now turn to the characteristic symptoms of rage. Under this powerful emotion the action of the heart is much accelerated,* or it may be much disturbed. The face reddens, or

* I am much indebted to Mr A. H. Garrod for having informed me of M. Lorain's work on the pulse, in which a sphygmogram of a woman in a rage is given; and this shows much difference in the rate and other characters from that of the same woman in her ordinary state.

it becomes purple from the impeded return of the blood, or may turn deadly pale. The respiration is laboured, the chest heaves, and the dilated nostrils quiver. The whole body often trembles. The voice is affected. The teeth are clenched or ground together, and the muscular system is commonly stimulated to violent, almost frantic action. But the gestures of a man in this state usually differ from the purposeless writhings and struggles of one suffering from an agony of pain; for they represent more or less plainly the act of striking or fighting with an enemy.

All these signs of rage are probably in large part, and some of them appear to be wholly, due to the direct action of the excited sensorium. But animals of all kinds, and their progenitors before them, when attacked or threatened by an enemy, have exerted their utmost powers in fighting and in defending themselves. Unless an animal does thus act, or has the intention, or at least the desire, to attack its enemy, it cannot properly be said to be enraged. An inherited habit of muscular exertion will thus have been gained in association with rage; and this will directly or indirectly affect various organs, in nearly the same manner as does great bodily suffering.

The heart no doubt will likewise be affected in a direct manner; but it will also in all probability be affected through habit; and all the more so from not being under the control of the will. We know that any great exertion which we voluntarily make, affects the heart, through mechanical and other principles which need not here be considered; and it was shown in the first chapter that nerve-force flows readily through habitually used channels – through the nerves of voluntary or involuntary movement, and through those of sensation. Thus even a moderate amount of exertion will tend to act on the heart; and on the principle of association, of which so many instances have been given, we may feel nearly sure that any sensation or emotion, as great pain or rage, which has habitually led to much muscular action, will immediately influence the flow of nerve-force to the heart, although there may not be at the time any muscular exertion.

Until recently most psychologists believed that emotions did not differ in terms of the changes that occur in the bodily organs governed by the Autonomic Nervous System (ANS), such as heart rate, sweating, respiration, blood flow to the hands or feet, etc. It was only what one thought, one's interpretations of events, that were said to distinguish one emotion from another, not distinctive physiological changes or expressions. 'I think, therefore I have an emotion, and which emotion I have depends upon what I think', might be the motto of this work, which has been quite influential for the past thirty years. Recent research[C22] has found contrary evidence: not only distinctive expressions for anger, fear, sadness and disgust, but different patterns of bodily changes for each of these emotions. Research with my colleague, the American psychologist Robert Levenson, has shown such emotion-specific changes in ANS activity. We believe that the particular changes that occur are preparing us to engage in actions which in the course of our evolutionary history have been most adaptive. For example, we found that in both anger and fear the heart rate accelerates. This prepares the person for strong exertions, as Darwin says, with the blood going to the hands in anger (preparatory to hitting), and to the limbs in fear (preparatory to flight).

The heart, as I have said, will be all the more readily affected through habitual associations, as it is not under the control of the will. A man when moderately angry, or even when enraged, may command the movements of his body, but he cannot prevent his heart from beating rapidly. His chest will perhaps give a few heaves, and his nostrils just quiver, for the movements of respiration are only in part voluntary. In like manner those muscles of the face which are least obedient to the will, will sometimes alone betray a slight and passing emotion. The glands again are wholly independent of the will, and a man suffering from grief may command his features, but cannot always prevent the tears from coming into his eyes. A hungry man, if tempting food is placed before him, may not show his hunger by any outward gesture, but he cannot check the secretion of saliva.

Under a transport of joy or of vivid pleasure, there is a strong tendency to various purposeless movements, and to the utterance of various sounds. We see this in our young children, in their loud laughter, clapping of hands, and jumping for joy; in the bounding and barking of a dog when going out to walk with his master; and in the frisking of a horse when turned out into an open field.* Joy quickens the circulation, and this stimulates the brain, which again reacts on the whole body. The above purpose-less movement and increased heart action may be attributed in chief part to the excited state of the sensorium,† and to the conse-quent undirected overflow, as Mr Herbert Spencer insists, of nerve-force. It deserves notice, that it is chiefly the anticipation of a pleasure, and not its actual enjoyment, which leads to pur-poseless and extravagant movements of the body, and to the utterance of various sounds. We see this in our children when they expect any great pleasure or treat; and dogs, which have been bounding about at the sight of a plate of food, when they get it do not show their delight by any outward sign, not even by wagging their tails. Now with animals of all kinds, the acquire-ment of almost all their pleasures, with the exception of those of

* [Mr Bain criticizes this passage in his review of Darwin on expression: being a postscript to *Senses and the Intellect*, 1873, p. 699.]

† How powerfully intense joy excites the brain, and how the brain reacts on the body, is well shown in the rare cases of psychical intoxication. Dr J. Crichton Browne (*Medical Mirror*, 1865) records the case of a young man of strongly nervous temperament, who, on hearing by a telegram that a fortune had been bequeathed him, first became pale then exhilarated, and soon in the highest spirits, but flushed and very restless. He then took a walk with a friend for the sake of tranquillizing himself, but returned staggering in his gait, uproariously laughing, yet irritable in temper, incessantly talking, and singing loudly in the public streets. It was positively ascertained that he had not touched any spirituous liquor, though every one thought that he was intoxicated. Vomiting after a time came on, and the half-digested contents of his stomach were examined, but no odour of alcohol could be detected. He then slept heavily, and on awakening was well, except that he suffered from headache, nausea, and prostration of strength.

warmth and rest, are associated, and have long been associated with active movements, as in the hunting or search for food, and in their courtship. Moreover, the mere exertion of the muscles after long rest or confinement is in itself a pleasure, as we ourselves feel, and as we see in the play of young animals. Therefore on this latter principle alone we might perhaps expect that vivid pleasure would be apt to show itself conversely in muscular movements.

The 6 November 1873 issue of *Nature* magazine published an anonymous rebuttal to Bain's review of *Expression*, which said: 'Darwin has instanced the frisking of a horse when turned into an open field as an example of joyful expression; on which it is remarked [by Bain] this is "almost pure spontaneity – it does not necessarily express joy or pleasure at all." How curious! One must really be a psychologist [Bain was a psychologist] before he can see common things in such an uncommon light.' (See also commentary p. 87.) The English historian Janet Browne believes this was written by William Hugh Spottiswoode. The English art historian Phillip Prodger has noted that Spottiswoode was very active during this time at the Royal Institution and the British Association for the Advancement of Science.

With all or almost all animals, even with birds, terror causes the body to tremble. The skin becomes pale, sweat breaks out, and the hair bristles. The secretions of the alimentary canal and of the kidneys are increased, and they are involuntarily voided, owing to the relaxation of the sphincter muscles,* as is known to be the case with man, and as I have seen with cattle, dogs,

---

* [Dr Lange, professor of medicine at Copenhagen, states that this is not due to the relaxation of the sphincters, but to a spasm of the viscera. See his *Gemüthsbewegungen*, translated into German by Kuralla, Leipzig, 1887, p. 85, where references to his previous writings on this subject are given. Mosso takes the same view; see his *La Peur*, p. 137, where he refers to a paper by Pellacani and himself, 'Sur les Fonctions de la Vessie' (*Archives Italiennes de Biologie*, 1882). See also Tuke, *Influence of the Mind on the Body*, p. 273.]

cats, and monkeys. The breathing is hurried. The heart beats quickly, wildly, and violently; but whether it pumps the blood more efficiently through the body may be doubted, for the surface seems bloodless and the strength of the muscles soon fails. In a frightened horse I have felt through the saddle the beating of the heart so plainly that I could have counted the beats. The mental faculties are much disturbed. Utter prostration soon follows, and even fainting. A terrified canary-bird has been seen not only to tremble and to turn white about the base of the bill, but to faint,[6] and I once caught a robin in a room, which fainted so completely, that for a time I thought it dead.

Most of these symptoms are probably the direct result, independently of habit, of the disturbed state of the sensorium; but it is doubtful whether they ought to be wholly thus accounted for. When an animal is alarmed it almost always stands motionless for a moment, in order to collect its senses and to ascertain the source of danger, and sometimes for the sake of escaping detection. But headlong flight soon follows, with no husbanding of the strength as in fighting, and the animal continues to fly as long as the danger lasts, until utter prostration, with failing respiration and circulation, with all the muscles quivering and profuse sweating, renders further flight impossible. Hence it does not seem improbable that the principle of associated habit may in part account for, or at least augment, some of the above-named characteristic symptoms of extreme terror.

That the principle of associated habit has played an important part in causing the movements expressive of the foregoing several strong emotions and sensations, we may, I think, conclude from considering firstly, some other strong emotions which do not ordinarily require for their relief or gratification any voluntary movement; and secondly the contrast in nature between the so-called exciting and depressing states of the mind. No emotion is stronger than maternal love; but a mother may feel deepest love for her helpless infant, and yet not show it any outward sign; or only by slight caressing movements, with a gentle smile and tender eyes. But let any one intentionally injure her infant, and see what a change! how she starts up with threatening aspect, how her eyes sparkle and her face reddens, how her bosom heaves, nostrils dilate, and heart beats; for anger, and not maternal love, has habitually led to action. The love between the opposite sexes is widely different from maternal love; and when lovers meet, we know that their hearts beat quickly, their breathing is hurried, and their faces flush; for this love is not inactive like that of a mother for her infant.

A man may have his heart filled with the blackest hatred or suspicion, or be corroded with envy or jealousy; but as these feelings do not at once lead to action, and as they commonly last for some time, they are not shown by any outward sign, excepting that a man in this state assuredly does not appear cheerful or good-tempered. If indeed these feelings break out into overt acts, rage takes their place, and will be plainly exhibited. Painters can hardly portray suspicion, jealousy, envy, etc., except by the aid of accessories which tell the tale; and poets use such vague and fanciful expressions as 'green-eyed jealousy'. Spenser describes suspicion as 'Foul, ill-favoured, and grim, under his eyebrows looking still askance', etc.; Shakespeare speaks of envy 'as lean-faced in her loathsome ease'; and in another place he says, 'no black envy shall make my grave'; and again as 'above pale envy's threatening reach'.

I believe Darwin is correct that there is no facial expression for maternal love, romantic love, hatred, envy or jealousy. That is not to say that we can't tell when these experiences occur; just that there is no momentary facial expression or vocalization unique to these feelings. Although the feelings are strong in each experience, I differ from Darwin in not regarding them as emotions.[C23] Emotions are brief and episodic, lasting seconds or minutes. Parental love, romantic love, hatred, envy or jealousy last for much longer periods – months, years, a lifetime for love and hatred, and at least hours or days for envy or jealousy. In each of these there is a strong commitment, an important attachment (negatively in the case of hatred, envy and jealousy). They also differ from emotions in specifying something about the cast of characters involved. The angry expression does not reveal who is the target, nor can one know from the expression itself what brought forth the anger. Not so with most of these experiences: the object is an offspring in parental love, a desired sexual object in romantic love, and a person who has something wanted by another in envy. In sexual jealousy there are two people involved: the person towards whom romantic love is felt and the rival for the affections of the loved one.

Emotions and sensations have often been classed as exciting or depressing. When all the organs of the body and mind – those of voluntary and involuntary movement, of perception, sensation, thought, etc. – perform their functions more energetically and rapidly than usual, a man or animal may be said to be excited, and, under an opposite state, to be depressed. Anger and joy are from the first exciting emotions, and they naturally lead, more especially the former, to energetic movements, which react on the heart and this again on the brain. A physician once remarked to me as a proof of the exciting nature of anger, that a man when excessively jaded will sometimes invent imaginary offences and put himself into a passion, unconsciously for the sake of reinvigorating himself; and since hearing this remark, I have occasionally recognized its full truth.

Several other states of mind appear to be at first exciting, but soon become depressing to an extreme degree. When a mother suddenly loses her child, sometimes she is frantic with grief, and must be considered to be in an excited state; she walks wildly about, tears her hair or clothes, and wrings her hands. This latter action is perhaps due to the principle of antithesis, betraying an inward sense of helplessness and that nothing can be done. The other wild and violent movements may be in part explained by the relief experienced through muscular exertion, and in part by the undirected overflow of nerve-force from the excited sensorium. But under the sudden loss of a beloved person, one of the first and commonest thoughts which occurs, is that something more might have been done to save the lost one. An excellent observer,[7] in describing the behaviour of a girl at the sudden death of her father, says she 'went about the house wringing her hands* like a creature demented, saying "it was her fault"; "I should never have left him"; "If I had only sat up with him",' etc. With such ideas vividly present before the mind, there would arise, through the principle of associated habit, the strongest tendency to energetic action of some kind.

As soon as the sufferer is fully conscious that nothing can be done, despair or deep sorrow takes the place of frantic grief. The sufferer sits motionless, or gently rocks to and fro; the circulation becomes languid; respiration is almost forgotten, and deep sighs are drawn.[†] All this reacts on the brain, and prostration soon follows with collapsed muscles and dulled eyes. An associated habit no longer prompts the sufferer to action, he is urged by his friends to voluntary exertion, and not to give way to silent, motionless, grief. Exertion stimulates the heart, and this reacts on the brain, and aids the mind to bear its heavy load.

Pain, if severe, soon induces extreme depression[‡] or prostration; but it is at first a stimulant and excites to action, as we

---

* [A correspondent writes: 'What does this common phrase mean? I asked three men yesterday.

'A. grasped his left hand with his right, and caused the latter to revolve round the former.

'B. clasped his hands so that the fingers interlaced, and then squeezed them.

'C. did not know what it meant.

'I said that I understood it to mean shaking the hands rapidly from the wrists, but that I had never seen the action; whereupon B. said that he had seen a lady do it more than once.']

† [Henle has written on the 'Natural History of Sighing', in his *Anthropologische Vorträge*, 1876, vol. i, p. 43. He divides emotions into the *depressing* and the *exciting*. Depressing emotions, such as disgust, fear, or horror, cause contraction of the unstriped muscles, while the exciting passions, such as joy or anger, paralyse them. Thus it comes about that a depressing state of mind, such as anxiety or nervousness, causes, by means of the contraction of the small bronchi, an unpleasant sensation in the chest, as if there were an obstacle to free breathing. The insufficiency of the diaphragmal respiration forces itself on our attention, and by calling in the voluntary muscles of respiration we draw a deep breath or sigh.]

‡ [Mantegazza, 'Azione del Dolore sulla Calorificazione', in the *Gazzetta medica Italiana Lombardia*, vol. 5, Milan, 1866, shows that pain causes a 'lasting and serious' lowering of the temperature. It is interesting to note that in some animals fear produces analogous effects.]

see when we whip a horse, and as is shown by the horrid tortures inflicted in foreign lands on exhausted dray-bullocks, to rouse them to renewed exertion. Fear again is the most depressing of all the emotions; and it soon induces utter, helpless prostration, as if in consequence of, or in association with, the most violent and prolonged attempts to escape from the danger, though no such attempts have actually been made. Nevertheless, even extreme fear often acts at first as a powerful stimulant. A man or animal driven through terror to desperation, is endowed with wonderful strength, and is notoriously dangerous in the highest degree.

On the whole we may conclude that the principle of the direct action of the sensorium on the body, due to the constitution of the nervous system, and from the first independent of the will, has been highly influential in determining many expressions. Good instances are afforded by the trembling of the muscles, the sweating of the skin, the modified secretions of the alimentary canal and glands, under various emotions and sensations. But actions of this kind are often combined with others, which follow from our first principle, namely, that actions which have often been of direct or indirect service, under certain states of the mind, in order to gratify or relieve certain sensations, desires, etc., are still performed under analogous circumstances through mere habit, although of no service. We have combinations of this kind, at least in part, in the frantic gestures of rage, and in the writhings of extreme pain; and, perhaps, in the increased action of the heart and of the respiratory organs. Even when these and other emotions or sensations are aroused in a very feeble manner, there will still be a tendency to similar actions, owing to the force of long-associated habit; and those actions which are least under voluntary control will generally be longest retained. Our second principle of antithesis has likewise occasionally come into play.

Porges has commented: 'Although Darwin provided insight into the neural regulation of visceral organs during emotional states, his insights are less provocative or prophetic with regard to the mechanisms underlying facial expressions. Today we know that facial expressivity is consistent with the evolution of the cranial nerves. The cranial nerves that regulate facial expression evolved from the branchial arches (i.e., ancient gill arches associated with the extraction of oxygen from water) and the brainstem areas that regulate these nerves have evolved through phylogenetic processes to become integrated with specific and identifiable pathways that regulate visceral states.'

Finally, so many expressive movements can be explained, as I trust will be seen in the course of this volume, through the three principles which have now been discussed, that we may hope hereafter to see all thus explained, or by closely analogous principles. It is, however, often impossible to decide how much weight ought to be attributed, in each particular case, to one of our principles, and how much to another; and very many points in the theory of expression remain inexplicable.

Darwin wrote to Bain, a psychologist who had written a negative review of *Expression*: 'Your criticisms are all written in a quite fair spirit, and indeed no one who knows you or your work would expect anything else. What you say about the vagueness of what I have called the direct action of the nervous system is perfectly just. I felt it so at the time, and even more of late ... Did you read a review in a late Edin. [*Edinburgh Review*]? It was magnificently contemptuous towards myself and many others.'

CHAPTER IV

Means of Expression in Animals

The emission of sounds – Vocal sounds – Sounds otherwise produced – Erection of the dermal appendages, hairs, feathers, etc., under the emotions of anger and terror – The drawing back of the ears as a preparation for fighting, and as an expression of anger – Erection of the ears and raising the head, a sign of attention.

In this and the following chapter I will describe, but only in sufficient detail to illustrate my subject, the expressive movements, under different states of the mind, of some few well-known animals. But before considering them in due succession, it will save much useless repetition to discuss certain means of expression common to most of them.

The emission of sounds. With many kinds of animals, man included, the vocal organs are efficient in the highest degree as a means of expression. We have seen, in the last chapter, that when the sensorium is strongly excited, the muscles of the body are generally thrown into violent action; and as a consequence, loud sounds are uttered, however silent the animal may generally be, and although the sounds may be of no use. Hares* and rabbits, for instance, never, I believe, use their vocal organs except in the extremity of suffering; as, when a wounded hare is killed by the sportsman, or when a young rabbit is caught by a stoat. Cattle and horses suffer great pain in silence; but when this is excessive,

* [Mr J. Brander Dunbar, in a letter to Charles Darwin, states that hares cry to their young, and that the cry can be called forth by removing the young hare from where the mother left it. The cry is said to be quite different from the scream of the hunted hare.]

and especially when associated with terror, they utter fearful sounds. I have often recognized, from a distance on the pampas, the agonized death-bellow of the cattle, when caught by the lasso and hamstrung. It is said that horses, when attacked by wolves, utter loud and peculiar screams of distress.*

Involuntary and purposeless contractions of the muscles of the chest and glottis, excited in the above manner, may have first given rise to the emission of vocal sounds. But the voice is now largely used by many animals for various purposes; and habit seems to have played an important part in its employment under other circumstances. Naturalists have remarked, I believe with truth, that social animals, from habitually using their vocal organs as a means of intercommunication, use them on other occasions much more freely that other animals. But there are marked exceptions to this rule, for instance, with the rabbit. The principle, also, of association, which is so widely extended in its power, has likewise played its part. Hence it follows that the voice, from having been habitually employed as a serviceable aid under certain conditions, inducing pleasure, pain, rage, etc., is commonly used whenever the same sensations or emotions are excited, under quite different conditions, or in a lesser degree.

The sexes of many animals incessantly call for each other during the breeding season; and in not a few cases, the male endeavours thus to charm or excite the female. This, indeed, seems to have been the primeval use and means of development of the voice, as I have attempted to show in my *Descent of Man*. Thus the use of the vocal organs will have become associated with the anticipation of the strongest pleasure which animals are capable of feeling. Animals which live in society often call to each other when separated, and evidently feel much joy at meeting; as we see with a horse, on the return of his companion, for whom he has been neighing. The mother calls incessantly for her lost young ones; for instance, a cow for her calf; and the young of many

---

* [A lady communicated the following description of a horse screaming: 'In a crowd in London the horse fell and got under the wheel of a carriage; the scream rang in our ears for days after, as the most expressive of agony that we had ever heard.']

animals call for their mothers. When a flock of sheep is scattered, the ewes bleat incessantly for their lambs, and their mutual pleasure at coming together is manifest. Woe betide the man who meddles with the young of the larger and fiercer quadrupeds, if they hear the cry of distress from their young. Rage leads to the violent exertion of all the muscles, including those of the voice; and some animals, when enraged, endeavour to strike terror into their enemies by its power and harshness, as the lion does by roaring, and the dog by growling. I infer that their object is to strike terror, because the lion at the same time erects the hair of its mane, and the dog the hair along its back, and thus they make themselves appear as large and terrible as possible. Rival males try to excel and challenge each other by their voices, and this leads to deadly contests. Thus the use of the voice will have become associated with the emotion of anger, however it may be aroused. We have also seen that intense pain, like rage, leads to violent outcries, and the exertion of screaming by itself gives some relief; and thus the use of the voice will have become associated with suffering of any kind.

The German psychologist Klaus Scherer, an expert in the study of how the human voice shows emotion, commented: 'A strong aspect of Darwin's discussion of vocal sounds is his point that some of the acoustic variables, intensity and pitch, are similar across species. This is, in fact, a point that has been empirically established by people studying animal vocalization documented in a recent chapter I wrote.[C24] In particular the claim of motivational-structural similarity has been well established.'

The cause of widely different sounds being uttered under different emotions and sensations is a very obscure subject. Nor does the rule always hold good that there is any marked difference. For instance with the dog, the bark of anger and that of joy do not differ much, though they can be distinguished. It is not probable that any precise explanation of the cause or source of each particular sound, under different states of mind, will ever be given. We know that some animals, after being domesticated, have acquired the habit of uttering sounds which were not natural to them.[1] Thus domestic dogs, and even tamed jackals, have learnt to bark, which is a noise not proper to any species of the genus, with the exception of the *Canis latrans* of North America, which is said to bark. Some breeds, also, of the domestic pigeon have learnt to coo in a new and quite peculiar manner.

The character of the human voice, under the influence of various emotions, has been discussed by Mr Herbert Spencer[2] in his interesting essay on music. He clearly shows that the voice alters much under different conditions, in loudness and quality, that is, in resonance and timbre, in pitch and intervals. No one can listen to an eloquent orator or preacher, or to a man calling angrily to another, or to one expressing astonishment, without being struck with the truth of Mr Spencer's remarks. It is curious how early in life the modulation of the voice becomes expressive. With one of my children, under the age of two years, I clearly perceived that his humph of assent was rendered by a slight modulation strongly emphatic; and that by a peculiar whine his negative expressed obstinate determination. Mr Spencer further shows that emotional speech, in all the above respects is intimately related to vocal music, and consequently to instrumental music; and he attempts to explain the characteristic qualities of both on physiological grounds – namely, on 'the general law that a feeling is a stimulus to muscular action'. It may be admitted that the voice is affected through this law; but the explanation appears to me too general and vague to throw much light on the various differences, with the exception of that of loudness, between ordinary speech and emotional speech, or singing.

Scherer comments, 'Darwin produces the music-as-origin-of-speech theory, which Helmholtz also mentions. I agree with this.'[C25] It is likely that emotional changes of non-linguistic affect sounds or bursts are at the origin of both music and speech, in parallel or in sequence. But speech origin theories are notoriously speculative and have been frequently banned from discussion. I believe

> this is still a worthy issue and should be taken up by comparative studies of animal vocalizations, human affective bursts or interjects in different languages, and other prosoid manifestations, as well as emotional aspects of musical sounds.'

This remark holds good, whether we believe that the various qualities of the voice originated in speaking under the excitement of strong feelings, and that these qualities have subsequently been transferred to vocal music; or whether we believe, as I maintain, that the habit of uttering musical sounds was first developed as a means of courtship, in the early progenitors of man, and thus became associated with the strongest emotions of which they were capable – namely, ardent love, rivalry and triumph. That animals utter musical notes is familiar to every one, as we may daily hear in the singing of birds. It is a more remarkable fact that an ape, one of the Gibbons, produces an exact octave of musical sounds, ascending and descending the scale by half-tones; so that this monkey 'alone of brute mammals may be said to sing'.* From this fact, and from the analogy of other animals, I have been led to infer that the progenitors of man probably uttered musical tones before they had acquired the power of articulate speech; and that consequently, when the voice is used under any strong emotion, it tends to assume, through the principle of association, a musical character. We can plainly perceive, with some of the lower animals, that the males employ their voices to please the females, and that they themselves take pleasure in their own vocal utterances; but why particular sounds are uttered, and why these give pleasure cannot at present be explained.

That the pitch of the voice bears some relation to certain states of feeling is tolerably clear. A person gently complaining of ill-treatment, or slight suffering, almost always speaks in a

---

* *The Descent of Man*, 1870, vol. ii, p. 332. The words quoted are from Professor Owen. It has lately been shown that some quadrupeds much lower in the scale than monkeys, namely rodents, are able to produce correct musical tones; see the account of a singing hesperomys, by the Rev. S. Lockwood, in the *American Naturalist*, vol. v, December, 1871, p. 761.

high-pitched voice. Dogs, when a little impatient, often make a high piping note through their noses, which at once strikes us as plaintive;[3] but how difficult it is to know whether the sound is essentially plaintive, or only appears so in this particular case, from our having learnt by experience what it means! Rengger states[4] that the monkeys (*Cebus azarae*), which he kept in Paraguay, expressed astonishment by a half-piping, half-snarling noise; anger or impatience, by repeating the sound *hu hu* in a deeper, grunting voice; and fright, or pain, by shrill screams. On the other hand, with mankind, deep groans and high piercing screams equally express an agony of pain. Laughter may be either high or low; so that, with adult men, as Haller long ago remarked,[5] the sound partakes of the character of the vowels (as pronounced in German) *O* and *A*; whilst with children and women, it has more of the character of *E* and *I*; and these latter vowel-sounds naturally have, as Helmholtz has shown, a higher pitch than the former; yet both tones of laughter equally express enjoyment or amusement.

In my work with Scherer, we found that pitch became higher when people lied.[C26] It is an increase in muscle tension which drives pitch up, according to Scherer. He believes that the signal value is that of submissiveness or of an infant-like help call. In other studies I and my colleagues have found that lower pitch is perceived by others to be a sign of dominance.[C27] The Israeli zoologist Zahavi discussed[C28] a number of vocal signals in animals: 'Clutton-Brock and Albeon suggested that a stronger deer may roar louder and more frequently than a weaker one, hence the correlation between the potential to win and the pattern of roaring.[C29] Morton[C30] suggested that the pitch of the voice correlates with the potential to win because larger individuals tend to emit lower sounds. Scherer agrees that in general there is a larger vocal apparatus in larger individuals, making for a deeper pitch. Davies and Halliday[C31] demonstrated the correlation between the pitch of the vocal threat signal of toads and their potential to win.' I do not know whether or not lower pitch is associated with greater size or strength, or the likelihood of winning a fight, in humans.

In considering the mode in which vocal utterances express emotion, we are naturally led to enquire into the cause of what is called 'expression' in music. Upon this point Mr Litchfield, who has long attended to the subject of music, has been so kind as to give me the following remarks: 'The question, what is the essence of musical "expression" involves a number of obscure points, which, so far as I am aware, are as yet unsolved enigmas. Up to a certain point, however, any law which is found to hold as to the expression of the emotions by simple sounds must apply to the more developed mode of expression in song, which may be taken as the primary type of all music. A great part of the emotional effect of a song depends on the character of the action by which the sounds are produced. In songs, for instance, which express great vehemence of passion, the effect often chiefly depends on the forcible utterance of some one or two characteristic passages which demand great exertion of vocal force; and it will be frequently noticed that a song of this character fails of its proper effect when sung by a voice of sufficient power and range to give the characteristic passages without much exertion. This is, no doubt, the secret of the loss of effect so often produced by the transposition of a song from one key to another. The effect is thus seen to depend not merely on the actual sounds, but also in part on the nature of the action which produces the sounds. Indeed it is obvious that whenever we feel the "expression" of a song to be due to its quickness or slowness of movement – to smoothness of flow, loudness of utterance, and so on – we are, in fact, interpreting the muscular actions which produce sound, in the same way in which we interpret muscular action generally. But this leaves unexplained the more subtle and more specific effect which we call the *musical* expression of the song – the delight given by its melody, or even by the separate sounds which make up the melody. This is an effect indefinable in language – one which, so far as I am aware, no one has been able to analyse, and which the ingenious speculation of Mr Herbert Spencer as to the origin of music leaves quite unexplained. For it is certain that the *melodic* effect of a series of sounds does not depend in the least on their loudness or softness, or on their *absolute* pitch. A tune is always the same tune, whether it is sung loudly or softly, by a child or a man; whether it is played on a flute or on a trombone. The purely musical effect of any sound depends on its place in what is technically called a "scale"; the same sound producing absolutely different effects on the ear, according as it is heard in connection with one or another series of sounds.

'It is on this *relative* association of the sounds that all the essentially characteristic effects which are summed up in the phrase "musical expression", depend. But why certain associations of sounds have such-and-such effects, is a problem which yet remains to be solved. These effects must indeed, in some way or other, be connected with the well-known arithmetical relations between the rates of vibration of the sounds which form a musical scale. And it is possible – but this is merely a suggestion – that the greater or less mechanical facility with which the vibrating apparatus of the human larynx passes from one state of vibration to another, may have been a primary cause of the greater or less pleasure produced by various sequences of sounds.'

But leaving aside these complex questions and confining ourselves to the simpler sounds, we can, at least, see some reasons for the association of certain kinds of sounds with certain states of mind. A scream for instance, uttered by a young animal, or by one of the members of a community, as a call for assistance, will naturally be loud, prolonged and high, so as to penetrate to a distance. For Helmholtz has shown* that, owing to the shape of the internal cavity of the human ear and its consequent power of resonance, high notes produce a particularly strong impression. When male animals utter sounds in order to please the females, they would naturally employ those which are sweet to the ears of the species; and it appears that the same sounds are often pleasing to widely different animals, owing to the similarity of

* *Théorie Physiologique de la Musique*, Paris, 1868, p. 146. Helmholtz has also fully discussed in this profound work the relation of the form of the cavity of the mouth to the production of vowel sounds.

their nervous systems, as we ourselves perceive in the singing of birds and even in the chirping of certain tree-frogs giving us pleasure. On the other hand, sounds produced in order to strike terror into an enemy, would naturally be harsh or displeasing.

Whether the principle of antithesis has come into play with sounds, as might perhaps have been expected, is doubtful. The interrupted, laughing or tittering sounds made by man and by various kinds of monkeys when pleased, are as different as possible from the prolonged screams of these animals when distressed. The deep grunt of satisfaction uttered by a pig, when pleased with its food, is widely different from its harsh scream of pain or terror. But with the dog, as lately remarked, the bark of anger and that of joy are sounds which by no means stand in opposition to each other; and so it is in some other cases.

There is another obscure point, namely, whether the sounds which are produced under various states of the mind determine the shape of the mouth, or whether its shape is not determined by independent causes, and the sound thus modified. When young infants cry they open their mouths widely, and this, no doubt, is necessary for pouring forth a full volume of sound; but the mouth then assumes, from a quite distinct cause, an almost quadrangular shape, depending, as will hereafter be explained, on the firm closing of the eyelids, and consequent drawing up of the upper lip. How far the square shape of the mouth modifies the wailing or crying sound, I am not prepared to say; but we know from the researches of Helmholtz and others that the form of the cavity of the mouth and lips determines the nature and pitch of the vowel sounds which are produced.

Scherer and I did some preliminary work in which I tried to emit a continuous sound while changing the contraction of different muscles around my mouth. Scherer's analysis of the vocalizations I produced showed that tensing different parts of the muscle which orbits the mouth (*orbicularis oris*) had an appreciable effect on the power spectrum. Regrettably, we did not continue or publish that work.

It will also be shown in a future chapter that, under the feeling of contempt, or disgust, there is a tendency, from intelligible causes, to blow out of the mouth or nostrils, and this process sounds like *pooh* or *pish*. When any one is startled or suddenly astonished, there is an instantaneous tendency, likewise from an intelligible cause, namely, to be ready for prolonged exertion, to open the mouth widely, so as to draw a deep and rapid inspiration. When the next full expiration follows, the mouth is slightly closed, and the lips, from causes hereafter to be discussed, are somewhat protruded; and this form of the mouth, if the voice be at all exerted, produces, according to Helmholtz, the sound of the vowel *O*. Certainly a deep sound of a prolonged *Oh!* may be heard from a whole crowd of people immediately after witnessing an astonishing spectacle. If, together with surprise, pain be felt, there is a tendency to contract all the muscles of the body, including those of the face, and the lips will then be drawn back; and this will perhaps account for the sound becoming higher and assuming the character of *Ah!* or *Ach!* As fear causes all the muscles of the body to tremble, the voice naturally becomes tremulous, and at the same time husky from the dryness of the mouth, owing to the salivary glands failing to act. Why the laughter of man and the tittering of monkeys should be a rapidly reiterated sound, cannot be explained. During the utterance of these sounds, the mouth is transversely elongated by the corners being drawn backwards and upwards; and of this fact an explanation will be attempted in a future chapter. But the whole subject of the differences of sounds produced under different states of the mind is so obscure, that I have succeeded in throwing hardly any light on it; and the remarks which I have made, have but little significance.

In the next few lines, Darwin describes stamping by rabbits. Humans also sometimes stamp their feet when angry. My daughter tells me that I stamp my foot when I become angry or am arguing forcibly. I am never aware of doing this, but I have seen other men do so.

All the sounds hitherto noticed depend on the respiratory organs; but sounds produced by wholly different means are likewise expressive. Rabbits stamp loudly on the ground as a signal to their comrades; and if a man knows how to do so properly, he may on a quiet evening hear the rabbits answering him all around. These animals, as well as some others, also stamp on the ground when made angry. Porcupines rattle their quills and vibrate their tails when angered; and one behaved in this manner when a live snake was placed in its compartment. The quills on the tail are very different from those on the body; they are short, hollow, thin like a goose-quill, with their ends transversely truncated, so that they are open; they are supported on long, thin, elastic foot-stalks. Now, when the tail is rapidly shaken, these hollow quills strike against each other and produce, as I heard in the presence of Mr Bartlett, a peculiar continuous sound. We can, I think, understand why porcupines have been provided, through the modification of their protective spines, with this special sound-producing instrument. They are nocturnal animals, and if they scented or heard a prowling beast of prey, it would be a great advantage to them in the dark to give warning to their enemy what they were, and that they were furnished with dangerous spines. They would thus escape being attacked. They are, as I may add, so fully conscious of the power of their weapons, that when enraged they will charge backwards with their spines erected, yet still inclined backwards.

Many birds during their courtship produce diversified sounds by means of specially adapted feathers. Storks, when excited, make a loud clattering noise with their beaks. Some snakes produce a grating or rattling noise. Many insects stridulate by rubbing together specially modified parts of their hard integuments. This stridulation generally serves as a sexual charm or call; but it is likewise used to express different emotions.* Every one who has attended to bees knows that their humming changes when they are angry; and this serves as a warning that there is danger of

---

* I have given some details on this subject in my *Descent of Man*, 2nd edit., vol. i, pp. 434, 468.

Fig. 11 Sound-producing
quills from the tail of
the porcupine

being stung. I have made these few remarks because some writers
have laid so much stress on the vocal and respiratory organs as
having been specially adapted for expression, that it was advisable
to show that sounds otherwise produced serve equally well for
the same purpose.

Erection of the dermal appendages. Hardly any expressive movement
is so general as the involuntary erection of the hairs, feathers and
other dermal appendages; for it is common throughout three of
the great vertebrate classes.* These appendages are erected under

* [Rev. S. J. Whitmee (*Proc. Zool. Soc.*, 1878, pt. i, p. 132) describes the erection
of the dorsal and anal fins of fishes in anger and fear. He suggests that the
erection of the spines gives protection against carnivorous fish, and, if this is so,
it is not hard to understand the association of such movements with these emotions. Mr F. Day (*Proc. Zool. Soc.*, 1878, pt. i, p. 219) criticizes Mr Whitmee's
conclusions, but the description by Mr Whitmee of a spiny fish sticking in the
throat of a bigger fish and being finally ejected, seems to prove that the spines
are useful.]

the excitement of anger or terror; more especially when these emotions are combined, or quickly succeed each other. The action serves to make the animal appear larger and more frightful to its enemies or rivals, and is generally accompanied by various voluntary movements adapted for the same purpose, and by the utterance of savage sounds. Mr Barlett, who has had such wide experience with animals of all kinds, does not doubt that this is the case; but it is a different question whether the power of erection was primarily acquired for this special purpose.

I will first give a considerable body of facts showing how general this action is with mammals, birds and reptiles; retaining what I have to say in regard to man for a future chapter. Mr Sutton, the intelligent keeper in the Zoological Gardens, carefully observed for me the chimpanzee and orang; and he states that when they are suddenly frightened, as by a thunderstorm, or when they are made angry, as by being teased, their hair becomes erect. I saw a chimpanzee who was alarmed at the sight of a black coalheaver, and the hair rose all over his body; he made little starts forward as if to attack the man, without any real intention of doing so, but with the hope, as the keeper remarked, of frightening him. The gorilla, when enraged, is described by Mr Ford,[6] as having his crest of hair 'erect and projecting forward, his nostrils dilated, and his underlip thrown down; at the same time uttering his characteristic yell, designed, it would seem, to terrify his antagonists'. I saw the hair on the Anubis baboon, when angered, bristling along the back, from the neck to the loins, but not on the rump or other parts of the body. I took a stuffed snake into the monkey-house, and the hair on several of the species instantly became erect; especially on their tails, as I particularly noticed with the *Cercopithecus nictitans*. Brehm states[7] that the *Midas oedipus* (belonging to the American division) when excited erects its mane, in order, as he adds, to make itself as frightful as possible.

With the Carnivora the erection of the hair seems to be almost universal, often accompanied by threatening movements, the uncovering of the teeth and the utterance of savage growls. In the Herpestes, I have seen the hair on end over nearly the whole

body, including the tail; and the dorsal crest is erected in a conspicuous manner by the hyaena and Proteles. The enraged lion
erects his mane. The bristling of the hair along the neck and
back of the dog, and over the whole body of the cat, especially
on the tail, is familiar to every one. With the cat it apparently
occurs only under fear; with the dog, under anger and fear; but
not, as far as I have observed, under abject fear, as when a dog
is going to be flogged by a severe gamekeeper. If, however, the
dog shows fight, as sometimes happens, up goes his hair. I have
often noticed that the hair of a dog is particularly liable to rise,
if he is half angry and half afraid, as on beholding some object
only indistinctly seen in the dusk.

I have been assured by a veterinary surgeon that he has often
seen the hair erected on horses and cattle, on which he had
operated and was again going to operate. When I showed a stuffed
snake to a peccary, the hair rose in a wonderful manner along its
back; and so it does with a boar when enraged. An elk which
gored a man to death in the United States, is described as first
brandishing his antlers, squealing with rage and stamping on the
ground; 'at length his hair was seen to rise and stand on end',
and then he plunged forward to the attack.[8] The hair likewise
becomes erect on goats, and, as I hear from Mr Blyth, on some
Indian antelopes. I have seen it erected on the hairy anteater; and
on the agouti, one of the rodents. A female bat,[9] which reared
her young under confinement, when anyone looked into the cage
'erected the fur on her back, and bit viciously at intruding fingers'.

Birds belonging to all the chief Orders ruffle their feathers
when angry or frightened. Every one must have seen two cocks,
even quite young birds, preparing to fight with erected neck-
hackles; nor can these feathers when erected serve as a means
of defence, for cockfighters have found by experience that it is
advantageous to trim them. The male ruff (*Machetes pugnax*) likewise erects its collar of feathers when fighting. When a dog
approaches a common hen with her chickens, she spreads out
her wings, raises her tail, ruffles all her feathers, and looking as
ferocious as possible, dashes at the intruder. The tail is not always
held in exactly the same position; it is sometimes so much erected,

Fig. 12. Hen driving away a dog from her chickens.
Drawn from life by Mr Wood

that the central feathers, as in the accompanying drawing, almost touch the back. Swans, when angered, likewise raise their wings and tail, and erect their feathers. They open their beaks, and make by paddling little rapid starts forwards, against any one who approaches the water's edge too closely. Tropic-birds[10] when disturbed on their nests are said not to fly away, but 'merely to stick out their feathers and scream'. The barn-owl, when approached, 'instantly swells out its plumage, extends its wings and tail, hisses and clacks its mandibles with force and rapidity'.* So do other kinds of owls. Hawks, as I am informed by Mr Jenner Weir, likewise ruffle their feathers, and spread out their wings and tail under similar circumstances. Some kinds of parrots erect their feathers; and I have seen this action in the cassowary, when angered at the sight of an anteater. Young cuckoos in the nest,

---

* On the *Strix flammea*, Audubon, *Ornithological Biography*, 1864, vol. ii, p. 407. I have observed other cases in the Zoological Gardens.

raise their feathers, open their mouths widely, and make themselves as frightful as possible.

Small birds, also, as I hear from Mr Weir, such as various finches, buntings and warblers, when angry, ruffle all their feathers, or only those round the neck; or they spread out their wings and tail-feathers. With their plumage in this state, they rush at each other with open beaks and threatening gestures. Mr Weir concludes from his large experience that the erection of the feathers is caused much more by anger than by fear. He gives as an instance a hybrid goldfinch of a most irascible disposition, which, when approached too closely by a servant, instantly assumes the appearance of a ball of ruffled feathers. He believes that birds when frightened, as a general rule, closely adpress all their feathers, and their consequently diminished size is often astonishing. As soon as they recover from their fear or their surprise, the first thing which they do is to shake out their

Fig. 13. Swan driving away an intruder. Drawn from life by Mr Wood

feathers. The best instances of this adpression of the feathers and apparent shrinking of the body from fear, which Mr Weir has noticed, has been in the quail and grass-parrakeet.[11] The habit is intelligible in these birds from their being accustomed, when in danger, either to squat on the ground or to sit motionless on a branch, so as to escape detection. Though, with birds, anger may be the chief and commonest cause of the erection of the feathers, it is probable that young cuckoos when looked at in the nest, and a hen with her chickens when approached by a dog, feel at least some terror. Mr Tegetmeier informs me that with game-cocks, the erection of the feathers on the head has long since been recognized in the cock-pit as a sign of cowardice.

The males of some lizards, when fighting together during their courtship, expand their throat pouches or frills, and erect their dorsal crests.* But Dr Günther does not believe that they can erect their separate spines or scales.

We thus see how generally throughout the two higher vertebrate classes, and with some reptiles, the dermal appendages are erected under the influence of anger and fear. The movement is effected, as we know from Kölliker's interesting discovery, by the contraction of minute, unstriped, involuntary muscles,† often called *arrectores pili*, which are attached to the capsules of the separate hairs, feathers, etc. By the contraction of these muscles the hairs can be instantly erected, as we see in a dog, being at the same time a little drawn out of their sockets; they are afterwards quickly depressed. The vast number of the minute muscles over the whole body of a hairy quadruped is astonishing. The erection of the hair is, however, aided in some cases, as with that on the head of a man, by the striped and voluntary muscles of the underlying *panniculus carnosus*. It is by the action of these latter muscles that the hedgehog erects its spines. It appears, also, from the researches of Leydig[12] and others, that striped fibres

---

* See, for instance, the account which I have given (*Descent of Man*, 2nd edit., vol. ii, p. 36), of an anolis and draco.

† These muscles are described in his well-known works. I am greatly indebted to this distinguished observer for having given me in a letter information on this same subject.

extend from the *fanniculus* to some of the larger hairs, such as the *vibrissae* of certain quadrupeds. The *arrectores pili* contract not only under the above emotions, but from the application of cold to the surface. I remember that my mules and dogs, brought from a lower and warmer country, after spending a night on the bleak Cordillera, had the hair all over their bodies as erect as under the greatest terror. We see the same action in our own *goose-skin* during the chill before a fever-fit. Mr Lister has also found[13] that tickling a neighbouring part of the skin causes the erection and protrusion of the hairs.

From these facts it is manifest that the erection of the dermal appendages is a reflex action, independent of the will; and this action must be looked at, when, occurring under the influence of anger or fear, not as a power acquired for the sake of some advantage, but as an identical result, at least to a large extent, of the sensorium being affected. The result, in as far as it is incidental, may be compared with the profuse sweating from an agony of pain or terror. Nevertheless, it is remarkable how slight an excitement often suffices to cause the hair to become erect; as when two dogs pretend to fight together in play. We have, also, seen in a large number of animals, belonging to widely distinct classes, that the erection of the hair or feathers is almost always accompanied by various voluntary movements – by threatening gestures, opening the mouth, uncovering the teeth, spreading out of the wings and tail by birds, and by the utterance of harsh sounds; and the purpose of these involuntary movements is unmistakable. Therefore it seems hardly credible that the co-ordinated erection of the dermal appendages, by which the animal is made to appear larger and more terrible to its enemies or rivals, should be altogether an incidental and purposeless result of the disturbance of the sensorium. This seems almost as incredible as that the erection by the hedgehog of its spines, or of the quills by the porcupine, or of the ornamental plumes by many birds during their courtship, should all be purposeless actions.

We here encounter a great difficulty. How can the contraction of the unstriped and involuntary *arrectores pili* have been co-ordinated with that of various voluntary muscles for the same special purpose? If we could believe that the *arrectores* primordially had been voluntary muscles, and had since lost their stripes and become involuntary, the cause would be comparatively simple. I am not, however, aware that there is any evidence in favour of this view; although the reversed transition would not have presented any great difficulty, as the voluntary muscles are in an unstriped condition in the embryos of the higher animals, and in the larvae of some crustaceans. Moreover in the deeper layers of the skin of adult birds, the muscular network is, according to Leydig,[14] in a transitional condition; the fibres exhibiting only indications of transverse striation.

Another explanation seems possible. We may admit that originally the *arrectores pili* were slightly acted on in a direct manner, under the influence of rage and terror, by the disturbance of the nervous system; as is undoubtedly the case with our so-called *goose-skin* before a fever-fit. Animals have been repeatedly excited by rage and terror during many generations; and consequently the direct effects of the disturbed nervous system on the dermal appendages will almost certainly have been increased through habit and through the tendency of nerve-force to pass readily along accustomed channels. We shall find this view of the force of habit strikingly confirmed in a future chapter, where it will be shown that the hair of the insane is affected in an extraordinary manner, owing to their repeated accesses of fury and terror. As soon as with animals the power of erection had thus been strengthened or increased, they must often have seen the hairs or feathers erected in rival and enraged males, and the bulk of their bodies thus increased. In this case it appears possible that they might have wished to make themselves appear larger and more terrible to their enemies, by voluntarily assuming a threatening attitude and uttering harsh cries; such attitudes and utterances after a time becoming through habit instinctive. In this manner actions performed by the contraction of voluntary muscles might have been combined for the same special purpose with those effected by involuntary muscles. It is even possible that animals, when excited and dimly conscious of some change in the state of their hair, might act on it by repeated exertions of their attention and will; for we have reason to believe that the will is able to influence in an obscure manner the action of some unstriped or involuntary muscles, as in the period of the peristaltic movements of the intestines, and in the contraction of the bladder. Nor must we overlook the part which variation and Natural Selection may have played; for the males which succeeded in making themselves appear the most terrible to their rivals, or to their other enemies, if not of overwhelming power, will on an average have left more offspring to inherit their characteristic qualities, whatever these may be and however first acquired, than have other males.*

The inflation of the body, and other means of exciting fear in an enemy. Certain amphibians and reptiles, which either have no spines to erect, or no muscles by which they can be erected, enlarge themselves when alarmed or angry by inhaling air. This is well known to be the case with toads and frogs. The latter animal is made, in Aesop's fable of the 'Ox and the Frog', to blow itself up from vanity and envy until it burst. This action must have been observed during the most ancient times, as, according to Mr Hensleigh Wedgwood,[15] the word *toad* expresses in some of the languages of Europe the habit of swelling. It has been observed with some of the exotic species in the Zoological Gardens; and Dr Günther believes that it is general throughout the group. Judging from analogy, the primary purpose probably was to make the body appear as large and frightful as possible to an enemy; but another, and perhaps more important secondary advantage is thus gained. When frogs are seized by snakes, which are their chief enemies, they enlarge themselves wonderfully; so that if the snake be of small size, as Dr Günther informs me, it cannot swallow the frog, which thus escapes being devoured.

Chameleons and some other lizards inflate themselves when

* [Dr T. Clay Shawe, in the *Journal of Mental Science*, April 1873, is inclined to doubt that the bristling of the hairs is due to the *panniculus carnosus* rather than to the *arrectores*. But the hair on a cat's tail bristles with anger or fear; and here, as Professor Macalister tells me, the effect must be due to the *arrectores*, there being no *panniculus*.]

angry. Thus a species inhabiting Oregon, the *Tapaya Douglasii*, is slow in its movements and does not bite, but has a ferocious aspect; 'when irritated it springs in a most threatening manner at anything pointed at it, at the same time opening its mouth wide and hissing audibly, after which it inflates its body, and shows other marks of anger'.[16]

Several kinds of snakes likewise inflate themselves when irritated. The puff-adder (*Clotho arietans*) is remarkable in this respect; but I believe, after carefully watching these animals, that they do not act thus for the sake of increasing their apparent bulk, but simply for inhaling a large supply of air, so as to produce their surprisingly loud, harsh, and prolonged hissing sound. The cobras-de-capello, when irritated, enlarge themselves a little, and hiss moderately; but, at the same time, they lift their heads aloft, and dilate by means of their elongated anterior ribs the skin on each side of the neck into a large flat disk – the so-called hood. With their widely-opened mouths, they then assume a terrific aspect. The benefit thus derived ought to be considerable, in order to compensate for the somewhat lessened rapidity (though this is still great) with which, when dilated, they can strike at their enemies or prey; on the same principle that a broad, thin piece of wood cannot be moved through the air so quickly as a small round stick. An innocuous snake, the *Tropidonotus macrophthalmus*, an inhabitant of India, likewise dilates its neck when irritated; and consequently is often mistaken for its compatriot, the deadly cobra.[17] This resemblance perhaps serves as some protection to the Tropidonotus. Another innocuous species, the Dasypeltis of South Africa, blows itself out, distends its neck, hisses and darts at an intruder.[18] Many other snakes hiss under similar circumstances. They also rapidly vibrate their protruded tongues; and this may aid in increasing their terrific appearance.

Snakes possess other means of producing sounds besides hissing. Many years ago I observed in South America that a venomous Trigonocephalus, when disturbed, rapidly vibrated the end of its tail, which, striking against the dry grass and twigs, produced a rattling noise that could be distinctly heard at the distance of six feet.* The deadly and fierce *Echis carinata* of India produces 'a curious prolonged, almost hissing sound' in a very different manner, namely by rubbing 'the sides of the folds of its body against each other', whilst the head remains in almost the same position. The scales on the sides, and not on other parts of the body, are strongly keeled, with the keels toothed like a saw; and as the coiled-up animal rubs its sides together, these grate against each other.[19] Lastly, we have the well-known case of the rattle-snake. He who has merely shaken the rattle of a dead snake can form no idea of the sound produced by the living animal. Professor Shaler states that it is indistinguishable from that made by the male of a large cicada (an homopterous insect), which inhabits the same district.† In the Zoological Gardens, when the rattle-snakes and puff-adders were greatly excited at the same time, I was much struck at the similarity of the sound produced by them; and although that made by the rattle-snake is louder and shriller than the hissing of the puff-adder, yet when standing at some yards distance I could scarcely distinguish the two. For whatever purpose the sound is produced by the one species, I can hardly doubt that it serves for the same purpose in the other species; and I conclude from the threatening gestures made at the same time by many snakes, that their hissing – the rattling of the rattle-snake and of the tail of the Trigonocephalus – the grating of the scales of the echis – and the dilatation of the hood of the

* *Journal of Researches during the Voyage of the* Beagle, 1845, p. 96. I here compared the rattling thus produced with that of the rattle-snake.

† The *American Naturalist*, January 1872, p. 32. I regret that I cannot follow Professor Shaler in believing that the rattle has been developed, by the aid of Natural Selection, for the sake of producing sounds which deceive and attract birds, so that they may serve as prey to the snake. I do not, however, wish to doubt that the sounds may occasionally subserve this end. But the conclusion at which I have arrived, viz. that the rattling serves as a warning to would-be devourers, appears to me much more probable, as it connects together various classes of facts. If this snake had acquired its rattle and the habit of rattling, for the sake of attracting prey, it does not seem probable that it would have invariably used its instrument when angered or disturbed. Professor Shaler takes nearly the same view as I do of the manner of development of the rattle; and I have always held this opinion since observing the Trigonocephalus in South America.

cobra – all subserve the same end, namely, to make them appear terrible to their enemies.*

It seems at first a probable conclusion that venomous snakes, such as the foregoing, from being already so well defended by their poison-fangs, would never be attacked by any enemy; and consequently would have no need to excite additional terror. But this is far from being the case, for they are largely preyed on in all quarters of the world by many animals. It is well known that pigs are employed in the United States to clear districts infested with rattle-snakes, which they do most effectually.† In England the hedgehog attacks and devours the viper. In India, as I hear from Dr Jerdon, several kinds of hawks, and at least one mammal, the herpestes, kill cobras and other venomous species;‡ and so it is in South Africa. Therefore it is by no means improbable that any sounds or signs by which the venomous species could instantly make themselves recognized as dangerous, would be of more service to them than to the innocuous species which would not be able, if attacked, to inflict any real injury.

Having said thus much about snakes, I am tempted to add a few remarks on the means by which the rattle of the rattle-snake was probably developed. Various animals, including some lizards, either curl or vibrate their tails when excited. This is the case with many kinds of snakes.¶ In the Zoological Gardens, an innocuous

* From the accounts lately collected, and given in the *Journal of the Linnaean Society*, by Mrs Barber, on the habits of the snakes of South Africa; and from the accounts published by several writers, for instance by Lawson, of the rattle-snake in North America – it does not seem improbable that the terrific appearance of snakes and the sounds produced by them, may likewise serve in procuring prey, by paralysing, or as it is sometimes called fascinating, the smaller animals.

† See the account by Dr R. Brown, in *Proc. Zool. Soc. 1871*, p. 39. He says that as soon as a pig sees a snake it rushes upon it; and a snake makes off immediately on the appearance of a pig.

‡ Dr Günther remarks (*Reptiles of British India*, p. 340) on the destruction of cobras by the ichneumon or herpestes, and whilst the cobras are young by the jungle-fowl. It is well known that the peacock also eagerly kills snakes.

¶ Professor Cope enumerates a number of kinds in his *Method of Creation of Organic Types*, read before the American Phil. Soc., 15 December, 1871, p. 20. Professor Cope takes the same view as I do of the use of the gestures and sounds made by snakes. I briefly alluded to this subject in the last edition of my *Origin* species, the *Coronella sayi*, vibrates its tail so rapidly that it becomes almost invisible. The Trigonocephalus, before alluded to, has the same habit; and the extremity of its tail is a little enlarged or bead-like or ends in a bead. In the Lachesis, which is so closely allied to the rattle-snake that it was placed by Linnaeus in the same genus, the tail ends in a single, large, lancet-shaped point or scale. With some snakes the skin, as Professor Shaler remarks, 'is more imperfectly detached from the region about the tail than at other parts of the body'. Now if we suppose that the end of the tail of some ancient American species was enlarged, and was covered by a single large scale, this could hardly have been cast off at the successive moults. In this case it would have been permanently retained, and at each period of growth, as the snake grew larger, a new scale, larger than the last, would have been formed above it, and would likewise have been retained. The foundation for the development of a rattle would thus have been laid; and it would have been habitually used, if the species, like so many others, vibrated its tail whenever it was irritated. That the rattle has since been specially developed to serve as an efficient sound-producing instrument, there can hardly be a doubt: for even the vertebrae included within the extremity of the tail have been altered in shape and cohere. But there is no greater improbability in various structures, such as the rattle of the rattle-snake – the lateral scales of the echis – the neck with the included ribs of the cobra – and the whole body of the puff-adder – having been modified for the sake of warning and frightening away their enemies, than in a bird, namely, the wonderful Secretary-hawk (*Gypogeranus*) having had its whole frame modified for the sake of killing snakes with impunity. It is highly probable, judging from what we have before seen, that this bird would ruffle its feathers whenever it attacked a snake; and it is certain that the herpestes, when it eagerly rushes to attack a snake,

---

of Species. Since the passages in the text above have been printed, I have been pleased to find that Mr Henderson (*The American Naturalist*, May, 1872, p. 260) also takes a similar view of the use of the rattle, namely 'in preventing an attack from being made'.

erects the hair all over its body, and especially that on its tail.[20] We have also seen that some porcupines, when angered or alarmed at the sight of a snake, rapidly vibrate their tails, thus producing a peculiar sound by the striking together of the hollow quills. So that here both the attackers and the attacked endeavour to make themselves as dreadful as possible to each other; and both possess for this purpose specialized means, which, oddly enough, are nearly the same in some of these cases. Finally we can see that if, on the one hand, those individual snakes, which were best able to frighten away their enemies, escaped best from being devoured; and if, on the other hand, those individuals of the attacking enemy survived in larger numbers which were the best fitted for the dangerous task of killing and devouring venomous snakes: then in the one case as in the other, beneficial variations, supposing the characters in question to vary, would commonly have been preserved through the survival of the fittest.

The drawing back and pressure of the ears to the head. The ears through their movements are highly expressive in many animals; but in some, such as man, the higher apes, and many ruminants, they fail in this respect. A slight difference in position serves to express in the plainest manner a different state of mind, as we may daily see in the dog; but we are here concerned only with the ears being drawn closely backwards and pressed to the head. A savage frame of mind is thus shown, but only in the case of those animals which fight with their teeth; and the care which they take to prevent their ears being seized by their antagonists, accounts for this position. Consequently, through habit and association, whenever they feel slightly savage, or pretend in their play to be savage, their ears are drawn back. That this is the true explanation may be inferred from the relation which exists in very many animals between their manner of fighting and the retraction of their ears.

All the Carnivora fight with their canine teeth, and all, as far as I have observed, draw their ears back when feeling savage. This may be continually seen with dogs when fighting in earnest, and with puppies fighting in play. The movement is different from the falling down and slight drawing back of the ears, when a dog feels pleased and is caressed by his master. The retraction of the ears may likewise be seen in kittens fighting together in their play, and in full-grown cats when really savage, as before illustrated in Fig. 9 (p. 61). Although their ears are thus to a large extent protected, yet they often get much torn in old male cats during their battles. The same movement is very striking in tigers, leopards, etc., whilst growling over their food in menageries. The lynx has remarkably long ears; and their retraction, when one of these animals is approached in its cage, is very conspicuous, and is eminently expressive of its savage disposition. Even one of the Eared seals, the *Otaria pusilla*, which has very small ears, draws them backwards, when it makes a savage rush at the legs of its keeper.

When horses fight together they use their incisors for biting, and their fore-legs for striking, much more than they do their hind-legs for kicking backwards. This has been observed when stallions have broken loose and have fought together, and may likewise be inferred from the kinds of wounds which they inflict on each other. Every one recognizes the vicious appearance which the drawing back of the ears gives to a horse. This movement is very different from that of listening to a sound behind. If an ill-tempered horse in a stall is inclined to kick backwards, his ears are retracted from habit, though he has no intention or power to bite. But when a horse throws up both hind-legs in play, as when entering an open field, or when just touched by the whip, he does not generally depress his ears, for he does not then feel vicious. Guanacoes fight savagely with their teeth; and they must do so frequently, for I found the hides of several which I shot in Patagonia deeply scored. So do camels; and both these animals, when savage, draw their ears closely backwards. Guanacoes, as I have noticed, when not intending to bite, but merely spit out their offensive saliva from a distance at an intruder, retract their ears. Even the hippopotamus, when threatening with its widely-open enormous mouth a comrade, draws back its small ears, just like a horse.

Now what a contrast is presented between the foregoing

animals and cattle, sheep, or goats, which never use their teeth in fighting, and never draw back their ears when enraged!* Although sheep and goats appear such placid animals, the males often join in furious contests. As deer form a closely related family, and as I did not know that they ever fought with their teeth, I was much surprised by the account given by Major Ross King of the Moose-deer in Canada. He says, when 'two males chance to meet, laying back their ears and gnashing their teeth together, they rush at each other with appalling fury'.[21] But Mr Bartlett informs me that some species of deer fight savagely with their teeth, so that the drawing back of the ears by the moose accords with our rule. Several kinds of kangaroos, kept in the Zoological Gardens, fight by scratching with their fore-feet and by kicking with their hind-legs; but they never bite each other, and the keepers have never seen them draw back their ears when angered. Rabbits fight chiefly by kicking and scratching, but they likewise bite each other; and I have known one to bite off half the tail of its antagonist. At the commencement of their battles they lay back their ears, but afterwards, as they bound over and kick each other, they keep their ears erect, or move them much about.

Mr Bartlett watched a wild boar quarrelling rather savagely with his sow; and both had their mouths open and their ears drawn backwards.[22] But this does not appear to be a common action with domestic pigs when quarrelling. Boars fight together by striking upwards with their tusks; and Mr Bartlett doubts whether they then draw back their ears. Elephants, which in like manner fight with their tusks, do not retract their ears, but, on the contrary, erect them while rushing at each other or at an enemy.

The rhinoceroses in the Zoological Gardens fight with their nasal horns, and have never been seen to attempt biting each other except in play; and the keepers are convinced that they do not draw back their ears, like horses and dogs, when feeling savage. The following statement, therefore, by Sir S. Baker[23] is

* [The following note is in Charles Darwin's handwriting, and seems to be from an early note-book: 'The giraffe kicks with its front legs, and knocks with the back of its head, yet never puts down its ears. Good to contrast with horses.']

inexplicable, namely, that a rhinoceros, which he shot in North Africa, 'had no ears; they had been bitten off close to the head by another of the same species while fighting; and this mutilation is by no means uncommon'.

Lastly, with respect to monkeys. Some kinds, which have moveable ears, and which fight with their teeth – for instance the *Cercopithecus ruber* – draw back their ears when irritated just like dogs; and they then have a very spiteful appearance. Other kinds, as the *Inuus ecaudatus*, apparently do not thus act. Again, other kinds – and this is a great anomaly in comparison with most other animals – retract their ears, show their teeth and jabber, when they are pleased by being caressed. I observed this in two or three species of macacus, and in the *Cynopithecus niger*. This expression, owing to our familiarity with dogs, would never be recognized as one of joy or pleasure by those unacquainted with monkeys.

Erection of the ears. This movement requires hardly any notice. All animals which have the power of freely moving their ears, when they are startled, or when they closely observe any object, direct their ears to the point towards which they are looking, in order to hear any sound from this quarter. At the same time they generally raise their heads, as all their organs of sense are there situated, and some of the smaller animals rise on their hind legs. Even those kinds which squat on the ground or instantly flee away to avoid danger, generally act momentarily in this manner, in order to ascertain the source and nature of the danger. The head being raised, with erected ears and eyes directed forwards, gives an unmistakable expression of close attention to any animal.

CHAPTER V

Special Expressions of Animals

The dog, various expressive movements of – Cats – Horses – Ruminants – Monkeys, their expressions of joy and affection – Of pain – Anger – Astonishment and terror.

The dog. I have already described (Figs 5 and 7) the appearance of a dog approaching another dog with hostile intentions, namely, with erected ears, eyes intently directed forwards, hair on the neck and back bristling, gait remarkably stiff, with the tail upright and rigid. So familiar is this appearance to us, that an angry man is sometimes said 'to have his back up'. Of the above points, the stiff gait and upright tail alone require further discussion. Sir C. Bell remarks[1] that, when a tiger or wolf is struck by its keeper and is suddenly roused to ferocity, 'every muscle is in tension, and the limbs are in an attitude of strained exertion, prepared to spring'. This tension of the muscles and consequent stiff gait may be accounted for on the principle of associated habit, for anger has continually led to fierce struggles, and consequently to all the muscles of the body having been violently exerted. There is also reason to suspect that the muscular system requires some short preparation, or some degree of innervation, before being brought into strong action. My own sensations lead me to this inference; but I cannot discover that it is a conclusion admitted by physiologists. Sir J. Paget, however, informs me that when muscles are suddenly contracted with the greatest force, without any preparation, they are liable to be ruptured, as when a man slips unexpectedly; but that this rarely occurs when an action, however violent, is deliberately performed.

Klinghammer questioned Darwin's explanation based on associated habits. Instead, he remarked, 'threat behavior which is well established in social contexts in animals, is simply elicited by any number of external stimuli (if learned), or releasers (if innate). Nothing more needs to be said.'

With respect to the upright position of the tail, it seems to depend (but whether this is really the case I know not) on the elevator muscles being more powerful than the depressors, so that when all the muscles of the hinder part of the body are in a state of tension, the tail is raised. A dog in cheerful spirits, and trotting before his master with high, elastic steps, generally carries his tail aloft, though it is not held nearly so stiffly as when he is angered. A horse when first turned out into an open field, may be seen to trot with long elastic strides, the head and tail being held high aloft. Even cows, when they frisk about from pleasure,

Fig. 14. Head of a snarling dog. From life, by Mr Wood

throw up their tails in a ridiculous fashion. So it is with various animals in the Zoological Gardens. The position of the tail, however, in certain cases, is determined by special circumstances; thus as soon as a horse breaks into a gallop, at full speed, he always lowers his tail, so that as little resistance as possible may be offered to the air.*

When a dog is on the point of springing on his antagonist, he utters a savage growl; the ears are pressed closely backwards, and the upper lip (Fig. 14) is retracted out of the way of his teeth, especially of his canines. These movements may be observed with dogs and puppies in their play. But if a dog gets really savage in his play, his expression immediately changes. This, however, is simply due to the lips and ears being drawn back with much greater energy. If a dog only snarls at another, the lip is generally retracted on one side alone, namely towards his enemy.

The movements of a dog whilst exhibiting affection towards his master were described (Figs 6 and 8) in our second chapter. These consist in the head and whole body being lowered and thrown into flexuous movements, with the tail extended and wagged from side to side. The ears fall down and are drawn somewhat backwards, which causes the eyelids to be elongated, and alters the whole appearance of the face. The lips hang loosely, and the hair remains smooth. All these movements or gestures are explicable, as I believe, from their standing in complete antithesis to those naturally assumed by a savage dog under a directly opposite state of mind. When a man merely speaks to, or just notices, his dog, we see the last vestige of these movements in a slight wag of the tail, without any other movement of the body, and without even the ears being lowered. Dogs also exhibit their affection by desiring to rub against their masters, and to be rubbed or patted by them.

Gratiolet explains the above gestures of affection in the

* [Mr Wallace suggests (*Quarterly Journal of Science*, January, 1873, p. 116) a different explanation. 'As a whole available nervous energy is being expended in locomotion, all special muscular contractions not aiding the motion cease.']

following manner: and the reader can judge whether the explanation appears satisfactory. Speaking of animals in general, including the dog, he says:[2] 'C'est toujours la partie la plus sensible de leurs corps qui recherche les caresses ou les donne. Lorsque toute la longueur des flancs et du corps est sensible, l'animal serpente et rampe sous les caresses; et ces ondulations se propageant le long des muscles analogues des segments jusqu'aux extrémités de la colonne vertébrale, la queue se ploie et s'agite.' ['It is always the most sensitive parts of the bodies that seek the endearments. When the whole length of the flanks and body are sensitive, the animal twists and crawls under the caresses, and these undulations spread along the muscles and segments to the end of the spine, the tail bending and waving.'] Further on, he adds that dogs, when feeling affectionate, lower their ears in order to exclude all sounds, so that their whole attention may be concentrated on the caresses of their master!

Dogs have another and striking way of exhibiting their affection, namely, by licking the hands or the faces of their masters. They sometimes lick other dogs, and then it is always their chops. I have also seen dogs licking cats with whom they were friends. This habit probably originated in the females carefully licking their puppies – the dearest object of their love – for the sake of cleansing them. They also often give their puppies, after a short absence, a few cursory licks, apparently from affection. Thus the habit will have become associated with the emotion of love, however it may afterwards be aroused. It is now so firmly inherited or innate, that it is transmitted equally to both sexes. A female terrier of mine lately had her puppies destroyed, and though at all times a very affectionate creature, I was much struck with the manner in which she then tried to satisfy her instinctive maternal love by extending it on me; and her desire to lick my hands rose to an insatiable passion.*

---

* [M. Baudry has pointed out, in a letter, a passage in the *Rāmāyana*, where a mother, finding the dead body of her son, 'lèche avec sa langue le visage du mort en gémissant comme une vache privée de son veau' ['licks with her tongue the dead boy's face, moaning like a cow deprived of her calf'].]

Klinghammer agreed with Darwin's interpretation of the origin of licking, but questions whether we should call it 'love'.

The same principle probably explains why dogs, when feeling affectionate, like rubbing against their masters and being rubbed or patted by them, for from the nursing of their puppies, contact with a beloved object has become firmly associated in their minds with the emotion of love.

Klinghammer said that rubbing against the owner is probably triggered by an odor, and represents 'scent-rolling'.

The feeling of affection of a dog towards his master is combined with a strong sense of submission, which is akin to fear. Hence dogs not only lower their bodies and crouch a little as they approach their masters, but sometimes throw themselves on the ground with their bellies upwards. This is a movement as completely opposite as is possible to any show of resistance. I formerly possessed a large dog who was not at all afraid to fight with other dogs; but a wolf-like shepherd-dog in the neighbourhood, though not ferocious and not so powerful as my dog, had a strange influence over him. When they met on the road, my dog used to run to meet him, with his tail partly tucked in between his legs and hair not erected; and then he would throw himself on the ground, belly upwards. By this action he seemed to say more plainly than by words, 'Behold, I am your slave.'

A pleasurable and excited state of mind, associated with affection, is exhibited by some dogs in a very peculiar manner; namely, by grinning.* This was noticed long ago by Somerville, who says,

* [A correspondent in the E. I. Gov. Telegraph Department, states (letter, 14 February, 1875), that in cattle the uncovering of the teeth is connected with the sexual instinct. 'I was buying a bull, and wished to examine his teeth, but this he would by no means allow; the natives suggested a cow should be brought', when 'the bull immediately stretched out his neck and opened his lips so as to expose his teeth.' He states that the practice of bringing a cow to make a bull show his teeth is a common one in India.]

'And with a courtly grin, the fawning hound
Salutes thee cow'ring, his wide op'ning nose
Upward he curls, and his large sloe-black eyes
Melt in soft .blandishments, and humble joy.'

The Chase, book i.

Sir W. Scott's famous Scotch greyhound, Maida, had this habit, and it is common with terriers. I have also seen it in a spitz and in a sheep-dog. Mr Riviere, who has particularly attended to this expression, informs me that it is rarely displayed in a perfect manner, but it is quite common in a lesser degree. The upper lip during the act of grinning is retracted, as in snarling, so that the canines are exposed, and the ears are drawn backwards; but the general appearance of the animal clearly shows that anger is not felt. Sir C. Bell[3] remarks, 'Dogs, in their expression of fondness, have a slight eversion of the lips, and grin and sniff amidst their gambols, in a way that resembles laughter.' Some persons speak of the grin as a smile, but if it had been really a smile, we should see a similar, though more pronounced, movement of the lips and ears, when dogs utter their bark of joy; but this is not the case, although a bark of joy often follows a grin. On the other hand, dogs, when playing with their comrades or masters, almost always pretend to bite each other; and they then retract, though not energetically, their lips and ears. Hence I suspect that there is a tendency in some dogs, whenever they feel lively pleasure combined with affection, to act through habit and association on the same muscles, as in playfully biting each other, or their master's hands.

I have described, in the second chapter, the gait and appearance of a dog when cheerful, and the marked antithesis presented by the same animal when dejected and disappointed, with his head, ears, body, tail, and chops drooping, and eyes dull. Under the expectation of any great pleasure, dogs bound and jump about in an extravagant manner, and bark for joy. The tendency to bark under this state of mind is inherited, or runs in the breed; greyhounds rarely bark, whilst the spitz-dog barks so incessantly on starting for a walk with his master that he becomes a nuisance.

An agony of pain is expressed by dogs in nearly the same way as by many other animals, namely, by howling, writhing, and contortions of the whole body.

Attention is shown by the head being raised, with the ears erected, and eyes intently directed towards the object or quarter under observation. If it be a sound and the source is not known, the head is often turned obliquely from side to side in a most significant manner, apparently in order to judge with more exactness from what point the sound proceeds. But I have seen a dog greatly surprised at a new noise, turning his head to one side through habit, though he clearly perceived the source of the noise. Dogs, as formerly remarked, when their attention is in any way aroused, whilst watching some object, or attending to some sound, often lift up one paw (Fig. 4) and keep it doubled up, as if to make a slow and stealthy approach.

A dog under extreme terror will throw himself down, howl, and void his excretions; but the hair, I believe, does not become erect unless some danger is felt. I have seen a dog much terrified at a band of musicians who were playing loudly outside the house, with every muscle of his body trembling, with his heart palpitating so quickly that the beats could hardly be counted, and panting for breath with widely open mouth, in the same manner as a terrified man does. Yet this dog had not exerted himself; he had only wandered slowly and restlessly about the room, and the day was very cold.

Even a very slight degree of fear is invariably shown by the tail being tucked in* between the legs.† This tucking in of the

* [It appears probable that the tucking in of the tail is not so much an attempt to protect the tail as a part of a general attempt to make the surface exposed as small as possible (cf. the kneeling of hyaenas described in the next page). A correspondent compares it to the crouching of a fives player, who is forced to be idle while a 'bully' is being played out by his companions. It would thus be analogous to the shrugging of the shoulders, if M. Baudry (see ch. xi, p. 203) is right in connecting this gesture with an effort to tuck in the head.]

† [In a cuneiform inscription, nearly 5000 years old, giving an account of the Deluge, there is a description of the terror of the gods at the tempest. And 'the gods like dogs with tails hidden crouched down'. This note is taken from a newspaper clipping, preserved by Charles Darwin, but without date or title.]

tail is accompanied by the ears being drawn backwards; but they are not pressed closely to the head, as in snarling, and they are not lowered, as when a dog is pleased or affectionate. When two young dogs chase each other in play, the one that runs away always keeps his tail tucked inwards. So it is when a dog, in the highest spirits, careers like a mad creature round and round his master in circles, or in figures of eight. He then acts as if another dog were chasing him. This curious kind of play, which must be familiar to every one who has attended to dogs, is particularly apt to be excited, after the animal has been a little startled or frightened, as by his master suddenly jumping out on him in the dusk. In this case, as well as when two young dogs are chasing one another in play, it appears as if the one that runs away was afraid of the other catching him by the tail; but as far as I can find out, dogs very rarely catch each other in this manner. I asked a gentleman, who had kept foxhounds all his life, and he applied to other experienced sportsmen, whether they had ever seen hounds thus seize a fox; but they never had. It appears that when a dog is chased, or when in danger of being struck behind, or of anything falling on him, in all these cases he wishes to withdraw as quickly as possible his whole hind-quarters, and that from some sympathy or connection between the muscles, the tail is then drawn closely inwards.

A similarly connected movement between the hind-quarters and the tail may be observed in the hyaena. Mr Bartlett informs me that when two of these animals fight together, they are mutually conscious of the wonderful power of each other's jaws, and are extremely cautious. They well know that if one of their legs were seized, the bone would instantly be crushed into atoms; hence they approach each other kneeling, with their legs turned as much as possible inwards and with their whole bodies bowed, so as not to present any salient point; the tail at the same time being closely tucked in between the legs. In this attitude they approach each other sideways, or even partly backwards. So again with deer, several of the species, when savage and fighting, tuck in their tails. When one horse in a field tries to bite the hind-quarters of another in play, or when a rough boy strikes a donkey from behind, the hind-quarters and the tail are drawn in, though it does not appear as if this were done merely to save the tail from being injured. We have also seen the reverse of these movements; for when an animal trots with high elastic steps, the tail is almost always carried aloft.

As I have said, when a dog is chased and runs away, he keeps his ears directed backwards but still open; and this is clearly done for the sake of hearing the footsteps of his pursuer. From habit the ears are often held in this same position, and the tail tucked in, when the danger is obviously in front. I have repeatedly noticed, with a timid terrier of mine, that when she is afraid of some object in front, the nature of which she perfectly knows and does not need to reconnoitre, yet she will for a long time hold her ears and tail in this position, looking the image of discomfort. Discomfort, without any fear, is similarly expressed: thus, one day I went out of doors, just at the time when this same dog knew that her dinner would be brought. I did not call her, but she wished much to accompany me, and at the same time she wished much for her dinner; and there she stood, first looking one way and then the other, with her tail tucked in and ears drawn back, presenting an unmistakable appearance of perplexed discomfort.

Almost all the expressive movements now described, with the exception of the grinning from joy, are innate or instinctive, for they are common to all the individuals, young and old, of all the breeds. Most of them are likewise common to the aboriginal parents of the dog, namely the wolf and jackal; and some of them to other species of the same group.* Tamed wolves and jackals, when caressed by their masters, jump about for joy, wag their tails, lower their ears, lick their masters' hands, crouch down, and even throw themselves on the ground belly upwards.† I have

---

* [Mr Arthur Nicols, writing in *The Country*, 31 December, 1874, p. 588, states that for nearly two years he had 'intimate knowledge' of a pure bred dingo (which had been reared from a litter of wild pups), and that during this time he never saw it wag its tail or erect it when approaching a strange dog.]

† Many particulars are given by Gueldenstädt in his account of the jackal in *Nov. Comm. Acad. Sc. Imp. Petrop.* 1775, vol. xx, p. 449. See also another excellent

seen a rather fox-like African jackal, from the Gaboon, depress its ears when caressed. Wolves and jackals, when frightened, certainly tuck in their tails; and a tamed jackal has been described as careering round his master in circles and figures of eight, like a dog, with his tail between his legs.

It has been stated[4] that foxes, however tame, never display any of the above expressive movements; but this is not strictly accurate. Many years ago I observed in the Zoological Gardens, and recorded the fact at the time, that a very tame English fox, when caressed by the keeper, wagged its tail, depressed its ears, and then threw itself on the ground, belly upwards. The black fox of North America likewise depressed its ears in a slight degree. But I believe that foxes never lick the hands of their masters,* and I have been assured that when frightened they never tuck in their tails. If the explanation I have given of the expression of affection in dogs be admitted, then it would appear that animals which have never been domesticated – namely wolves, jackals, and even foxes – have nevertheless acquired, through the principle of antithesis, certain expressive gestures; for it is not probable that these animals, confined in cages, should have learnt them by imitating dogs.

Klinghammer, an expert on wolves, agreed with Darwin's observations, but emphasized that dominance and submission, or attack and fleeing, are extremes on a continuum.

Cats. I have already described the actions of a cat (Fig. 9), when feeling savage and not terrified. She assumes a crouching attitude and occasionally protrudes her fore-feet, with her claws exserted ready for striking. The tail is extended, being curled or lashed

---

account of the manners of this animal and of its play, in *Land and Water*, October, 1869. Lieut. Annesley, R. A., has also communicated to me some particulars with respect to the jackal. I have made many inquiries about wolves and jackals in the Zoological Gardens, and have observed them for myself.

* [Mr R. M. Lloyd, of Birmingham, describes (letter, 14 June, 1881) a tame fox licking the hands and face of its master.]

from side to side. The hair is not erected – at least it was not so in the few cases observed by me. The ears are drawn closely backwards and the teeth are shown. Low savage growls are uttered. We can understand why the attitude assumed by a cat when preparing to fight with another cat, or in any way greatly irritated, is so widely different from that of a dog approaching another dog with hostile intentions; for the cat uses her fore-feet for striking, and this renders a crouching position convenient or necessary. She is also much more accustomed than a dog to lie concealed and suddenly spring on her prey. No cause can be assigned with certainty for the tail being lashed or curled from side to side. This habit is common to many other animals – for instance, to the puma, when prepared to spring;[5] but it is not common to dogs, or to foxes, as I infer from Mr St John's account of a fox lying in wait and seizing a hare. We have already seen that some kinds of lizards and various snakes, when excited, rapidly vibrate the tips of their tails. It would appear as if, under strong excitement, there existed an uncontrollable desire for movement of some kind, owing to nerve-force being freely liberated from the excited sensorium; and that as the tail is left free, and as its movement does not disturb the general position of the body, it is curled or lashed about.

All the movements of a cat, when feeling affectionate, are in complete antithesis to those just described. She now stands upright, with slightly arched back, tail perpendicularly raised, and ears erected; and she rubs her cheeks and flanks against her master or mistress. The desire to rub something is so strong in cats under this state of mind, that they may often be seen rubbing themselves against the legs of chairs or tables, or against door-posts. The manner of expressing affection probably originated through association, as in the case of dogs, from the mother nursing and fondling her young; and perhaps from the young themselves loving each other and playing together. Another and very different gesture, expressive of pleasure, has already been described, namely the curious manner in which young and even old cats, when pleased, alternately protrude their fore-feet, with separated toes, as if pushing against and sucking their mother's teats. The habit is so far analogous to that of rubbing against something, that both apparently are derived from actions performed during the nursing period. Why cats should show affection by rubbing so much more than do dogs, though the latter delight in contact with their masters, and why cats only occasionally lick the hands of their friends, whilst dogs always do so, I cannot say. Cats cleanse themselves by licking their own coats more regularly than do dogs. On the other hand, their tongues seem less well fitted for the work than the longer more flexible tongues of dogs.

Cats, when terrified, stand at full height, and arch their backs in a well-known and ridiculous fashion. They spit, hiss, or growl.

Fig. 15. Cat terrified at a dog. From life, by Mr Wood

The hair over the whole body, and especially on the tail, becomes erect. In the instances observed by me, the basal part of the tail was held upright, the terminal part being thrown on one side; but sometimes the tail (see Fig. 15) is only a little raised, and is bent almost from the base to one side. The ears are drawn back, and the teeth exposed. When two kittens are playing together, the one often thus tries to frighten the other. From what we have seen in former chapters, all the above points of expression are intelligible, except the extreme arching of the back. I am inclined to believe that, in the same manner as many birds, while they ruffle their feathers, spread out their wings and tail, to make themselves look as big as possible, so cats stand upright at their full height, arch their backs, often raise the basal part of the tail, and erect their hair, for the same purpose. The lynx, when attacked, is said to arch its back, and is thus figured by Brehm. But the keepers in the Zoological Gardens have never seen any tendency to this action in the larger feline animals, such as tigers, lions, etc.; and these have little cause to be afraid of any other animal.

Cats use their voices much as a means of expression, and they utter, under various emotions and desires, at least six or seven different sounds. The purr of satisfaction, which is made during both inspiration and expiration, is one of the most curious. The puma, cheetah, and ocelot likewise purr; but the tiger, when pleased, 'emits a peculiar sort of snuffle, accompanied by the close of the eyelids'.[6] It is said that the lion, jaguar, and leopard, do not purr.

Freedman commented that 'purring is a signal of well-being in another's presence (normally a conspecific), and it probably evolved in the service of fostering social closeness.' It would be interesting to know whether or not cats purr when they are alone.

Horses. Horses when savage draw their ears closely back, protrude their heads, and partially uncover their incisor teeth, ready for biting. When inclined to kick behind, they generally, through habit, draw back their ears; and their eyes are turned backwards in a peculiar manner.* When pleased, as when some coveted food is brought to them in the stable, they raise and draw in their heads, prick their ears, and looking intently towards their friend, often whinny. Impatience is expressed by pawing the ground.

The actions of a horse when much startled are highly express-ive. One day my horse was much frightened at a drilling machine, covered by a tarpaulin, and lying in an open field. He raised his head so high, that his neck became almost perpendicular: and this he did from habit, for the machine lay on a slope below, and could not have been seen with more distinctness through the raising of the head; nor if any sound had proceeded from it, could the sound have been more distinctly heard. His eyes and ears were directed intently forwards; and I could feel through the saddle the palpitations of his heart. With red dilated nostrils he snorted violently, and whirling round, would have dashed off at full speed, had I not prevented him. The distension of the nostrils is not for the sake of scenting the source of danger, for when a horse smells carefully at any object and is not alarmed, he does not dilate his nostrils. Owing to the presence of a valve in the throat, a horse when panting does not breathe through his open mouth, but through his nostrils; and these consequently have become endowed with great powers of expansion. The expansion of the nostrils as well as the snorting, and the palpitations of the heart, are actions which have become firmly associated during a long series of generations with the emotion of terror; for terror has habitually led the horse to the most violent exertion in dashing away at full speed from the cause of danger.

Ruminants. Cattle and sheep are remarkable from displaying in so slight a degree their emotions or sensations, excepting that of extreme pain. A bull when enraged exhibits his rage only by the manner in which he holds his lowered head, with distended nostrils, and by bellowing. He also often paws the ground; but

* Sir C. Bell, *Anatomy of Expression*, 3rd edit., p. 123. See also p. 126, on horses not breathing through their mouths, with reference to their distended nostrils.

this pawing seems quite different from that of an impatient horse, for when the soil is loose, he throws up clouds of dust. I believe that bulls act in this manner when irritated by flies, for the sake of driving them away. The wilder breeds of sheep and the chamois when startled stamp on the ground, and whistle through their noses; and this serves as a danger signal to their comrades. The musk-ox of the Arctic regions, when encountered, likewise stamps on the ground.[7] How this stamping action arose I cannot conjecture; for from enquiries which I have made, it does not appear that any of these animals fight with their fore-legs.*

Some species of deer, when savage, display far more expression than do cattle, sheep, or goats, for, as has already been stated, they draw back their ears, grind their teeth, erect their hair, squeal, stamp on the ground, and brandish their horns. One day in the Zoological Gardens, the Formosan deer (*Cervus pseudaxis*) approached me in a curious attitude, with his muzzle raised high up, so that the horns were pressed back on his neck; the head being held rather obliquely. From the expression of his eye I felt sure that he was savage; he approached slowly, and as soon as he came close to the iron bars, he did not lower his head to butt at me, but suddenly bent it inwards, and struck his head with great force against the railings. Mr Bartlett informs me that some other species of deer place themselves in the same attitude when enraged.

Monkeys. The various species and genera of monkeys express their feelings in many different ways; and this fact is interesting, as in some degree bearing on the question, whether the so-called races of man should be ranked as distinct species or varieties; for, as we shall see in the following chapters, the different races of man

---

* [Mr G. Hookham, of Hall Green, states in a letter that he has seen sheep 'strike viciously with their fore-feet at a small dog'. It seems doubtful, however, as Mr Hookham remarks, whether this action can have given rise to the stamping of an angry sheep.

Is it possible that the stamping may be simply a signal, and be understood as such from its resemblance to the sound of the frightened scamper of a startled sheep?]

express their emotions and sensations with remarkable uniformity throughout the world.

> In Darwin's time some who claimed that Caucasians were superior to other races had proposed that the different races had descended not from one but from different progenitors – the Caucasians from more advanced progenitors than the negroid race. Darwin's evidence that the expression of emotions is the same for all mankind was strong evidence for the opposite view – that all human beings have common progenitors – challenging the opinion that any race is superior to another. Nevertheless, the American historian Frederick Burkhardt pointed out that Darwin does speak of 'higher' and 'lower' races in *Descent of Man*.

Some of the expressive actions of monkeys are interesting in another way, namely from being closely analogous to those of man.

> The American primatologist Sue Parker remarked that instead of using the term 'analogous' '. . . to describe the similarities between human and nonhuman primates, modern biologists would describe those that are due to common ancestry as "homologous" or as "shared derived" characters'.

As I have had no opportunity of observing any one species of the group under all circumstances, my miscellaneous remarks will be best arranged under different states of the mind.

Pleasure, joy, affection.[8] It is not possible to distinguish in monkeys, at least without more experience than I have had, the expression of pleasure or joy from that of affection. Young chimpanzees make a kind of barking noise, when pleased by the return of any one to whom they are attached. When this noise, which the keepers call a laugh, is uttered, the lips are protruded; but so they are under various other emotions. Nevertheless I could perceive that when they were pleased the form of the lips differed a little from that assumed when they were angered. If a young chimpanzee be tickled – and the armpits are particularly sensitive to tickling, as in the case of our children – a more decided chuckling or laughing sound is uttered: though the laughter is sometimes noiseless. The corners of the mouth are then drawn backwards; and this sometimes causes the lower eyelids to be slightly wrinkled. But this wrinkling, which is so characteristic of our own laughter, is more plainly seen in some other monkeys. The teeth in the upper jaw in the chimpanzee are not exposed when they utter their laughing noise, in which respect they differ from us. But their eyes sparkle and grow brighter, as Mr W. L. Martin,[9] who has particularly attended their expression, states.

Young orangs, when tickled, likewise grin and make a chuckling sound; and Mr Martin says that their eyes grow brighter. As soon as their laughter ceases, an expression may be detected passing over their faces, which, as Mr Wallace remarked to me, may be called a smile. I have also noticed something of the same kind with the chimpanzee. Dr Duchenne – and I cannot quote a better authority – informs me that he kept a very tame monkey in his house for a year; and when he gave it during meal-times some choice delicacy, he observed that the corners of its mouth were slightly raised; thus an expression of satisfaction, partaking of the nature of an incipient smile, and resembling that often seen on the face of a man, could be plainly perceived in this animal.

Parker commented that because of '. . . his limited sample, Darwin sometimes describes gestures in one species without noting that they are common to several species. The laughter-like response to tickling is found in gorillas as well as chimpanzees and orangutans.'

Parker also noted that Darwin used the term 'monkey' to refer to both monkeys and apes, and did not '. . . distinguish between Old World Monkeys, who are closer relatives of great apes, and New World Monkeys. Some of the species names and some of the genera are archaic. For example, *Cebus azarae* = *Cebus appella* or *Cebus olivaceous*.'

The *Cebus azarae*,* when rejoiced at seeing a beloved person, utters a peculiar tittering (*kichernden*) sound. It also expresses agreeable sensation, by drawing back the corners of its mouth, without producing any sound. Rengger calls this movement laughter, but it would be more appropriately called a smile. The form of the mouth is different when either pain or terror is expressed, and high shrieks are uttered. Another species of Cebus in the Zoological Gardens (*C. hypoleucus*), when pleased, makes a reiterated shrill note, and likewise draws back the corners of its mouth, apparently through the contraction of the same muscles as with us. So does the Barbary ape (*Inuus ecaudatus*) to an extraordinary degree; and I observed on this monkey that the skin of the lower eyelids then became much wrinkled. At the same time it rapidly moved its lower jaw or lips in a spasmodic manner, the teeth being exposed; but the noise produced was hardly more distinct than that which we sometimes call silent laughter. Two of the keepers affirmed that this slight sound was the animal's laughter, and when I expressed some doubt on this head (being at the time quite inexperienced), they made it attack or rather threaten a hated Entellus monkey, living in the same compartment. Instantly the whole expression of the face of the Inuus changed; the mouth was opened much more widely, the canine teeth were fully exposed, and a hoarse barking noise was uttered.

The Anubis baboon (*Cynocephalus anubis*) was first insulted and put into a furious rage, as was easily done, by his keeper, who then made friends with him and shook hands. As the reconciliation was effected the baboon rapidly moved up and down his jaws and lips, and looked pleased. When we laugh heartily, a similar movement, or quiver, may be observed more or less distinctly in our jaws; but with man the muscles of the chest are more particularly acted on, whilst with this baboon, and with some other monkeys, it is the muscles of the jaws and lips which are spasmodically affected.

I have already had occasion to remark on the curious manner

---

* Rengger (*Säugethiere von Paraguay*, 1830, p. 46) kept these monkeys in confinement for seven years in their native country of Paraguay.

in which two or three species of the Macacus and *Cynopithecus niger* draw back their ears and utter a slight jabbering noise, when they are pleased by being caressed. With the Cynopithecus (Fig. 17), the corners of the mouth are at the same time drawn backwards and upwards, so that the teeth are exposed. Hence this expression would never be recognized by a stranger as one of pleasure.

The American primatologist William Mason said that Darwin is wrong about Figure 17. 'Although monkeys show a diversity of vocal and facial expressions within a broad range of circumstances, the relation of these behaviors to human emotions and emotional expressions is usually tenuous. In some cases the similarities in form may even be misleading, as in the Niger macaque shown in Darwin's Figure 17, which he implies is indicating pleasure. This expression is shown by many species of macaques and is generally considered today as expressing fear or tension. A stronger case for similar expressions can be made for chimps.'

The crest of long hairs on the forehead is depressed, and apparently the skin of the whole head drawn backwards. The eyebrows are thus raised a little, and the eyes also become slightly wrinkled; but this wrinkling is not conspicuous, owing to the permanent transverse furrows on the face.

Painful emotions and sensations. With monkeys the expression of slight pain, or of any painful emotion, such as grief, vexation, jealousy, etc., is not easily distinguished from that of moderate anger; and these states of mind readily and quickly pass into each other. Grief, however, with some species is certainly exhibited by weeping. A woman, who sold a monkey to the Zoological Society, believed to have come from Borneo (*Macacus maurus* or *M. inornatus* of Gray), said that it often cried; and Mr Bartlett, as well as the keeper Mr Sutton, have repeatedly seen it, when grieved, or even when much pitied, weeping so copiously that

Fig. 16. *Cynopithecus niger*, in a placid condition.
Drawn from life by Mr Wolf

Fig. 17. The same, when pleased by being caressed.
[In the First Edition, fig. 17 appeared as an engraving. This is
the previously unpublished drawn version on which the engraving
was based.]

the tears rolled down its cheeks. There is, however, something strange about this case, for two specimens subsequently kept in the Gardens, and believed to be the same species, have never been seen to weep, though they were carefully observed by the keeper and myself when much distressed and loudly screaming. Rengger states[10] that the eyes of the *Cebus azarae* fill with tears, but not sufficiently to overflow, when it is prevented getting some much desired object, or is much frightened. Humboldt also asserts that the eyes of *Callithrix sciureus* 'instantly fill with tears when it is seized with fear'; but when this pretty little monkey in the Zoological Gardens was teased, so as to cry out loudly, this did not occur. I do not, however, wish to throw the least doubt on the accuracy of Humboldt's statement.

Mason commented that sobbing and pouting are not likely to occur in monkeys.

The appearance of dejection in young orangs and chimpanzees, when out of health, is as plain and almost as pathetic as in the case of our own children. This state of mind and body is shown by their listless movements, fallen countenances, dull eyes, and changed complexion.

Anger. This emotion is often exhibited by many kinds of monkeys, and is expressed, as Mr Martin remarks,[11] in many different ways, 'Some species, when irritated, pout the lips, gaze with a fixed and savage glare on their foe, and make repeated short starts as if about to spring forward, uttering at the same time inward guttural sounds. Many display their anger by suddenly advancing, making abrupt starts, at the same time opening the mouth and pursing up the lips, so as to conceal the teeth, while the eyes are daringly fixed on the enemy, as if in savage defiance. Some again, and principally the long-tailed monkeys, or guenons, display their teeth, and accompany their malicious grins with a sharp, abrupt, reiterated cry.' Mr Sutton confirms the statement that some species uncover their teeth when enraged, whilst others conceal them by the protrusion of their lips; and some kinds draw back their ears. The *Cynopithecus niger*, lately referred to, acts in this manner, at the same time depressing the crest of hair on its forehead, and showing its teeth; so that the movements of the features from anger are nearly the same as those from pleasure; and the two expressions can be distinguished only by those familiar with the animal.

Baboons often show their passion and threaten their enemies in a very odd manner, namely by opening their mouths widely, as in the act of yawning. Mr Bartlett has often seen two baboons, when first placed in the same compartment, sitting opposite to each other and thus alternately opening their mouths; and this action seems frequently to end in a real yawn. Mr Bartlett believes that both animals wish to show to each other that they are provided with a formidable set of teeth, as is undoubtedly the case.* As I could hardly credit the reality of this yawning gesture, Mr Bartlett insulted an old baboon and put him into a violent passion; and he almost immediately thus acted. Some species of Macacus and of Cercopithecus[12] behave in the same manner. Baboons likewise show their anger, as was observed by Brehm with those which he kept alive in Abyssinia, in another manner, namely by striking the ground with one hand, 'like an angry man striking the table with his fist'. I have seen this movement with the baboons in the Zoological Gardens; but sometimes the action seems rather to represent the searching for a stone or other object in their beds of straw.

Parker commented that the baboon gesture of striking one hand on the ground involves the flat of the hand, and is common among other Old World monkeys.

Mr Sutton has often observed the face of the *Macacus rhesus*, when much enraged, growing red. As he was mentioning this to me, another monkey attacked a rhesus, and I saw its face redden

* ['Baboons seem to act consciously when they threaten by opening their mouths . . . for Mr Bartlett has had specimens with their canine teeth sawn off, and these never acted in this manner; they would not show their comrades that they were powerless' – *Note by C. Darwin*, dated 14 November 1873.]

as plainly as that of a man in a violent passion. In the course of a few minutes, after the battle, the face of this monkey recovered its natural tint. At the same time that the face reddened, the naked posterior part of the body, which is always red, seemed to grow still redder; but I cannot positively assert that this was the case. When the mandrill is in any way excited, the brilliantly coloured, naked parts of the skin are said to become still more vividly coloured.

With several species of baboons the ridge of the forehead projects much over the eyes, and is studded with a few long hairs, representing our eyebrows. These animals are always looking about them, and in order to look upwards they raise their eyebrows. They have thus, as it would appear, acquired the habit of frequently moving their eyebrows. However this may be, many kinds of monkeys, especially baboons, when angered or in any way excited, rapidly and incessantly move their eyebrows up and down, as well as the hairy skin of their foreheads.* As we associate in the case of man the raising and lowering of the eyebrows with definite states of the mind, the almost incessant movement of the eyebrows by monkeys gives them a senseless expression. I once observed a man who had a trick of continually raising his eyebrows without any corresponding emotion, and this gave to him a foolish appearance; so it is with some persons who keep the corners of their mouths a little drawn backwards and upwards, as if by an incipient smile, though at the time they are not amused or pleased.

I believe that Darwin mistakenly combined two very different phenomena. The first is a facial *tic*, a movement that occurs spontaneously and seems to be unrelated to either emotion or what the person is saying. The most common facial tic is the tightening of the muscle which orbits the eye, *orbicularis oculi*, producing a wincing appearance. Brow-raising, brow-lowering and various lip movements can also occur as tics, which sometimes appear

---

* Brehm remarks (*Thierleben*, p. 68) that the eyebrows of the *Inuus ecaudatus* are frequently moved up and down when the animal is angered.

Fig. 18. Chimpanzee disappointed and sulky.
Drawn from life by Mr Wood

more frequently when a person is under stress. Some psychotherapists believe that tics have a psychogenic basis, but I don't believe there has been much success in treating tics with psychotherapy. A second quite different type of facial movement is what appears to be a habitual partial expression, as if in anticipation of feeling a particular emotion. An expression such as a smile, or a brow-raise, may be shown frequently or may be maintained for long time periods in a slight contraction.

A young orang, made jealous by her keeper attending to another monkey, slightly uncovered her teeth, and, uttering a peevish noise like *tish-shisht*, turned her back on him. Both orangs and chimpanzees, when a little more angered, protrude their lips greatly, and make a harsh barking noise. A young female chimpanzee, in a violent passion, presented a curious semblance to a child in the same state. She screamed loudly with wide open mouth, the lips being retracted so that the teeth were fully exposed. She threw her arms wildly about, sometimes clasping them over her head. She rolled on the ground, sometimes on her back, sometimes on her belly, and bit everything within reach. A young gibbon (*Hylobates syndactylus*) in a passion has been described[13] as behaving in almost exactly the same manner.

The lips of young orangs and chimpanzees are protruded, sometimes to a wonderful degree, under various circumstances. They act thus, not only when slightly angered, sulky, or dis-appointed, but when alarmed at anything – in one instance, at the sight of a turtle[14] – and likewise when pleased. But neither the degree of protrusion nor the shape of the mouth is exactly the same, as I believe, in all cases; and the sounds which are then uttered are different. The accompanying drawing represents a chimpanzee made sulky by an orange having been offered him, and then taken away. A similar protrusion or pouting of the lips, though to a much slighter degree, may be seen in sulky children.

Mason commented that the pout face in which the lips are protruded '. . . may occur as a prelude to vocalization in both adult and immature chimps. In adults, the pout face is the beginning of the elaborate threat display, which includes prolonged vocalization. In young animals it is usually the beginning of whining or screaming from an individual experiencing some distress, such as fear or frustration.'

Many years ago, in the Zoological Gardens, I placed a looking-glass on the floor between two young orangs, who, as far as it was known, had never before seen one. At first they gazed at their own images with the most steady surprise, and often changed their point of view. They then approached close and protruded their lips towards the image, as if to kiss it, in exactly the same manner as they had previously done towards each other, when first placed, a few days before, in the same room. They next made all sorts of grimaces, and put themselves in various attitudes before the mirror; they pressed and rubbed the surface; they placed their hands at different distances behind it; looked behind it; and finally seemed almost frightened, started a little, became cross, and refused to look any longer.

Parker said that Darwin's description of the responses of the orangutan to his mirror image is consistent with modern descriptions, '. . . but Darwin does not mention that some individual orangutans, chimpanzees, and gorillas show evidence that they recognize the image as their own, whereas monkeys do not.'

When we try to perform some little action which is difficult and requires precision, for instance, to thread a needle, we generally close our lips firmly, for the sake, I presume, of not disturbing our movements by breathing; and I noticed the same action in a young orang. The poor little creature was sick, and was amusing itself by trying to kill the flies on the window-panes with his knuckles; this was difficult as the flies buzzed about, and at each attempt the lips were firmly compressed, and at the same time slightly protruded.

Although the countenances, and more especially the gestures, of orangs and chimpanzees are in some respects highly expressive, I doubt whether on the whole they are so expressive as those of some other kinds of monkeys. This may be attributed in part to their ears being immovable, and in part to the nakedness of their eyebrows, of which the movements are thus rendered less conspicuous. When, however, they raise their eyebrows their foreheads become, as with us, transversely wrinkled. In comparison with man, their faces are inexpressive, chiefly owing to their not frowning under any emotion of the mind – that is, as far as I have been able to observe, and I carefully attended to this point. Frowning, which is one of the most important of all the expressions in man, is due to the contraction of the corrugators by which the eyebrows are lowered and brought together, so that vertical furrows are formed on the forehead. Both the orang and chimpanzee are said* to possess this muscle, but it seems rarely brought into action, at least in a conspicuous manner. I made my hands into a sort of cage, and placing some tempting fruit within, allowed both a young orang and chimpanzee to try their utmost to get it out; but although they grew rather cross, they showed not a trace of a frown. Nor was there any frown when they were enraged. Twice I took two chimpanzees from their rather dark room suddenly into bright sunshine, which would certainly have caused us to frown; they blinked and winked their eyes, but only once did I see a very slight frown. On another occasion, I tickled the nose of a chimpanzee with a straw, and as it crumpled up its face, slight vertical furrows appeared between the eyebrows. I have never seen a frown on the forehead of an orang.

The gorilla, when enraged, is described as erecting its crest of hair, throwing down its under lip, dilating its nostrils, and uttering terrific yells. Messrs Savage and Wyman[15] state that the scalp can be freely moved backwards and forwards, and that when the animal is excited it is strongly contracted; but I presume that they mean by this latter expression that the scalp is lowered; for they likewise speak of the young chimpanzee, when crying out, 'as having the eyebrows strongly contracted'. The great power of movement in the scalp of the gorilla, of many baboons and other monkeys, deserves notice in relation to the power possessed by some few men, either through reversion or persistence, of voluntarily moving their scalps.[16]

Astonishment, terror. A living fresh-water turtle was placed at my request in the same compartment in the Zoological Gardens with many monkeys; and they showed unbounded astonishment, as well as some fear. This was displayed by their remaining motionless, staring intently with widely opened eyes, their eyebrows being often moved up and down. Their faces seemed somewhat lengthened. They occasionally raised themselves on their hind-

---

* Professor Owen on the orang, *Proc. Zool. Soc.*, 1830, p. 28. On the chimpanzee, see Professor Macalister, in *Annals and Mag. of Nat. Hist.*, vol. vii, 1871, p. 342, who states that the *corrugator supercilii* is inseparable from the *orbicularis palpebrarum*.

legs to get a better view. They often retreated a few feet, and then turning their heads over one shoulder, again stared intently. It was curious to observe how much less afraid they were of the turtle than of a living snake which I had formerly placed in their compartment;[17] for in the course of a few minutes some of the monkeys ventured to approach and touch the turtle. On the other hand, some of the larger baboons were greatly terrified, and grinned as if on the point of screaming out. When I showed a little dressed-up doll to the *Cynopithecus niger*, it stood motionless, stared intently with widely opened eyes and advanced its ears a little forwards. But when the turtle was placed in its compartment, this monkey also moved its lips in an odd, rapid, jabbering manner, which the keeper declared was meant to conciliate or please the turtle.

I was never able clearly to perceive that the eyebrows of astonished monkeys were kept permanently raised, though they were frequently moved up and down. Attention, which precedes astonishment, is expressed by man by a slight raising of the eyebrows; and Dr Duchenne informs me that when he gave to the monkey formerly mentioned some quite new article of food, it elevated its eyebrows a little, thus assuming an appearance of close attention. It then took the food in its fingers, and, with lowered or rectilinear eyebrows, scratched, smelt, and examined it – an expression of reflection being thus exhibited. Sometimes it would throw back its head a little, and again with suddenly raised eyebrows re-examine and finally taste the food.

In no case did any monkey keep its mouth open when it was astonished. Mr Sutton observed for me a young orang and chimpanzee during a considerable length of time; and however much they were astonished, or whilst listening intently to some strange sound, they did not keep their mouths open. This fact is surprising, as with mankind hardly any expression is more general than a widely open mouth under the sense of astonishment. As far as I have been able to observe, monkeys breathe more freely through their nostrils than men do; and this may account for their not opening their mouths when they are astonished; for, as we shall see in a future chapter, man apparently acts in this manner when startled, at first for the sake of quickly drawing a full inspiration, and afterwards for the sake of breathing as quietly as possible.

Terror is expressed by many kinds of monkeys by the utterance of shrill screams; the lips being drawn back so that the teeth are exposed. The hair becomes erect, especially when some anger is likewise felt. Mr Sutton has distinctly seen the face of the *Macacus rhesus* grow pale from fear. Monkeys also tremble from fear; and sometimes they void their excretions. I have seen one which, when caught, almost fainted from an excess of terror.

Sufficient facts have now been given with respect to the expressions of various animals. It is impossible to agree with Sir C. Bell when he says[18] that 'the faces of animals seem chiefly capable of expressing rage and fear'; and again, when he says that all their expressions 'may be referred, more or less plainly, to their acts of volition or necessary instincts'. He who will look at a dog preparing to attack another dog or a man, and at the same animal when caressing his master, or will watch the countenance of a monkey when insulted, and when fondled by his keeper, will be forced to admit that the movements of their features and their gestures are almost as expressive as those of man. Although no explanation can be given of some of the expressions in the lower animals, the greater number are explicable in accordance with the three principles given at the commencement of the first chapter.

The American primatologist Suzanne Chevalier-Skolnikoff reviewed the research on facial expression in non-human primates in the century after Darwin wrote this chapter. She said: 'Darwin's central hypothesis – that the facial expressions of non-human primates and man are similar – has been strikingly confirmed, strongly supporting his theory that human facial expressions have evolved from those of man's non human primate ancestors.' The American primatologist William Redican, who also reviewed the findings on expression in non-human primates proposed that they and we have similar expressions for fear/surprise, anger, happiness and sadness. The most precise comparisons of specific expressions have been in regard to the smile. The German primatologist Signe Preuschoft documents how monkeys show the same expressions as humans do, but argues the smile is not a diminished version of the laughter face, as Darwin suggests (see Chapter VIII), but a distinct expression.[C32]

CHAPTER VI

Special Expressions of Man: Suffering and Weeping

The screaming and weeping of infants – Form of features
– Age at which weeping commences – The effects of habitual
restraint on weeping – Sobbing – Cause of the contraction
of the muscles round the eyes during screaming – Cause of
the secretion of tears.

In this and the following chapters the expressions exhibited by
man under various states of the mind will be described and
explained, as far as lies in my power. My observations will be
arranged according to the order which I have found the most
convenient; and this will generally lead to opposite emotions and
sensations succeeding each other.

Suffering of the body and mind: weeping. I have already described
in sufficient detail, in the third chapter, the signs of extreme pain,
as shown by screams or groans, with the writhing of the whole
body and the teeth clenched or ground together. These signs
are often accompanied or followed by profuse sweating, pallor,
trembling, utter prostration, or faintness. No suffering is greater
than that from extreme fear or horror, but here a distinct emotion
comes into play, and will be elsewhere considered. Prolonged
suffering, especially of the mind, passes into low spirits, grief,
dejection, and despair, and these states will be the subject of the
following chapter. Here I shall almost confine myself to weeping
or crying, more especially in children.

Infants, when suffering even slight pain, or discomfort, utter
violent and prolonged screams. Whilst thus screaming their eyes

are firmly closed, so that the skin round them is wrinkled, and the forehead contracted into a frown. The mouth is widely opened with the lips retracted in a peculiar manner, which causes it to assume a squarish form: the gums or teeth being more or less exposed. The breath is inhaled almost spasmodically. It is easy to observe infants whilst screaming; but I have found photographs made by the instantaneous process the best means for observation, as allowing more deliberation. I have collected twelve, most of them made purposely for me; and they all exhibit the same general characteristics. I have, therefore, had six of them* (Plate 1) reproduced by the heliotype process.

Phillip Prodger wrote of Fig. 1 in Plate 1: 'An enlargement of that image was displayed in the popular press, under the title "Ginx's Baby" after the name of a popular novel. In total Rejlander [the photographer who took many of the photographs in *Expression*] sold approximately [300,000 prints] . . . to the general public. "Ginx's Baby" was hailed as one of the first "momentary" images widely distributed in Victorian England. Rejlander appeared to have succeeded in capturing the child's appearance while his body and facial muscles were in vigorous movement. This was unusual in photography of the time, causing one critic to suggest that prior artistic portrayals of the emotions had "finally been scattered to the winds by the wonderful photographs of the late O. G. Rejlander", especially noting the illustrations in Dr Darwin's work on expression, and "Ginx's Baby", as examples. Those who admired the photographic quality of "Ginx's Baby" may have been surprised to discover that it was not, strictly speaking, really a photograph. Rather, it was a photographic copy of a drawing *after* an original photograph . . . By *transcribing* the photograph into a drawing, Rejlander would have been free to high-

---

* The best photographs in my collection are by Mr Rejlander, of Victoria Street, London, and by Herr Kindermann, of Hamburg. Figs 1, 3, 4 and 6 are by the former; and Figs 2 and 5 by the latter gentleman. Fig. 6 is given to show moderate crying in an older child.

light elements of the image Darwin sought to express . . . [I]n the drawn copy Rejlander rendered the child perched in a conspicuous padded chair that is completely missing from the original photograph. The chair itself seems unnaturally small for the child, giving him a larger-than-life appearance. It also serves to ground the child in a domestic setting that would have been instantly recognizable to Darwin's audience. It helps to make the image seem plausible, and provides it with a personal intimacy lacking in the photographic original. By inserting a chair into the drawn rendition of the image, Rejlander created an illustration which would have seemed persuasive to Darwin's readers: It appeared to capture a perceptible moment from everyday life which readers could sympathize with and mentally verify. Darwin refers to "Ginx's Baby" as a photograph in the text, but fails to explain that it is actually a drawn and altered copy of a photograph. He would certainly have known of Rejlander's alterations of this image, as he had both versions in his possession prior to publication of *The Expression* . . .'[C33]

In Figs 19, 20, and 21 Darwin also took some liberties with the accuracy of the illustration, as I explain later.

The firm closing of the eyelids and consequent compression of the eyeball – and this is a most important element in various expressions – serves to protect the eyes from becoming too much gorged with blood, as will presently be explained in detail. With respect to the order in which the several muscles contract in firmly compressing the eyes I am indebted to Dr Langstaff, of Southampton, for some observations which I have since repeated. The best plan for observing the order is to make a person first raise his eyebrows, and this produces transverse wrinkles across the forehead; and then very gradually to contract all the muscles round the eyes with as much force as possible. The reader who is unacquainted with the anatomy of the face, ought to refer to pp. 29–30, and look at the woodcuts 1 to 3. The corrugators of the brow (*corrugatores supercilii*) seem to be the first muscles to contract; and these draw the eyebrows downwards and inwards

PLATE I

1

2

3

4

5

6

towards the base of the nose, causing vertical furrows, that is a frown, to appear between the eyebrows; at the same time they cause the disappearance of the transverse wrinkles across the forehead. The orbicular muscles contract almost simultaneously with the corrugators, and produce wrinkles all round the eyes; they appear, however, to be enabled to contract with greater force, as soon as the contraction of the corrugators has given them some support. Lastly, the pyramidal muscles of the nose contract; and these draw the eyebrows and the skin of the forehead still lower down, producing short transverse wrinkles across the base of the nose.* For the sake of brevity these muscles will generally be spoken of as the orbiculars, or as those surrounding the eyes.

When these muscles are strongly contracted, those running to the upper lip† likewise contract and raise the upper lip. This might have been expected from the manner in which at least one of them, the *malaris*, is connected with the orbiculars. Any one who will gradually contract the muscles round the eyes, will feel, as he increases the force, that his upper lip and the wings of his nose (which are partly acted on by one of the same muscles) are almost always a little drawn up. If he keeps his mouth firmly shut whilst contracting the muscles round the eyes, and then suddenly relaxes his lips, he will feel that the pressure on his eyes immediately increases. So again when a person on a bright, glaring day wishes to look at a distant object, but is compelled partially to close his eyelids, the upper lip may almost always be observed to be somewhat raised. The mouths of some very short-sighted persons, who are forced habitually to reduce the aperture of their eyes, wear from this same reason a grinning expression.

* Henle (*Handbuch d. Syst. Anat.*, 1858, vol. i, p. 139) agrees with Duchenne that this is the effect of the contraction of the *pyramidalis nasi*.
† These consist of the *levator labii superioris alaeque nasi*, the *levator labii proprius*, the *malaris*, and the *zygomaticus minor*, or little zygomatic. This latter muscle runs parallel to and above the great zygomatic, and is attached to the outer part of the upper lip. It is represented in Fig. 2, p. 29, but not in Figs 1 and 3. Dr Duchenne first showed (*Mécanisme de la Physionomie Humaine*, Album, 1862, p. 39) the importance of the contraction of this muscle in the shape assumed by the features in crying. Henle considers the above-named muscles (excepting the *malaris*) as subdivisions of the *quadratus labii superioris*.

I agree with Darwin about which muscles raise the upper lip during the cry, but he is wrong in his claim, below that this must happen whenever the *orbicularis oculi* muscle is contracted. If that muscle only is strongly contracted, it will very slightly raise the upper lip but it will not deepen the naso-labial fold. That requires as well the action of the other muscles he mentions.

The raising of the upper lip draws upwards the flesh of the upper parts of the cheeks, and produces a strongly marked fold on each cheek – the naso-labial fold – which runs from near the wings of the nostrils to the corners of the mouth and below them. This fold or furrow may be seen in all the photographs, and is very characteristic of the expression of a crying child; though a nearly similar fold is produced in the act of laughing or smiling.*

As the upper lip is much drawn up during the act of screaming, in the manner just explained, the depressor muscles of the angles of the mouth (see K in woodcuts 1 and 2 [p. 24]) are strongly

* Although Dr Duchenne has so carefully studied the contraction of the different muscles during the act of crying, and the furrows on the face thus produced, there seems to be something incomplete in his account; but what that is I cannot say. He has given a figure (Fig. 19) in which one half of the face is made, by galvanizing the proper muscles, to smile; whilst the other half is similarly made to begin crying. Almost all those (viz. nineteen out of twenty-one persons) to whom I showed the smiling half of the face instantly recognized the expression; but, with respect to the other half, only six persons out of twenty-one recognized it – that is, if we accept such terms as 'grief', 'misery', 'annoyance', as correct – whereas, fifteen persons were ludicrously mistaken; some of them saying the face expressed 'fun', 'satisfaction', 'cunning', 'disgust', etc. We may infer from this that there is something wrong in the expression. Some of the fifteen persons may, however, have been partly misled by not expecting to see an old man crying, and by tears not being secreted.

With respect to another figure by Dr Duchenne (Fig. 20), in which the muscles of half the face are galvanized in order to represent a man beginning to cry, with the eyebrow on the same side rendered oblique, which is characteristic of misery, the expression was recognized by a greater proportional number of persons. Out of twenty-three persons, fourteen answered correctly, 'sorrow', 'distress', 'grief', 'just going to cry', 'endurance of pain', etc. On the other hand, nine persons either could form no opinion or were entirely wrong, answering, 'cunning leer', 'jocund', 'looking at an intense light', 'looking at a distant object', etc.

contracted in order to keep the mouth widely open, so that a full volume of sound may be poured forth.

Earlier [commentary, p. 151] I expressed disagreement with part of what Darwin said the *orbicularis oculi* muscle contraction did to the appearance of the lower face. A further disagreement is with his claim that when this muscle contracts, it is necessary to contract *depressor anguli oris* to keep the mouth wide open.

Fig. 19. [Ekman comments: 'Darwin included many of Duchenne's photographs, which appear in Chapters 7, 8, and 12, and engravings made from Duchenne's photographs in Chapter 12. I don't know why he did not include the photographs he discusses in this original footnote; perhaps it was because of the cost involved. My research suggests that Duchenne is correct in saying that the muscle he activated on the right side of the face, *zygomatic minor*, is contracted at the beginning of a cry, but it is not the only muscle which is activated. That may explain why Darwin found this half of the expression was ambiguous when he showed it to observers.]

The action of these opposed muscles, above and below, tends to give to the mouth an oblong, almost squarish outline, as may be seen in the accompanying photographs. An excellent observer,[1] in describing a baby crying whilst being fed, says, 'it made its mouth like a square, and let the porridge run out at all four corners.' I believe, but we shall return to this point in a future chapter, that the depressor muscles of the angles of the mouth are less under the separate control of the will than the adjoining muscles; so that if a young child is only doubtfully inclined to

Fig. 20. [Ekman comments: here Duchenne has added the contraction of the inner part of the *frontalis* muscle, pulling the inner corner of the eyebrow up and producing furrows in the center of the forehead. This is a very clear signal of sadness or distress, as Darwin found.]

cry, this muscle is generally the first to contract, and is the last to cease contracting. When older children commence crying, the muscles which run to the upper lip are often the first to contract; and this may perhaps be due to older children not having so strong a tendency to scream loudly; and consequently to keep their mouths widely open; so that the above-named depressor muscles are not brought into such strong action.

Our evidence[C34] supports Darwin's hunch that most people cannot deliberately contract the muscle which pulls the lip corners down. However, in my observations it is not just this muscle which precedes a cry, but a very slight contraction of the *mentalis* muscle in the chin, which pushes the lower lip up slightly.

With one of my own infants, from his eighth day and for some time afterwards, I often observed that the first sign of a screaming-fit, when it could be observed coming on gradually, was a little frown, owing to the contraction of the corrugators of the brows; the capillaries of the naked head and face becoming at the same time reddened with blood. As soon as the screaming-fit actually began, all the muscles round the eyes were strongly contracted, and the mouth widely opened in the manner above described; so that at this early period the features assumed the same form as at a more advanced age.

Dr Piderit[2] lays great stress on the contraction of certain muscles which draw down the nose and narrow the nostrils, as eminently characteristic of a crying expression. The *depressores anguli oris*, as we have just seen, are usually contracted at the same time, and they indirectly tend, according to Dr Duchenne, to act in this same manner on the nose. With children having bad colds a similar pinched appearance of the nose may be noticed, which is at least partly due, as remarked to me by Dr Langstaff, to their constant snuffling, and the consequent pressure of the atmosphere on two sides. The purpose of this contraction of the nostrils by children having bad colds, or whilst crying, seems to be to check the downward flow of the mucus and tears, and to prevent these fluids spreading over the upper lip.

After a prolonged and severe screaming-fit, the scalp, face, and eyes are reddened, owing to the return of the blood from the head having been impeded by the violent expiratory efforts; but the redness of the stimulated eyes is chiefly due to the copious effusion of tears. The various muscles of the face which have been strongly contracted, still twitch a little, and the upper lip is still slightly drawn up or everted,[3] with the corners of the mouth still a little drawn downwards. I have myself felt, and have observed in other grown-up persons, that when tears are restrained with difficulty, as in reading a pathetic story, it is almost impossible to prevent the various muscles, which with young children are brought into strong action during their screaming-fits, from slightly twitching or trembling.

Infants whilst young do not shed tears or weep,[*] as is well known to nurses and medical men. This circumstance is not exclusively due to the lacrymal glands being as yet incapable of secreting tears. I first noticed this fact from having accidentally brushed with the cuff of my coat the open eye of one of my infants, when seventy-seven days old, causing this eye to water freely; and though the child screamed violently, the other eye remained dry, or was only slightly suffused with tears. A similar slight effusion occurred ten days previously in both eyes during a screaming-fit. The tears did not run over the eyelid and roll down the cheeks of this child, whilst screaming badly, when 122 days old. This first happened 17 days later, at the age of 139 days. A few other children have been observed for me, and the period of free weeping appears to be very variable. In one case, the eyes became slightly suffused at the age of only 20 days; in another at 62 days. With two other children, the tears did *not* run down the face at the ages of 84 and 110 days; but in a third child they did run down at the age of 104 days. In one instance, as I was positively assured, tears ran down at the unusually early age of 42 days.[†] It would appear as if the lacrymal glands required some practice in the individual before they are easily excited

---

* [According to Maffei and Rösch, *Untersuchungen über den Cretinismus*, Erlangen, 1844, vol. ii, p. 110, quoted by F. W. Hagen, *Psychologische Untersuchungen*, Brunswick, 1847, p. 16, cretins never shed tears, but merely howl and shriek on occasions which would naturally produce weeping.]

† [A reviewer (*Lancet*, 14 December, 1872, p. 852) states that in one instance he saw tears roll freely down the cheeks of a child under one month old.]

into action, in somewhat the same manner as various inherited consensual movements and tastes require some exercise before they are fixed and perfected. This is all the more likely with a habit like weeping, which must have been acquired since the period when man branched off from the common progenitor of the genus Homo and of the non-weeping anthropomorphous apes.

> The American psychologist Harriet Oster, who has specialized in the study of facial expressions in infants, confirms Darwin's observation that in the first two to three months infants do not shed tears.

The fact of tears not being shed at a very early age from pain or any mental emotion is remarkable, as, later in life, no expression is more general or more strongly marked than weeping. When the habit has once been acquired by an infant, it expresses in the clearest manner suffering of all kinds, both bodily pain and mental stress, even though accompanied by other emotions, such as fear or rage. The character of the crying, however, changes at a very early age, as I noticed in my own infants – the passionate cry differing from that of grief. A lady informs me that her child, nine months old, when in a passion screams loudly, but does not weep; tears, however, are shed when she is punished by her chair being turned with its back to the table. This difference may perhaps be attributed to weeping being restrained, as we shall immediately see, at a more advanced age, under most circumstances excepting grief; and to the influence of such restraint being transmitted to an earlier period of life, than that at which it was first practised.

With adults, especially of the male sex, weeping soon ceases to be caused by, or to express, bodily pain. This may be accounted for by its being thought weak and unmanly by men, both of civilized and barbarous races, to exhibit bodily pain by any outward sign. With this exception, savages weep copiously from very slight causes, of which fact Sir J. Lubbock[4] has collected instances. A New Zealand chief 'cried like a child because the sailors spoilt his favourite cloak by powdering it with flour'. I saw in Terra del Fuego a native who had lately lost a brother, and who alternately cried with hysterical violence, and laughed heartily at anything which amused him. With the civilized nations of Europe there is also much difference in the frequency of weeping. Englishmen rarely cry, except under the pressure of the acutest grief; whereas in some parts of the Continent the men shed tears much more readily and freely.

The insane notoriously give way to all their emotions with little or no restraint; and I am informed by Dr J. Crichton Browne, that nothing is more characteristic of simple melancholia, even in the male sex, than a tendency to weep on the slightest occasions, or from no cause. They also weep disproportionately on the occurrence of any real cause of grief. The length of time during which some patients weep is astonishing, as well as the amount of tears which they shed. One melancholic girl wept for a whole day, and afterwards confessed to Dr Browne that it was because she remembered that she had once shaved off her eyebrows to promote their growth. Many patients in the asylum sit for a long time rocking themselves backwards and forwards, 'and if spoken to, they stop their movements, purse up their eyes, depress the corners of the mouth, and burst out crying'. In some of these cases, the being spoken to or kindly greeted appears to suggest some fanciful and sorrowful notion; but in other cases an effort of any kind excites weeping, independently of any sorrowful idea. Patients suffering from acute mania likewise have paroxysms of violent crying or blubbering, in the midst of their incoherent ravings. We must not, however, lay too much stress on the copious shedding of tears by the insane, as being due to the lack of all restraint; for certain brain-diseases, as hemiplegia, brain-wasting, and senile decay, have a special tendency to induce weeping. Weeping is common in the insane, even after a complete state of fatuity has been reached and the power of speech lost. Persons born idiotic likewise weep;[5] but it is said that this is not the case with cretins [see footnote p. 155].

Weeping seems to be the primary and natural expression, as we see in children, of suffering of any kind, whether bodily pain short of extreme agony, or mental distress. But the foregoing facts and common experience show us that a frequently repeated effort to restrain weeping, in association with certain states of the mind, does much in checking the habit. On the other hand, it appears that the power of weeping can be increased through habit; thus the Rev. R. Taylor,[6] who long resided in New Zealand, asserts that the women can voluntarily shed tears in abundance; they meet for this purpose to mourn for the dead, and they take pride in crying 'in the most affecting manner'.

A single effort of repression brought to bear on the lacrymal glands does little, and indeed seems often to lead to an opposite result. An old and experienced physician told me that he had always found that the only means to check the occasional bitter weeping of ladies who consulted him, and who themselves wished to desist, was earnestly to beg them not to try, and to assure them that nothing would relieve them so much as prolonged and copious crying.

The screaming of infants consists of prolonged expirations, with short and rapid, almost spasmodic inspirations, followed at somewhat more advanced age by sobbing. According to Gratiolet,[7] the glottis is chiefly affected during the act of sobbing. The sound is heard 'at the moment when the inspiration conquers the resistance of the glottis, and the air rushes into the chest'. But the whole act of respiration is likewise spasmodic and violent. The shoulders are at the same time generally raised, as by this movement respiration is rendered easier. With one of my infants, when seventy-seven days old, the inspirations were so rapid and strong that they approached in character to sobbing; when 138 days old I first noticed distinct sobbing, which subsequently followed every bad crying-fit. The respiratory movements are partly voluntary and partly involuntary, and I apprehend that sobbing is at least in part due to children having some power to command after early infancy their vocal organs and to stop their screams, but from having less power over their respiratory muscles, these continue for a time to act in an involuntary or spasmodic manner, after having been brought into violent action. Sobbing seems to be peculiar to the human species; for the keepers in the Zoological

Gardens assure me that they have never heard a sob from any kind of monkey; though monkeys often scream loudly whilst being chased and caught, and then pant for a long time. We thus see that there is a close analogy between sobbing and the free shedding of tears; for with children sobbing does not commence during early infancy, but afterwards comes on rather suddenly and then follows every bad crying-fit until the habit is checked with advancing years.

Mason said he had seen something '. . . reminiscent of sobbing in young chimpanzees, which seemed to occur during an extreme state of fear or during a temper tantrum. As Darwin said about sobbing, the behavior is definitely involuntary and spasmodic.'

On the cause of the contraction of the muscles round the eyes during screaming. We have seen that infants and young children, whilst screaming, invariably close their eyes firmly, by the contraction of the surrounding muscles, so that the skin becomes wrinkled all around. With older children, and even with adults, whenever there is violent and unrestrained crying, a tendency to the contraction of these same muscles may be observed; though this is often checked in order not to interfere with vision.

Sir C. Bell explains[8] this action in the following manner: 'During every violent act of expiration, whether in hearty laughter, weeping, coughing, or sneezing, the eyeball is firmly compressed by the fibres of the orbicularis; and this is a provision for supporting and defending the vascular system of the interior of the eye from a retrograde impulse communicated to the blood in the veins at that time. When we contract the chest and expel the air, there is a retardation of the blood in the veins of the neck and head; and in the more powerful acts of expulsion, the blood not only distends the vessels, but is even regurgitated into the minute branches. Were the eye not properly compressed at that time, and a resistance given to the shock, irreparable injury might be inflicted on the delicate textures of the interior of the eye.' He further adds, 'If we separate the eyelids of a child to examine the eye, while it cries and struggles with passion, by taking off the support of the vascular system to the eye, and means of guarding it against the rush of blood then occurring, the conjunctiva becomes suddenly filled with blood, and the eyelid everted.'

Not only are the muscles round the eyes strongly contracted, as Sir C. Bell states, and as I have often observed, during screaming, loud laughter, coughing, and sneezing, but during several other analogous actions. A man contracts these vessels when he violently blows his nose. I asked one of my boys to shout as loudly as he possibly could, and as soon as he began, he firmly contracted his orbicular muscles; I observed this repeatedly, and on asking him why he had every time so firmly closed his eyes, I found that he was quite unaware of the fact: he had acted instinctively or unconsciously.*

It is not necessary, in order to lead to the contraction of these muscles, that air should actually be expelled from the chest; it suffices that the muscles of the chest and abdomen should contract with great force, whilst by the closure of the glottis no air escapes. In violent vomiting or retching the diaphragm is made to descend by the chest being filled with air; it is then held in this position by the closure of the glottis, 'as well as by the contraction of its own fibres'.[9] The abdominal muscles now contract strongly upon the stomach, its proper muscles likewise contracting, and the contents are thus ejected. During each effort of vomiting 'the head becomes greatly congested, so that the features are red and swollen, and the large veins of the face and temples visibly dilate'. At the same time, as I know from observation, the muscles round the eyes are strongly contracted. This is likewise the case when

---

* '[Chaucer, in describing a cock crowing, wrote:

> 'This chaunteclere stood high upon his toos,
> Stretching his necke and held his eyen cloos,
> And gan to crowen loude for the nones.'
> *The Nonnes Priestes Tale*

The author's attention was called to this passage by Sir W. Gull.]

the abdominal muscles act downwards with *unusual* force in expelling the contents of the intestinal canal.

The greatest exertion of the muscles of the body, if those of the chest are not brought into strong action in expelling or compressing the air within the lungs, does not lead to the contraction of the muscles round the eyes. I have observed my sons using great force in gymnastic exercises, as in repeatedly raising their suspended bodies by their arms alone, and in lifting heavy weights from the ground, but there was hardly any trace of contraction in the muscles round the eyes.

In the next few lines, Darwin hints that the role of *orbicularis oculi* in protecting the eye is crucial to the rationale he will develop in the next chapter about the movements in the eyebrows which signal sadness or grief. For that reason, he went to some lengths to verify whether Bell was correct.

As the contraction of these muscles for the protection of the eyes during violent expiration is indirectly, as we shall hereafter see, a fundamental element in several of our most important expressions, I was extremely anxious to ascertain how far Sir C. Bell's view could be substantiated. Professor Donders, of Utrecht,* well known as one of the highest authorities in Europe on vision and on the structure of the eye, has most kindly undertaken for me this investigation with the aid of the many ingenious mechanisms of modern science, and has published the results.[10] He shows that during violent expiration the external, the intra-ocular, and the retro-ocular vessels of the eye are all affected in two ways, namely by the increased pressure of the blood in the arteries, and by the return of the blood in the veins being impeded. It is, therefore, certain that both the arteries and the veins of the eye are more or less distended during violent

---

* I am greatly indebted to Mr Bowman for having introduced me to Professor Donders, and for his aid in persuading this great physiologist to undertake the investigation of the present subject. I am likewise much indebted to Mr Bowman for having given me, with the utmost kindness, information on many points.

expiration. The evidence in detail may be found in Professor Donders' valuable memoir. We see the effects on the veins of the head, in their prominence, and in the purple colour of the face of a man who coughs violently from being half choked. I may mention, on the same authority, that the whole eye certainly advances a little during each violent expiration. This is due to the dilatation of the retro-ocular vessels, and might have been expected from the intimate connection of the eye and brain; the brain being known to rise and fall with each respiration, when a portion of skull has been removed; and as may be seen along the unclosed sutures of infants' heads. This also, I presume, is the reason that the eyes of a strangled man appear as if they were starting from their sockets.*

With respect to the protection of the eye during violent expiratory efforts by the pressure of the eyelids, Professor Donders concludes from his various observations, that this action certainly limits or entirely removes the dilatation of the vessels.† At such times, he adds, we not infrequently see the hand involuntarily laid upon the eyelids, as if the better to support and defend the eyeball.

Nevertheless much evidence cannot at present be advanced to

---

* [Dr Keen, of Philadelphia, calls attention (letter n. d.), to his paper in the *Med. and Surg. History of the War of the Rebellion (Surgical Part)*, vol. i, pp. 206–7, bearing on this point. A patient lost part of his skull by a gunshot wound, and recovered with a concavity on the surface of his head, into which the scalp dipped to the depth of an inch. Ordinary respiration did not affect the concavity, but on moderate coughing a little cone bulged up, and a severe cough changed the concavity into a convex surface rising above the surface of the head.]

† Professor Donders remarks (ibid., p. 28), that, 'After injury to the eye, after operations, and in some forms of internal inflammation, we attach great value to the uniform support of the closed eyelids, and we increase this in many instances by the application of a bandage. In both cases we carefully endeavour to avoid great expiratory pressure, the disadvantage of which is well known.' Mr Bowman informs me that in the excessive photophobia, accompanying what is called scrofulous ophthalmia in children, when the light is so very painful that during weeks or months it is constantly excluded by the more forcible closure of the lids, he has often been struck on opening the lids by the paleness of the eye – not an unnatural paleness, but an absence of the redness that might have been expected when the surface is somewhat inflamed, as is then usually the case; and this paleness he is inclined to attribute to the forcible closure of the eyelids.

prove that the eye actually suffers injury from the want of support during violent expiration; but there is some. It is 'a fact that forcible expiratory efforts in violent coughing or vomiting, and especially in sneezing, sometimes give rise to ruptures of the little (external) vessels' of the eye.[11] With respect to the internal vessels, Dr Gunning has lately recorded a case of exophthalmos in consequence of whooping-cough, which in his opinion depended on the rupture of the deeper vessels; and another analogous case has been recorded. But a mere sense of discomfort would probably suffice to lead to the associated habit of protecting the eyeball by the contraction of the surrounding muscles. Even the expectation or chance of injury would probably be sufficient, in the same manner as an object moving too near the eye induces involuntary winking of the eyelids. We may, therefore, safely conclude from Sir C. Bell's observations, and more especially from the more careful investigations by Professor Donders, that the firm closure of the eyelids during the screaming of children is an action full of meaning and of real service.

Although some subsequent writers[C35] on facial expression doubted Darwin's account of the importance of contracting *orbicularis oculi* to prevent the vessels in the eyeball from rupturing, more recent experts support Darwin. The American ophthalmologist David Heiden wrote to me that what Darwin said '. . . seems to make sense, and we often see patients with benign subcon-junctival hemorrhages after coughing bouts, and occasionally after violent bouts of emesis [vomiting]'. The Australian vision researcher Andrew Cuthbertson commented, 'Bell's explanation, that contraction of the *orbicularis oculi* muscles during vigorous effort, such as the Valsalva manoeuvre seems quite sound. (The Valsalva effect is created by attempting to expel air from the lungs against a closed glottis.) Interestingly enough, the blood vessels within the eyeball itself are relatively protected from sudden pressure changes, as these changes in vascular pressure are accompanied by a rise in surrounding intraocular pressure. More vulnerable are the vessels outside the eye, such as those beneath the conjunctiva, or in the orbit, which may rupture during acute episodes of coughing, vomiting, defecation, labor, etc.

'[The Dutchman] Francisco Cornelius Donders (1818–1889), was indeed one of the greatest European ophthalmologists ... His most enduring contributions were to the science of the optics of refraction.'

We have already seen that the contraction of the orbicular muscles leads to the drawing up of the upper lip, and consequently, if the mouth is kept widely open, to the drawing down of the corners by the contraction of the depressor muscles. The formation of the naso-labial fold on the cheeks likewise follows from the drawing up of the upper lip. Thus all the chief expressive movements of the face during crying apparently result from the contraction of the muscles round the eyes. We shall also find that the shedding of tears depends on, or at least stands in some connection with, the contraction of these same muscles.

In some of the foregoing cases, especially in those of sneezing and coughing, it is possible that the contraction of the orbicular muscles may serve in addition to protect the eyes from too severe a jar or vibration. I think so, because dogs and cats, in crunching hard bones, always close their eyelids, and at least sometimes in sneezing; though dogs do not do so whilst barking loudly. Mr Sutton carefully observed for me a young orang and chimpanzee, and he found that both always closed their eyes in sneezing and coughing, but not whilst screaming violently. I gave a small pinch of snuff to a monkey of the American division, namely, a Cebus, and it closed its eyelids whilst sneezing; but not on a subsequent occasion whilst uttering loud cries.

*Cause of the secretion of tears.** It is an important point which must be considered in any theory of the secretion of tears from the

---

* [Henle, *Anthropologische Vorträge*, 1876, vol. i, p. 66, discusses the effect of the emotions on certain bodily actions, and points out that whether we look at muscular contractions, or vascular changes, or glandular secretions, there is a general tendency for the symptoms of the emotional state to begin near the head

mind being affected, that whenever the muscles round the eyes are strongly and involuntarily contracted in order to compress the blood-vessels and thus to protect the eyes, tears are secreted, often in sufficient abundance to roll down the cheeks. This occurs under the most opposite emotions, and under no emotion at all. The sole exception, and this is only a partial one, to the existence of a relation between the involuntary and strong contraction of the muscles and the secretion of tears, is that of young infants, who, whilst screaming violently with their eyelids firmly closed, do not commonly weep until they have attained the age of from two to three or four months. Their eyes, however, become suffused with tears at a much earlier age. It would appear, as already remarked, that the lacrymal glands do not, from the want of practice or some other cause, come to full functional activity at a very early period of life. With children at a somewhat later age, crying out or wailing from any distress is so regularly accompanied by the shedding of tears, that weeping and crying are synonymous terms.*

Cuthbertson wrote that Darwin's '. . . explanation of shedding tears during *orbicularis oculi* contraction also seems valid. Contraction of *orbicularis oculi* during a Valsalva manoeuvre will compress the major lachrymal gland and its ducts, as the gland lies behind the muscle and orbital septum within the orbit. Furthermore, raised

---

and spread downwards. As an example of the law applying to secretion he points out that in terror the sweat first breaks out on the forehead. In the same way he says that in strong emotion the flow of tears is the first effect, then follows the saliva, and in still more violent mental states the liver and other abdominal viscera are affected. Henle relies on anatomy entirely, for he says, 'If by bad luck the origin of the nerve which excites the salivary gland had been nearer to the cerebral hemispheres than the nerves of lachrymation, poets must have celebrated salivation instead of weeping'.

This kind of generalization leaves unexplained the *specific* action of different emotions – why should we not perspire with grief, instead of with terror?]

* Mr Hensleigh Wedgwood (*Dict. of English Entymology*, 1859, vol. i, p. 410) says, 'the verb to weep comes from the Anglo-Saxon *wop*, the primary meaning of which is simply outcry'.

orbital pressure and *orbicular oculi* contraction, will tend to squeeze tears out of the conjunctival sack to spill out onto the cheek.'

Under the opposite emotion of great joy or amusement, so long as laughter is moderate there is hardly any contraction of the muscles round the eyes, so that there is no frowning; but when peals of loud laughter are uttered, with rapid and violent spasmodic expirations, tears stream down the face. I have more than once noticed the face of a person, after a paroxysm of violent laughter, and I could see that the orbicular muscles and those running to the upper lip were still partially contracted, which together with the tear-stained cheeks gave to the upper half of the face an expression not to be distinguished from that of a child still blubbering from grief. The fact of tears streaming down the face during violent laughter is common to all races of mankind, as we shall see in a future chapter.

In violent coughing, especially when a person is half-choked, the face becomes purple, the veins distended, the orbicular muscles strongly contracted, and tears run down the cheeks. Even after a fit of ordinary coughing, almost every one has to wipe his eyes. In violent vomiting or retching, as I have myself experienced and seen in others, the orbicular muscles are strongly contracted, and tears sometimes flow freely down the cheeks. It has been suggested to me that this may be due to irritating matter being injected into the nostrils, and causing by reflex action the secretion of tears. Accordingly I asked one of my informants, a surgeon, to attend to the effects of retching when nothing was thrown up from the stomach; and, by an odd coincidence, he himself suffered the next morning from an attack of retching, and three days subsequently observed a lady under a similar attack; and he is certain that in neither case an atom of matter was ejected from the stomach; yet the orbicular muscles were strongly contracted, and tears freely secreted. I can also speak positively to the energetic contraction of these same muscles round the eyes, and to the coincident free secretion of tears, when the abdominal muscles act with unusual force in a downward direction on the intestinal canal.

Yawning commences with a deep inspiration, followed by a long and forcible expiration; and at the same time almost all the muscles of the body are strongly contracted, including those round the eyes. During this act tears are often secreted, and I have seen them even rolling down the cheeks.

I have frequently observed that when persons scratch some point which itches intolerably, they forcibly close their eyelids; but they do not, as I believe, first draw a deep breath and then expel it with force; and I have never noticed that the eyes then become filled with tears; but I am not prepared to assert that this does not occur. The forcible closure of the eyelids is, perhaps, merely a part of that general action by which almost all the muscles of the body are at the same time rendered rigid. It is quite different from the gentle closure of the eyes which often accompanies, as Gratiolet remarks,[12] the smelling a delicious odour, or the tasting a delicious morsel, and which probably originates in the desire to shut out any disturbing impression through the eyes.

Professor Donders writes to me to the following effect: 'I have observed some cases of a very curious affection when, after a slight rub (*attouchement*), for example, from the friction of a coat, which caused neither a wound nor a contusion, spasms of the orbicular muscles occurred, with a very profuse flow of tears, lasting about an hour. Subsequently, sometimes after an interval of several weeks, violent spasms of the same muscles re-occurred, accompanied by the secretion of tears, together with primary or secondary redness of the eye.' Mr Bowman informs me that he has occasionally observed closely analogous cases, and that, in some of these, there was no redness or inflammation of the eyes.

I was anxious to ascertain whether there existed in any of the lower animals a similar relation between the contraction of the orbicular muscles during violent expiration and the secretion of tears; but there are very few animals which contract these muscles in a prolonged manner, or which shed tears. The *Macacus maurus*, which formerly wept so copiously in the Zoological Gardens, would have been a fine case for observation; but the two monkeys now there, and which are believed to belong to the same species, do not weep. Nevertheless they were carefully observed by Mr Bartlett and myself, whilst screaming loudly, and they seemed to contract these muscles; but they moved about their cages so rapidly, that it was difficult to observe with certainty. No other monkey, as far as I have been able to ascertain, contracts its orbicular muscles whilst screaming.

The Indian elephant is known sometimes to weep. Sir E. Tennent, in describing those which he saw captured and bound in Ceylon, says, some 'lay motionless on the ground, with no other indication of suffering than the tears which suffused their eyes and flowed incessantly'. Speaking of another elephant he says, 'When overpowered and made fast, his grief was most affecting; his violence sank to utter prostration, and he lay on the ground, uttering choking cries, with tears trickling down his cheeks.'* In the Zoological Gardens the keeper of the Indian elephants positively asserts that he has several times seen tears rolling down the face of the old female, when distressed by the removal of the young one. Hence I was extremely anxious to ascertain, as an

---

* *Ceylon*, 3rd edit., 1859, vol. ii, pp. 364, 376. I applied to Mr Thwaites, in Ceylon, for further information with respect to the weeping of the elephant; and in consequence received a letter from the Rev. Mr Glenie, who, with others, kindly observed for me a herd of recently captured elephants. These, when irritated, screamed violently; but it is remarkable that they never when thus screaming contracted the muscles round the eyes. Nor did they shed tears; and the native hunters asserted that they had never observed elephants weeping. Nevertheless, it appears to me impossible to doubt Sir E. Tennent's distinct details about their weeping, supported as they are by the positive assertion of the keeper in the Zoological Gardens. It is certain that the two elephants in the Gardens, when they began to trumpet loudly, invariably contracted their orbicular muscles. I can reconcile these conflicting statements only by supposing that the recently captured elephants in Ceylon, from being enraged or frightened, desired to observe their persecutors, and consequently did not contract their orbicular muscles, so that their vision might not be impeded. Those seen weeping by Sir E. Tennent were prostrate, and had given up the contest in despair. The elephants which trumpeted in the Zoological Gardens at the word of command, were, of course, neither alarmed nor enraged.

[Gordon Cumming (*The Lion Hunter of South Africa*, 1856, p. 227), in describing the behaviour of an African elephant severely hit with rifle bullets, says that 'large tears now trickled from his eyes, which he slowly shut and opened'. Mr W. G. Walker called the author's attention to this fact.]

extension of the relation between the contraction of the orbicular muscles and the shedding of tears in man, whether elephants when screaming or trumpeting loudly contract these muscles. At Mr Bartlett's desire the keeper ordered the old and the young elephant to trumpet; and we repeatedly saw in both animals that, just as the trumpeting began, the orbicular muscles, especially the lower ones, were distinctly contracted. On a subsequent occasion the keeper made the old elephant trumpet much more loudly, and invariably both the upper and lower orbicular muscles were strongly contracted, and now in an equal degree. It is a singular fact that the African elephant, which, however, is so different from the Indian species that it is placed by some naturalists in a distinct sub-genus, when made on two occasions to trumpet loudly, exhibited no trace of the contraction of the orbicular muscles.

From the several foregoing cases with respect to Man, there can, I think, be no doubt that the contraction of the muscles round the eyes, during violent expiration or when the expanded chest is forcibly compressed, is, in some manner, intimately connected with the secretion of tears. This holds good under widely different emotions, and independently of any emotion. It is not, of course, meant that tears cannot be secreted without the contraction of these muscles; for it is notorious that they are often freely shed with the eyelids not closed, and with the brows unwrinkled. The contraction must be both involuntary and prolonged, as during a choking fit, or energetic, as during a sneeze. The more involuntary winking of the eyelids, though often repeated, does not bring tears into the eyes. Nor does the voluntary and prolonged contraction of the several surrounding muscles suffice. As the lacrymal glands of children are easily excited, I persuaded my own and several other children of different ages to contract these muscles repeatedly with their utmost force, and to continue doing so as long as they possibly could: but this produced hardly any effect. There was sometimes a little moisture in the eyes, by the squeezing out of the already secreted tears within the glands.

The nature of the relation between the involuntary and

energetic contraction of the muscles round the eyes, and the secretion of tears, cannot be positively ascertained, but a probable view may be suggested. The primary function of the secretion of tears, together with some mucus, is to lubricate the surface of the eye; and a secondary one, as some believe, is to keep the nostrils damp, so that the inhaled air may be moist,[13] and likewise to favour the power of smelling. But another, and at least equally important function of tears, is to wash out particles of dust or other minute objects which may get into the eyes. That this is of great importance is clear from the cases in which the cornea has been rendered opaque through inflammation, caused by particles of dust not being removed, in consequence of the eye and eyelid becoming immovable.[14] The secretion of tears from the irritation of any foreign body in the eye is a reflex action – that is, the body irritates a peripheral nerve which sends an impression to certain sensory nerve-cells; these transmit an influence to other cells, and these again to the lacrymal glands. The influence transmitted to these glands causes, as there is good reason to believe, the relaxation of the muscular coats of the smaller arteries; this allows more blood to permeate the glandular tissue, and this induces a free secretion of tears. When the small arteries of the face, including those of the retina, are relaxed under very different circumstances, namely, during an intense blush, the lacrymal glands are sometimes affected in a like manner, for the eyes become suffused with tears.

It is difficult to conjecture how many reflex actions have originated, but, in relation to the present case of the affection of the lacrymal glands through irritation of the surface of the eye, it may be worth remarking that, as soon as some primordial form became semiterrestrial in its habits, and was liable to get particles of dust into its eyes, if these were not washed out they would cause much irritation; and on the principle of the radiation of nerve-force to adjoining nerve-cells, the lacrymal glands would be stimulated to secretion. As this would often recur, and as nerve-force readily passes along accustomed channels, a slight irritation would ultimately suffice to cause a free secretion of tears.

As soon as by this, or by some other means, a reflex action of this nature had been established and rendered easy, other stimulants applied to the surface of the eye – such as cold wind, slow inflammatory action, or a blow on the eyelids – would cause a copious secretion of tears, as we know to be the case. The glands are also excited into action through the irritation of adjoining parts. Thus when the nostrils are irritated by pungent vapors, though the eyelids may be kept firmly closed, tears are copiously secreted; and this likewise follows from a blow on the nose, for instance from a boxing-glove. A stinging switch on the face produces, as I have seen, the same effect. In these latter cases the secretion of tears is an incidental result, and of no direct service. As all these parts of the face, including the lacrymal glands, are supplied with branches of the same nerve, namely, the fifth, it is in some degree intelligible that the effects of the excitement of any one branch should spread to the nerve-cells or roots of the other branches.

The internal parts of the eye likewise act, under certain conditions, in a reflex manner on the lacrymal glands. The following statements have been kindly communicated to me by Mr Bowman; but the subject is a very intricate one, as all the parts of the eye are so intimately related together, and are so sensitive to various stimulants. A strong light acting on the retina, when in a normal condition, has very little tendency to cause lacrymation; but with unhealthy children having small, old-standing ulcers on the cornea, the retina becomes excessively sensitive to light, and exposure even to common daylight causes forcible and sustained closure of the lids, and a profuse flow of tears. When persons who ought to begin the use of convex glasses habitually strain the waning power of accommodation, an undue secretion of tears very often follows, and the retina is liable to become unduly sensitive to light. In general, morbid affections of the surface of the eye, and of the ciliary structures concerned in the accommodative act, are prone to be accompanied with excessive secretion of tears. Hardness of the eyeball, not rising to inflammation, but implying a want of balance between the fluids poured out and again taken up by the intra-ocular vessels, is not usually attended with any lacrymation. When the balance is on the other side, and the eye becomes too soft, there is a greater tendency to lacrymation. Finally, there are numerous morbid states and structural alterations of the eyes, and even terrible inflammations, which may be attended with little or no secretion of tears.

It also deserves notice, as indirectly bearing on our subject, that the eye and adjoining parts are subject to an extraordinary number of reflex and associated movements, sensations, and actions, besides those relating to the lacrymal glands. When a bright light strikes the retina of one eye alone, the iris contracts, but the iris of the other eye moves after a measurable interval of time. The iris likewise moves in accommodation to near or distant vision, and when the two eyes are made to converge.[15] Every one knows how irresistibly the eyebrows are drawn down under an intensely bright light. The eyelids also involuntarily wink when an object is moved near the eyes, or a sound is suddenly heard. The well-known case of a bright light causing some persons to sneeze is even more curious; for nerve-force here radiates from certain nerve-cells in connection with the retina, to the sensory nerve-cells of the nose, causing it to tickle; and from these, to the cells which command the various respiratory muscles (the orbiculars included) which expel the air in so peculiar a manner that it rushes through the nostrils alone.

To return to our point: why are tears secreted during a screaming-fit or other violent expiratory efforts? As a slight blow in the eyelids causes a copious secretion of tears, it is at least possible that the spasmodic contraction of the eyelids, by pressing strongly on the eyeball, should in a similar manner cause some secretion. This seems possible, although the voluntary contraction of the same muscles does not produce any effect. We know that a man cannot voluntarily sneeze or cough with nearly the same force as he does automatically; and so it is with the contraction of the orbicular muscles: Sir C. Bell experimented on them, and found that by suddenly and forcibly closing the eyelids in the dark, sparks of light are seen, like those caused by tapping the eyelids with the fingers; 'but in sneezing the compression is both more rapid and more forcible, and the sparks more brilliant'. That these sparks are due to the contraction of the eyelids is clear, because if they 'are held open during the act of sneezing, no sensation of light will be experienced'. In the peculiar cases referred to by Professor Donders and Mr Bowman, we have seen that some weeks after the eye has been very slightly injured, spasmodic contractions of the eyelids ensue, and these are accompanied by a profuse flow of tears. In the act of yawning, the tears are apparently due solely to the spasmodic contraction of the muscles round the eyes. Notwithstanding these latter cases, it seems hardly credible that the pressure of the eyelids on the surface of the eye, although effected spasmodically and therefore with much greater force than can be done voluntarily, should be sufficient to cause by reflex action the secretion of tears in the many cases in which this occurs during violent expiratory efforts.

Another cause may come conjointly into play. We have seen that the internal parts of the eye, under certain conditions, act in a reflex manner on the lacrymal glands. We know that during violent expiratory efforts the pressure of the arterial blood within the vessels of the eye is increased, and that the return of the venous blood is impeded. It seems, therefore, not improbable that the distension of the ocular vessels, thus induced, might act by reflection on the lacrymal glands – the effects due to the spasmodic pressure of the eyelids on the surface of the eye being thus increased.

In considering how far this view is probable, we should bear in mind that the eyes of infants have been acted on in this double manner during numberless generations, whenever they have screamed; and on the principle of nerve-force readily passing along accustomed channels, even a moderate compression of the eyeballs and a moderate distension of the ocular vessels would ultimately come, through habit, to act on the glands. We have an analogous case in the orbicular muscles being almost always contracted in some slight degree, even during a gentle crying-fit, when there can be no distension of the vessels and no uncomfortable sensation excited within the eyes.

Moreover, when complex actions or movements have long been performed in strict association together, and these are from any cause at first voluntarily and afterwards habitually checked, then if the proper exciting conditions occur, any part of the action or movement which is least under the control of the will, will often still be involuntarily performed. The secretion by a gland is remarkably free from the influence of the will; therefore, when the advancing age of the individual, or with the advancing culture of the race, the habit of crying out or screaming is restrained, and there is consequently no distension of the blood-vessels of the eye, it may nevertheless well happen that tears should still be secreted. We may see, as lately remarked, the muscles round the eyes of a person who reads a pathetic story, twitching or trembling in so slight a degree as hardly to be detected. In this case there has been no screaming and no distension of the blood-vessels, yet through habit certain nerve-cells send a small amount of nerve-force to the cells commanding the muscles round the eyes; and they likewise send some to the cells commanding the lacrymal glands, for the eyes often become at the same time just moistened with tears. If the twitching of the muscles round the eyes and the secretion of tears had been completely prevented, nevertheless it is almost certain that there would have been some tendency to transmit nerve-force in these same directions; and as the lacrymal glands are remarkably free from the control of the will, they would be eminently liable still to act, thus betraying, though there were no other outward signs, the pathetic thoughts which were passing through the person's mind.

As a further illustration of the view here advanced, I may remark that if, during an early period of life, when habits of all kinds are readily established, our infants, when pleased, had been accustomed to utter loud peals of laughter (during which the vessels of their eyes are distended) as often and as continuously as they have yielded when distressed to screaming-fits, then it is probable that in after life tears would have been as copiously and as regularly secreted under the one state of mind as under the other. Gentle laughter, or a smile, or even a passing thought, would have sufficed to cause a moderate secretion of tears. There does indeed exist an evident tendency in this direction, as will be seen in a future chapter, when we treat of the tender feelings. With the Sandwich Islanders, according to Freycinet,[16] tears are actually recognized as a sign of happiness; but we should require better evidence on this head than that of a passing voyager. So again if our infants, during many generations, and each of them during several years, had almost daily suffered from prolonged choking-fits, during which the vessels of the eye are distended and tears copiously secreted, then it is probable, such is the force of associated habit, that during after life the mere thought of a choke, without any distress of mind, would have sufficed to bring tears into our eyes.

To sum up this chapter, weeping is probably the result of some such chain of events as follows. Children when wanting food or suffering in any way, cry out loudly, like the young of most other animals, partly as a call to their parents for aid, and partly from any great exertion serving as a relief. Prolonged screaming inevitably leads to the gorging of the blood-vessels of the eye; and this will have led, at first consciously and at last habitually, to the contraction of the muscles round the eyes in order to protect them. At the same time the spasmodic pressure on the surface of the eye, and the distension of the vessels within the eye, without necessarily entailing any conscious sensation, will have affected, through reflex action, the lacrymal glands. Finally, through the three principles of nerve-force readily passing along accustomed channels of association, which is so widely extended in its power – and of certain actions, being more under the control of the will than others – it has come to pass that suffering readily causes the secretion of tears, without being necessarily accompanied by any other action.

Although in accordance with this view we must look at weeping as an incidental result, as purposeless as the secretion of tears from a blow outside the eye, or as a sneeze from the retina being affected by a bright light, yet this does not present any difficulty in our understanding how the secretion of tears serves as a relief to suffering. And by as much as the weeping is more violent or hysterical, by so much will the relief be greater – on the same principle that the writhing of the whole body, the grinding of the teeth, and the uttering of piercing shrieks, all give relief under an agony of pain.

CHAPTER VII

Low Spirits, Anxiety, Grief, Dejection, Despair

General effect of grief on the system – Obliquity of the eyebrows under suffering – On the cause of the obliquity of the eyebrows – On the depression of the corners of the mouth.

After the mind has suffered from an acute paroxysm of grief, and the cause still continues, we fall into a state of low spirits; or we may be utterly cast down and dejected. Prolonged bodily pain, if not amounting to an agony, generally leads to the same state of mind. If we expect to suffer, we are anxious; if we have no hope of relief, we despair.

The words for closely related feelings can be confusing. In the next paragraph Darwin uses the term *grief* (which the dictionary says is sorrow or anguish in response to a loss) as a general term for two more specific emotions: distress and sadness. We[C36] have suggested that the term *distress* be used for what Darwin describes as the violent and almost frantic movements of grief. We reserve the term *sadness* for the state which often follows distress, when, as Darwin observes, the person no longer wishes for action but becomes passively resigned to the feelings of grief.

Persons suffering from excessive grief often seek relief by violent and almost frantic movements, as described in a former chapter; but when their suffering is somewhat mitigated, yet prolonged, they no longer wish for action, but remain motionless and passive, or may occasionally rock themselves to and fro. The circulation becomes languid; the face pale; the muscles flaccid; the eyelids droop; the head hangs on the contracted chest; the lips, cheeks, and lower jaw all sink downwards from their own weight. Hence all the features are lengthened; and the face of a person who hears bad news is said to fall. A party of natives in Tierra del Fuego endeavoured to explain to us that their friend, the captain of a sealing vessel, was out of spirits, by pulling down their cheeks with both hands, so as to make their faces as long as possible. Mr Bunnet informs me that the Australian aborigines when out of spirits have a chop-fallen appearance. After prolonged suffering the eyes become dull and lack expression, and are often slightly suffused with tears. The eyebrows not rarely are rendered oblique, which is due to their inner ends being raised. This produces peculiarly-formed wrinkles on the forehead which are very different from those of a simple frown; though in some cases a frown alone may be present. The corners of the mouth are drawn downwards, which is so universally recognized as a sign of being out of spirits, that it is almost proverbial.

The breathing becomes slow and feeble, and is often interrupted by deep sighs. As Gratiolet remarks, whenever our attention is long concentrated on any subject, we forget to breathe, and then revive ourselves by a deep inspiration;[1] but the sighs of a sorrowful person, owing to his slow respiration and languid circulation, are eminently characteristic.[2] As the grief of a person in this state occasionally recurs and increases into a paroxysm, spasms affect the respiratory muscles, and he feels as if something, the so-called *globus hystericus*, was rising in his throat. These spasmodic movements are clearly allied to the sobbing of children, and are remnants of those severer spasms which occur when a person is said to choke from excessive grief.[3]

Obliquity of the eyebrows. Two points alone in the above description require further elucidation, and these are very curious ones; namely, the raising of the inner ends of the eyebrows, and the drawing down of the corners of the mouth. With respect to the eyebrows, they may occasionally be seen to assume an oblique position in persons suffering from deep dejection or anxiety; for instance, I have observed this movement in a mother whilst speaking about her sick son; and it is sometimes excited by quite trifling or momentary causes of real or pretended distress. The eyebrows assume this position owing to the contraction of certain muscles (namely, the orbiculars, corrugators, and pyramidals of the nose which together bend to lower and contract the eyebrows) being partially checked by the more powerful action of the central fasciae of the frontal muscle. These latter fasciae by their contraction raise the inner ends alone of the eyebrows; and as the corrugators at the same time draw the eyebrows together, their inner ends become puckered into a fold or lump. This fold is a highly characteristic point in the appearance of the eyebrows when rendered oblique, as may be seen in Figs 2 and 5, Plate II. The eyebrows are at the same time somewhat roughened, owing to the hairs being made to project. Dr J. Crichton Browne has also often noticed in melancholic patients who keep their eyebrows persistently oblique, 'a peculiar acute arching of the upper eyelid'. A trace of this may be observed by comparing the right and left eyelids of the young man in the photograph (Fig. 2, Plate II); for he was not able to act equally on both eyebrows. This is also shown by the unequal furrows on the two sides of his forehead. The acute arching of the eyelids depends, I believe, on the inner end alone of the eyebrows being raised; for when the whole eyebrow is elevated and arched, the upper eyelid follows in a slight degree the same movement.

I believe Darwin is wrong in his description in the above paragraph of the muscular actions necessary to produce the appearance shown in Figures 2 and 5, Plate II. The combined action of *corrugator* and the inner portion of *frontalis* produce the oblique positioning of the eyebrow; *orbicularis oculi* and the *pyramidals* need not be involved.

But the most conspicuous result of the opposed contraction of the above-named muscles, is exhibited by the peculiar furrows formed on the forehead. These muscles, when thus in conjoint yet opposed action, may be called, for the sake of brevity, the grief-muscles. When a person elevates his eyebrows by the contraction of the whole frontal muscle, transverse wrinkles extend across the whole breadth of the forehead; but in the present case the middle fasciae alone are contracted; consequently, transverse furrows are formed across the middle part alone of the forehead. The skin over the exterior parts of both eyebrows is at the same time drawn downwards and smoothed, by the contraction of the outer portions of the orbicular muscles. The eyebrows are likewise brought together through the simultaneous contraction of the corrugators,* and this latter action generates vertical furrows, separating the exterior and lowered part of the skin of the forehead from the central and raised part. The union of these vertical furrows with the central and transverse furrows (see Figs 2 and 3) produces a mark on the forehead which has been compared to a horse-shoe; but the furrows more strictly form three sides of a quadrangle. They are often conspicuous on the foreheads of

---

* In the foregoing remarks on the manner in which the eyebrows are made oblique, I have followed what seems to be the universal opinion of all the anatomists, whose works I have consulted on the action of the above-named muscles, or with whom I have conversed. Hence throughout this work I shall take a similar view of the action of the *corrugator supercilii, orbicularis, pyramidalis nasi,* and *frontalis* muscles. Dr Duchenne, however, believes, and every conclusion at which he arrives deserves serious consideration, that it is the corrugator, called by him the *sourcilier,* which raises the inner corner of the eyebrows and is antagonistic to the upper and inner part of the orbicular muscle, as well as to the *pyramidalis nasi* (see *Mécanisme de la Phys. Humaine,* 1862, folio, art, v, text and figures 19 to 29: octavo edit, 1862, p. 43 text). He admits, however, that the corrugator draws together the eyebrows, causing vertical furrows above the base of the nose, or a frown. He further believes that towards the outer two-thirds of the eyebrow the corrugator acts in conjunction with the upper orbicular muscle; both here standing in antagonism to the frontal muscle. I am unable to understand, judging from Henle's drawings (woodcut, Fig. 3), how the corrugator can act in the manner described by Duchenne. See, also, on this subject, Professor Donders' remarks in the *Archives of Medicine,* 1870, vol. v, p. 34. Mr J. Wood, who is so well known for his careful study of the muscles of the human frame, informs me that he believes the account which I have given of the action of the corrugator to be correct. But this is not a point of any importance with respect to the expression which is caused by the obliquity of the eyebrows, nor of much importance to the theory of its origin.

adult or nearly adult persons, when their eyebrows are made oblique; but with young children, owing to their skin not easily wrinkling, they are rarely seen or mere traces of them can be detected.

Not everyone will show the horse-shoe. The wrinkling in the middle of the forehead is almost always apparent, but in some people the lines going down, which form the horse-shoe, are not evident.

These peculiar furrows are best represented in Fig. 3, Plate II, on the forehead of a young lady who has the power in an unusual degree of voluntarily acting on the requisite muscles. As she was absorbed in the attempt, whilst being photographed, her expression was not at all one of grief; I have therefore given the forehead alone. Fig. 1 on the same plate, copied from Dr Duchenne's work,* represents, on a reduced scale, the face, in its natural state, of a young man who was a good actor. In Fig. 2 he is shown simulating grief, but the two eyebrows, as before remarked, are not equally acted on. That the expression is true, may be inferred from the fact that out of fifteen persons, to whom the original photograph was shown, without any clue to what was intended being given them, fourteen immediately answered, 'despairing sorrow', 'suffering endurance', 'melancholy', and so forth. The history of Fig. 5 is rather curious: I saw the photograph in a shop-window, and took it to Mr Rejlander for the sake of finding out by whom it had been made; remarking to him how pathetic the expression was. He answered, 'I made it, and it was likely to be pathetic, for the boy in a few minutes burst out crying.' He then showed me a photograph of the same boy in a placid state, which I have had (Fig. 4) reproduced. In Fig. 6, a trace of obliquity in the eyebrows may be detected; but this figure,

---

* I am greatly indebted to Dr Duchenne for permission to have these two photographs (Figs 1 and 2) reproduced by the heliotype process from his work in folio. Many of the foregoing remarks on the furrowing of the skin, when the eyebrows are rendered oblique, are taken from his excellent discussion on this subject.

PLATE II

1 2 3

4 5

6 7

[Digital reconstruction of Figure 3 © Phillip Prodger and Daniel Hillman.]

as well as Fig. 7, is given to show the depression of the corners of the mouth, to which subject I shall presently refer.

We[C37] have found that when people deliberately make a muscle movement, as this actor did, it often is stronger on one side of the face, although the difference is slight and not easy to detect. By contrast, most spontaneous facial expressions of emotion are more symmetrical. While we use measurement of asymmetry as one index that a facial movement is not emotional but deliberately made, the differences are so subtle that I expect most people would not notice this clue during a conversation. There are other less subtle signs – in morphology and timing – to distinguish involuntary from deliberately made expressions that some people can and do notice.[C38]

Few persons, without some practice, can voluntarily act on their grief-muscles; but after repeated trials a considerable number succeed, whilst others never can. The degree of obliquity in the eyebrows, whether assumed voluntarily or unconsciously, differs much in different persons. With some who apparently have unusually strong pyramidal muscles, the contraction of the central fasciae of the frontal muscle, although it may be energetic, as shown by the quadrangular furrows on the forehead, does not raise the inner ends of the eyebrows, but only prevents their being so much lowered as they otherwise would have been. As far as I have been able to observe, the grief-muscles are brought into action much more frequently by children and women than by men. They are rarely acted on, at least, with grown-up persons, from bodily pain, but almost exclusively from mental distress. Two persons who, after some practice, succeeded in acting on their grief-muscles, found by looking at a mirror that when they made their eyebrows oblique, they unintentionally at the same time depressed the corners of their mouths; and this is often the case when the expression is naturally assumed.

The power to bring the grief-muscles freely into play appears to be hereditary, like almost every other human faculty. A lady belonging to a family famous for having produced an extraordinary number of great actors and actresses, and who can herself give this expression 'with singular precision', told Dr Crichton Browne that all her family had possessed the power in a remarkable degree. The same hereditary tendency is said to have extended, as I likewise hear from Dr Browne, to the last descendant of the family, which gave rise to Sir Walter Scott's novel of 'Red Gauntlet'; but the hero is described as contracting his forehead into a horse-shoe mark from any strong emotion. I have also seen a young woman whose forehead seemed almost habitually thus contracted, independently of any emotion being at the same time felt.

In work not yet published I have confirmed Darwin's belief that the ability to move the grief-muscles voluntarily is hereditary. I found that if one identical twin could make these movements so could the other, but not so for fraternal twins. All of these twins had been reared apart since early infancy.

The grief-muscles are not very often brought into play; and as the action is often momentary, it easily escapes observation. Although the expression, when observed, is universally and instantly recognized as that of grief or anxiety, yet not one person out of a thousand who has never studied the subject, is able to say precisely what change passes over the sufferer's face. Hence probably it is that this expression is not even alluded to, as far as I have noticed, in any work of fiction, with the exception of 'Red Gauntlet' and of one other novel; and the authoress of the latter, as I am informed, belongs to the famous family of actors just alluded to; so that her attention may have been specially called to the subject.

The ancient Greek sculptors were familiar with the expression, as shown in the statues of the Laocoon and Arretino; but, as Duchenne remarks, they carried the transverse furrows across the whole breadth of the forehead, and thus committed a great anatomical mistake: this is likewise the case in some modern statues. It is, however, more probable that these wonderfully accurate observers intentionally sacrificed truth for the sake of beauty, than that they made a mistake; for rectangular furrows on the forehead would not have had a grand appearance on the marble. The expression, in its fully developed condition, is, as far as I can discover, not often represented in pictures by the old masters, no doubt owing to the same cause; but a lady who is perfectly familiar with this expression, informs me that in Fra Angelico's 'Descent from the Cross' in Florence, it is clearly exhibited in one of the figures on the right-hand; and I could add a few other instances.

Dr Crichton Browne, at my request, closely attended to this expression in the numerous insane patients under his care in the West Riding Asylum; and he is familiar with Duchenne's photographs of the action of the grief-muscles. He informs me that they may be constantly seen in energetic action in cases of melancholia, and especially of hypochondria; and that the persistent lines or furrows, due to their habitual contraction, are characteristic of the physiognomy of the insane belonging to these two classes. Dr Browne carefully observed for me during a considerable period three cases of hypochondria, in which the grief-muscles were persistently contracted. In one of these, a widow, aged 51, fancied that she had lost all her viscera, and that her whole body was empty. She wore an expression of great distress, and beat her semi-closed hands rhythmically together for hours. The grief-muscles were permanently contracted, and the upper eyelids arched. This condition lasted for months; she then recovered, and her countenance resumed its natural expression. A second case presented nearly the same peculiarities, with the addition that the corners of the mouth were depressed.

Mr Patrick Nicol has also kindly observed for me several cases in the Sussex Lunatic Asylum, and has communicated to me full details with respect to three of them; but they need not here be given. From his observations on melancholic patients, Mr Nicol concludes that the inner ends of the eyebrows are almost always more or less raised, with the wrinkles on the forehead more or less plainly marked. In the case of one young woman, these wrinkles were observed to be in constant slight play or movement.

In some cases the corners of the mouth are depressed, but often only in a slight degree. Some amount of difference in the expression of the several melancholic patients could almost always be observed. The eyelids generally droop; and the skin near their outer corners and beneath them is wrinkled. The naso-labial fold, which runs from the wings of the nostrils to the corners of the mouth, and which is so conspicuous in blubbering children, is often plainly marked in these patients.

Although with the insane the grief-muscles often act persistently; yet in ordinary cases they are sometimes brought unconsciously into momentary action by ludicrously slight causes. A gentleman rewarded a young lady by an absurdly small present; she pretended to be offended, and as she upbraided him, her eyebrows became extremely oblique, with the forehead properly wrinkled. Another lady and a youth, both in the highest spirits, were eagerly talking together with extraordinary rapidity; and I noticed that, as often as the young lady was beaten, and could not get out her words fast enough, her eyebrows went obliquely upwards, and rectangular furrows were formed on her forehead. She thus each time hoisted a flag of distress; and this she did half-a-dozen times in the course of a few minutes. I made no remark on the subject, but on a subsequent occasion I asked her to act on her grief-muscles; another girl who was present, and who could do so voluntarily, showing her what was intended. She tried repeatedly, but utterly failed; yet so light a cause of distress as not being able to talk quickly enough, sufficed to bring these muscles over and over again into energetic action.

The expression of grief, due to the contraction of the grief-muscles, is by no means confined to Europeans, but appears to be common to all the races of mankind. I have, at least, received trustworthy accounts in regard to Hindoos, Dhangars (one of the aboriginal hill-tribes of India, and therefore belonging to a quite distinct race from the Hindoos), Malays, Negroes and Australians. With respect to the latter, two observers answer my query in the affirmative, but enter into no details. Mr Taplin, however, appends to my descriptive remarks the words 'this is exact'. With respect to negroes, the lady who told me of Fra Angelico's picture, saw a negro towing a boat on the Nile, and as he encountered an obstruction, she observed his grief-muscles in strong action, with the middle of the forehead well wrinkled. Mr Geach watched a Malay man in Malacca, with the corners of his mouth much depressed, the eyebrows oblique, with deep short grooves on the forehead. This expression lasted for a very short time; and Mr Geach remarks it 'was a strange one, very much like a person about to cry at some loss'.

In India Mr H. Erskine found that the natives were familiar with this expression; and Mr J. Scott, of the Botanic Gardens, Calcutta, has obligingly sent me a description of two cases. He observed during some time, himself unseen, a very young Dhangar woman from Nagpore, the wife of one of the gardeners nursing her baby who was at the point of death; and he distinctly saw the eyebrows raised at the inner corners, the eyelids drooping, the forehead wrinkled in the middle, the mouth slightly open, with the corners much depressed. He then came from behind a screen of plants and spoke to the poor woman, who started, burst into a bitter flood of tears, and besought him to cure her baby. The second case was that of a Hindustani man, who from illness and poverty was compelled to sell his favourite goat. After receiving the money, he repeatedly looked at the money in his hand and then at the goat, as if doubting whether he would not return it. He went to the goat, which was tied up ready to be led away, and the animal reared up and licked his hands. His eyes then wavered from side to side; his 'mouth was partially closed, with the corners very decidedly depressed'. At last the poor man seemed to make up his mind that he must part with his goat, and then, as Mr Scott saw, the eyebrows became slightly oblique, with the characteristic puckering or swelling at the inner ends, but the wrinkles on the forehead were not present. The man stood thus for a minute, then heaving a deep sigh, burst into tears, raised up his two hands, blessed the goat, turned round, and without looking again, went away.

On the cause of the obliquity of the eyebrows under suffering. During several years no expression seemed to me so utterly perplexing as this which we are here considering. Why should grief or anxiety cause the central fasciae alone of the frontal muscle together with those round the eyes, to contract? Here we seem to have a complex movement for the sole purpose of expressing grief; and yet it is a comparatively rare expression, and often overlooked. I believe the explanation is not so difficult as it at first appears. Dr Duchenne gives a photograph of the young man before referred to, who, when looking upwards at a strongly illuminated surface, involuntarily contracted his grief-muscles in an exaggerated manner. I had entirely forgotten this photograph, when on a very bright day with the sun behind me, I met, whilst on horseback, a girl whose eyebrows, as she looked up at me, became extremely oblique, with the proper furrows on her forehead. I have observed the same movement under similar circumstances on several subsequent occasions. On my return home I made three of my children, without giving them any clue to my object, look as long and attentively as they could, at the summit of a tall tree standing against an extremely bright sky. With all three, the orbicular, corrugator, and pyramidal muscles were energetically contracted, through reflex action, from the excitement of the retina, so that their eyes might be protected from the bright light. But they tried their utmost to look upwards; and now a curious struggle, with spasmodic twitchings, could be observed between the whole or only the central portion of the frontal muscle, and the several muscles which serve to lower the eyebrows and close the eyelids. The involuntary contraction of the pyramidal caused the basal part of their noses to be transversely and deeply wrinkled. In one of the three children, the whole eyebrows were momentarily raised and lowered by the alternate contraction of the whole frontal muscle and of the muscles surrounding the eyes, so that the whole breadth of the forehead was alternately wrinkled and smoothed. In the other two children the forehead became wrinkled in the middle part alone, rectangular furrows being thus produced; and the eyebrows were rendered oblique, with their inner extremities puckered and swollen – in the one child in a slight degree, in the other in a strongly marked manner. This difference in the obliquity of the eyebrows apparently depended on a difference in their general mobility, and in the strength of the pyramidal muscles. In both these cases the eyebrows and forehead were acted on under the influence of a strong light, in precisely the same manner, in every characteristic detail, as under the influence of grief or anxiety.

Duchenne states that the pyramidal muscle of the nose is less under the control of the will than are the other muscles round the eyes. He remarks that the young man who could so well act on his grief-muscles, as well as on most of his other facial muscles, could not contract the pyramidals.[4] This power, however, no doubt differs in different persons. The pyramidal muscle serves to draw down the skin of the forehead between the eyebrows, together with their inner extremities. The central fasciae of the frontal are the antagonists of the pyramidal; and if the action of the latter is to be specially checked, these central fasciae must be contracted. So that with persons having powerful pyramidal muscles, if there is under the influence of a bright light an unconscious desire to prevent the lowering of the eyebrows, the central fasciae of the frontal muscle must be brought into play; and their contraction, if sufficiently strong to overmaster the pyramidals, together with the contraction of the corrugator and orbicular muscles, will act in the manner just described on the eyebrows and forehead.*

When children scream, or cry out, they contract, as we know, the orbicular, corrugator, and pyramidal muscles, primarily for the sake of compressing their eyes, and thus protecting them from being gorged with blood, and secondarily through habit. I therefore expected to find with children, that when they endeavoured either to prevent a crying-fit from coming on, or to stop crying, they would check the contraction of the above-named muscles, in the same manner as when looking upwards at a bright light; and consequently that the central fasciae of the frontal

* [Dr Keen had the opportunity of faradizing the muscles of a criminal immediately after his execution by hanging. His experiments confirm the conclusion that the *pyramidalis nasi* is the 'direct antagonist of the central portion of the occipito-frontal, and vice-versa'.[5]]

muscle would often be brought into play. Accordingly, I began myself to observe children at such times, and asked others, including some medical men, to do the same. It is necessary to observe carefully, as the peculiar opposed action of these muscles is not nearly so plain in children, owing to their foreheads not easily wrinkling, as in adults. But I soon found that the grief-muscles were very frequently brought into distinct action on these occasions. It would be superfluous to give all the cases which have been observed; and I will specify only a few. A little girl, a year and a half old, was teased by some other children, and before bursting into tears her eyebrows became decidedly oblique. With an older girl the same obliquity was observed, with the inner ends of the eyebrows plainly puckered; and at the same time the corners of the mouth were drawn downwards. As soon as she burst into tears, the features all changed and this peculiar expression vanished. Again, after a little boy had been vaccinated, which made him scream and cry violently, the surgeon gave him an orange brought for the purpose, and this pleased the child much; as he stopped crying all the characteristic movements were observed, including the formation of rectangular wrinkles in the middle of the forehead. Lastly, I met on the road a little girl three or four years old, who had been frightened by a dog, and when I asked her what was the matter, she stopped whimpering, and her eyebrows instantly became oblique to an extraordinary degree.

Here then, as I cannot doubt, we have the key to the problem why the central fasciae of the frontal muscle and the muscles round the eyes contract in opposition to each other under the influence of grief – whether their contraction be prolonged, as with the melancholic insane, or momentary, from some trifling cause of distress. We have all of us, as infants, repeatedly contracted our orbicular, corrugator, and pyramidal muscles, in order to protect our eyes whilst screaming; our progenitors before us have done the same during many generations; and though with advancing years we easily prevent, when feeling distressed, the utterance of screams, we cannot from long habit always prevent a slight contraction of the above-named muscles; nor indeed do we observe their contraction in ourselves, or attempt to stop it, if slight. But the pyramidal muscles seem to be less under the command of the will than the other related muscles; and if they be well developed, their contraction can be checked only by the antagonistic contraction of the central fasciae of the frontal muscle. The result which necessarily follows, if these fasciae contract energetically, is the oblique drawing up of the eyebrows, the puckering of their inner ends, and the formation of rectangular furrows on the middle of the forehead. As children and women cry much more freely than men, and as grown-up persons of both sexes rarely weep except from mental distress, we can understand why the grief-muscles are more frequently seen in action, as I believe to be the case, with children and women than with men; and with adults of both sexes from mental distress alone. In some of the cases before recorded, as in that of the poor Dhangar woman and of the Hindustani man, the action of the grief-muscles was quickly followed by bitter weeping. In all cases of distress, whether great or small, our brains tend through long habit to send an order to certain muscles to contract, as if we were still infants on the point of screaming out; but this order we, by the wondrous power of the will, and through habit, are able partially to counteract; although this is effected unconsciously, as far as the means of counteraction are concerned.

This is an ingenious explanation, but I think it is wrong. Darwin is correct about the grief eyebrows – the oblique positioning of the brows by the actions of the inner part of *frontalis* and what Darwin calls the pyramidals – occurring from early life when crying stops (the distress abates) and the unhappiness or sadness continues. But the combination of facial movements for this state is not likely to originate in deliberate and habitual attempts to control the cry, as Darwin argues. One reason why this is improbable is that most people cannot deliberately make this movement. Contracting the inner part of the *frontalis* muscle is one of the most difficult movements to perform voluntarily.[C39] A second reason for doubting Darwin's explanation is the early appearance of this expression in infancy. If Darwin were correct, we would not expect to see the grief-muscle displayed until the infant attempts to control crying, but it is apparent much earlier. Camras, an expert on expressions in early life, has seen the grief-eyebrow at four weeks of life. Oster, who has specialized in studying the neonate, has observed this expression in the newborn. It is unlikely that newborns are deliberately attempting to control their cries. Oster commented that this grief-eyebrow display may index 'some primitive self-regulatory mechanism'; in this sense, Oster agrees with Darwin's explanation.

On the depression of the corners of the mouth. This action is effected by the *depressores anguli oris* (see letter K in Figs 1 and 2 [p. 29]). The fibres of this muscle diverge downwards, with the upper convergent ends attached round the angles of the mouth, and to the lower lip a little way within the angles.[6] Some of the fibres appear to be antagonistic to the great zygomatic muscle, and others to the several muscles running to the outer part of the upper lip. The contraction of this muscle draws downwards and outwards the corners of the mouth, including the outer part of the upper lip, and even in a slight degree the wings of the nostrils. When the mouth is closed and this muscle acts, the commissure or line of junction of the two lips forms a curved line with the concavity downwards,[7] and the lips themselves are generally somewhat protruded, especially the lower one. The mouth in this state is well-represented in the two photographs (Plate II, Figs 6 and 7) by Mr Rejlander. The upper boy (Fig. 6) had just stopped crying, after receiving a slap on the face from another boy; and the right moment was seized for photographing him.

The expression of low spirits, grief or dejection, due to the contraction of this muscle has been noticed by every one who has written on this subject. To say that a person is 'down in the mouth', is synonymous with saying that he is out of spirits. The depression of the corners may often be seen, as already stated on the authority of Dr Crichton Browne and Mr Nicol, with the melancholic insane, and was well exhibited in some photographs sent to me by the former gentleman, of patients with a strong tendency to suicide. It has been observed with men belonging to various races, namely with Hindoos, the dark hill-tribes of India, Malays, and, as the Rev. Mr Hagenauer informs me, with the aborigines of Australia.

When infants scream they firmly contract the muscles round their eyes, and this draws up the upper lip; and as they have to keep their mouths widely open, the depressor muscles running to the corners are likewise brought in to strong action. This generally, but not invariably, causes a slight angular bend in the lower lip on both sides, near the corners of the mouth. The result of the upper and lower lip thus being acted on, is that the mouth assumes a squarish outline. The contraction of the depressor muscle is best seen in infants when not screaming violently, and especially just before they begin, or when they cease to scream. Their little faces then acquire an extremely piteous expression, as I continually observed with my own infants between the ages of about six weeks and two or three months. Sometimes, when they are struggling against a crying-fit, the outline of the mouth is curved in so exaggerated a manner as to be like a horse shoe; and the expression of misery then becomes a ludicrous caricature.

The explanation of the contraction of this muscle, under the influence of low spirits or dejection, apparently follows from the same general principles as in the case of the obliquity of the eyebrows. Dr Duchenne informs me that he concludes from his observations, now prolonged during many years, that this is one of the facial muscles which is least under the control of the will. This fact may indeed be inferred from what has just been stated with respect to infants when doubtfully beginning to cry, or endeavouring to stop crying; for they then generally command all the other facial muscles more effectually than they do the depressors of the corners of the mouth. Two excellent observers who had no theory on the subject, one of them a surgeon, carefully watched for me some older children and women as with some opposed struggling they very gradually approached the point of bursting out into tears; and both observers felt sure that the depressors began to act, before any of the other muscles.

Now as the depressors have been repeatedly brought into strong action during infancy in many generations, nerve-force will tend to flow, on the principle of long associated habit, to these muscles as well as to various other facial muscles, whenever in after life even a slight feeling of distress is experienced. But as the depressors are somewhat less under the control of the will than most of the other muscles, we might expect that they would often slightly contract, whilst the others remained passive. It is remarkable how small a depression of the corners of the mouth gives to the countenance an expression of low spirits or dejection, so that an extremely slight contraction of these muscles would be sufficient to betray this state of mind.

I may here mention a trifling observation, as it will serve to sum up our present subject. An old lady with a comfortable but absorbed expression sat nearly opposite to me in a railway carriage. Whilst I was looking at her, I saw that her *depressores anguli oris* became very slightly, yet decidedly, contracted; but as her countenance remained as placid as ever, I reflected how meaningless was this contraction, and how easily one might be deceived. The thought had hardly occurred to me when I saw that her eyes suddenly became suffused with tears almost to overflowing, and her whole countenance fell. There could now be no doubt that some painful recollection, perhaps that of a long-lost child, was passing through her mind. As soon as her sensorium was thus affected, certain nerve-cells from long habit instantly transmitted an order to all the respiratory muscles, and to those round the mouth, to prepare for a fit of crying. But the order was countermanded by the will, or rather by a later acquired habit, and all the muscles were obedient, excepting in a slight degree the *depressores anguli oris*. The mouth was not even opened; the respiration was not hurried; and no muscle was affected except those which draw down the corners of the mouth.

As soon as the mouth of this lady began, involuntarily and unconsciously on her part, to assume the proper form for a crying-fit, we may feel almost sure that some nerve-influence would have been transmited through the long accustomed channels to the various respiratory muscles, as well as to those round the eyes, and to the vaso-motor centre which governs the supply of blood sent to the lacrymal glands. Of this latter fact we have indeed clear evidence in her eyes becoming suffused with tears; and we can understand this, as the lacrymal glands are less under the control of the will than the facial muscles. No doubt there existed at the same time some tendency in the muscles round the eyes to contract, as if for the sake of protecting them from being gorged with blood, but this contraction was completely over-mastered, and her brow remained unruffled. Had the pyramidal, corrugator, and orbicular muscles been as little obedient to the will, as they are in many persons, they would have been slightly acted on; and then the central fasciae of the frontal muscle would have contracted in antagonism, and her eyebrows would have become oblique, with rectangular furrows on her forehead. Her countenance would then have expressed still more plainly than it did a state of dejection, or rather one of grief.

Through steps such as these we can understand how it is, that as soon as some melancholy thought passes through the brain, there occurs a just perceptible drawing down of the corners of the mouth, or a slight raising up of the inner ends of the eyebrows, or both movements combined, and immediately afterwards a slight suffusion of tears. A thrill of nerve-force is transmitted along several habitual channels, and produces an effect on any point where the will has not acquired through long habit much power of interference. The above actions may be considered as rudimental vestiges of the screaming-fits, which are so frequent and prolonged during infancy. In this case, as well as in many others, the links are indeed wonderful which connect cause and effect in giving rise to various expressions on the human countenance; and they explain to us the meaning of certain movements, which we involuntarily and unconsciously perform, whenever certain transitory emotions pass through our minds.

CHAPTER VIII

Joy, High Spirits, Love, Tender Feelings, Devotion

Laughter primarily the expression of joy – Ludicrous ideas – Movements of the features during laughter – Nature of the sound produced – The secretion of tears during loud laughter – Gradation from loud laughter to gentle smiling – High spirits – The expression of love – Tender feelings – Devotion.

Joy, when intense, leads to various purposeless movements – to dancing about, clapping the hands, stamping, etc., and to loud laughter. Laughter seems to be the expression of mere joy or happiness. We clearly see this in children at play, who are almost incessantly laughing. With young persons past childhood, when they are in high spirits, there is always much meaningless laughter. The laughter of the gods is described by Homer as 'the exuberance of their celestial joy after their daily banquet'. A man smiles – and smiling, as we shall see, graduates into laughter – at meeting an old friend in the street, as he does at any trifling pleasure, such as smelling a sweet perfume.[1] Laura Bridgman, from her blindness and deafness, could not have acquired any expression through imitation, yet when a letter from a beloved friend was communicated to her by gesture-language, she 'laughed and clapped her hands, and the colour mounted to her cheeks'. On other occasions she was seen to stamp for joy.[2]

Idiots and imbecile persons likewise afford good evidence that laughter or smiling primarily expresses mere happiness or joy. Dr Crichton Browne, to whom, as on so many other occasions, I am indebted for the results of his wide experience, informs me that with idiots laughter is the most prevalent and frequent of all the emotional expressions. Many idiots are morose, passionate, restless, in a painful state of mind, or utterly stolid, and these never laugh. Others frequently laugh in a quite senseless manner. Thus an idiot boy, incapable of speech, complained to Dr Browne, by the aid of signs, that another boy in the asylum had given him a black eye; and this was accompanied by 'explosions of laughter and with his face covered with the broadest of smiles'. There is another large class of idiots who are persistently joyous or benign, and who are constantly laughing or smiling.[3] Their countenances often exhibit a stereotyped smile; their joyousness is increased, and they grin, chuckle, or giggle, whenever food is placed before them, or when they are caressed, are shown bright colours, or hear music. Some of them laugh more than usual when they walk about, or attempt any muscular exertion. The joyousness of most of these idiots cannot possibly be associated, as Dr Browne remarks, with any distinct ideas: they simply feel pleasure, and express it, by laughter or smiles. With imbeciles rather higher in the scale, personal vanity seems to be the commonest cause of laughter, and next to this, pleasure arising from the approbation of their conduct.

With grown-up persons laughter is excited by causes considerably different from those which suffice during childhood; but this remark hardly applies to smiling. Laughter in this respect is analogous with weeping, which with adults is almost confined to mental distress, whilst with children it is excited by bodily pain or any suffering, as well as by fear or rage. Many curious discussions have been written on the causes of laughter with grown-up persons. The subject is extremely complex. Something incongruous or unaccountable, exciting surprise and some sense of superiority in the laugher, who must be in a happy frame of mind, seems to be the commonest cause.[4] The circumstances must not be of a momentous nature: no poor man would laugh or smile on suddenly hearing that a large fortune had been bequeathed to him. If the mind is strongly excited by pleasurable feelings, and any little unexpected event or thought occurs, then, as Mr Herbert Spencer remarks,[5] 'a large amount of nervous energy, instead of being allowed to expend itself in producing an equivalent amount of the new thoughts and emotion which were nascent, is suddenly checked in its flow' ... 'The excess must discharge itself in some other direction, and there results an efflux through the motor nerves to various classes of the muscles, producing the half-convulsive actions we term laughter'. An observation, bearing on this point, was made by a correspondent during the recent siege of Paris, namely, that German soldiers, after strong excitement from exposure to extreme danger, were particularly apt to burst out into loud laughter at the smallest joke. So again when young children are just beginning to cry, an unexpected event will sometimes suddenly turn their crying into laughter, which apparently serves equally well to expend their superfluous nervous energy.*

The German psychologist Willibald Ruch, a specialist in the study of humor and expression, commented that no one has yet verified Darwin's idea that the causes of laughter, but not smiling, change with age. Ruch acknowledges jokes funny enough to elicit laughter in children but not in adults, but often, he says, the difference between smiling and laughter is a matter of how intense the emotion is. Preuschoft (whose opinion I mentioned in an earlier commentary, p. 145) takes the opposite position; she says that smiling is not a diminished form of laughing. They may both be right; Preuschoft about the monkeys she has studied, and Ruch about humans.

The imagination is sometimes said to be tickled by a ludicrous idea; and this so-called tickling of the mind is curiously analogous with that of the body. Every one knows how immoderately children laugh, and how their whole bodies are convulsed, when they are tickled. The anthropoid apes, as we have seen, likewise utter

* [Mr C. Hinton, of San Francisco (letter, 15 June, 1873), describes himself as alternately screaming for help and laughing when alone in a position of great danger on the cliffs near the Golden Gate.]

a reiterated sound, corresponding with our own laughter, when they are tickled, especially under the armpits. I touched with a bit of paper the sole of the foot of one of my infants, when only seven days old, and it was suddenly jerked away and the toes curled about, as in an older child. Such movements, as well as laughter from being tickled, are manifestly reflex actions; and this is likewise shown by the minute unstriped muscles, which serve to erect the separate hairs on the body, contracting near a tickled surface.[6] Yet laughter from a ludicrous idea, though involuntary, cannot be called a strictly reflex action. In this case, and in that of laughter from being tickled, the mind must be in a pleasurable condition; a young child, if tickled by a strange man, would scream from fear. The touch must be light, and an idea or event, to be ludicrous, must not be of grave import. The parts of the body which are most easily tickled are those which are not commonly touched, such as the armpits or between the toes, or parts such as the soles of the feet, which are habitually touched by a broad surface; but the surface on which we sit offers a marked exception to this rule. According to Gratiolet,[7] certain nerves are much more sensitive to tickling than others. From the fact that a child can hardly tickle itself, or in a much less degree than when tickled by another person, it seems that the precise point to be touched must not be known; so with the mind, something unexpected – a novel or incongruous idea which breaks through an habitual train of thought – appears to be a strong element in the ludicrous.*

Ruch commented: 'According to Hecker[C40] [cited by Darwin in the second edition, see footnote] and Wundt,[C41] tickling is the most common elicitor of laughter other than humor. Chimpanzees also show a facial display, a respiration pattern, and vocal sounds compar-

* [L. Dumont (*Théorie Scientifique de la Sensibilité*, 2nd edit., 1877, p. 202) seeks to show that tickling depends on *unexpected* variations in the nature of the contact; he, too, believes that it is this unexpectedness which allies tickling with the ludicrous, as a cause of laughter. Hecker (*Physiologie und Psychologie des Lachens*, 1872) connects tickling with the ludicrous as a cause of laughter, but from a different point of view.]

able to those associated with human laughter when being tickled or expecting to be tickled. From their survey on laughter, Hall and Allin[C42] concluded that the areas where children are most ticklish are the following: soles of the feet, under the arms, the neck, under the chin, the waist and ribs, and the cheeks.'

The sound of laughter is produced by a deep inspiration followed by short, interrupted, spasmodic contractions of the chest, and especially of the diaphragm.[8] Hence we hear of 'laugher holding both his sides'. From the shaking of the body, the head nods to and fro. The lower jaw often quivers up and down, as is likewise the case with some species of baboons, when they are much pleased.

Ruch said: 'With increasing levels in the intensity of exhilaration, changes in the respiration pattern occur . . . which form the basis for the characteristic "ha-ha" vocalization. . . . The most distinctive feature of laughter respiration is its expiratory nature. The extent of expiration during laughter not only exceeds the level of a normal exhalation but typically reaches the limit of the maximal voluntary expiration and sometimes even exceeds it.'

During laughter the mouth is opened more or less widely, with the corners drawn much backwards, as well as a little upwards; and the upper lip is somewhat raised. The drawing back of the corners is best seen in moderate laughter, and especially in a broad smile – the latter epithet showing how the mouth is widened. In the accompanying Figs 1 – 3, Plate III, different degrees of moderate laughter and smiling have been photographed. The figure of the little girl, with the hat, is by Dr Wallich, and the expression was a genuine one; the other two are by Mr Rejlander. Dr Duchenne repeatedly insists[9] that, under the emotion of joy, the mouth is acted on exclusively by the great zygomatic muscles, which serve to draw the corners backwards and upwards; but judging from the manner in which the upper teeth are always

PLATE III

1

4

2

5

3

6

exposed during laughter and broad smiling, as well as from my own sensations, I cannot doubt that some of the muscles running to the upper lip are likewise brought into moderate action. The upper and lower orbicular muscles of the eyes are at the same time more or less contracted; and there is an intimate connection, as explained in the chapter on weeping, between the orbiculars, especially the lower ones, and some of the muscles running to the upper lip. Henle remarks,[10] on this head, that when a man closely shuts one eye he cannot avoid retracting the upper lip on the same side; conversely, if any one will place his finger on his lower eyelid, and then uncover his upper incisors as much as possible, he will feel, as his upper lip is drawn strongly upwards, that the muscles of the lower eyelid contract. In Henle's drawing, given in woodcut, Fig. 2 [p. 29], the *muscularis malaris* (H) which runs to the upper lip may be seen to form an almost integral part of the lower orbicular muscle.

I disagree with Darwin on the anatomical basis for the facial movements he proposes in this paragraph. I believe Duchenne was right and Darwin was wrong about why the upper lip is often raised in a strong smile. My research suggests that with enjoyment the *zygomatic major* muscle is the principal muscle in the lower face, and may be the only active muscle in the lower face. The exposure of the teeth and raising of the upper lip noted by Darwin can occur by strong activation of *zygomatic major* alone, and does not, as Darwin proposed, require the activation of a second muscle. The strong action of the *zygomatic* muscle stretches the upper lip, and in most people this also slightly raises the lip. Of course, additional muscles can be activated which will raise the upper lip further, but this is not typical or necessary in a smile of enjoyment. I believe Darwin was also mistaken in accepting Henle's claim that eye-closures raise the upper lip. The upper lip is often slightly raised, particularly at the outer edges, but it is the action of *orbicularis oculi* alone which stretches the skin and causes this change in the upper lip, not the activation of another muscle in the lower face.

The man who appears in Figures 4, 5 and 6 also appears in later illustrations. Duchenne wrote about him, 'The individual I chose as my principal subject for the experiments ... was an old toothless man, with a thin face, whose features without being absolutely ugly, approached triviality and whose facial expression was in perfect agreement with his inoffensive character and his restricted intelligence. ... There are few people who are willing to submit to this type of experiment, because, without being extremely painful, electrilization of the facial muscles often provokes involuntary movements resulting in contortion of the facial features. This subject had reduced sensations. He was suffering from a complicated anesthetic [unable to sense pain] condition of the face. I was able to experiment on his face without causing him much pain, to the extent that I could stimulate his individual muscles with as much precision and accuracy as if I were working with a still irritable cadaver.'[C43]

Dr Duchenne has given a large photograph of an old man (reduced on Plate III, Fig. 4), in his usual passive condition, and another of the same man (Fig. 5), naturally smiling. The latter was instantly recognized by every one to whom it was shown as true to nature. He has also given, as an example of an unnatural or false smile, another photograph (Fig. 6) of the same old man, with the corners of his mouth strongly retracted by the galvanization of the great zygomatic muscles. That the expression is not natural is clear, for I showed this photograph to twenty-four persons, of whom three could not in the least tell what was meant, whilst the others, though they perceived that the expression was of the nature of a smile, answered in such words as 'a wicked joke', 'trying to laugh', 'grinning laughter', 'half-amazed laughter' etc. Dr Duchenne attributes the falseness of the expression altogether to the orbicular muscles of the lower eyelids not being sufficiently contracted; for he justly lays great stress on their contraction in the expression of joy. No doubt there is much truth in this view, but not, as it appears to me, the whole truth. The contraction of the lower orbiculars is always accompanied, as we have seen, by the drawing up of the upper lip. Had the upper lip, in Fig. 6, been thus acted on to a slight extent, its curvature would have been less rigid, the naso-labial furrow would have been slightly different, and the whole expression would, as I believe, have been more natural, independently of the more conspicuous effect from the stronger contraction of the lower eyelids. The corrugator muscle, moreover, in Fig. 6, is too much contracted, causing a frown; and this muscle never acts under the influence of joy except during strongly pronounced or violent laughter.

The distinction between the smile with and without the *orbicularis oculi* muscle, which Duchenne proposed would distinguish the smile of enjoyment from a simulated smile, has proven extremely robust. For example, five-month-old infants show the eye-muscle smile when the mother approaches, but a smile without the eye muscle when approached by a stranger.[C44] When the eye-muscle smile is shown the pattern of brain activity found with genuine enjoyment, occurs, but that brain activity pattern is not found when the smile alone is shown.[C45] Happily married couples when they meet at the end of the day show eye-muscle smiles, while unhappily married couples do not show the eye-muscle activity when they smile at each other.[C46] To pay tribute to Duchenne for this discovery, I proposed the smile which involves the action of both *zygomatic major* and *orbicularis oculi* muscles, be called the Duchenne smile, or D-smile for short.[C47]

By the drawing backwards and upwards of the corners of the mouth, through the contraction of the great zygomatic muscles, and by the raising of the upper lip, the cheeks are drawn upwards. Wrinkles are thus formed under the eyes, and, with old people, at their outer ends; and these are highly characteristic of laughter or smiling. As a gentle smile increases into a strong one, or into a laugh, every one may feel and see, if he will attend to his own sensations and look at himself in a mirror, that as the upper lip is drawn up and the lower orbiculars contract, the wrinkles in the lower eyelids and those beneath the eyes are much strengthened or increased. At the same time, as I have repeatedly observed, the eyebrows are slightly lowered, which shows that the upper as well as the lower orbiculars contract at least to some degree, though this passes unperceived, as far as our sensations are concerned. If the original photograph of the old man, with his countenance in its usual placid state (Fig. 4), be compared with that (Fig. 5) in which he is naturally smiling, it may be seen that the eyebrows in the latter are a little lowered. I presume that this is owing to the upper orbiculars being impelled, through the force of long-associated habit, to act to a certain extent in concert with the lower orbiculars, which themselves contract in connection with the drawing up of the upper lip.

Darwin correctly emphasized that the clue to recognizing the true smile of enjoyment (Duchenne's smile) is the lowering of the outer portion of the eyebrow. Though a subtle change, it (together with a lowering of the skin between the eyebrow and the upper eyelid – the eye-cover fold) is a reliable sign that the outer portions of *orbicularis oculi* have been contracted, and enjoyment is occurring. Crow's-feet wrinkles, and the bagging of the skin below the eye can be produced by a strong action of *zygomatic major* alone, without any action of *orbicularis oculi*. Tensing or raising the lower eyelid, produced by tightening the inner part of *orbicularis oculi – pars palpebralis –* we found *not* to be a reliable sign of enjoyment.[C48]

The tendency in the zygomatic muscles to contract under pleasurable emotions is shown by a curious fact, communicated to me by Dr Browne, with respect to patients suffering from *general paralysis of the insane*.[11] 'In this malady there is almost invariably optimism – delusions as to wealth, rank, grandeur – insane joyousness, benevolence, and profusion, while its very earliest physical symptom is trembling at the corners of the mouth and at the outer corners of the eyes. This is a well-recognized fact. Constant tremulous agitation of the inferior palpebral and great zygomatic muscles is pathognomic of the earlier stages of general paralysis. The countenance has a pleased and benevolent expression. As the disease advances other muscles become involved, but until complete fatuity is reached, the prevailing expression is that of feeble benevolence.'

As in laughing and broadly smiling the cheeks and upper lip are much raised, the nose appears to be shortened, and the skin on the bridge becomes finely wrinkled in transverse lines, with other oblique longitudinal lines on the sides. The upper front teeth are commonly exposed. A well-marked naso-labial fold is formed, which runs from the wing of each nostril to the corner of the mouth; and this fold is often double in old persons.

A bright and sparkling eye is as characteristic of a pleased or amused state of mind, as is the retraction of the corners of the mouth and upper lip with the wrinkles thus produced. Even the eyes of microcephalus idiots, who are so degraded that they never learn to speak, brighten slightly when they are pleased.[12] Under extreme laughter the eyes are too much suffused with tears to sparkle; but the moisture squeezed out of the glands during moderate laughter or smiling may aid in giving them lustre; though this must be of altogether subordinate importance, as they become dull from grief, though they are then often moist. Their brightness seems to be chiefly due to their tenseness,[13] owing to the contraction of the orbicular muscles and to the pressure of the raised cheeks. But, according to Dr Piderit, who has discussed this point more fully than any other writer,[14] the tenseness may be largely attributed to the eyeballs becoming filled with blood and other fluids, from the acceleration of the circulation, consequent on the excitement of pleasure. He remarks on the contrast in the appearance of the eyes of a hectic patient with a rapid circulation, and of a man suffering from cholera with almost all the fluids of his body drained from him. Any cause which lowers the circulation deadens the eye. I remember seeing a man utterly prostrated by prolonged and severe exertion during a very hot day, and a bystander compared his eyes to those of a boiled codfish.

To return to the sounds produced during laughter. We can

see in a vague manner how the utterance of sound of some kind would naturally become associated with a pleasurable state of mind; for throughout a large part of the animal kingdom vocal or instrumental sounds are employed either as a call or as a charm by one sex for the other. They are also employed as the means for a joyful meeting between the parents and their offspring, and between the attached members of the same social community. But why the sounds which man utters when he is pleased have the peculiar reiterated character of laughter we do not know. Nevertheless we can see that they would naturally be as different as possible from the screams or cries of distress; and as in the production of the latter, the expirations are prolonged and continuous, with the inspirations short and interrupted, so it might perhaps have been expected with the sounds uttered from joy, that the expirations would have been short and broken with the inspirations prolonged; and this is the case.

It is an equally obscure point why the corners of the mouth are retracted and the upper lip raised during ordinary laughter. The mouth must not be opened to its utmost extent, for when this occurs during a paroxysm of excessive laughter hardly any sound is emitted; or it changes its tone and seems to come from deep down in the throat. The respiratory muscles, and even those of the limbs, are at the same time thrown into rapid vibratory movements. The lower jaw often partakes of this movement, and this would tend to prevent the mouth from being widely opened. But as a full volume of sound has to be poured forth, the orifice of the mouth must be large; and it is perhaps to gain this end that the corners are retracted and the upper lip raised. Although we can hardly account for the shape of the mouth during laughter, which leads to wrinkles being formed beneath the eyes, nor for the peculiar reiterated sound of laughter, nor for the quivering of the jaws, nevertheless we may infer that all these effects are due to some common cause. For they are all characteristic and expressive of a pleased state of mind in various kinds of monkeys.

A graduated series can be followed from violent to moderate laughter, to a broad smile, to a gentle smile, and to the expression of mere cheerfulness. During excessive laughter the whole body is often thrown backward and shakes, or is almost convulsed; the respiration is much disturbed; the head and face become gorged with blood, with the veins distended; and the orbicular muscles are spasmodically contracted in order to protect the eyes. Tears are freely shed. Hence, as formerly remarked, it is scarcely possible to point out any difference between the tear-stained face of a person after a paroxysm of excessive laughter and after a bitter crying-fit.* It is probably due to the close similarity of the spasmodic movements caused by these widely different emotions that hysteric patients alternately cry and laugh with violence, and that young children sometimes pass suddenly from one to the other state. Mr Swinhoe informs me that he has often seen the Chinese, when suffering from deep grief, burst out into hysterical fits of laughter.

I was anxious to know whether tears are freely shed during excessive laughter by most of the races of men, and I hear from my correspondents that this is the case. One instance was observed with the Hindoos, and they themselves said that it often occurred. So it is with the Chinese. The women of a wild tribe of Malays in the Malacca peninsula, sometimes shed tears when they laugh heartily, though this seldom occurs. With the Dyaks of Borneo it must frequently be the case, at least with women, for I hear from the Rajah C. Brooke that it is a common expression with them to say 'we nearly made tears from laughter'. The aborigines of Australia express their emotions freely, and they are described by my correspondents as jumping about and clapping their hands for joy, and as often roaring with laughter. No less than four observers have seen their eyes freely watering on such occasions; and in one instance the tears rolled down their cheeks. Mr Bulmer, a missionary in a remote part of Victoria, remarks, 'that they have a keen sense of the ridiculous; they are excellent mimics, and when one of them is able to imitate the peculiarities of some absent member of the tribe, it is very

---

* Sir J. Reynolds remarks (*Discourses*, xii, p. 100), 'It is curious to observe, and it is certainly true, that the extremes of contrary passions are, with very little variation, expressed by the same action.' He gives as an instance the frantic joy of a Bacchante and the grief of a Mary Magdalen.

common to hear all in the camp convulsed with laughter.' With Europeans hardly anything excites laughter so easily as mimicry; and it is rather curious to find the same fact with the savages of Australia, who constitute one of the most distinct races in the world.

In Southern Africa with two tribes of Kafirs, especially with the women, their eyes often fill with tears during laughter. Gaika, the brother of the chief Sandilli, answers my query on this head, with the words, 'Yes, that is their common practice.' Sir Andrew Smith has seen the painted face of a Hottentot woman all furrowed with tears after a fit of laughter. In Northern Africa, with the Abyssinians, tears are secreted under the same circumstances. Lastly, in North America, the same fact has been observed in a remarkably savage and isolated tribe, but chiefly with the women; in another tribe it was observed only on a single occasion.*

Excessive laughter, as before remarked, graduates into moderate laughter. In this latter case the muscles round the eyes are much less contracted, and there is little or no frowning. Between a gentle laugh and a broad smile there is hardly any difference, excepting that in smiling no reiterated sound is uttered, though a single rather strong expiration, or slight noise – a rudiment of a laugh – may often be heard at the commencement of a smile. On a moderately smiling countenance the contraction of the upper orbicular muscles can still just be traced by a slight lowering of the eyebrows. The contraction of the lower orbicular and palpebral muscles is much plainer, and is shown by the wrinkling of the lower eyelids and of the skin beneath them, together with a slight drawing up of the upper lip. From the broadest smile we pass by the finest steps into the gentlest one. In this latter case the features are moved in a much less degree, and much more slowly, and the mouth is kept closed. The curvature of the naso-labial furrow is also slightly different in the two cases. We thus see that no abrupt line of demarcation can be drawn between the

---

* [Mr B. F. Hartshorne (*Fortnightly Review*, March, 1876, p. 410) states in the most positive manner that the Weddas of Ceylon never laugh. Every conceivable incitive to laughter was used in vain. When asked whether they ever laughed, they replied, 'No, what is there to laugh at?']

movement of the features during the most violent laughter and a very faint smile.*

A smile, therefore, may be said to be the first stage in the development of a laugh. But a different and more probable view may be suggested; namely, that the habit of uttering loud reiterated sounds from a sense of pleasure, first led to the retraction of the corners of the mouth and of the upper lip, and to the contraction of the orbicular muscles; and that now, through association and long-continued habit, the same muscles are brought into slight play whenever any cause excites in us a feeling which, if stronger, would have led to laughter; and the result is a smile.†

Whether we look at laughter as the full development of a smile, or, as is more probable, at a gentle smile as the last trace of a habit, firmly fixed during many generations, of laughing whenever we are joyful, we can follow in our infants the gradual passage of the one into the other. It is well known to those who have the charge of young infants, that it is difficult to feel sure when certain movements about their mouths are really expressive; that is, when they really smile. Hence I carefully watched my own infants. One of them at the age of forty-five days, and being at the time in a happy frame of mind, smiled; that is, the corners of the mouth were retracted, and simultaneously the eyes became decidedly bright. I observed the same thing on the following day; but on the third day the child was not quite well and there was no trace of a smile, and this renders it probable that the previous smiles were real. Eight days subsequently and during the next succeeding week, it was remarkable how his eyes brightened whenever he smiled, and his nose became at the same time transversely wrinkled. This was now accompanied by a little bleating noise, which perhaps represented a laugh. At the age of 113 days these little noises, which were always made during expiration,

* Dr Piderit has come to the same conclusion, ibid., p. 99.
† [It appears from a manuscript note of the author's that his final opinion was that the contraction of the orbiculars in gentle laughter and smiling cannot be wholly explained as a 'trace of the contraction during loud laughter, for this does not explain the contraction chiefly of the lower orbiculars' in smiling.]

assumed a slightly different character, and were more broken or interrupted, as in sobbing; and this was certainly incipient laughter. The change in tone seemed to me at the time to be connected with the greater lateral extension of the mouth as the smiles became broader.

In a second infant the first real smile was observed at about the same age, viz. forty-five days; and in a third, at a somewhat earlier age. The second infant, when sixty-five days old, smiled much more broadly and plainly than did the one first mentioned at the same age; and even at this early age uttered noises very like laughter. In this gradual acquirement, by infants, of the habit of laughing, we have a case in some degree analogous to that of weeping. As practice is requisite with the ordinary movements of the body, such as walking, so it seems to be with laughing and weeping. The art of screaming, on the other hand, from being of service to infants, has become finely developed from the first days.

High spirits, cheerfulness. A man in high spirits, though he may not actually smile, commonly exhibits some tendency to the retraction of the corners of his mouth. From the excitement of pleasure, the circulation becomes more rapid; the eyes are bright, and the colour of the face rises. The brain, being stimulated by the increased flow of blood, reacts on the mental powers; lively ideas pass still more rapidly through the mind, and the affections are warmed. I heard a child, a little under four years old, when asked what was meant by being in good spirits, answer, 'It is laughing, talking, and kissing'. It would be difficult to give a truer and more practical definition. A man in this state holds his body erect, his head upright, and his eyes open. There is no drooping of the features, and no contractions of the eyebrows. On the contrary, the frontal muscle, as Moreau observes;[15] tends to contract slightly; and this smooths the brow, removes every trace of a frown, arches the eyebrows a little, and raises the eyelids. Hence the Latin phrase, *exporrigere frontem* – to unwrinkle the brow – means, to be cheerful or merry. The whole expression of a man in good spirits is exactly the opposite of that of one suffering from sorrow. According to Sir C. Bell, 'In all the exhilarating emotions the eyebrows, eyelids, the nostrils, and the angles of the mouth are raised. In the depressing passions it is the reverse'. Under the influence of the latter the brow is heavy, the eyelids, cheeks, mouth, and whole head droop; the eyes are dull; the countenance pallid, and the respiration slow. In joy the face expands, in grief it lengthens. Whether the principle of antithesis has here come into play in producing these opposite expressions, in aid of the direct causes which have been specified and which are sufficiently plain, I will not pretend to say.

With all the races of man the expression of good spirits appears to be the same, and is easily recognized. My informants, from various parts of the Old and New Worlds, answer in the affirmative to my queries on this head, and they give some particulars with respect to Hindoos, Malays, and New Zealanders. The brightness of the eyes of the Australians has struck four observers, and the same fact has been noticed with Hindoos, New Zealanders, and the Dyaks of Borneo.

Savages sometimes express their satisfaction not only by smiling, but by gestures derived from the pleasure of eating. Thus Mr Wedgwood[16] quotes Petherick that the negroes on the Upper Nile began a general rubbing of their bellies when he displayed his beads; and Leichardt says that the Australians smacked and clacked their mouths at the sight of his horses and bullocks, and more especially of his kangaroo dogs. The Greenlanders, 'when they affirm anything with pleasure, suck down air with a certain sound';[17] and this may be an imitation of the act of swallowing savoury food.

Laughter is suppressed by the firm contraction of the orbicular muscles of the mouth, which prevents the great zygomatic and other muscles from drawing the lips backwards and upwards. The lower lip is also sometimes held by the teeth, and this gives a roguish expression to the face, as was observed with the blind and deaf Laura Bridgman.[18] The great zygomatic muscle is sometimes variable in its course, and I have seen a young woman in whom the *depressores anguli oris* were brought into strong action in suppressing a smile; but this by no means gave to her countenance a melancholy expression, owing to the brightness of her eyes.

Laughter is frequently employed in a forced manner to conceal or mask some other states of mind, even anger. We often see persons laughing in order to conceal their shame or shyness. When a person purses up his mouth, as if to prevent the possibility of a smile, though there is nothing to excite one, or nothing to prevent its free indulgence, an affected, solemn, or pedantic expression is given; but of such hybrid expressions nothing more need here be said. In the case of derision, a real or pretended smile or laugh is often blended with the expression proper to contempt, and this may pass into angry contempt or scorn. In such cases the meaning of the laugh or smile is to show the offending person that he excites only amusement.

Love, tender feelings, etc. Although the emotion of love, for instance that of a mother for her infant, is one of the strongest of which the mind is capable, it can hardly be said to have any proper or peculiar means of expression; and this is intelligible, as it has not habitually led to any special line of action. No doubt, as affection is a pleasurable sensation, it generally causes a gentle smile and some brightening of the eyes. A strong desire to touch the beloved person is commonly felt; and love is expressed by this means more plainly than by any other.* Hence we long to clasp in our arms those whom we tenderly love. We probably owe this desire to inherited habit, in association with the nursing and tending of our children, and with the mutual caresses of lovers.

I agree with Darwin that there is no distinctive facial expression for love. He said this is because there is no action required for love, and therefore no movements from which the expression would have evolved. My explanation is different: it is because love is not an emotion. Emotions come and go in a matter of seconds or minutes. Parental love or romantic love are not so transitory, and

---

* Mr Bain remarks (*Mental and Moral Science*, 1868, p. 239), 'Tenderness is a pleasurable emotion, variously stimulated, whose effort is to draw human beings into mutual embrace.'

clearly different from momentary emotions. Love is an affective commitment, in which many emotions are felt. What is distinctive is the extent of commitment and attachment to a particular person and the strength of the various emotions – not just happiness – which are felt towards that person. (See my earlier discussion of this in Chapter 3, p. 83).[C49]

With the lower animals we see the same principle of pleasure derived from contact in association with love. Dogs and cats manifestly take pleasure in rubbing against their masters and mistresses, and in being rubbed or patted by them. Many kinds of monkeys, as I am assured by the keepers in the Zoological Gardens, delight in fondling and being fondled by each other, and by persons to whom they are attached. Mr Bartlett has described to me the behaviour of two chimpanzees, rather older animals than those generally imported into this country, when they were first brought together. They sat opposite, touching each other with their much protruded lips; and the one put his hand on the shoulder of the other. They then mutually folded each other in their arms. Afterwards they stood up, each with one arm on the shoulder of the other, lifted up their heads, opened their mouths, and yelled with delight.

We Europeans are so accustomed to kissing as a mark of affection, that it might be thought to be innate in mankind; but this is not the case. Steele was mistaken when he said 'Nature was its author, and it began with the first courtship.' Jemmy Button, the Fuegian, told me that this practice was unknown in his land. It is equally unknown with the New Zealanders, Tahitians, Papuans,* Australians, Somals of Africa, and the Esquimaux.† But it is so far innate or natural that it apparently depends on pleasure from

---

* [Mantegazza (*La Physionomie*, p. 198) quotes Wyatt Gill, who has seen kissing among the Papuans.]

† Sir J. Lubbock, *Prehistoric Times*, 2nd edit., 1869, p. 552, gives full authorities for these statements. The quotation from Steele is taken from this work. [Mr Winwood Reade (Letter, 5 November, 1872) says that kissing is unknown throughout West Africa, 'which is probably the largest non-kissing region on the whole globe'.]

close contact with a beloved person; and it is replaced in various parts of the world, by the rubbing of noses, as with the New Zealanders and Laplanders, by the rubbing or patting of the arms, breasts, or stomachs, or by one man striking his own face with the hands or feet of another. Perhaps the practice of blowing, as a mark of affection, on various parts of the body may depend on the same principle.[19]

The feelings which are called tender are difficult to analyse; they seem to be compounded of affection, joy, and especially of sympathy. These feelings are in themselves of a pleasurable nature, excepting when pity is too deep, or horror is aroused, as in hearing of a tortured man or animal. They are remarkable under our present point of view from so readily exciting the secretion of tears. Many a father and son have wept on meeting after a long separation, especially if the meeting has been unexpected. No doubt extreme joy by itself tends to act on the lacrymal glands; but on such occasions as the foregoing vague thoughts of the grief which would have been felt had the father and son never met, will probably have passed through their minds; and grief naturally leads to the secretion of tears. Thus on the return of Ulysses:

> 'Telemachus
> Rose, and clung weeping round his father's breast.
> There the pent grief rained o'er them, yearning thus.
>
> Thus piteously they wailed in sore unrest,
> And on their weepings had gone down the day,
> But that at last Telemachus found words to say.'
>
> *Worsley's Translation of the Odyssey*,
> Book xvi, st. 27.

So, again, when Penelope at last recognized her husband:

> 'Then from her eyelids the quick tears did start
> And she ran to him from her place, and threw
> Her arms about his neck, and a warm dew
> Of kisses poured upon him, and thus spake.'
>
> Book xxiii, st. 27.

The vivid recollection of our former home, or of long-past happy days, readily causes the eyes to be suffused with tears; but here, again, the thought naturally occurs that these days will never return. In such cases we may be said to sympathize with ourselves in our present, in comparison with our former, state. Sympathy with the distresses of others, even with the imaginary distresses of a heroine in a pathetic story, for whom we feel no affection, readily excites tears. So does sympathy with the happiness of others, as with that of a lover, at last successful after many hard trials in a well-told tale.

Sympathy appears to constitute a separate or distinct emotion; and it is especially apt to excite the lacrymal glands. This holds good whether we give or receive sympathy. Every one must have noticed how readily children burst out crying if we pity them for some small hurt. With the melancholic insane, as Dr Crichton Browne informs me, a kind word will often plunge them into unrestrained weeping. As soon as we express our pity for the grief of a friend, tears often come into our own eyes. The feeling of sympathy is commonly explained by assuming that, when we see or hear of suffering in another, the idea of suffering is called up so vividly in our minds that we ourselves suffer. But this explanation is hardly sufficient, for it does not account for the intimate alliance between sympathy and affection. We undoubtedly sympathize far more deeply with a beloved than with an indifferent person; and the sympathy of the one gives us far more relief that that of the other. Yet assuredly we can sympathize with those for whom we feel no affection.

Why suffering, when actually experienced by ourselves, excites weeping, has been discussed in a former chapter. With respect to joy, its natural and universal expression is laughter; and with all the races of man loud laughter leads to the secretion of tears more freely than does any other cause excepting distress. The suffusion of the eyes with tears, which undoubtedly occurs under great joy, though there is no laughter, can, as it seems to me, be explained through habit and association on the same principles as the effusion of tears from grief, although there is no screaming. Nevertheless it is not a little remarkable that sympathy with the distresses of others should excite tears more freely than our own distress; and this is certainly the case. Many a man, from whose eyes no suffering of his own could wring a tear, has shed tears at the sufferings of a beloved friend. It is still more remarkable that sympathy with the happiness or good fortune of those whom we tenderly love should lead to the same result, whilst a similar happiness felt by ourselves would leave our eyes dry. We should, however, bear in mind that the long-continued habit of restraint which is so powerful in checking the free flow of tears from bodily pain, has not been brought into play in preventing a moderate effusion of tears in sympathy with the sufferings or happiness of others.

Music has a wonderful power, as I have elsewhere attempted to show,[20] of recalling in a vague and indefinite manner, those strong emotions which were felt during long-past ages, when, as is probable, our early progenitors courted each other by the aid of vocal tones. And as several of our strongest emotions – grief, great joy, love, and sympathy – lead to the free secretion of tears, it is not surprising that music should be apt to cause our eyes to become suffused with tears, especially when we are already soft-ened by any of the tenderer feelings. Music often produces another peculiar effect. We know that every strong sensation, emotion, or excitement – extreme pain, rage, terror, joy, or the passion of love – all have a special tendency to cause the muscles to tremble; and the thrill or slight shiver which runs down the backbone and limbs of many persons when they are powerfully affected by music, seems to bear the same relation to the above trembling of the body, as a slight suffusion of tears from the power of music does to weeping from any strong and real emotion.

Devotion. As devotion is, in some degree, related to affection, though mainly consisting of reverence, often combined with fear, the expression of this state of mind may here be briefly noticed. With some sects, both past and present, religion and love have been strangely combined; and it has even been maintained, lam-entable as the fact may be, that the holy kiss of love differs but little from that which a man bestows on a woman, or a woman on a man.[21] Devotion is chiefly expressed by the face being directed towards the heavens, with the eyeballs upturned. Sir C. Bell remarks that, at the approach of sleep, or of a fainting-fit, or of death, the pupils are drawn upwards and inwards; and he believes that 'when we are wrapt in devotional feelings, and outward impressions are unheeded, the eyes are raised by an action neither taught nor acquired'; and that this is due to the same cause as in the above cases.[22] That the eyes are upturned during sleep is, as I hear from Professor Donders, certain. With babies, whilst sucking their mother's breast, this movement of the eyeballs often gives to them an absurd appearance of ecstatic delight; and here it may be clearly perceived that a struggle is going on against the position naturally assumed during sleep. But Sir C. Bell's explanation of the fact, which rests on the assumption that certain muscles are more under the control of the will than others is, as I hear from Professor Donders, incorrect. As the eyes are often turned up in prayer, without the mind being so much absorbed in thought as to approach to the unconsciousness of sleep, the movement is probably a conventional one – the result of the common belief that Heaven, the source of Divine power to which we pray, is seated above us.

A humble kneeling posture, with the hands upturned and palms joined appears to us, from long habit, a gesture so appropriate to devotion, that it might be thought to be innate; but I have not met with any evidence to this effect with the various extra-European races of mankind. During the classical period of Roman history it does not appear, as I hear from an excellent classic, that the hands were thus joined during prayer. Mr Hensleigh Wedgwood has apparently given* the true explanation, though this implies that the attitude is one of slavish subjection. 'When the suppliant kneels and holds up his hands with the palms joined, he represents a captive who proves the completeness of his sub-mission by offering up his hands to be bound by the victor. It is

---

* *The Origin of Language*, 1866, p. 146. Mr Tylor (*Early History of Mankind*, 2nd edit., 1870, p. 48) gives a more complex origin to the position of the hands during prayer.

the pictorial representation of the Latin *dare manus*, to signify submission.' Hence it is not probable that either the uplifting of the eyes or the joining of the open hands, under the influence of devotional feelings, are innate or truly expressive actions; and this could hardly have been expected, for it is very doubtful whether feelings such as we should now rank as devotional, affected the hearts of men, whilst they remained during past ages in an uncivilized condition.

CHAPTER IX

Reflection – Meditation – Ill-temper – Sulkiness – Determination

The act of frowning – Reflection with an effort, or with the perception of something difficult or disagreeable – Abstracted meditation – Ill-temper – Moroseness – Obstinacy – Sulkiness and pouting – Decision or determination – The firm closure of the mouth.

The corrugators, by their contraction, lower the eyebrows and bring them together, producing vertical furrows on the forehead – that is, a frown. Sir C. Bell, who erroneously thought that the corrugator was peculiar to man, ranks it as 'the most remarkable muscle of the human face. It knits the eyebrows with an energetic effort, which unaccountably, but irresistibly, conveys the idea of mind.' Or, as he elsewhere says, 'when the eyebrows are knit, energy of mind is apparent, and there is the mingling of thought and emotion with the savage and brutal rage of the mere animal.'*

* *Anatomy of Expression*, pp. 137, 139. It is not surprising that the corrugators should have become much more developed in man than in the anthropoid apes; for they are brought into incessant action by him under various circumstances, and will have been strengthened and modified by the inherited effects of use. We have seen how important a part they play, together with the orbiculars, in protecting the eyes from being too much gorged with blood during violent expiratory movements. When the eyes are closed as quickly and as forcibly as possible, to save them from being injured by a blow, the corrugators contract. With savages or other men whose heads are uncovered, the eyebrows are continually lowered and contracted to serve as a shade against a too strong light; and this is effected partly by the corrugators. This movement would have been more especially serviceable to man, as soon as his early progenitors held their heads erect. Lastly, Professor Donders believes (*Archives of Medicine*, ed. by L. Beale, 1870, vol. v, p. 34) that the corrugators are brought into action in causing the eyeball to advance in accommodation for proximity in vision.

There is much truth in these remarks, but hardly the whole truth. Dr Duchenne has called the corrugator the muscle of reflection;[1] but this name, without some limitation, cannot be considered as quite correct.

A man may be absorbed in the deepest thought, and his brow will remain smooth until he encounters some obstacle in his train of reasoning, or is interrupted by some disturbance, and then a frown passes like a shadow over his brow. A half-starved man may think intently how to obtain food, but he probably will not frown unless he encounters either in thought or action some difficulty, or finds the food when obtained nauseous. I have noticed that almost everyone instantly frowns if he perceives a strange or bad taste in what he is eating. I asked several persons, without explaining my object, to listen intently to a very gently tapping sound, the nature and source of which they all perfectly knew, and not one frowned; but a man who joined us, and who could not conceive what we were all doing in profound silence, when asked to listen, frowned much, though not in an ill-temper, and said he could not in the least understand what we all wanted. Dr Piderit,[2] who has published remarks to the same effect, adds that stammerers generally frown in speaking; and that a man, in doing even so trifling a thing as pulling on a boot, frowns if he finds it too tight. Some persons are such habitual frowners, that the mere effort of speaking almost always causes their brows to contract.

Men of all races frown when they are in any way perplexed in thought, as I infer from the answers which I have received to my queries; but I framed them badly, confounding absorbed meditation with perplexed reflection. Nevertheless, it is clear that the Australians, Malays, Hindoos, and Kafirs of South Africa frown, when they are puzzled. Dobritzhoffer remarks that the Guaranies of South America on like occasions knit their brows.[3]

From these considerations, we may conclude that frowning is not the expression of simple reflection, however profound, or of attention, however close, but of something difficult or displeasing encountered in a train of thought or in action. Deep reflection can, however, seldom be long carried on without some difficulty, so that it will generally be accompanied by a frown. Hence it is that frowning commonly gives to the countenance, as Sir C. Bell remarks, an aspect of intellectual energy. But in order that this effect may be produced, the eyes must be clear and steady, or they may be cast downwards, as often occurs in deep thought. The countenance must not be otherwise disturbed, as in the case of an ill-tempered or peevish man, or of one who shows the effects of prolonged suffering, with dulled eyes and drooping jaw, or who perceives a bad taste in his food, or who finds it difficult to perform some trifling act, such as threading a needle. In these cases a frown may often be seen but it will be accompanied by some other expression, which will entirely prevent the countenance having an appearance of intellectual energy or of profound thought.

We may now enquire how it is that a frown should express the perception of something difficult or disagreeable, either in thought or action. In the same way as naturalists find it advisable to trace the embryological development of an organ in order fully to understand its structure, so with the movements of expression it is advisable to follow as nearly as possible the same plan. The earliest and almost sole expression seen during the first days of infancy, and then often exhibited, is that displayed during the act of screaming; and screaming is excited, both at first and for some time afterwards, by every distressing or displeasing sensation and emotion — by hunger, pain, anger, jealousy, fear, etc. At such times the muscles round the eyes are strongly contracted; and this, as I believe, explains to a large extent the act of frowning during the remainder of our lives. I repeatedly observed my own infants, from under the age of one week to that of two or three months, and found that when a screaming-fit came on gradually, the first sign was the contraction of the corrugators, which produced a slight frown, quickly followed by the contraction of the other muscles round the eyes. When an infant is uncomfortable or unwell, little frowns — as I record in my notes — may be seen incessantly passing like shadows over its face; these being generally, but not always, followed sooner or later by a crying-fit. For instance, I watched for some time a baby, between seven and eight weeks old, sucking some milk which was cold, and therefore displeasing to him; and a steady little frown was maintained all the time. This was never developed into an actual crying-fit, though occasionally every stage of close approach could be observed.

As the habit of contracting the brows has been followed by infants during innumerable generations, at the commencement of every crying- or screaming-fit, it has become firmly associated with the incipient sense of something distressing or disagreeable. Hence under similar circumstances it would be apt to be continued during maturity, although never then developed into a crying-fit. Screaming or weeping begins to be voluntarily restrained at an early period of life, whereas frowning is hardly ever restrained at any age. It is perhaps worth notice that with children much given to weeping, anything which perplexes their minds, and which would cause most other children merely to frown, readily makes them weep. So with certain classes of the insane, any effort of mind, however slight, which with an habitual frowner would cause a slight frown, leads to their weeping in an unrestrained manner. It is not more surprising that the habit of contracting the brows at the first perception of something distressing, although gained during infancy, should be retained during the rest of our lives, than that many other associated habits acquired at an early age should be permanently retained both by man and the lower animals. For instance, full-grown cats, when feeling warm and comfortable, often retain the habit of alternately protruding their fore-feet with extended toes, which habit they practised for a definite purpose whilst sucking their mothers.

Another and distinct cause has probably strengthened the habit of frowning, whenever the mind is intent on any subject and encounters some difficulty. Vision is the most important of all the senses, and during primeval times the closest attention must have been incessantly directed towards distant objects for the sake of obtaining prey and avoiding danger. I remember being struck, whilst travelling in parts of South America, which were dangerous from the presence of Indians, how incessantly, yet as it appeared unconsciously, the half-wild Gauchos closely scanned the whole horizon. Now, when any one with no covering on his head (as must have been aboriginally the case with mankind) strives to the utmost to distinguish in broad daylight, and especially if the sky is bright, a distant object, he almost invariably contracts his brows to prevent the entrance of too much light; the lower eyelids, cheeks, and upper lip being at the same time raised, so as to lessen the orifice of the eyes. I have purposely asked several persons, young and old, to look, under the above circumstances, at distant objects, making them believe that I only wished to test the power of their vision; and they all behaved in the manner just described. Some of them, also, put their open, flat hands over their eyes to keep out the excess of light.* Gratiolet, after making some remarks to nearly the same effect,† says, 'Ce sont là des attitudes de vision difficile.' ['This is the posture when it is difficult to see.'] He concludes that the muscles round the eyes contract partly for the sake of excluding too much light (which appears to me the more important end), and partly to prevent all rays striking the retina, except those which come direct from the object that is scrutinized. Mr Bowman, whom I consulted on this point, thinks that the contraction of the surrounding muscles may, in addition, 'partly sustain the consensual movements of the two eyes, by giving a firmer support while the globes are brought to binocular vision by their own proper muscles'.

As the effort of viewing with ease under a bright light a distant object is both difficult and irksome, and as this effort has been habitually accompanied, during numberless generations, by the contraction of the eyebrows, the habit of frowning will thus have been much strengthened; although it was originally practised

---

* [Mr Henry Recks (letter, 3 March 1873) writes: 'I have seen the black bear, *U. americanus*, sit on its haunches and shade its eyes with both fore-paws when trying to make out a distant object, and I hear that it is a frequent habit of that species.']

† *De la Physionomie*, pp. 15, 144, 146. Mr Herbert Spencer accounts for frowning exclusively by the habit of contracting the brows as a shade to the eyes in a bright light: see *Principles of Psychology*, 2nd edit., 1872, p. 546. The Rev H. H. Blair, Principal of the Worcester College, states that the born-blind have little or no control over the *corrugator supercilii* so that they cannot frown when told to do so; nevertheless, they frown involuntarily. They can, however, smile at command.

during infancy from a quite independent cause, namely as the first step in the protection of the eyes during screaming. There is, indeed, much analogy, as far as the state of the mind is concerned, between intently scrutinizing a distant object, and following out an obscure train of thought, or performing some little and troublesome mechanical work. The belief that the habit of contracting the brows is continued when there is no need whatever to exclude too much light, receives support from the cases formerly alluded to, in which the eyebrows or eyelids are acted on under certain circumstances in a useless manner, from having been similarly used, under analogous circumstances, for a serviceable purpose. For instance, we voluntarily close our eyes when we do not wish to see any object, and we are apt to close them, when we reject a proposition, as if we could not or would not see it; or when we think about something horrible. We raise our eyebrows when we wish to see quickly all round us, and we often do the same, when we earnestly desire to remember something; acting as if we endeavoured to see it.

Darwin's explanation assumes that infants learn to lower their brows to decrease the light entering the eye. If blind infants showed this movement, Darwin's theory would be wrong, and the movement not a product of learning but genetically linked to the psychological states Darwin describes. The second footnote on the previous page suggests this might be so, but there is as yet no objective evidence to settle this question.

Abstraction, meditation. When a person is lost in thought with his mind absent, or, as it is sometimes said, 'when he is in a brown study', he does not frown, but his eyes appear vacant. The lower eyelids are generally raised and wrinkled, in the same manner as when a short-sighted person tries to distinguish a distant object; and the upper orbicular muscles are at the same time slightly contracted. The wrinkling of the lower eyelids under these circumstances has been observed with some savages, as by Mr Dyson Lacy with the Australians of Queensland, and several times by

Mr Geach with the Malays of the interior of Malacca. What the meaning or cause of this action may be, cannot at present be explained; but here we have another instance of movement round the eyes in relation to the state of the mind.

The vacant expression of the eyes is very peculiar, and at once shows when a man is completely lost in thought. Professor Donders has, with his usual kindness, investigated this subject for me. He has observed others in this condition, and has been himself observed by Professor Engelmann. The eyes are not then fixed on any object, and therefore not, as I had imagined, on some distant object. The lines of vision of the two eyes even often become slightly divergent; the divergence, if the head be held vertically, with the plane of vision horizontal, amounting to an angle of 2° as a maximum. This was ascertained by observing the crossed doubled image of a distant object. When the head droops forward, as often occurs with a man absorbed in thought, owing to the general relaxation of his muscles, if the plane of vision be still horizontal, the eyes are necessarily a little turned upwards, and then the divergence is as much as 3°, or 3°5': if the eyes are turned still more upwards, it amounts to between 6° and 7°. Professor Donders attributes this divergence to the almost complete relaxation of certain muscles of the eyes, which would be apt to follow from the mind being wholly absorbed.* The active condition of the muscles of the eyes is that of convergence; and Professor Donders remarks, as bearing on their divergence during a period of complete abstraction, that when one eye becomes blind, it almost always, after a short lapse of time, deviates outwards: for its muscles are no longer used in moving the eyeball inwards for the sake of binocular vision.

Perplexed reflection is often accompanied by certain movements or gestures. At such times we commonly raise our hands to our foreheads, mouths, or chins; but we do not act thus, as

* Gratiolet remarks (*De la Phys.*, p. 35), 'Quand l'attention est fixée sur quelque image intérieure, l'oeil regarde dans le vide et s'associe automatiquement à la contemplation de l'esprit.' ['When the attention is fixed on some inner image, the eye stares into the void and automatically joins the contemplation of the spirit.'] But this view hardly deserves to be called an explanation.

far as I have seen, when we are quite lost in meditation, and no difficulty is encountered. Plautus, describing in one of his plays[4] a puzzled man, says, 'Now look, he has pillared his chin upon his hand.' Even so trifling and apparently unmeaning a gesture as the raising of the hand to the face has been observed with some savages. Mr J. Mansel Weale has seen it with the Kafirs of South Africa; and the native chief Gaika adds, that men then 'sometimes pull their beards'. Mr Washington Matthews, who attended to some of the wildest tribes of Indians in the western regions of the United States, remarks that he has seen them when concentrating their thoughts, bring their 'hands, usually the thumb and index finger, in contact with some part of the face, commonly the upper lip'. We can understand why the forehead should be pressed or rubbed, as deep thought tries the brain; but why the hand should be raised to the mouth or face is far from clear.

Ill-temper. We have seen that frowning is the natural expression of some difficulty encountered, or of something disagreeable experienced either in thought or action, and he whose mind is often and readily affected in this way, will be apt to be ill-tempered, or slightly angry, or peevish, and will commonly show it by frowning. But a cross expression, due to a frown, may be counteracted, if the mouth appears sweet, from being habitually drawn into a smile, and the eyes are bright and cheerful. So it will be if the eye is clear and steady, and there is the appearance of earnest reflection. Frowning, with some depression of the corners of the mouth, which is a sign of grief, gives an air of peevishness. If a child (see Plate IV, Fig. 1)* frowns much whilst crying, but does not strongly contract in the usual manner the orbicular muscles, a well-marked expression of anger or even of rage, together with misery, is displayed.

If the whole frowning brow can be drawn much downward by the contraction of the pyramidal muscles of the nose, which

---

* The original photograph by Herr Kindermann is much more expressive than this copy, as it shows the frown on the brow more plainly.

PLATE IV

I

2

[In Fig. 1. in the First and Second Editions of *Expression*, Darwin had the poodle and chair cropped out of the picture. Fig. 2. was not in the First or Second Editions, but it is certain from Darwin's description that this is the photograph he is discussing.]

produces transverse wrinkles or folds across the base of the nose, the expression becomes one of moroseness. Duchenne believes that the contraction of this muscle, without any frowning, gives the appearance of extreme and aggressive hardness.[5] But I much doubt whether this is true or natural expression. I have shown Duchenne's photograph of a young man (Plate IV, Fig. 2), with this muscle strongly contracted by means of galvanism, to eleven persons, including some artists, and none of them could form an idea of what was intended, except one, a girl, who answered correctly, 'surly reserve'. When I first looked at this photograph, knowing what was intended, my imagination added, as I believe, what was necessary, namely, a frowning brow; and consequently the expression appeared to me true and extremely morose.

A firmly closed mouth, in addition to a lowered and frowning brow, gives determination to the expression, or may make it obstinate and sullen. How it comes that the firm closure of the mouth gives the appearance of determination will presently be discussed. An expression of sullen obstinacy has been clearly recognized by my informants, in the natives of six different regions of Australia. It is well marked, according to Mr Scott, with the Hindoos. It has been recognized with the Malays, Chinese, Kafirs, Abyssinians, and in a conspicuous degree, according to Dr Rothrock, with the wild Indians of North America, and according to Mr D. Forbes, with the Aymaras of Bolivia. I have also observed it with the Araucanos of southern Chili. Mr Dyson Lacy remarks that the natives of Australia, when in this frame of mind, sometimes fold their arms across their breasts, an attitude which may be seen with us. A firm determination, amounting to obstinacy, is, also, sometimes expressed by both shoulders being kept raised, the meaning of which gesture will be explained in the following chapter.

With young children sulkiness is shown by pouting, or, as it is sometimes called, 'making a snout'.[6] When the corners of the mouth are much depressed, the lower lip is a little everted and protruded; and this is likewise called a pout. But the pouting here referred to, consists of the protrusion of both lips into a tubular form, sometimes to such an extent as to project as far as the end of the nose, if this be short. Pouting is generally accompanied by frowning, and sometimes by the utterance of a booing or whooing noise. This expression is remarkable, as almost the sole one, as far as I know, which is exhibited much more plainly during childhood, at least with Europeans, than during maturity. There is, however, some tendency to the protrusion of the lips with the adults of all races under the influence of great rage. Some children pout when they are shy, and they can then hardly be called sulky.

Darwin described a very strong protrusion for the pout, but I have more commonly found a very slight protrusion of just the lower lip as the first sign of distress or sadness.

From enquiries which I have made in several large families, pouting does not seem very common with European children; but it prevails throughout the world, and must be both common and strongly marked with most savage races, as it has caught the attention of many observers. It has been noticed in eight different districts of Australia; and one of my informants remarks how greatly the lips of the children are then protruded. Two observers have seen pouting with the children of Hindoos; three, with those of the Kafirs and Fingoes of South Africa, and with the Hottentots; and two, with the children of the wild Indians of North America. Pouting has also been observed with the Chinese, Abyssinians, Malays of Malacca, Dyaks of Borneo, and often with the New Zealanders. Mr Mansel Weale informs me that he has seen the lips much protruded, not only with the children of the Kafirs, but with the adults of both sexes when sulky; and Mr Stack has sometimes observed the same thing with the men, and very frequently with the women of New Zealand. A trace of the same expression may occasionally be detected even with adult Europeans.

We thus see that the protrusion of the lips, especially with young children, is characteristic of sulkiness throughout the greater part of the world. This movement apparently results from the retention, chiefly during youth, of a primordial habit, or from an occasional reversion to it. Young orangs and chimpanzees protrude their lips to an extraordinary degree, as described in a former chapter, when they are discontented, somewhat angry, or sulky; also when they are surprised, a little frightened, and even when slightly pleased. Their mouths are protruded apparently for the sake of making the various noises proper to these several states of mind; and its shape, as I observed with the chimpanzee, differed slightly when the cry of pleasure and that of anger were uttered. As soon as these animals become enraged, the shape of the mouth wholly changes, and the teeth are exposed. The adult orang when wounded is said to emit 'a singular cry, consisting at first of high notes which at length deepen into a low roar. While giving out the high notes he thrusts out his lips into a funnel shape, but in uttering the low notes he holds his mouth wide open.'[7] With the gorilla, the lower lip is said to be capable of great elongation. If then our semi-human progenitors protruded their lips when sulky or a little angered, in the same manner as do the existing anthropoid apes, it is not an anomalous, though a curious fact, that our children should exhibit, when similarly affected, a trace of the same expression, together with some tendency to utter a noise. For it is not at all unusual for animals to retain, more or less perfectly, during early youth, and subsequently to lose, characters which were aboriginally possessed by their adult progenitors, and which are still retained by distinct species, their near relations.

Nor is it an anomalous fact that the children of savages should exhibit a stronger tendency to protrude their lips, when sulky, than the children of civilized Europeans; for the essence of savagery seems to consist in the retention of a primordial condition, and this occasionally holds good even with bodily peculiarities.* It may be objected to this view of the origin of pouting, that the anthropoid apes likewise protrude their lips when astonished and even when a little pleased; whilst with us this expression is generally confined to a sulky frame of mind. But we shall see in a future chapter that with men of various races surprise does

---

* I have given several instances in my *Descent of Man*, vol. i, chap. ii.

sometimes lead to a slight protrusion of the lips, though great surprise or astonishment is more commonly shown by the mouth being widely opened. As when we smile or laugh we draw back the corners of the mouth, we have lost any tendency to protrude the lips, when pleased, if indeed our early progenitors thus expressed pleasure.

A little gesture made by sulky children may here be noticed, namely, their 'showing a cold shoulder'. This has a different meaning, as, I believe, from the keeping both shoulders raised. A cross child, sitting on its parent's knee, will lift up the near shoulder, then jerk it away as if from a caress, and afterwards give a backward push with it, as if to push away the offender. I have seen a child, standing at some distance from any one, clearly express its feeling by raising one shoulder, giving it a little back-ward movement, and then turning away its whole body.

Decision or determination. The firm closure of the mouth tends to give an expression of determination or decision to the counten-ance. No determined man probably had an habitually gaping mouth. Hence, also, a small and weak lower jaw, which seems to indicate that the mouth is not habitually and firmly closed, is commonly thought to be characteristic of feebleness of character. A prolonged effort of any kind, whether of body or mind, implies previous determination; and if it can be shown that the mouth is generally closed with firmness before and during a great and continued exertion of the muscular system, then, through the principle of association, the mouth would almost certainly be closed as soon as any determined resolution was taken. Now several observers have noticed that a man, in commencing any violent muscular effort, invariably first distends his lungs with air, and then compresses it by the strong contraction of the muscles of the chest; and to effect this the mouth must be firmly closed. Moreover, as soon as the man is compelled to draw breath, he still keeps his chest as much distended as possible.

Various causes have been assigned for this manner of acting. Sir C. Bell maintains[8] that the chest is distended with air, and is kept distended at such times, in order to give a fixed support to the muscles which are thereto attached. Hence as he remarks, when two men are engaged in a deadly contest, a terrible silence prevails, broken only by hard stifled breathing. There is silence, because to expel the air in the utterance of any sound would be to relax the support for the muscles of the arms. If an outcry is heard, supposing the struggle to take place in the dark, we at once know that one of the two has given up in despair.

Gratiolet admits[9] that when a man has to struggle with another to his utmost, or has to support a great weight, or to keep for a long time the same forced attitude, it is necessary for him to first make a deep inspiration, and then to cease breathing; but he thinks that Sir C. Bell's explanation is erroneous. He maintains that arrested respiration retards the circulation of the blood, of which I believe there is no doubt, and he adduces some curious evidence from the structure of the lower animals, showing, on one hand, that a retarded circulation is necessary for prolonged muscular exertion, and, on the other hand, that a rapid circulation is necessary for rapid movements. According to this view, when we commence any great exertion, we close our mouths and stop breathing, in order to retard the circulation of the blood. Gratiolet sums up the subject by saying, 'C'est là la vraie théorie de l'effort continu' ['That is the true theory of continued effort'], but how far this theory is admitted by other physiologists I do not know.

Dr Piderit accounts[10] for the firm closure of the mouth during strong muscular exertion, on the principle that the influence of the will spreads to other muscles besides those necessarily brought into action in making any particular exertion; and it is natural that the muscles of respiration and of the mouth, from being so habitually used, should be especially liable to be thus acted on. It appears to me that there probably is some truth in this view, for we are apt to press the teeth hard together during violent exertion, and this is not requisite to prevent expiration, whilst the muscles of the chest are strongly contracted.

Lastly, when a man has to perform some delicate and difficult operation, not requiring the exertion of any strength, he nevertheless generally closes his mouth and ceases for a time to breathe;

but he acts thus in order that the movement of his chest may not disturb those of his arms. A person, for instance, whilst threading a needle, may be seen to compress his lips and either to stop breathing, or to breathe as quietly as possible. So it was, as formerly stated, with a young and sick chimpanzee, whilst it amused itself by killing flies with its knuckles, as they buzzed about on the window-panes. To perform an action, however trifling, if difficult, implies some amount of previous determination.

There appears nothing improbable in all the above assigned causes having come into play in different degrees, either conjointly or separately, on various occasions. The result would be a well-established habit, now perhaps inherited, of firmly closing the mouth at the commencement of and during any violent and prolonged exertion, or any delicate operation. Through the principle of association there would also be a strong tendency towards this same habit, as soon as the mind had resolved on any particular action or line of conduct, even before there was any bodily exertion, or if none were requisite. The habitual and firm closure of the mouth would thus come to show decision of character; and decision readily passes into obstinacy.

CHAPTER X

Hatred and Anger

Hatred – Rage, effects of, on the system – Uncovering of the teeth – Rage in the insane – Anger and indignation – As expressed by the various races of man – Sneering and defiance – The uncovering of the canine tooth on one side of the face.

If we have suffered or expect to suffer some wilful injury from a man, or if he is in any way offensive to us, we dislike him; and dislike easily rises into hatred. Such feelings, if experienced in a moderate degree, are not clearly expressed by any movement of the body or features, excepting perhaps by a certain gravity of behaviour, or by some ill-temper. Few individuals, however, can long reflect about a hated person, without feeling and exhibiting signs of indignation or rage. But if the offending person be quite insignificant, we experience merely disdain or contempt. If, on the other hand, he is all-powerful, then hatred passes into terror, as when a slave thinks about a cruel master, or a savage about a bloodthirsty malignant deity.[1] Most of our emotions are so closely connected with their expression, that they hardly exist if the body remains passive – the nature of the expression depending in chief part on the nature of the actions which have been habitually performed under this particular state of the mind. A man, for instance, may know that his life is in the extremest peril, and may strongly desire to save it, yet may exclaim as did Louis XVI, when surrounded by a fierce mob, 'Am I afraid? feel my pulse.' So a man may intensely hate another, but until his bodily frame is affected he cannot be said to be enraged.

Darwin's description of when one feels anger, contempt or terror is beautifully succinct and accurate. I disagree, however, with how he characterizes hatred. That word is better reserved for a more enduring attitude towards another person, albeit one identified with intense anger, but it can be distinguished from the transitory emotions. We can be very angry with people we don't hate, which perhaps Darwin was implying when he wrote that you can hate someone, but until the body is affected, rage (or anger, for that matter) cannot be felt.

Rage. I have already had occasion to treat of this emotion in the third chapter, when discussing the direct influence of the excited sensorium on the body, in combination with the effects of habitually associated actions. Rage exhibits itself in the most diversified manner. The heart and circulation are always affected; the face reddens or becomes purple, with the veins on the forehead and neck distended. The reddening of the skin has been observed with the copper-coloured Indians of South America,[2] and even, as it is said, on the white cicatrices left by old wounds on negroes.* Monkeys also redden from passion. With one of my own infants, under four months old, I repeatedly observed that the first symptom of an approaching passion was the rushing of the blood into his bare scalp. On the other hand, the action of the heart is sometimes so much impeded by great rage, that the countenance becomes pallid or livid,[3] and not a few men with heart disease have dropped down dead under this powerful emotion.

Our studies[C50] of patients with cardiovascular disease confirm that the experience of anger, in a person who has cardiovascular disease, can put them at risk for a heart attack.

* Sir C. Bell, *Anatomy of Expression*, p. 96. On the other hand, Dr Burgess (*Physiology of Blushing*, 1839, p. 31) speaks of the reddening of a cicatrix in a negress as of the nature of a blush.

The respiration is likewise affected; the chest heaves, and the dilated nostrils quiver.* As Tennyson writes, 'sharp breaths of anger puffed her fairy nostrils out'. Hence we have such expressions as 'breathing out vengeance', and 'fuming with anger'.† The excited brain gives strength to the muscles, and at the same time energy to the will. The body is commonly held erect ready for instant action, but sometimes it is bent forward towards the offending person, with the limbs more or less rigid. The mouth is generally closed with firmness, showing fixed determination, and the teeth are clenched or ground together. Such gestures as the raising of the arms, with the fists clenched, as if to strike the offender, are common. Few men in a great passion, and telling some one to be gone, can resist acting as if they intended to strike or punch the man violently away. The desire, indeed, to strike often becomes so intolerably strong, that inanimate objects are struck or dashed to the ground; but the gestures frequently become altogether purposeless or frantic. Young children, when in a violent rage, roll on the ground on their backs or bellies, screaming, kicking, scratching or biting everything within reach. So it is, as I hear from Mr Scott, with Hindoo children; and, as we have seen, with the young of the anthropomorphous apes.

But the muscular system is often affected in a wholly different way; for trembling is a frequent consequence of extreme rage.

* Sir C. Bell (*Anatomy of Expression*, pp. 91, 107) has fully discussed this subject. Moreau remarks (in the edit. of 1820 of *La Physionomie*, by G. Lavater, vol. iv, p. 237), and quotes Portal in confirmation, that asthmatic patients acquire permanently expanded nostrils, owing to the habitual contraction of the elevatory muscles of the wings of the nose. The explanation by Dr Piderit (*Mimik und Physiognomik*, p. 82) of the distension of the nostrils, namely, to allow free breathing whilst the mouth is closed and the teeth clenched, does not appear to be nearly so correct as that by Sir C. Bell, who attributes it to the sympathy (i.e. habitual co-action) of all the respiratory muscles. The nostrils of an angry man may be seen to become dilated, although his mouth is open. [Homer, according to Mr H. Jackson, notices the effect of rage upon the nostrils.]
† Mr Wedgwood, *On the Origin of Language*, 1866, p. 76. He also observes that the sound of hard breathing 'is represented by the syllables *puff*, *huff*, *whiff*, whence *a huff* is a fit of ill-temper'.

The paralysed lips then refuse to obey the will, 'and the voice sticks in the throat';* or it is rendered loud, harsh, and discordant. If there be much and rapid speaking, the mouth froths. The hair sometimes bristles; but I shall return to this subject in another chapter, when I treat of the mingled emotions of rage and terror. There is in most cases a strongly-marked frown on the forehead; for this follows from the sense of anything displeasing or difficult, together with concentration of the mind. But sometimes the brow, instead of being much contracted and lowered, remains smooth, with the glaring eyes kept widely open. The eyes are always bright, or may, as Homer expresses it, be like a blazing fire.[4] They are sometimes blood-shot, and are said to protrude from their sockets – the result, no doubt, of the head being gorged with blood, as shown by the veins being distended. According to Gratiolet,[5] the pupils are always contracted in rage, and I hear from Dr Crichton Browne that this is the case in the fierce delirium of meningitis; but the movements of the iris under the influence of the different emotions is a very obscure subject.

Shakespeare sums up the chief characteristics of rage as follows:

> 'In peace there's nothing so becomes a man,
> As modest stillness and humility;
> But when the blast of war blows in our ears,
> Then imitate the action of the tiger:
> Stiffen the sinews, summon up the blood,
>
> Then lend the eye a terrible aspect;
> Now set the teeth, and stretch the nostril wide,
> Hold hard the breath, and bend up every spirit
> To his full height! On, on, you noblest English.'
>
> *Henry V*, iii, 1

In my study of a preliterate people in the highlands of Papua New Guinea, I asked the men to show me what they would do if they were angry and about to attack

---

* Sir C. Bell (*Anatomy of Expression*, p. 95) has some excellent remarks on the expression of rage. [For an interesting case of temporary aphasia produced by rage, see Tuke's *Influence of the Mind on the Body*, 1872, p. 223.]

another man. They pressed their lips together. This fits Darwin's suggestion. When I asked them to show me what they would do if they were angry at a woman or child, but would not attack, they then showed me the open square-mouth anger. I found the reverse pattern in Americans, although what I asked them to do was slightly different. When asked to show uncontrolled anger, middle-class Americans showed the square-mouth anger as if shouting; to show controlled anger, they pressed their lips together. I believe the difference is due to what follows in uncontrolled anger for these two groups: for the New Guineans it is physical attack, for the Americans it is shouting.

The lips are sometimes protruded during rage in a manner, the meaning of which I do not understand, unless it depends on our descent from some ape-like animal. Instances have been observed, not only with Europeans, but with the Australians and Hindoos. The lips, however, are much more commonly retracted, the grinning or clenched teeth being thus exposed. This has been noticed by almost every one who has written on expression.* The appearance is as if the teeth were uncovered, ready for seizing or tearing an enemy, though there may be no intention of acting in this manner. Mr Dyson Lacy has seen this grinning expression with the Australians, when quarrelling, and so has Gaika with the Kafirs of South Africa.† Dickens,[6] in speaking of an atrocious

---

* Sir C. Bell, *Anatomy of Expression*, p. 177. Gratiolet (*De la Phys.*, p. 369) says, 'les dents se découvrent, et imitent symboliquement l'action de déchirer et de mordre'. ['the teeth are bared, and imitate symbolically the action of tearing and biting'.] If, instead of using the vague term *symboliquement*, Gratiolet had said that the action was a remnant of a habit acquired during primeval times when our semi-human progenitors fought together with their teeth, like gorillas and orangs at the present day, he would have been more intelligible. Dr Piderit (*Mimik*, etc., p. 82) also speaks of the retraction of the upper lip during rage. In an engraving of one of Hogarth's wonderful pictures [Fig. 21], passion is represented in the plainest manner by the open glaring eyes, frowning forehead, and exposed grinning teeth.
† [Dr Comrie (*Journal of Anthropological Institute*, vol. vi, p. 108) describes the natives of New Guinea as showing their canine teeth and spitting when angry.]

Fig. 21. [William Hogarth, *Rake's Progress*, Plate I, 1735 (Fitzwilliam Museum). Phillip Prodger believes this is probably the Hogarth picture Darwin describes in the first footnote on p. 238.]

murderer who had just been caught, and was surrounded by a furious mob, describes 'the people as jumping up one behind another, snarling with their teeth, and making at him like wild beasts'. Everyone who has had much to do with young children must have seen how naturally they take to biting, when in a passion. It seems as instinctive in them as in young crocodiles, who snap their little jaws as soon as they emerge from the egg.

A grinning expression and the protrusion of the lips appear sometimes to go together. A close observer says that he has seen many instances of intense hatred (which can hardly be distinguished from rage, more or less expressed) in Orientals, and once in an elderly English woman. In all these cases there 'was a grin, not a scowl – the lips lengthening, the cheeks settling downwards, the eyes half closed, whilst the brow remained perfectly calm'.[7]

The word *grin* has two meanings: to draw back the lips exposing the teeth; and, to smile. In Old English, 'grin' meant a grimace of pleasure or displeasure. Darwin is probably using the word grin in the first meaning, just to describe the exposure of the teeth, without implying that it is related to smiling.

This retraction of the lips and uncovering of the teeth during paroxysms of rage, as if to bite the offender, is so remarkable, considering how seldom the teeth are used by men in fighting, that I enquired from Dr J. Crichton Browne whether the habit was common in the insane whose passions are unbridled. He informs me that he has repeatedly observed it both with the insane and idiotic, and has given me the following illustrations:

Shortly before receiving my letter, he witnessed an uncontrollable outbreak of anger and delusive jealousy in an insane lady. At first she vituperated her husband, and whilst doing so foamed at the mouth. Next she approached close to him with compressed lips, and a virulent set frown. Then she drew back her lips, especially the corners of the upper lip, and showed her teeth, at the same time aiming a vicious blow at him. A second case is that of an old soldier, who, when he is requested to conform to the rules of the establishment, gives way to discontent, terminating in fury. He commonly begins by asking Dr Browne whether he is not ashamed to treat him in such a manner. He then swears and blasphemes, paces up and down, tosses his arms widely about, and menaces any one near him. At last, as his exasperation culminates, he rushes up towards Dr Browne with a peculiar sidelong movement, shaking his doubled fist, and threatening destruction. Then his upper lip may be seen to be raised, especially at the corners, so that his huge canine teeth are exhibited. He hisses forth his curses through his set teeth, and his whole expression assumes the character of extreme ferocity. A similar description is applicable to another man, excepting that he generally foams at the mouth and spits, dancing and jumping about in a strange rapid manner, shrieking out his maledictions in a shrill falsetto voice.

Dr Browne also informs me of the case of an epileptic idiot, incapable of independent movements, and who spends the whole day in playing with some toys; but his temper is morose and easily roused into fierceness. When any one touches his toys, he slowly raises his head from its natural downward position, and fixes his eyes on the offender, with a tardy yet angry scowl. If the annoyance be repeated, he draws back his thick lips and reveals a prominent row of hideous fangs (large canines being especially noticeable), and then makes a quick and cruel clutch with his open hand at the offending person. The rapidity of this clutch, as Dr Browne remarks, is marvellous in a being ordinarily so torpid that he takes about fifteen seconds, when attracted by any noise, to turn his head from one side to the other. If when thus incensed, a handkerchief, book, or other article, be placed into his hands, he drags it to his mouth and bites it. Mr Nicol has likewise described to me two cases of insane patients, whose lips are retracted during paroxysms of rage.

Dr Maudsley, after detailing various strange animal-like traits in idiots, asks whether these are not due to the reappearance of primitive instincts – 'a faint echo from a far-distant past, testifying to a kinship which man has almost outgrown'. He adds, that as every human brain passes, in the course of its development, through the same stages as those occurring in the lower vertebrate animals, and as the brain of an idiot is in arrested condition, we may presume that it 'will manifest its most primitive functions, and no higher functions'. Dr Maudsley thinks that the same view may be extended to the brain in its degenerated condition in some insane patients: and asks, whence come 'the savage snarl, the destructive disposition, the obscene language, the wild howl, the offensive habits, displayed by some of the insane? Why should a human being, deprived of his reason, ever become so brutal in character, as some do, unless he has the brute nature within him?'[8] The question must, as it would appear, be answered in the affirmative.

*

Anger, indignation. These states of the mind differ from rage only in degree, and there is no marked distinction in their character-istic signs. Under moderate anger the action of the heart is a little increased, the colour heightened, and the eyes become bright. The respiration is likewise a little hurried; and as all the muscles serving for this function act in association, the wings of the nostrils are somewhat raised to allow of a free indraught of air; and this is a highly characteristic sign of indignation. The mouth is commonly compressed, and there is almost always a frown on the brow. Instead of the frantic gestures of extreme rage, an indignant man unconsciously throws himself into an attitude ready for attacking or striking his enemy, whom he will perhaps scan from head to foot in defiance. He carries his head erect, with his chest well expanded, and the feet planted firmly on the ground. He holds his arms in various positions, with one or both elbows squared, or with the arms rigidly suspended by his sides. With Europeans the fists are commonly clenched.* The figures 1 and 2 in Plate V are fairly good representations of men simulating indignation. Any one may see in a mirror, if he will vividly imagine that he has been insulted and demands an explanation in an angry tone of voice, that he suddenly and unconsciously throws himself into some such attitude.

Rage, anger, and indignation are exhibited in nearly the same manner throughout the world: and the following descriptions may be worth giving as evidence of this, and as illustrations of some of the foregoing remarks. There is, however, an exception with respect to clenching the fists, which seems confined chiefly to the men who fight with their fists. With the Australians only one of my informants has seen the fists clenched. All agree about the body being held erect; and all, with two exceptions, state that the brows are heavily contracted. Some of them allude to the firmly-compressed mouth, the distended nostrils, and flashing

* Le Brun, in his well-known *Conférence sur L'Expression* (*La Physionomie*, by Lavater, edit. of 1820, vol. ix, p. 268), remarks that anger is expressed by the clenching of the fists. See, to same effect, Huschke, *Mimices et Physiognomices, Fragmentum Physiologicum*, 1824, p. 20. Also Sir C. Bell, *Anatomy of Expression*, p. 219.

PLATE V

eyes. According to the Rev. Mr Taplin, rage, with the Australians, is expressed by the lips being protruded, the eyes being widely open; and in the case of the women by their dancing about and casting dust into the air. Another observer speaks of the native men, when enraged, throwing their arms wildly about.

I have received similar accounts, except as to the clenching of the fists, in regard to the Malays of the Malacca peninsula, the Abyssinians and the natives of South Africa. So it is with Dakota Indians of North America; and, according to Mr Matthews, they then hold their heads erect, frown, and often stalk away with long strides. Mr Bridges states that the Fuegians, when enraged, frequently stamp on the ground, walk distractedly about, sometimes cry and grow pale. The Rev. Mr Stack watched a New Zealand man and woman quarrelling, and made the following entry in his note-book: 'Eyes dilated, body swayed violently backwards and forwards, head inclined forwards, fists clenched, now thrown behind the body, now directed towards each other's faces.' Mr Swinhoe says that my description agrees with what he has seen of the Chinese, excepting that an angry man generally inclines his body towards his antagonist, and pointing at him pours forth a volley of abuse.

Lastly, with respect to the natives of India, Mr J. Scott has sent me a full description of their gestures and expressions when enraged. Two low-caste Bengalees disputed about a loan. At first they were calm, but soon grew furious and poured forth the grossest abuse on each other's relations and progenitors for many generations past. Their gestures were very different from those of Europeans; for though their chests were expanded and shoulders squared, their arms remained rigidly suspended, with the elbows turned inwards and the hands alternately clenched and opened. Their shoulders were often raised high, and then again lowered. They looked fiercely at each other from under their lowered and strongly wrinkled brows, and their protruded lips were firmly closed. They approached each other, with heads and necks stretched forwards, and pushed, scratched, and grasped at each other. This protrusion of the head and body seems a common gesture with the enraged; and I have noticed it with degraded English women whilst quarrelling violently in the streets. In such cases it may be presumed that neither party expects to receive a blow from the other.*

A Bengalee employed in the Botanic Gardens was accused, in the presence of Mr Scott, by the native overseer, of having stolen a valuable plant. He listened silently and scornfully to the accusation; his attitude erect, chest expanded, mouth closed, lips protruding, eyes firmly set and penetrating. He then defiantly maintained his innocence, with upraised and clenched hands, his head now being pushed forwards, with the eyes widely open and eyebrows raised. Mr Scott also watched two Mechis, in Sikhim,

---

* ['May not the protruding of the head and body towards the offender by the enraged be a remnant of attacking an enemy with the teeth?' – Note by C. Darwin.

H. N. Moseley (*J. Anthropolog. Institute*, vol. vi, 1876–7) gives a good account of an Admiralty Islander in a 'furious rage'; he describes the man's head as 'lowered and jerked towards the object of his wrath as if he meant to attack him with his teeth'.]

quarrelling about their share of payment. They soon got into a furious passion, and then their bodies became less erect, with their heads pushed forwards; they made grimaces at each other; their shoulders were raised; their arms rigidly bent inwards at the elbows, and their hands spasmodically closed, but not properly clenched. They continually approached and retreated from each other, and often raised their arms as if to strike, but their hands were open, and no blow was given. Mr Scott made similar observations on the Lepchas whom he often saw quarrelling, and he noticed that they kept their arms rigid and almost parallel to their bodies, with the hands pushed somewhat backwards and partially closed, but not clenched.

Sneering, defiance: uncovering the canine tooth on one side. The expression which I wish here to consider differs but little from that already described, when the lips are retracted and the grinning teeth exposed. The difference consists solely in the upper lip being retracted in such a manner that the canine tooth on one side of the face alone is shown; the face itself being generally a little upturned and half everted from the person causing offence. The other signs of rage are not necessarily present. The expression may occasionally be observed in a person who sneers at or defies another, though there may be no real anger; as when any one is playfully accused of some fault, and answers, 'I scorn the imputation'. The expression is not a common one, but I have seen it exhibited with perfect distinctness by a lady who was being quizzed by another person. It was described by Parsons as long ago as 1746, with an engraving, showing the uncovered canine on one side.[9] Mr Rejlander, without my having made any allusion to the subject, asked me whether I had ever noticed this expression, as he had been much struck by it. He has photographed for me (Fig. 22) a lady, who sometimes unintentionally displays the canine on one side, and who can do so voluntarily with unusual distinctness.

The expression of a half-playful sneer graduates into one of great ferocity when, together with a heavily frowning brow and fierce eye, the canine tooth is exposed. A Bengalee boy was

Fig. 22. [Darwin's photographer Rejlander used his wife as the model for this picture.[C51] Rejlander himself appears in the next plate, in Figures 2 and 3 and again in Plate 7.]

accused before Mr Scott of some misdeed. The delinquent did not dare to give vent to his wrath in words, but it was plainly shown on his countenance, sometimes by a defiant frown, and sometimes 'by a thoroughly canine snarl'. When this was exhibited, 'the corner of the lip over the eye-tooth, which happened in the case to be large and projecting, was raised on the side of his accuser, a strong frown being still retained on the brow'. Sir C. Bell states* that the actor Cooke could express the most determined hate 'when with the oblique cast of his eyes he drew up the outer part of the upper lip, and discovered a sharp angular tooth'.

The uncovering the canine tooth is the result of a double movement. The angle or corner of the mouth is drawn a little backwards, and at the same time a muscle which runs parallel to and near the nose draws up the outer part of the upper lip, and

---

* *Anatomy of Expression*, p. 136. Sir C. Bell calls (p. 131) the muscles which uncover the canines the *snarling muscles*.

exposes the canine on this side of the face. The contraction of this muscle makes a distinct furrow on the cheek, and produces strong wrinkles under the eye, especially at its inner corner. The action is the same as that of a snarling dog; and a dog when pretending to fight often draws up the lip on one side alone, namely that facing his protagonist. Our word *sneer* is in fact the same as *snarl*, which was originally *snar*, the *l* 'being merely an element implying continuance of action'.[10]

I suspect that we see a trace of this same expression in what is called a derisive or sardonic smile. The lips are then kept joined or almost joined, but one corner of the mouth is retracted on the side towards the derided person; and this drawing back of a corner is part of a true sneer. Although some persons smile more on one side of their face than on the other, it is not easy to understand why in cases of derision the smile, if a real one, should so commonly be confined to one side. I have also on these occasions noticed a slight twitching of the muscle which draws up the outer part of the upper lip; and this movement, if fully carried out, would have uncovered the canine, and would have produced a true sneer.

Mr Bulmer, an Australian missionary in a remote part of Gipp's Land, says, in answer to my query about the uncovering of the canine on one side, 'I find that the natives in snarling at each other speak with the teeth closed, the upper lip drawn to one side, and a general angry expression of face; but they look direct at the person addressed.' Three other observers in Australia, one in Abyssinia, and one in China, answer my query on this head in the affirmative; but as the expression is rare, and as they enter into no details, I am afraid of implicitly trusting them. It is, however, by no means improbable that this animal-like expression may be more common with savages than with civilized races. Mr Geach is an observer who may be fully trusted, and he has observed it on one occasion in a Malay in the interior of Malacca. The Rev. S. O. Glenie answers, 'We have observed this expression with the natives of Ceylon, but not often.' Lastly, in North America, Dr Rothrock has seen it with some wild Indians, and often in a tribe adjoining the Atnahs.

Although the upper lip is certainly sometimes raised on one side alone in sneering at or defying any one, I do not know that this is always the case, for the face is commonly half averted, and the expression is often momentary. The movement being confined to one side may not be an essential part of the expression, but may depend on the proper muscles being incapable of movement excepting on one side. I asked four persons to endeavour to act voluntarily in this manner; two could expose the canine only on the left side, one only on the right side, and the fourth on neither side. Nevertheless it is by no means certain that these same persons, if defying any one in earnest, would not unconsciously have uncovered their canine tooth on one side, whichever it might be, towards the offender. For we have seen that some persons cannot voluntarily make their eyebrows oblique, yet instantly act in this manner when affected by any real, although most trifling, cause of distress. The power of voluntarily uncovering the canine on one side of the face being thus often wholly lost, indicates that it is a rarely used and almost abortive action. It is indeed a surprising fact that man should possess the power, or should exhibit any tendency to its use; for Mr Sutton has never noticed a snarling action in our nearest allies, namely the monkeys in the Zoological Gardens, and he is positive that the baboons, though furnished with great canines, never act thus, but uncover all their teeth when feeling savage and ready for an attack. Whether the adult anthropomorphous apes, in the males of whom the canines are much larger than in the females, uncover them when prepared to fight, is not known.

The expression here considered, whether that of a playful sneer or ferocious snarl, is one of the most curious which occurs in man. It reveals his animal descent; for no one, even if rolling on the ground in a deadly grapple with his enemy, and attempting to bite him, would try to use his canine teeth more than his other teeth. We may readily believe from our affinity to the anthropomorphous apes that our male semi-human progenitors possessed great canine teeth, and men are now occasionally born having them of unusually large size, with interspaces in the opposite jaw for their reception.[11] We may further suspect, notwithstanding that we have no support from analogy, that our semi-human progenitors uncovered their canine teeth when prepared for battle, as we still do when feeling ferocious, or when merely sneering at or defying some one, without any intention of making a real attack with our teeth.

CHAPTER XI

Disdain – Contempt – Disgust – Guilt – Pride, Etc. – Helplessness – Patience – Affirmation and Negation

Contempt, scorn and disdain, variously expressed – Derisive smile – Gestures expressive of contempt – Disgust – Guilt, deceit, pride, etc. – Helplessness or impotence – Patience – Obstinacy – Shrugging the shoulders common to most of the races of man – Signs of affirmation and negation.

Scorn and disdain can hardly be distinguished from contempt, excepting that they imply a rather more angry frame of mind. Nor can they be clearly distinguished from the feelings discussed in the last chapter under the terms of sneering and defiance. Disgust is a sensation rather more distinct in its nature, and refers to something revolting, primarily in relation to the sense of taste, as actually perceived or vividly imagined; and secondarily to anything which causes a similar feeling, through the sense of smell, touch, and even of eyesight. Nevertheless, extreme contempt, or, as it is often called, loathing contempt, hardly differs from disgust. These several conditions of the mind are, therefore, nearly related; and each of them may be exhibited in many different ways. Some writers have insisted chiefly on one mode of expression, and others on a different mode. From this circumstance M. Lemoine has argued[1] that their descriptions are not trustworthy. But we shall immediately see that it is natural that the feelings which we have here to consider should be expressed in many different ways, inasmuch as various habitual actions serve equally well, through the principle of association, for their expression.

Scorn and disdain, as well as sneering and defiance, may be displayed by a slight uncovering of the canine tooth on one side of the face; and this movement appears to graduate into one closely like a smile. Or the smile or laugh may be real, although one of derision; and this implies that the offender is so insignificant that he excites only amusement; but the amusement is generally a pretence. Gaika in his answers to my queries remarks, that contempt is commonly shown by his countrymen, the Kafirs, by smiling; and the Rajah Brooke makes the same observation with respect to the Dyaks of Borneo. As laughter is primarily the expression of simple joy, very young children do not, I believe, ever laugh in derision.

The partial closure of the eyelids, as Duchenne* insists, or the turning away of the eyes or of the whole body, are likewise highly expressive of disdain. These actions seem to declare that the despised person is not worth looking at, or is disagreeable to behold. The accompanying photograph (Plate VI, Fig. 1) by Mr Rejlander, shows this form of disdain. It represents a young lady, who is supposed to be tearing up the photograph of a despised lover.†

---

* *Physionomie Humaine*, Album, légende viii, p. 35. Gratiolet also speaks (*De la Phys.*, 1865, p. 52) of the turning away of the eyes and the body.

† [Mr H. Holbeach (*St Paul's Magazine*, February, 1873, p. 202) suggests that when 'the head is lifted upwards and backwards in order to give the feeling of as much distance in the way of height as possible being placed between the despiser and the despised, the eyelids partake of the general movement, and the eyes are made to look *down* upon the object of contempt'.

Professor Cleland gives a similar explanation in his *Evolution, Expression and Sensation*, 1881, p. 54, where he writes, 'In haughtiness the upward head contrasts with the somewhat downward glance, indicating that it is the height pertaining to self which occupies the mind and which looks down on others.'

Cleland points out (p. 60) that the expression of contempt in Fig. 1, Plate 6, depends essentially on the opposition between the direction of the eyes and the turn of the head – the head being held up, and the eyes cast down. In proof of this he recommends an experiment (which I have found perfectly successful) – namely, to cover the neck of the woman in Plate VI with a piece of paper on which a figure is drawn in such a manner that the head appears to droop; the contempt now dies out, giving place to an expression which is 'serious and quiet', and, it may be added, somewhat melancholy.

In this connection, compare what is said in the text under *Pride*, p. 262.]

The most common method of expressing contempt is by movements about the nose, or round the mouth; but the latter movements, when strongly pronounced, indicate disgust. The nose may be slightly turned up, which apparently follows from the turning up of the upper lip; or the movement may be abbreviated into the mere wrinkling of the nose. The nose is often slightly contracted, so as to partly close the passage;* and this is commonly accompanied by a slight snort or [nasal] expiration. All these actions are the same with those which we employ when we perceive an offensive odour, and wish to exclude or repel it. In extreme cases, as Dr Piderit remarks,[†] we protrude and raise both lips, or the upper lip alone, so as to close the nostrils as by a valve, the nose being thus turned up. We seem thus to say to the despised person that he smells offensively,[‡] in nearly the same manner as we express to him by half-closing our eyelids, or turning away our faces, that he is not worth looking at. It must not, however, be supposed that such ideas actually pass through the mind when we exhibit our contempt; but as whenever we have perceived a disagreeable odour or seen a disagreeable sight, actions of this kind have been performed, they have become habitual or fixed, and are now employed under any analogous state of mind.

---

* Dr W. Ogle, in an interesting paper on the sense of smell (*Medico-Chirurgical Transactions*, vol. liii, p. 268), shows that when we wish to smell carefully, instead of taking one deep nasal inspiration, we draw in the air by a succession of rapid short sniffs. If 'the nostrils be watched during this process, it will be seen that, so far from dilating, they actually contract at each sniff. The contraction does not include the whole anterior opening, but only the posterior portion.' He then explains the cause of this movement. When, on the other hand, we wish to exclude any odour, the contraction, I presume, affects only the anterior part of the nostrils.

† *Mimik und Physiognomik*, pp. 84, 93. Gratiolet (ibid., p. 155) takes nearly the same view as Dr Piderit respecting the expression of contempt and disgust.

‡ Scorn implies a strong form of contempt; and one of the roots of the word 'scorn' means, according to Mr Wedgwood (*Dict. of English Etymology*, vol. iii, p. 125), ordure or dirt. A person who is scorned is treated like dirt.

PLATE VI

I

2

3

Our research[C52] identified a different, universal expression for contempt, in which one lip corner is tightened and stretched obliquely. Cocking the head backward and looking downward adds to this expression but is not necessary. It is worth noting that this is the only facial expression of emotion which is asymmetrical. Because of this and its late appearance developmentally, I had expected to find that it was not universal, but the evidence suggests it is. The raising of the upper lip which Darwin describes is more characteristic of disgust than contempt, although when it occurs on just one side of the face it can also signify contempt.

The American otolaryngologist Roger Crumley said that Darwin is wrong about what we do to exclude an offensive odor. The contraction of the nostrils is accomplished by the dilator alae nasalis muscle, which '. . . pulls the lateral edge of the nostril (ala) laterally, thus opening the nasal chamber'. The wrinkling of the nose, according to Crumley, '. . . is not a respiratory movement . . . It is true that raising both lips will help to, as he says, "close the nostrils as by a valve" '.

Various odd little gestures likewise indicate contempt; for instance, *snapping one's fingers*. This, as Mr Tylor remarks,[2] 'is not very intelligible as we generally see it; but when we notice the same sign made quite gently, as if rolling some tiny object away between finger and thumb, or the sign of flipping it away with the thumb-nail and forefinger, as usual and well-understood deaf-and-dumb gestures, denoting anything tiny, insignificant, contemptible, it seems as though we had exaggerated and conventionalized a perfectly natural action, so as to lose sight of its original meaning'. There is a curious mention of this gesture by Strabo.* Mr Washington Matthews informs me that, with the

* [In the *Letters of Chauncey Wright* (privately printed, Cambridge, Mass., 1878, p. 309) is some interesting information on this point, given on the authority of a modern Greek – Mr Sophocles, at that time Professor of Greek at Harvard. Chauncey Wright wrote: 'A gesture which I had never seen him [Mr Sophocles] use unreflectively, but which, as I have since learned, others have seen in him,

Dakota Indians of North America, contempt is shown not only by movements of the face, such as those above described, but 'conventionally, by the hand being closed and held near the breast, then, as the forearm is suddenly extended, the hand is opened and the fingers separated from each other. If the person at whose expense the sign is made is present, the hand is moved towards him, and the head sometimes averted from him.' This sudden extension and opening of the hand perhaps indicates the dropping or throwing away a valueless object.

The term 'disgust', in its simplest sense, means something offensive to the taste. It is curious how readily this feeling is excited by anything unusual in the appearance, odour, or nature of our food. In Tierra del Fuego a native touched with his finger some cold preserved meat which I was eating at our bivouac, and plainly showed utter disgust at its softness; whilst I felt utter disgust at my food being touched by a naked savage, though his hands did not appear to be dirty. A smear of soup on a man's beard looks disgusting, though there is of course nothing disgusting in the soup itself. I presume that this follows from the strong association in our minds between the sight of food, however circumstanced, and the idea of eating it.

The American psychologist Silvan Tomkins, who was one of the first theorists in modern times to develop a theory of emotion that recognized Darwin (Plutchik[C53] is the other), agrees that disgust primarily involves taste and movements around the mouth, and contempt concerns smell. Tomkins contrasted contempt, which is based on what he termed dissmell, with disgust, which is based on distaste.[C54]

---

he explained to me as the Eastern equivalent of snapping the fingers to express contempt, and more abstractly to express minuteness, and secondarily, nothing or negation – namely, touching the upper front teeth with the thumb nail, and then snapping it away, as if throwing away a bit of nail.'

It is possible that the phrase, 'Do you bite your thumb at us, sir?' in *Romeo and Juliet*, i, 1, refers to a similar gesture of contempt.]

As the sensation of disgust primarily arises in connection with the act of eating or tasting it, it is natural that its expression should consist chiefly in movements round the mouth. But as disgust also causes annoyance, it is generally accompanied by a frown, and often by gestures as if to push away or to guard oneself against the offensive object. In the two photographs (Figs 2 and 3, on Plate VI) Mr Rejlander has simulated this expression with some success. With respect to the face, moderate disgust is exhibited in various ways; by the mouth being widely opened, as if to let an offensive morsel drop out; by spitting; by blowing out of the protruded lips; or by a sound as of clearing the throat. Such guttural sounds are written *ach* or *ugh*; and their utterance is sometimes accompanied by a shudder, the arms being pressed close to the sides and the shoulders raised in the same manner as when horror is experienced.[3] Extreme disgust is expressed by movements round the mouth identical with those preparatory to the act of vomiting. The mouth is opened widely, with the upper lip strongly retracted, which wrinkles the sides of the nose, and with the lower lip protruded and everted as much as possible. The latter movement requires the contraction of the muscles which draw downwards the corners of the mouth.*

I disagree with Darwin about both the expression and the anatomy of disgust. There are two disgust expressions. Darwin described one, but not the best one – in terms of people of various cultures agreeing that disgust, not contempt, is being shown. In this disgust expression the nose is wrinkled, the nostrils raised, and the inner corners of the brow lowered. These actions are produced primarily by the *levator labii superioris alaeque nasi* muscle. The expression Darwin did describe, in which the upper lip is raised and the lower lip lowered, does signal disgust but not as clearly across cultures as the other. Darwin said this second expression produces nose wrinkling as well, but that is not so unless the two sets of actions

---

* Duchenne believes that in the eversion of the lower lip, the corners are drawn downwards by the *depressores anguli oris*. Henle (*Handbuch d. Anat. des Menschen*, 1858, vol. i, p. 151) concludes that this is effected by the *musculus quadratus menti*.

merge, which can also happen. Darwin is also incorrect about the lip corners being pulled down when the lower lip is lowered. These are two separate actions, produced by separate muscles (lower lip lowering by *depressor labii*, and lip corners pulled down by *triangularis*). In the second disgust expression, the lowering of the lower lip need not involve any pulling down of the lip corners, although this can happen.

It is remarkable how readily and instantly retching or actual vomiting is induced in some persons by the mere idea of having partaken of any unusual food, as of an animal which is not commonly eaten; although there is nothing in such food to cause the stomach to reject it. When vomiting results, as a reflex action, for some real cause – as from too rich food, or tainted meat, or from an emetic – it does not ensue immediately, but generally after a considerable interval of time. Therefore, to account for retching or vomiting being so quickly and easily excited by a mere idea, the suspicion arises that our progenitors must formerly have had the power (like that possessed by ruminants and some other animals) of voluntarily rejecting food which disagreed with them, or which they thought would disagree with them,* and now, though this power has been lost, as far as the will is concerned, it is called into involuntary action, through the force of a formerly well-established habit, whenever the mind revolts at the idea of having partaken of any kind of food, or at anything disgusting. This suspicion receives support from the fact, of which I am assured by Mr Sutton, that the monkeys in the Zoological Gardens often vomit whilst in perfect health, which looks as if the act were voluntary. We can see that as a man is able to

---

* [The medical attendant at the Ballymahon Workhouse (letter, 3 January, 1873) describes the case of an idiot, by name Patrick Walsh, who had the power of regurgitating food from his stomach.

The author received another, and apparently trustworthy, account of a Scotch youth who had the power of voluntarily bringing up his food; the action was not accompanied by any pain or uneasiness.

Mr Cupples states that bitches often vomit up food for their young when these have reached a certain age.]

communicate by language to his children and others, the know-ledge of the kinds of food to be avoided, he would have had little occasion to use the faculty of voluntary rejection; so that this power would tend to be lost through disuse.*

As the sense of smell is so intimately connected with that of taste, it is not surprising that an excessively bad odour should excite retching or vomiting in some persons, quite as readily as the thought of revolting food does; and that, as a further consequence, a moderately offensive odour should cause the vari-ous expressive movements of disgust. The tendency to retch from a fetid odour is immediately strengthened in a curious manner by some degree of habit, though soon lost by longer familiarity with the cause of offence and by voluntary restraint. For instance, I wished to clean the skeleton of a bird, which had not been sufficiently macerated, and the smell made my servant and myself (we not having had much experience in such work) retch so violently, that we were compelled to desist. During the previous days I had examined some other skeletons, which smelt slightly; yet the odour did not in the least affect me, but, subsequently for several days, whenever I handled these same skeletons, they made me retch.

From the answer received from my correspondents it appears that the various movements, which have now been described as expressing contempt and disgust, prevail throughout a large part of the world. Dr Rothrock, for instance, answers with a decided affirmative with respect to certain wild Indian tribes of North America. Crantz says that when a Greenlander denies anything with contempt or horror he turns up his nose, and gives a slight sound through it.[4] Mr Scott has sent me a graphic description of the face of a young Hindoo at the sight of castor-oil, which he was compelled occasionally to take. Mr Scott has also seen the same expression on the faces of high-caste natives who have approached close to some defiling object. Mr Bridges says that

* [From pencilled notes in the author's copy of Dr Tuke's *Influence of the Mind on the Body* (p. 88), it appears that Charles Darwin considered himself to have been in error referring retching to habit. He seems to have been convinced that it might be due simply to the effect of the imagination.]

the Fuegians 'express contempt by shooting out the lips* and hissing through them, and by turning up the nose'. The tendency either to snort through the nose, or to make a noise expressed by *ugh* or *ach*, is noticed by several of my correspondents.

Spitting seems an almost universal sign of contempt or disgust; and spitting obviously represents the rejection of anything offensive from the mouth. Shakespeare makes the Duke of Norfolk say, 'I spit at him – call him a slanderous coward and a villain.' So, again, Falstaff says, 'Tell thee what, Hal – if I tell thee a lie, spit in my face.' Leichhardt remarks that the Australians 'interrupted their speeches by spitting, and uttering a noise like pooh! pooh! apparently expressive of their disgust.' And Captain Burton speaks of certain negroes 'spitting with disgust upon the ground'.[5] Captain Speedy informs me that this is likewise the case with the Abyssinians. Mr Geach says that with the Malays of Malacca the expression of disgust 'answers to spitting from the mouth'; and with the Fuegians, according to Mr Bridges, 'to spit at one is the highest mark of contempt'.

I never saw disgust more plainly expressed than on the face of one of my infants at the age of five months, when, for the first time, some cold water, and again a month afterwards, when a piece of ripe cherry was put into his mouth. This was shown by the lips and whole mouth assuming a shape which allowed the contents to run or fall quickly out; the tongue being likewise protruded. These movements were accompanied by a little shudder. It was all the more comical, as I doubt whether the child felt real disgust – the eyes and forehead expressing much surprise and consideration. The protrusion of the tongue in letting a nasty object fall out of the mouth, may explain how it is that lolling out the tongue universally serves as a sign of contempt and hatred.†

We have now seen that scorn, disdain, contempt, and disgust are expressed in many different ways, by movements of the

---

* [Dr Comrie (*Journal of Anthropological Institute*, vol. vi, p. 108) says that the inhabitants of New Guinea express disgust by pouting or by an imitation of vomiting.]

† This is stated to be the case by Mr Tylor (*Early Hist. of Mankind*, 2nd edit., 1870, p. 52); and he adds, 'it is not clear why this should be so'.

features, and by various gestures; and that these are the same throughout the world. They all consist of actions representing the rejection or exclusion of some real object which we dislike or abhor, but which does not excite in us certain other strong emotions, such as rage or terror; and through the force of habit and association similar actions are performed, whenever any analogous sensation arises in our minds.

Jealousy, *envy*, *avarice*, *revenge*, *suspicion*, *deceit*, *slyness*, *guilt*, *vanity*, *conceit*, *ambition*, *pride*, *humility*, *etc*. It is doubtful whether the greater number of the above complex states of mind are revealed by any fixed expression, sufficiently distinct to be described or delineated. When Shakespeare speaks of envy as *lean-faced*, or *black*, or *pale*, and jealousy as '*the green-eyed monster*'; and when Spenser describes suspicion as '*foul ill-favoured, and grim*', they must have felt this difficulty. Nevertheless, the above feelings – at least many of them – can be detected by the eye; for instance, conceit; but we are often guided in a much greater degree than we suppose by our previous knowledge of the persons or circumstances.

I agree with Darwin that there is no facial expression for jealousy (see following paragraph). I do not consider it to be an elemental emotion, such as anger, fear or disgust, but an emotion complex or plot. With jealousy we know there are three persons involved, and we know about the history of their relationships with one another.

This is far more information than we have if we are told someone is angry; we would not even know if anger were directed at a person, for one can become angry at the weather. In jealousy the various actors are likely to experience one or another of the elemental emotions: the person who fears being supplanted may feel anger or sadness at the loss, the person who is thought to be straying may feel anger or fear or disgust towards the jealous person, and so on. Sexual jealousy is what we most often think of, but there can be jealousy involving rivalry and loss which is not sexual. Much recent research suggests that in sexual jealousy males and females experience quite different emotions.[C55]

___

My correspondents almost unanimously answer in the affirmative to my query whether the expression of guilt and deceit can be recognized among the various races of man;* and I have confidence in their answers, as they generally deny that jealousy can thus be recognized. In the cases in which details are given, the eyes are almost always referred to. The guilty man is said to avoid looking at his accuser, or to give him stolen looks. The eyes are said 'to be turned askant', or 'to waver from side to side', or 'the eyelids to be lowered and partly closed'. This latter remark is made by Mr Hagenauer with respect to the Australians, and by Gaika with respect to the Kafirs. The restless movements of the eyes apparently follow, as will be explained when we treat of blushing, from the guilty man not enduring to meet the gaze of his accuser. I may add, that I have observed a guilty expression, without a shade of fear, in some of my own children at a very early age. In one instance the expression was unmistakably clear in a child two years and seven months old, and led to the detection of his little crime. It was shown, as I record in my notes made at the time, by an unnatural brightness in the eyes, and by an odd, affected manner, impossible to describe.

___

Searching through Darwin's notebooks on his children, I found the following description when his son, Willy, was the age when Darwin said this mishap occurred which I reproduce here, complete with its infelicities of expression: 'About a fortnight ago, I met Willy coming out of Dining Room, with an unnatural brightness of eye and an odd affected manner, so odd that I turned back to see if anyone was hiding behind the door – I then found out by marks that he had been taking the powdered

___

* [According to Sir Henry Maine, the natives of India when giving evidence are able to control the expression of their faces so that no indication is given as to whether they are speaking the truth or not; but they cannot control the toes, the contortions of which often reveal the fact that the witness is lying.]

sugar which he had once or twice he [sic] had been told he ought not to do – Now these singular grimaces and expressions not to be overlooked, certainly was not fear, for he was not afraid, but a kind of conscience. This day I met him coming out of dining room with his pianofore [sic] folded up carefully and he eyeing it – I asked him what he had got there: he said "nothing" looking all the while to see that his pianofor [sic] was well folded and as I came nearer he cried "go away" "Doddy [sic] going to send" "go away" – from his odd manner I determined to see what was concealed when I found he had stained with yellow pickle his pianofore, when taking pickle, like he had done sugar – Here was natural acting and deceit.' Michael Ghiselin pointed out that Darwin tells much of this story in 'A Biographical Sketch of an Infant', published in *Mind*, No. 7, July 1877, 285–94. In that account the grammar is, of course, better, but there is less detail about the incident. Darwin does say that 'Doddy' was William's nickname for himself.

Slyness is also, I believe, exhibited chiefly by movements about the eyes; for these are less under the control of the will, owing to the force of long-continued habit, than are the movements of the body. Mr Herbert Spencer remarks,[6] 'When there is a desire to see something on one side of the visual field without being supposed to see it, the tendency is to check the conspicuous movement of the head, and to make the required adjustment entirely with the eyes; which are, therefore, drawn very much to one side. Hence, when the eyes are turned to one side, while the face is not turned to the same side, we get the natural language of what is called slyness.'*

Of all the above-named complex emotions, pride, perhaps, is the most plainly expressed. A proud man exhibits his sense of

---

* [Professor Cleland (*Evolution, Expression and Sensation*, 1881, p. 55) points out that concealment or deceit is expressed by the face being directed downwards, while the eyes are turned upwards. 'The culprit sheltering himself by a lie ... hangs his head over his secret, while he steals upwards glances to see the effect which he distrusts.']

Fig. 23. [This photograph did not appear in the earlier editions of *Expression*]

superiority over others by holding his head and body erect. He is haughty (*haut*), or high, and makes himself appear as large as possible; so that metaphorically he is said to be swollen or puffed up with pride. A peacock or a turkey-cock strutting about with puffed-up feathers, is sometimes said to be an emblem of pride.[7] The arrogant man looks down on others, and with lowered eyelids hardly condescends to see them; or he may show his contempt by slight movements, such as those before described, about the nostrils or lips. Hence the muscle which everts the lower lip has been called the *musculus superbus*. In some photographs of patients affected by a monomania of pride, sent me by Dr Crichton Browne, the head and body were held erect, and the mouth firmly closed. This latter action, expressive of decision, follows, I presume, from the proud man feeling perfect self-confidence in himself. The whole expression of pride stands in direct

PLATE VII

I

2

antithesis to that of humility; so that nothing need here be said of the latter state of mind.

*Helplessness, impotence: shrugging the shoulders.** When a man wishes to show that he cannot do something, or prevent something being done, he often raises with a quick movement both shoulders. At the same time, if the whole gesture is completed, he bends his elbows closely inwards, raises his open hands, turning them outwards, with the fingers separated. The head is often thrown a little on one side; the eyebrows are elevated, and this causes wrinkles across the forehead. The mouth is generally opened. I may mention, in order to show how unconsciously the

* [Bulwer (*Pathomyotomia*, 1649, p. 85) describes shrugging the shoulders as follows: 'They who like not a thing that has happened for which there is no remedy but patience, or they who are taken tardy in the fact, and can no otherwise defend themselves but by a tacite confession; they who flatter, admire, doubt, deny, or are illiberall, or would frame an excuse, are wont to shrink the head and contracted neck between the shoulders.']

3

4

PLATE VII [Figures 1 and 2 appeared earlier in Plate V, on page 242 adjacent to the place where Darwin first described these two expressions. They are reproduced again here to allow the reader to more easily follow Darwin's description on page 272 of how the figures on the right (3 & 4) might be responding to the figures on the left. The layout of the photographs is as it appeared in the First Edition.]

features are thus acted on, that though I had often intentionally shrugged my shoulders to observe how my arms were placed, I was not at all aware that my eyebrows were raised and mouth opened, until I looked at myself in a glass; and since then I have noticed the same movements in the faces of others. In the accompanying Plate VII, Figs 3 and 4, Mr Rejlander has successfully acted the gesture of shrugging the shoulders.

Englishmen are much less demonstrative than the men of most other European nations, and they shrug their shoulders far less frequently and energetically than Frenchmen or Italians do. The gesture varies in all degrees from the complex movement, just described, to only a momentary and scarcely perceptible raising of both shoulders; or, as I have noticed in a lady sitting in an arm-chair, to the mere turning slightly outwards of the open hands with separated fingers. I have never seen very young English children shrug their shoulders, but the following case was observed with care by a medical professor and excellent observer, and has been communicated to me by him. The father of this gentleman was a Parisian, and his mother a Scotch lady. His wife is of British extraction on both sides, and my informant does not believe that she ever shrugged her shoulders in her life. His children have been reared in England, and the nursemaid is a thorough Englishwoman, who has never been seen to shrug her shoulders. Now, his eldest daughter was observed to shrug her shoulders at the age of between sixteen and eighteen months; mother exclaiming at the time, 'Look at the little French girl shrugging her shoulders!' At first she often acted thus, sometimes throwing her head a little backwards and on one side, but she did not, as far as was observed, move her elbows and hands in the usual manner. The habit gradually wore away, and now, when she is a little over four years old, she is never seen to act thus. The father is told that he sometimes shrugs his shoulders, especially when arguing with any one; but it is extremely improbable that his daughter should have imitated him at so early an age; for, as he remarks, she could not possibly have often seen this gesture in him. Moreover, if the habit had been acquired through imitation, it is not probable that it would so soon have been spontaneously discontinued by this child, and, as we shall immediately see, by a second child, though the father still lived with his family. This little girl, it may be added, resembles her Parisian grandfather in countenance to an almost absurd degree. She also presents another and very curious resemblance to him, namely by practising a singular trick. When she impatiently wants something, she holds out her little hand, and rapidly rubs the thumb against the index and middle finger: now this same trick was frequently performed under the same circumstances by her grandfather.

This gentleman's second daughter also shrugged her shoulders before the age of eighteen months, and afterwards discontinued the habit. It is of course possible that she may have imitated her elder sister; but she continued it after her sister had lost the habit. She at first resembled her Parisian grandfather in a less degree than did her sister at the same age, but now in a greater degree. She likewise practises to the present time the peculiar habit of rubbing together, when impatient, her thumb and two of her fingers.

In this latter case we have a good instance, like those given in a former chapter, of the inheritance of a trick or gesture; for no one, I presume, will attribute to mere coincidence so peculiar a habit as this, which was common to the grandfather and his two grandchildren who had never seen him.

Considering all the circumstances with reference to these children shrugging their shoulders, it can hardly be doubted that they have inherited the habit from their French progenitors, although they have only one quarter French blood in their veins, and although their grandfather did not often shrug his shoulders. There is nothing very unusual, though the fact is interesting, in these children having gained by inheritance a habit during early youth, and then discontinuing it; for it is of frequent occurrence with many kinds of animals that certain characters are retained for a period by the young, and are then lost.

As it appeared to me at one time improbable in a high degree that so complex a gesture as shrugging the shoulders, together with the accompanying movements, should be innate, I was anxious to ascertain whether the blind and deaf Laura Bridgman, who could not have learnt the habit by imitation, practised it. And I have heard through Dr Innes, from a lady who has lately had charge of her, that she does shrug her shoulders, turn in her elbows, and raise her eyebrows in the same manner as other people, and under the same circumstances. I was also anxious to learn whether this gesture was practised by the various races of man, especially by those who have never had much intercourse with Europeans. We shall see that they act in this manner; but it appears that the gesture is sometimes confined to merely raising or shrugging the shoulders, without the other movements.

Mr Scott has frequently seen this gesture in the Bengalees and Dhangars (the latter constituting a distinct race) who are employed in the Botanic Garden at Calcutta; when, for instance, they have declared that they could not do some work, such as lifting a heavy weight. He ordered a Bengalee to climb a lofty tree; but the man, with a shrug of his shoulders and a lateral shake of his head, said he could not. Mr Scott, knowing that the man was lazy, thought he could, and insisted on his trying. His face now became pale, his arms dropped to his sides, his mouth and eyes were widely opened, and again surveying the tree, he looked askant at Mr Scott, shrugged his shoulders, inverted his elbows, extended his open hands, and with a few quick lateral shakes of the head declared his inability. Mr H. Erskine has likewise seen the natives of India shrugging their shoulders; but he has never seen the elbows turned so much inwards as with us; and whilst shrugging their shoulders they sometimes lay their uncrossed hands on their breasts.*

With the wild Malays of the interior of Malacca, and with the Bugis (true Malays, though speaking a different language), Mr Geach has often seen this gesture. I presume that it is complete, as, in answer to my query descriptive of the movements of the shoulders, arms, hands, and face, Mr Geach remarks, 'it is performed in a beautiful style'. I have lost an extract from a scientific voyage, in which shrugging the shoulders by some natives (Micronesians) of the Caroline Archipelago in the Pacific Ocean, was well described. Captain Speedy informs me that the Abyssinians shrug their shoulders, but enters into no details. Mrs Asa Gray saw an Arab dragoman in Alexandria acting exactly as described in my query, when an old gentleman, on whom he attended, would not go in the proper direction which had been pointed out to him.

Mr Washington Matthews says, in reference to the wild Indian tribes of the western parts of the United States, 'I have on a few occasions detected men using a slight apologetic shrug, but the rest of the demonstration which you describe I have not

---

* ['A Bengalee', writing in the *Calcutta Englishman* (quoted in *Nature*, 6 March, 1873, p. 351), states that he has not noticed shrugging the shoulders among the unsophisticated Bengalee, although he has observed it among his countrymen who have adopted English ideas and habits.]

witnessed.' Fritz Müller informs me that he has seen the negroes in Brazil shrugging their shoulders,* but it is of course possible that they may have learnt to do so by imitating the Portuguese. Mrs Barber has never seen this gesture with the Kafirs of South Africa; and Gaika, judging from his answer, did not even understand what was meant by my description. Mr Swinhoe is also doubtful about the Chinese;† but he has seen them, under the circumstances which would make us shrug our shoulders, press their right elbow against their side, raise their eyebrows, lift up their hand with the palm directed towards the person addressed, and shake it from right to left. Lastly, with respect to the Australians, four of my informants answer by a simple negative, and one by a simple affirmative. Mr Bunnett, who has had excellent opportunities for observation on the borders of the Colony of Victoria, also answers by a 'yes', adding that the gesture is performed 'in a more subdued and less demonstrative manner than is the case with civilized nations'. This circumstance may account for its not having been noticed by four of my informants.

These statements, relating to Europeans, Hindoos, the hill-tribes of India, Malays, Micronesians, Abyssinians, Arabs, Negroes, Indians of North America, and apparently to the Australians – many of these natives having had scarcely any intercourse with Europeans – are sufficient to show that shrugging the shoulders, accompanied in some cases by the other proper movements, is a gesture natural to mankind.

This gesture implies an unintentional or unavoidable action on our own part, or one that we cannot perform; or an action performed by another person which we cannot prevent. It accompanies such speeches as, 'It was not my fault'; 'It is impossible for me to grant this favour'; 'He must follow his own course, I cannot stop him.' Shrugging the shoulders likewise expresses patience, or the absence of any intention to resist. Hence the

---

* [Mr Winwood Reade has also seen this gesture in negroes (letter, 5 November, 1872).]

† [In a letter of 26 March, 1873, Mr Swinhoe states with certainty that he has never seen a Chinese shrug his shoulders; the hands are outspread, but the elbows are kept away from the sides.]

muscles which raise the shoulders are sometimes called, as I have been informed by an artist, 'the patience muscles'. Shylock the Jew, says,

> 'Signor Antonio, many a time and oft
> In the Rialto have you rated me
> About my moneys and my usances;
> Still have I borne it with a patient shrug.'

Merchant of Venice, i, 3.

Sir C. Bell has given[8] a life-like figure of a man, who is shrinking back from some terrible danger, and is on the point of screaming out in abject terror. He is represented with his shoulders lifted up almost to his ears; and this at once declares that there is no thought of resistance.

As shrugging the shoulders generally implies 'I cannot do this or that,' so by a slight change, it sometimes implies 'I won't do it.' The movement then expresses a dogged determination not to act. Olmsted describes[9] an Indian in Texas as giving a great shrug to his shoulders, when he was informed that a party of men were Germans and not Americans, thus expressing that he would have nothing to do with them. Sulky and obstinate children may be seen with both their shoulders raised high up; but this movement is not associated with the others which generally accompany a true shrug. An excellent observer,[10] in describing a young man who was determined not to yield to his father's desire, says, 'He thrust his hands deep down into his pockets, and set up his shoulders to his ears, which was a good warning that, come right or wrong, this rock should fly from its firm base as soon as Jack would; and that any remonstrance on the subject was purely futile. As soon as the son got his own way, he put his shoulders into their natural position.'

Resignation is sometimes shown by the open hands being placed, one over the other, on the lower part of the body. I should not have thought this little gesture worth even a passing notice, had not Dr W. Ogle remarked to me that he had two or three times observed it in patients who were preparing for operations under chloroform. They exhibited no great fear, but seemed to declare by this posture of their hands, that they had made up their minds, and were resigned to the inevitable.

We may now enquire why men in all parts of the world when they feel – whether or not they wish to show this feeling – that they cannot or will not do something, or will not resist something if done by another, shrug their shoulders, at the same time often bending in their elbows, showing the palms of their hands with extended fingers, often throwing their heads a little on one side, raising their eyebrows, and opening their mouths. These states of the mind are either simply passive, or show a determination not to act. None of the above movements are of the least service. The explanation lies, I cannot doubt, in the principle of unconscious antithesis.* This principle here seems to come into play as clearly as in the case of a dog, who, when feeling savage, puts himself in the proper attitude for attacking and for making himself appear terrible to his enemy; but as soon as he feels affectionate, throws his whole body into a directly opposite attitude, though this is of no direct use to him.

Our research has shown[C56] that when people are attempting to conceal 'that they cannot or will not do something', the shrug is different from a shrug when a person is not trying to conceal this message. When it is suppressed or repressed, only a fragment of the shrug appears (such as one shoulder or one hand), and it is usually brief. Although not everyone shows a shrug

---

* [M. Baudry suggested in a letter (4 December, 1872) that the shrugging of the shoulders is not to be explained by the principle of antithesis, that it is the natural gesture of one who receives a blow without resistance. I think, however, that the shrug of a schoolboy who is being threatened with a box on the ears is distinct from the apologetic shrug. The action of shrinking from unseen danger, as when a cricket ball is coming towards one from behind, and someone shouts 'Heads!' is of the same nature as the protective shrug. M. Baudry describes it as a gesture of tucking in ('faire rentrer') the head and neck. A somewhat similar shrug is familiar as an expression of suffering from cold. Here it is a conscious repetition of the attitude instinctively assumed to economize the heat of the body. M. Baudry also suggests that the open hands express defencelessness, as showing that the actor has no weapons.]

fragment, when it *is* shown, it almost always signifies some attempt to conceal.

Let it be observed how an indignant man, who resents, and will not submit to some injury, holds his head erect, squares his shoulders, and expands his chest. He often clenches his fists, and puts one or both arms in the proper position for attack or defence, with the muscles of his limbs rigid. He frowns – that is, he contracts and lowers his brows – and, being determined, closes his mouth. The actions and attitude of a helpless man are, in every one of these respects, exactly the reverse. In Plate VII we may imagine one of the figures on the left side to have just said, 'What do you mean by insulting me?' and one of the figures on the right side to answer, 'I really could not help it.' The helpless man unconsciously contracts the muscles of his forehead which are antagonistic to those that cause a frown, and thus raises his eyebrows; at the same time he relaxes the muscles about the mouth, so that the lower jaw drops. The antithesis is complete in every detail, not only in the movements of the features, but in the position of the limbs and in the attitude of the whole body, as may be seen in Plate VII. As the helpless or apologetic man often wishes to show his state of mind, he then acts in a conspicuous or demonstrative manner.

In accordance with the fact that squaring the elbows and clenching the fists are gestures by no means universal with the men of all races, when they feel indignant and are prepared to attack their enemy, so it appears that a helpless or apologetic frame of mind is expressed in many parts of the world by merely shrugging the shoulders, without turning inwards the elbows and opening the hands. The man or child who is obstinate, or one who is resigned to some great misfortune, has in neither case any idea of resistance by active means; and he expresses this state of mind, by simply keeping his shoulders raised; or he may possibly fold his arms across his breast.

Signs of affirmation or approval, and of negation or disapproval: nodding and shaking the head. I was curious to ascertain how far the common signs used by us in affirmation and negation were general throughout the world. These signs are indeed to a certain extent expressive of our feelings, as we give a vertical nod of approval with a smile to our children, when we approve of their conduct; and shake our heads laterally with a frown, when we disapprove. With infants, the first act of denial consists in refusing food; and I repeatedly noticed with my own infants, that they did so by withdrawing their heads laterally from the breast, or from anything offered them in a spoon. In accepting food and taking it into their mouths, they incline their heads forwards. Since making these observations I have been informed that the same idea had occurred to Charma.[11] It deserves notice that in accepting or taking food, there is only a single movement forward, and a single nod implies an affirmation. On the other hand, in refusing food, especially if it be pressed on them, children frequently move their heads several times from side to side, as we do in shaking our heads in negation. Moreover, in the case of refusal, the head is not rarely thrown backwards, or the mouth is closed, so that these movements might likewise come to serve as signs of negation. Mr Wedgwood remarks on this subject,[12] that 'when the voice is exerted with closed teeth or lips, it produces the sound of the letter *n* or *m*. Hence we may account for the use of the particle *ne* to signify negation, and possibly also of the Greek μη in the same sense.'

That these signs are innate or instinctive, at least with Anglo-Saxons, is rendered highly probable by the blind and deaf Laura Bridgman 'constantly accompanying her *yes* with the common affirmative nod, and her *no* with our negative shake of the head.' Had not Mr Lieber stated to the contrary,[13] I should have imagined that these gestures might have been acquired or learnt by her, considering her wonderful sense of touch and appreciation of the movements of others. With microcephalous idiots, who are so degraded that they never learn to speak, one of them is described by Vogt,[14] as answering, when asked whether he wished for more food or drink, by inclining or shaking his head. Schmalz, in his remarkable dissertation on the education of the deaf and dumb, as well as of children raised only one degree above idiocy, assumes that they can always both make and understand the common signs of affirmation and negation.[15]

Nevertheless if we look to the various races of man, these signs are not so universally employed as I should have expected; yet they seem too general to be ranked as altogether conventional or artificial. My informants assert that both signs are used by the Malays, by the natives of Ceylon, the Chinese, the Negroes of the Guinea coast, and, according to Gaika, by the Kafirs of South Africa, though with these latter people Mrs Barber has never seen a lateral shake used as a negative. With respect to the Australians, seven observers agree that a nod is given in affirmation; five agree about a lateral shake in negation, accompanied or not by some word; but Mr Dyson Lacy has never seen this latter sign in Queensland, and Mr Bulmer says that in Gipp's Land a negative is expressed by throwing the head a little backwards and putting out the tongue. At the northern extremity of the continent, near Torres Straits, the natives when uttering a negative 'don't shake the head with it, but holding up the right hand, shake it by turning it half round and back again two or three times'.*[16] The throwing back of the head with a cluck of the tongue† is said to be used as a negative by the modern Greeks and Turks, the latter people expressing *yes* by a movement like that made by us when we shake our heads.‡ The Abyssinians, as I am informed

* [According to H. N. Moseley (*J. Anthropolog. Institute*, vol. vi, 1876–7), the Admiralty Islanders universally express negation by striking the nose on one side with the extended forefinger.]

† [Professor Victor Carus states, in a letter, that this movement is the regular sign of negation among the Neapolitans and Sicilians.]

‡ F. Lieber, *On the Vocal Sounds*, etc., p. 11. Tylor, ibid., p. 53.

[There is some obscurity on this point. Chauncey Wright (see his *Letters*, edited by J. B. Thayer, privately printed, Cambridge, Mass., 1878, p. 310) quotes the opinion of Mr Sophocles, a native of Greece, and at that time teacher of Modern and Ancient Greek at Harvard University, that the Turks never express affirmation by a shake of the head. Mr Sophocles describes Turks listening to a story and gravely bowing their heads in token of approval and assent, and throwing their heads back if anything is said to which they cannot assent. Vesalius, quoted in Bulwer's *Pathomyotia*, 1649, speaks of 'most of your Cretans' as expressing negation by an upward nod.

Mr Sophocles has often seen Turks and other Orientals shake their heads in by Captain Speedy, express a negative by jerking the head to the right shoulder, together with a slight cluck, the mouth being closed; an affirmation is expressed by the head being thrown backwards and the eyebrows raised for an instant. The Tagals of Luzon, in the Philippine Archipelago, as I hear from Dr Adolf Meyer, when they say *yes*, also throw the head backward.* According to the Rajah Brooke, the Dyaks of Borneo express an affirmation by raising the eyebrows, and a negation by slightly contracting them, together with a peculiar look from the eyes. With the Arabs on the Nile, Professor and Mrs Asa Gray concluded that nodding in affirmation was rare, whilst shaking the head in negation was never used, and was not even understood by them. With the Esquimaux[17] a nod means *yes* and a wink *no*. The New Zealanders 'elevate the head and chin in place of nodding acquiescence'.[18]

With the Hindoos Mr H. Erskine concludes from enquiries made from experienced Europeans, and from native gentlemen, that the signs of affirmation and negation vary – a nod and a lateral shake being sometimes used as we do; but a negative is more commonly expressed by the head being thrown suddenly backwards and a little to one side, with a cluck of the tongue. What the meaning may be of this cluck of the tongue, which has been observed with various people, I cannot imagine. A native

---

anger or strong disapprobation. This gesture is a familiar one with ourselves, and Chauncey Wright gives several instances of its occurrence in the Bible. Thus: Matt. xxvii, 39, 'And they that passed by reviled Him, wagging their heads'; compare also Psalms xxii, 7, and cix, 25.

Mr Chauncey Wright quotes Mr James Russell Lowell, who supports what is said in the text, for he has noticed in Italy a shake of the head like our sign of negation, used in an affirmative sense.

Mr Chauncey Wright, in attempting to reconcile the conflicting evidence as to an affirmatory shake of the head, is led to make an elaborate theory founded on the peculiar oblique position, first on one side and then on the other, which the head assumes in deliberation, e.g. when an artist is examining his work. He believes that from this gesture a symbol of deliberative assent would arise which might be confused with the rotation of the head on a vertical axis – our sign of negation.]

* [According to Moseley (loc. cit.), both the Fijians and the Admiralty Islanders express affirmation by an upward nod.]

gentleman stated that affirmation is frequently shown by the head being thrown to the left. I asked Mr Scott to attend particularly to this point, and, after repeated observations, he believes that a vertical nod is not commonly used by the natives in affirmation, but that the head is first thrown backwards either to the left or right, and then jerked obliquely forwards only once. This movement would perhaps have been described by a less careful observer as a lateral shake. He also states that in negation the head is usually held nearly upright, and shaken several times.

Mr Bridges informs me that the Fuegians nod their heads vertically in affirmation, and shake them laterally in denial. With the wild Indians of North America, according to Mr Washington Matthews, nodding and shaking the head have been learnt from Europeans, and are not naturally employed. They express affirmation 'by describing with the hand (all the fingers except the index being flexed) a curve downwards and outwards from the body, whilst negation is expressed by moving the open hand outwards, with the palm facing inwards'. Other observers state that the sign of affirmation with these Indians is the forefinger being raised, and then lowered and pointed to the ground, or the hand is waved straight forward from the face; and that the sign of negation is the finger or whole hand shaken from side to side.* This latter movement probably represents in all cases the lateral shaking of the head. The Italians are said in like manner to move the lifted finger from right to left in negation, as indeed we English sometimes do.

On the whole we find considerable diversity in the signs of affirmation and negation in the different races of man. With respect to negation, if we admit that the shaking of the finger or hand from side to side is symbolic of the lateral movement of the head; and if we admit that the sudden backward movement of the head represents one of the actions often practised by young children in refusing food, then there is much uniformity through-

* Lubbock, *The Origin of Civilization*, 1870, p. 277. Tylor, ibid., p. 38. Lieber (ibid., p. 11) remarks on the negative of the Italians. [Mr H. P. Lee (letter 17 January, 1873) describes a lateral shake of the index finger or of the whole hand as a common sign of negation in Japan.]

out the world in the signs of negation, and we can see how they originated. The most marked exceptions are presented by the Arabs, Esquimaux, some Australian tribes, and Dyaks. With the latter a frown is the sign of negation, and with us frowning often accompanies a lateral shake of the head.

With respect to nodding in affirmation, the exceptions are rather more numerous, namely with some of the Hindoos, with the Turks, Abyssinians, Dyaks, Tagals, and New Zealanders. The eyebrows are sometimes raised in affirmation, and as a person in bending his head forwards and downwards naturally looks up to the person whom he addresses, he will be apt to raise his eyebrows, and this sign may thus have arisen as an abbreviation. So again with the New Zealanders, the lifting up the chin and head in affirmation may perhaps represent in an abbreviated form the upward movement of the head after it has been nodded forwards and downwards.

CHAPTER XII

Surprise – Astonishment – Fear – Horror

Surprise, astonishment – Elevation of the eyebrows – Opening the mouth – Protrusion of the lips – Gestures accompanying surprise – Admiration – Fear – Terror – Erection
of the hair – Contraction of the platysma muscle – Dilatation
of the pupils – Horror – Conclusion.

Attention, if sudden and close, graduates into surprise; and this
into astonishment; and this into stupefied amazement. The latter
frame of mind is closely akin to terror. Attention is shown by the
eyebrows being slightly raised; and as this state increases into
surprise, they are raised to a much greater extent, with the eyes
and mouth widely open. The raising of the eyebrows is necessary
in order that the eyes should be opened quickly and widely; and
this movement produces transverse wrinkles across the forehead.
The degree to which the eyes and mouth are opened corresponds
with the degree of surprise felt: but these movements must be
co-ordinated; for a widely opened mouth with eyebrows only
slightly raised, results in a meaningless grimace, as Dr Duchenne
has shown in one of his photographs.[1] On the other hand, a
person may often be seen to pretend surprise by merely raising
his eyebrows.

Dr Duchenne has given a photograph of an old man with his
eyebrows well elevated and arched by the galvanization of the
frontal muscle; and with his mouth voluntarily opened (Fig. 24).
This figure expresses surprise with much truth. I showed it to
twenty-four persons without a word of explanation, and one alone
did not at all understand what was intended. A second person
answered terror, which is not far wrong; some of the others,

Fig. 24. [This figure did not appear in earlier editions, but it seems certain from Darwin's description that this is the picture he is discussing.]

however, added to the words surprise or astonishment, the epithets horrified, woeful, painful, or disgusted.

The eyes and mouth being widely open is an expression universally recognized as one of astonishment. Thus Shakespeare says, 'I saw a smith stand with open mouth swallowing a tailor's news.' (*King John*, iv, ii.) And again, 'They seemed almost, with staring on one another, to tear the cases of their eyes; there was speech in their dumbness, language in their very gesture; they looked as they had heard of a world destroyed.' (*Winter's Tale*, v, ii.)

My informants answer with remarkable uniformity to the same effect, with respect to the various races of man; the above movements of the features being often accompanied by certain gestures and sounds, presently to be described. Twelve observers in different parts of Australia agree on this head. Mr Winwood Reade has observed this expression with the negroes on the Guinea coast. The chief Gaika and others answer *yes* to my query with respect to the Kafirs of South Africa; and so do others emphatically with reference to the Abyssinians, Ceylonese, Chinese, Fuegians, various tribes of North America, and New Zealanders. With the latter, Mr Stack states that the expression is more plainly shown by certain individuals than by others, though all endeavour as much as possible to conceal their feelings. The Dyaks of Borneo are said by the Rajah Brooke to open their eyes widely, when astonished, often swinging their heads to and fro, and beating their breasts. Mr Scott informs me that the workmen in the Botanic Gardens at Calcutta are strictly ordered not to smoke; but they often disobey this order, and when suddenly surprised in the act, they first open their eyes and mouths widely. They then often slightly shrug their shoulders, as they perceive that discovery is inevitable, or frown and stamp on the ground from vexation. Soon they recover from their surprise, and abject fear is exhibited by the relaxation of all their muscles; their heads seem to sink between their shoulders; their fallen eyes wander to and fro; and they supplicate forgiveness.

The well-known Australian explorer, Mr Stuart, has given[2] a striking account of stupefied amazement together with terror in a native who had never before seen a man on horseback. Mr Stuart approached unseen and called to him from a little distance. 'He turned round and saw me. What he imagined I was I do not know; but a finer picture of fear and astonishment I never saw. He stood incapable of moving a limb, riveted to the spot, mouth open and eyes staring . . . He remained motionless until our black got within a few yards of him, when suddenly throwing down his waddies, he jumped into a mulga bush as high as he could get.' He could not speak, and answered not a word to the enquiries made by the black, but, trembling from head to foot, 'waved with his hand for us to be off'.

That the eyebrows are raised by an innate or instinctive impulse may be inferred from the fact that Laura Bridgman invariably acts thus when astonished, as I have been assured by the lady who has lately had charge of her. As surprise is excited by something unexpected or unknown, we naturally desire, when startled, to perceive the cause as quickly as possible; and we consequently open our eyes fully, so that the field of vision may be increased, and the eyeballs moved easily in any direction. But this hardly accounts for the eyebrows being so greatly raised as is the case, and for the wild staring of the open eyes. The explanation lies, I believe, in the impossibility of opening the eyes with great rapidity by merely raising the upper lids. To effect this the eyebrows must be lifted energetically. Any one who will try to open his eyes as quickly as possible before a mirror will find that he acts thus; and the energetic lifting up of the eyebrows open the eyes so widely that they stare, the white being exposed all round the iris. Moreover, the elevation of the eyebrows is an advantage in looking upwards; for as long as they are lowered they impede our vision in this direction. Sir C. Bell gives[3] a curious little proof of the part which the eyebrows play in opening the eyelids. In a stupidly drunken man all the muscles are relaxed, and the eyelids consequently droop, in the same manner as when we are falling asleep. To counteract this tendency the drunkard raises his eyebrows; and this gives to him a puzzled, foolish look, as is well represented in one of Hogarth's drawings. The habit of raising the eyebrows having once been gained in order to see as quickly as possible all around us, the movement would follow from the force of association whenever astonishment was felt from any cause, even from a sudden sound or an idea.

In a discussion of the origin of facial social signals,[C57] I criticized Darwin's explanation of the origin of brow raising in surprise. 'In discussing this action all commentators have emphasized that it increases visual input. Some have more specifically noted that this movement increases the superior portion of the visual field. Blurton Jones and Konner[C58] found that children show this action in visual search and when looking upwards at any adult, although children show 1+2 [those are the numbers used in our scoring system to refer to brow raise] on other occasions as well. Peiper[C59] pointed out that when a newborn's head is bent forward, a strong 1+2 is part of a reflexive response, together with eye opening and neck movements. The 1+2 action does increase the superior visual field, yet this influence of 1+2 is probably not uniform for all members of our species. The benefit of 1+2 would depend upon how deeply set the eyes are in the bony socket, the prominence of the brow ridge, and how well endowed with hair the eyebrows are. Oster[C60] suggests that infants' eyes are not deeply set and brow hair is sparse, so 1+2 should have less benefit. Generally there should be more benefit for males, Caucasians and adults, although obviously there will be individual differences as well. A number of other related functions of 1+2 have been described which are not supported by current knowledge of the neuroanatomy of vision.[C61] Darwin wrote that 1+2 helps to raise the upper eyelid quickly, and raising the upper eyelid helps to increase vision. There is no reason to believe that speed of upper lid action is enhanced by 1+2 unless the person has enormously drooping eye-cover folds, which hang down so far as to place pressure on the upper eyelid. Furthermore, the upper eyelid rarely comes down so far as to block vision unless the person is nodding off to sleep or *orbicularis oculi* has been contracted. Darwin noted that when someone becomes drowsy, he may use 1+2 to counteract the involuntary relaxation of the upper eyelid. This could provide the basis for a learned association between 1+2 and wanting to see. Less plausibly, Darwin suggested (and Andrew repeated) the idea that 1+2 helps to free the eyeball so that it can be moved around more quickly.'

With adult persons, when the eyebrows are raised, the whole forehead becomes much wrinkled in transverse lines; but with children this occurs only to a slight degree. The wrinkles run in lines concentric with each eyebrow, and are partially confluent in the middle. They are highly characteristic of the expression of surprise or astonishment. Each eyebrow, when raised, becomes also, as Duchenne remarks,[4] more arched than it was before.

The cause of the mouth being opened when astonishment is felt, is a much more complex affair; and several causes apparently concur in leading to this movement. It has often been supposed[5] that the sense of hearing is thus rendered more acute; but I have watched persons listening intently to a slight noise, the nature and source of which they knew perfectly, and they did not open their mouths. Therefore I at one time imagined that the open mouth might aid in distinguishing the direction whence a sound proceeded, by giving another channel for its entrance into the ear through the eustachian tube. But Dr W. Ogle[6] has been so kind as to search the best recent authorities on the functions of the eustachian tube; and he informs me that it is almost conclusively proved that it remains closed except during the act of deglutition; and that in persons in whom the tube remains abnormally open, the sense of hearing, as far as external sounds are concerned, is by no means improved; on the contrary, it is impaired by the respiratory sounds being rendered more distinct. If a watch be placed within the mouth, but not allowed to touch the sides, the ticking is heard much less plainly than when held outside. In persons in whom from disease or a cold the eustachian tube is permanently or temporarily closed, the sense of hearing is injured; but this may be accounted for by mucus accumulating within the tube, and the consequent exclusion of air. We may therefore infer that the mouth is not kept open under the sense of astonishment for the sake of hearing sounds more distinctly; notwithstanding that most deaf people keep their mouths open.

Every sudden emotion, including astonishment, quickens the action of the heart, and with it the respiration. Now we can breathe, as Gratiolet remarks[7] and as appears to me to be the case, much more quietly through the open mouth than through the nostrils. Therefore, when we wish to listen intently to any sound, we either stop breathing, or breathe as quietly as possible, by opening our mouths, at the same time keeping our bodies motionless. One of my sons was awakened in the night by a noise under circumstances which naturally led to great care, and after a few minutes he perceived that his mouth was widely open. He then became conscious that he had opened it for the sake of breathing as quietly as possible. This view receives support from the reversed case which occurs with dogs. A dog when panting after exercise, or on a hot day, breathes loudly; but if his attention be suddenly aroused, he instantly pricks his ears to listen, shuts his mouth, and breathes quietly, as he is enabled to do, through his nostrils.

When the attention is concentrated for a length of time with fixed earnestness on any object or subject, all the organs of the body are forgotten and neglected;[8] and as the nervous energy of each individual is limited in amount, little is transmitted to any part of the system, excepting that which is at the time brought into energetic action. Therefore many of the muscles tend to become relaxed, and the jaw drops from its own weight. This will account for the dropping of the jaw and open mouth of a man stupefied with amazement, and perhaps when less strongly affected. I have noticed this appearance, as I find recorded in my notes, in very young children when they were only moderately surprised.

There is still another and highly effective cause, leading to the mouth being opened, when we are astonished, and more especially when we are suddenly startled. We can draw a full and deep inspiration much more easily through the widely open mouth than through the nostrils. Now when we start at any sudden sound or sight, almost all the muscles of the body are involuntarily and momentarily thrown into strong action, for the sake of guarding ourselves against or jumping away from the danger, which we habitually associate with anything unexpected. But we always unconsciously prepare ourselves for any great exertion, as formerly explained, by first taking a deep and full inspiration, and we consequently open our mouths. If no exertion follows, and we still remain astonished, we cease for a time to breathe, or breathe as quickly as possible, in order that every sound may be distinctly heard. Or again, if our attention continues long and earnestly absorbed, all our muscles become relaxed, and the jaw, which was at first suddenly opened, remains dropped. Thus several causes concur towards this same movement, whenever surprise, astonishment or amazement is felt.*

* [Mr Wallace (*Quarterly Journal of Science*, January 1873, p. 116) suggests that among our savage ancestors, danger to themselves or others would often be associated with the cause of amazement, and that the open mouth may be the rudiment, as it were, of the cry of alarm or encouragement.

In this paragraph and earlier in this chapter, Darwin fails to differentiate the startled reaction from surprise, though they clearly vary in duration. Startle is much briefer, lasting no longer than 250 milliseconds, and the facial expressions are entirely different. In the startle reaction there is a very strong eye closure, horizontal stretching of the lips, and the contraction of the platysma muscle in the neck. My colleagues and I have argued that startle is a reflex not an emotion,[C62] although Tomkins[C63] does not agree.

Although when thus affected, our mouths are generally opened, yet the lips are often a little protruded. This fact reminds us of the same movement, though in a much more strongly marked degree, in the chimpanzee and orang when astonished. As a strong expiration naturally follows the deep inspiration which accompanies the first sense of startled surprise, and as the lips are often protruded, the various sounds which are then commonly uttered can apparently be accounted for. But sometimes a strong expiration alone is heard; thus Laura Bridgman, when amazed, rounds and protrudes her lips, opens them, and breathes strongly.[9] One of the commonest sounds is a deep *Oh*; and this would naturally follow, as explained by Helmholtz, from the mouth being moderately opened and the lips protruded. On a quiet night some rockets were fired from the *Beagle*, in a little creek at Tahiti, to amuse the natives; and as each rocket was let off there was absolute silence, but this was invariably followed by a deep groaning *Oh*, resounding all round the bay. Mr Washington Matthews says that the North American Indians express astonishment by a groan; and the negroes on the West Coast of Africa, according to Mr Winwood Reade, protrude their lips, and make a sound like *heigh*,

He explains the action of the hands as appropriate movements 'either to defend the observer's face or body or to prepare to give assistance to the person in danger'. He points out that nearly the same attitude of the hands is adopted when 'we rush to the assistance of some one in danger, the hands ready to grasp and save him'. But it should be noted that there is no tendency to open the mouth under these circumstances.]

heigh. If the mouth is not much opened, whilst the lips are considerably protruded, a blowing, hissing, or whistling noise is produced. Mr R. Brough Smyth informs me that an Australian from the interior was taken to the theatre to see an acrobat rapidly turning head over heels; 'he was greatly astonished, and protruded his lips, making a noise with his mouth as if blowing out a match.' According to Mr Bulmer the Australians, when surprised, utter the exclamation *korki*, 'and to do this the mouth is drawn out as if going to whistle'. We Europeans often whistle as a sign of surprise; thus, in a recent novel[10] it is said, 'here the man expressed his astonishment and disapprobation by a prolonged whistle'.* A Kafir girl, as Mr J. Mansel Weale informs me, 'on hearing of the high price of an article, raised her eyebrows and whistled just as a European would'. Mr Wedgwood remarks that such sounds are written down as *whew*, and they serve as interjections for surprise.

According to three other observers, the Australians often evince astonishment by a clucking noise. Europeans also sometimes express gentle surprise by a little clicking noise of nearly the same kind. We have seen that when we are startled, the mouth is suddenly opened; and if the tongue happens to be then pressed closely against the palate, its sudden withdrawal will produce a sound of this kind, which might thus come to express surprise.

Turning to gestures of the body. A surprised person often raises his opened hands high above his head, or by bending his arms only to the level of his face.† The flat palms are directed towards the person who causes this feeling, and the straightened fingers are separated. This gesture is represented by Mr Rejlander in Figure 25. In the 'Last Supper', by Leonardo da Vinci, two of

* [A correspondent points out that the 'whew' of surprise is produced by an inspiration, whereas the 'prolonged whistle' is a conscious imitation of it, which becomes with some people a trick.]

† [This gesture was observed in a child of 1 year 9 months. The author noted that 'C– brought for, and opened before one of her little grandchildren, 1 year 9 months old, a box of toys. The child immediately threw up both hands with palms forward and fingers extended on each side of her face, crying out, oh! or ah!']

Fig. 25. Surprised person.

the Apostles have their hands half uplifted, clearly expressive of their astonishment. A trustworthy observer told me that he had lately met his wife under most unexpected circumstances: 'She started, opened her mouth and eyes very widely, and threw up both her arms above her head.' Several years ago I was surprised by seeing several of my young children earnestly doing something together on the ground; but the distance was too great for me to ask what they were about. Therefore I threw up my open hands with extended fingers above my head; and as soon as I had done this, I became conscious of the action. I then waited, without saying a word, to see if my children had understood this gesture; and as they came running to me they cried out, 'We saw that you were astonished at us.' I do not know whether this gesture is common to the various races of man, as I neglected to make enquiries on this head. That it is innate or natural may be inferred from the fact that Laura Bridgman, when amazed, 'spreads her arms and turns her hands with extended fingers upwards';[11] nor is it likely, considering that the feeling of surprise is generally a brief one, that she should have learnt this gesture through her keen sense of touch.

Huschke describes[12] a somewhat different yet allied gesture, which he says is exhibited by persons when astonished. They hold themselves erect, with the features as before described, but with the straightened arms extended backwards – the stretched fingers being separated from each other. I have never myself seen this gesture; but Huschke is probably correct; for a friend asked another man how he would express great astonishment, and he at once threw himself into this attitude.

These gestures are, I believe, explicable on the principle of antithesis. We have seen that an indignant man holds his head erect, squares his shoulders, turns out his elbows, often clenches his fist, frowns, and closes his mouth; whilst the attitude of a helpless man is in every one of these details the reverse. Now, a man in an ordinary frame of mind, doing nothing and thinking of nothing in particular, usually keeps his two arms suspended laxly by his sides, with his hands somewhat flexed, and the fingers near together. Therefore, to raise the arms suddenly, either the whole arms or the fore-arms, to open the palms flat, and to separate the fingers – or, again, to straighten the arms, extending them backwards with separated fingers are movements in complete antithesis to those preserved under an indifferent frame of mind, and they are, in consequence, unconsciously assumed by an astonished man. There is, also, often a desire to display surprise in a conspicuous manner, and the above attitudes are well fitted for this purpose. It may be asked, why should surprise, and only a few other states of the mind, be exhibited by movements in antithesis to others. But this principle will not be brought into play in the case of these emotions, such as terror, great joy, suffering, or rage, which naturally lead to certain lines of action and produce certain effects on the body, for the whole system is thus preoccupied; and these emotions are already thus expressed with the greatest plainness.

There is another little gesture, expressive of astonishment, of which I can offer no explanation; namely, the hand being placed over the mouth;* or on some part of the head. This has been observed with so many races† of man that it must have some natural origin. A wild Australian was taken into a large room full of official papers, which surprised him greatly, and he cried out *cluck, cluck, cluck*, putting the back of his hand towards his lips. Mrs Barber says that the Kafirs and Fingoes express astonishment by a serious look and by placing the right hand upon the mouth, uttering the word *mawo*, which means 'wonderful'. The Bushmen are said[13] to put their right hands to their necks bending their heads backwards. Mr Winwood Reade has observed that the negroes on the West Coast of Africa when surprised, clap their hands to their mouths, saying at the same time, 'My mouth cleaves to me,' i.e. to my hands; and he has heard that this is their usual gesture on such occasions. Captain Speedy informs me that the Abyssinians place their right hand to the forehead, with the palm outside. Lastly, Mr Washington Matthews states that the conventional sign of astonishment with the wild tribes of the western parts of the United States 'is made by placing the half-closed hand over the mouth; in doing this, the head is often bent forwards, and words or low groans are sometimes uttered'. Catlin[14] makes the same remark about the hand being pressed over the mouth by the Mandans and other Indian tribes.

Admiration. Little need be said on this head. Admiration apparently consists of surprise associated with some pleasure and a sense of approval. When vividly felt, the eyes are opened and the eyebrows raised; the eyes become bright, instead of remaining blank, as under simple astonishment; and the mouth, instead of gaping open, expands into a smile.

* [Professor Gomperz, of Vienna, in a letter (25 August, 1873) suggests that in the life of a savage surprise would frequently occur on occasions when silence was needful, as on the sudden appearance or sound of an animal. The placing the hand over the mouth would thus have been originally a gesture enjoining silence which afterwards became associated with the feeling of surprise even when no need for silence existed, or when the percipient was alone.]
† [Cf. Job xii, 5: 'Mark me, and be astonished, and lay your hand upon your mouth.' Quoted by Mr H. Holbeach in *St Paul's Magazine*, February 1873, p. 211.]

Fear, terror. The word 'fear' seems to be derived from what is sudden and dangerous;[15] and that of terror from the trembling of the vocal organs and body. I use the word 'terror' for extreme fear; but some writers think it ought to be confined to cases in which the imagination is more particularly concerned. Fear is often preceded by astonishment, and is so far akin to it, that both lead to the senses of sight and hearing being instantly aroused. In both cases the eyes and mouth are widely opened,* and the eyebrows raised. The frightened man at first stands like a statue motionless and breathless, or crouches down as if instinctively to escape observation.

---

* [Mr A. J. Munby has given in a letter (9 December, 1872) a graphic description of terror: 'It was at Tabley Old Hall, in Cheshire, a mediaeval house, unoccupied except by a housekeeper who lives in the kitchens, but fully furnished with its ancient furniture, and preserved in *statu quo* by the family, as a memorial and museum. On one side of the great hall of the house is a noble oriel window, full of shields of arms: a balcony, overlooking the hall, runs round the other three sides, and into this balcony the doors of the first floor chambers open. I was in one of these chambers, an antique bedroom. I stood in the middle of the floor, with the window of the room behind me, and in front of me the open doorway, through which I was looking at the sunlight tinting the oriel window across the hall. Being in mourning, I wore a dark suit – shooting coat, knickerbockers, and leggings; and had on a black Louis XI wide-awake, the very shape of hat which Mephistopheles wears at the opera. The window behind me of course made my whole figure seem black to a spectator in front, and I was standing perfectly still, being absorbed in watching the sunlight on the oriel. Steps came shuffling along the balcony, and an old woman (she was, I believe, the housekeeper's sister) appeared crossing the doorway. Surprised at seeing the door open, she stopped and looked towards the room, and in looking round, she of course saw me, standing as I have described. In an instant, with a sort of galvanic jerk, she faced me, bringing her whole figure round so that it stood parallel to mine; immediately afterwards, as if she had not realized all my horrors, she rose to her full height (she was stooping before), and stood literally on the tips of her toes, and at the same moment she threw out both her arms, placing the upper-arm nearly at right angles to her body, and the forearm at right angles to the upper-arm, so that the forearms were vertical. Her hands, with the palms towards me, were spread wide, the thumbs and every finger stiff and standing apart. Her head was slightly thrown back, her eyes dilated and rounded, and her mouth wide open. She had a cap on, and I am not sure whether there was any visible erection of her hair. In opening her mouth she uttered a wild and piercing scream, which continued during the time (perhaps two or three seconds) that she stood on her toes, and long after that; for the moment she recovered herself somewhat, she

The heart beats quickly and violently, so that it palpitates or knocks against the ribs; but it is very doubtful whether it then works more efficiently than usual, so as to send a greater supply of blood to all parts of the body; for the skin instantly becomes pale, as during incipient faintness.* This paleness of the surface, however, is probably in large part, or exclusively, due to the vaso-motor centre being affected in such a manner as to cause the contraction of the small arteries of the skin. That the skin is much affected under the sense of great fear, we see in the marvellous and inexplicable manner in which perspiration immediately exudes from it. This exudation is all the more remarkable, as the surface is then cold, and hence the term a cold sweat; whereas, the sudorific glands are properly excited into action when the surface is heated. The hairs also on the skin stand erect; and the superficial muscles shiver. In connection with the disturbed action of the heart, the breathing is hurried. The salivary glands act imperfectly; the mouth becomes dry,† and is often opened and shut. I have also noticed that under slight fear there is a strong tendency to yawn. One of the best-marked symptoms is the trembling of all the muscles of the body; and this is often first seen in the lips. From this cause, and from the dryness of the mouth, the voice becomes husky or indistinct, or may altogether fail.

---

turned and fled, still screaming. She had taken me either for the devil or for a ghost, I forget which. All these details of her conduct were impressed on me, as you may suppose, most vividly, for I never saw anything so strange, of the kind, before or since. For myself, I stood gazing at her, and rooted to the spot: the reaction from my previous mood of quiet contemplation was so sudden, and her appearance so strange, that I half fancied *her* a thing "uncanny", being in a house so old and lonesome, and I felt my own eyes dilating and mouth opening, though I did not utter a sound until she had fled: and then I realized the oddity of the situation and ran after her to reassure her.']
* [Mosso (*La Peur*, French translation, 1886, p. 8) describes the ears of rabbits exhibiting a momentary pallor, followed by a blush when the animals are startled.]
† Mr Bain (*The Emotions and the Will*, 1865, p. 54) explains in the following manner the origin of the custom 'of subjecting criminals in India to the ordeal of the morsel of rice. The accused is made to take a mouthful of rice, and after a little time to throw it out. If the morsel is quite dry, the party is believed to be guilty – his own evil conscience operating to paralyse the salivating organs.'

'Obstupui, steteruntque comae, et vox faucibus haesit.' ['I was astounded, my hair stood on end, and my voice choked in my throat.']

In my research with Robert Levenson,[C64] we found that the hands get cold in fear and warm in anger. Blood goes to the legs in fear, we believe, to prepare us to flee, and to the hands in anger to prepare us to hit. We found no sex differences in these emotion-specific patterns of physiological activity.

Of vague fear there is a well-known and grand description in Job: 'In thoughts from the visions of the night, when deep sleep falleth on men, fear came upon me, and trembling, which made all my bones to shake. Then a spirit passed before my face; the hair of my flesh stood up: It stood still, but I could not discern the form thereof: an image was before mine eyes, there was silence, and I heard a voice, saying, Shall mortal man be more just than God? Shall a man be more pure than his Maker?' (Job iv, 13.)

As fear increases into an agony of terror, we behold, as under all violent emotions, diversified results. The heart beats wildly, or may fail to act, and faintness ensue; there is a death-like pallor; the breathing is laboured; the wings of the nostrils are widely dilated; 'there is a gasping and convulsive motion of the lips, a tremor on the hollow cheek, a gulping and catching of the throat';[16] the uncovered and protruding eyeballs are fixed on the object of terror; or they may roll restlessly from side to side, *huc illuc volvens oculos totumque pererrat* ['*rolling his eyes from side to side, he seemed completely lost*'].[17]

The pupils are said to be enormously dilated. All the muscles of the body may become rigid, or may be thrown into convulsive movements. The hands are alternately clenched and opened, often with a twitching movement. The arms may be protruded, as if to avert some dreadful danger, or may be thrown wildly over the head. The Rev. Mr Hagenauer has seen this latter action in a terrified Australian. In other cases there is a sudden and uncontrollable tendency to headlong flight; and so strong is this, that the boldest soldiers may be seized with a sudden panic.

As fear rises to an extreme pitch, the dreadful scream of terror is heard. Great beads of sweat stand on the skin. All the muscles of the body are relaxed. Utter prostration soon follows, and the mental powers fail. The intestines are affected. The sphincter muscles cease to act, and no longer retain the contents of the body.

Dr J. Crichton Browne has given me so striking an account of intense fear in an insane woman, aged thirty-five, that the description, though painful, ought not to be omitted. When a paroxysm seizes her, she screams out, 'This is hell!' 'There is a black woman!' 'I can't get out!' – and other such exclamations. When thus screaming, her movements are those of alternate tension and tremor. For one instant she clenches her hands, holds her arms out before her in a stiff semi-flexed position; then suddenly bends her body forwards, sways rapidly to and fro, draws her fingers through her hair, clutches at her neck, and tries to tear off her clothes. The sterno-cleido-mastoid muscles (which serve to bend the head on the chest) stand out prominently, as if swollen, and the skin in front of them is much wrinkled. Her hair, which is cut short at the back of her head, and is smooth when she is calm, now stands on end; that in front being dishevelled by the movements of her hands. The countenance expresses great mental agony. The skin is flushed over the face and neck, down to the clavicles, and the veins of the forehead and neck stand out like thick cords. The lower lip drops, and is somewhat everted. The mouth is kept half open, with the lower jaw projecting. The cheeks are hollow and deeply furrowed in curved lines running from the wings of the nostrils to the corners of the mouth. The nostrils themselves are raised and extended. The eyes are widely opened, and beneath them the skin appears swollen; the pupils are large. The forehead is wrinkled transversely in many folds, and at the inner extremities of the eyebrows it is strongly furrowed in diverging lines, produced by the powerful and persistent contraction of the corrugators.

Mr Bell has also described[18] an agony of terror and of despair, which he witnessed in a murderer, whilst carried to the place of execution in Turin. 'On each side of the car the officiating priests were seated; and in the centre sat the criminal himself. It was impossible to witness the condition of this unhappy wretch without terror; and yet, as if impelled by some strange infatuation, it was equally impossible not to gaze upon an object so wild, so full of horror. He seemed about thirty-five years of age; of large and muscular form; his countenance marked by strong and savage features; half-naked, pale as death, agonized with terror, every limb strained in anguish, his hands clenched convulsively, the sweat breaking out on his bent and contracted brow, he kissed incessantly the figure of our Saviour, painted on the flag which was suspended before him; but with an agony of wildness and despair, of which nothing ever exhibited on the stage can give the slightest conception.'

I will add only one other case, illustrative of a man utterly prostrated by terror. An atrocious murderer of two persons was brought into a hospital, under the mistaken impression that he had poisoned himself; and Dr W. Ogle carefully watched him the next morning, while he was being handcuffed and taken away by the police. His pallor was extreme, and his prostration so great that he was hardly able to dress himself. His skin perspired; and his eyelids and head drooped so much that it was impossible to catch even a glimpse of his eyes. His lower jaw hung down. There was no contraction of any facial muscle, and Dr Ogle is almost certain that the hair did not stand on end, for he observed it narrowly, as it had been dyed for the sake of concealment.*

With respect to fear, as exhibited by the various faces of man, my informants agree that the signs are the same as with Europeans. They are displayed in an exaggerated degree with the Hindoos[19] and natives of Ceylon. Mr Geach has seen Malays

* [Mr H. Jackson, in quoting the following passage from the *Odyssey*, remarks that Homer 'deliberately identifies the signs of despair with the symptoms of physical prostration'. The passage occurs where Telemachus (*Od*. xviii, 235–42) prays that he may see the suitors subdued, with bowed heads and loosened knees, even as now Irus (who has just been soundly beaten) sits nodding his head like a drunken man, unable to stand or to walk, with his knees loosened beneath him.]

when terrified turn pale and shake; and Mr Brough Smyth states that a native Australian 'being on one occasion much frightened, showed a complexion as nearly approaching to what we call paleness, as can well be conceived in the case of a very black man'.* Mr Dyson Lacy has seen extreme fear shown in an Australian, by a nervous twitching of the hands, feet, and lips; and by the perspiration standing on the skin. Many savages do not repress the signs of fear so much as Europeans; and they often tremble greatly. With the Kafirs, Gaika says, in his rather quaint English, the shaking 'of the body is much experienced, and the eyes are widely open'. With savages, the sphincter muscles are often relaxed, just as may be observed in much frightened dogs, and as I have seen with monkeys when terrified by being caught.

The erection of the hair. Some of the signs of fear deserve a little further consideration. Poets continually speak of the hair standing on end; Brutus says to the ghost of Caesar, 'that mak'st my blood cold, and my hair to stare'. And Cardinal Beaufort, after the murder of Gloucester exclaims, 'Comb down his hair; look, look, it stands upright.' As I did not feel sure whether writers of fiction might not have applied to man what they had often observed in animals, I begged for information from Dr Crichton Browne with respect to the insane. He states in answer that he has repeatedly seen their hair erected under the influence of sudden and extreme terror. For instance, it is occasionally necessary to inject morphia under the skin of an insane woman, who dreads the operation extremely, though it causes very little pain; for she believes that poison is being introduced into her system, and that her bones will be softened, and her flesh turned into dust. She becomes deadly pale; her limbs are stiffened by a sort of tetanic spasm, and her hair is partially erected on the front of the head.

Dr Browne further remarks that the bristling of the hair which is so common in the insane, is not always associated with

* [N. von Miklucho-Maclay states (*Natuurkundig Tijdschrift voor Nederlandsch Indie*, xxxiii, 1873) that the Papuans of New Guinea turn pale with fright or anger. He describes their normal colour as a dark chocolate-brown.]

terror.* It is perhaps most frequently seen in chronic maniacs, who rave incoherently and have destructive impulses; but it is during their paroxysms of violence that the bristling is most observable. The fact of the hair becoming erect under the influence both of rage and fear agrees perfectly with what we have seen in the lower animals. Dr Browne adduces several cases in evidence. Thus with a man now in the Asylum, before the recurrence of each maniacal paroxysm, 'the hair rises up from his forehead like the mane of a Shetland pony'. He has sent me photographs of two women, taken in the intervals between their

Fig. 26. From a photograph of an insane woman,
to show the condition of her hair.

* [M. Henri Stecki, a Polish gentleman of St Petersburg, describes (letter, March 1874) the case of a Caucasian lady whose hair became erect without the stimulus of any strong emotion. He observed her hair gradually becoming disordered, although the conversation was purposely directed by him to cheerful topics. The lady declared that when she was affected by strong emotion her hair stirred and rose 'as if it were alive', so that she herself was frightened at it. The lady was not at this time insane, but M. Stecki believes that she afterwards went mad.]

paroxysms, and he adds with respect to one of these women, 'that the state of her hair is a sure and convenient criterion of her mental condition'. I have had one of these photographs copied, and the engraving gives, if viewed from a little distance, a faithful

Fig. 27. {Ekman comments: in the Darwin materials in the Cambridge University library, I found the original photograph from which the engraving was made. In the photograph, one can see that the forehead does not contain the wrinkles that are apparent in the engraving. I can rule out the possibility that the wrinkles might have been in the photograph but faded with time, as the muscular action necessary to produce them (*corrugator* and inner portion of *frontalis*) would have triangulated her upper eyelid, of which there is no sign. The wrinkles were added by the engraver to fit with what we would expect in a woman who is upset. There is no record that Darwin instructed the engraver to make this change, though instructions for changes to many other illustrations do exist. Would the engraver have made it on his own initiative without Darwin noticing? Perhaps Darwin *did* notice but thought it unimportant, since he was commenting her hair, not her expression. Whatever his reason for allowing this change to stand, Darwin is using the engraving as an illustration, not as documentation or data.]

representation of the original, with the exception that the hair appears rather too coarse and too much curled. The extraordinary condition of the hair in the insane is due, not only to its erection, but to its dryness and harshness, consequent on the subcutaneous glands failing to act. Dr Bucknill has said[20] that a lunatic 'is a lunatic to his fingers' ends'; he might have added, and often to the extremity of each particular hair.

Dr Browne mentions as an empirical confirmation of the relation which exists in the insane between the state of their hair and minds, that the wife of a medical man, who has charge of a lady suffering from acute melancholia, with a strong fear of death, for herself, her husband and children, reported verbally to him the day before receiving my letter as follows, 'I think Mrs— will soon improve, for her hair is getting smooth; and I always notice that our patients get better whenever their hair ceases to be rough and unmanageable.'

Dr Browne attributes the persistently rough condition of the hair in many insane patients, in part to their minds being somewhat disturbed, and in part to the effects of habit – that is, to the hair being frequently and strongly erected during their many recurrent paroxysms. In patients in whom the bristling of the hair is extreme, the disease is generally permanent and mortal; but in others, in whom the bristling is moderate, as soon as they recover their health of mind the hair recovers its smoothness.

In a previous chapter we have seen that with animals the hairs are erected by the contraction of minute, unstriped, and involuntary muscles, which run to each separate follicle. In addition to this action, Mr J. Wood has clearly ascertained by experiment, as he informs me, that with man the hairs on the front of the head which slope forwards, and those on the back which slope backwards, are raised in opposite directions by the contraction of the occipito-frontalis or scalp muscle. So that this muscle seems to aid in the erection of the hairs on the head of man, in the same manner as the homologous *panniculus carnosus* aids, or takes the greater part, in the erection of the spines on the backs of some of the lower animals.

*

Contraction of the platysma myoides muscle. This muscle is spread over the sides of the neck, extending downwards to a little beneath the collar-bones, and upwards to the lower part of the cheeks. A portion, called the risorius, is represented in the woodcut Fig. 2 (M) [p. 29]. The contraction of this muscle draws the corners of the mouth and the lower parts of the cheeks downwards and backwards. It produces at the same time divergent, longitudinal, prominent ridges on the sides of the neck in the young; and, in old thin persons, fine transverse wrinkles. This muscle is some-times said not to be under the control of the will; but almost every one, if told to draw the corners of his mouth backwards and downwards with great force, brings it into action. I have, however, heard of a man who can voluntarily act on it only on one side of his neck.

Sir C. Bell[21] and others have stated that this muscle is strongly contracted under the influence of fear; and Duchenne insists so strongly on its importance in the expression of this emotion, that he calls it the *muscle of fright.*[22] He admits, however, that its contraction is quite inexpressive unless associated with widely open eyes and mouth. He has given a photograph [Fig. 29] (copied and reduced in the accompanying woodcut [Fig. 28]) of the same old man as on former occasions, with his eyebrows strongly raised, his mouth opened, and the platysma contracted, all by means of galvanism. The original photograph was shown to twenty-four persons, and they were separately asked, without any explanation being given, what expression was intended: twenty instantly answered, 'intense fright' or 'horror'; three said pain, and one extreme discomfort. Dr Duchenne has given another photograph of the same old man, with the platysma contracted, the eyes and mouth opened, and the eyebrows rendered oblique, by means of galvanism. The expression thus induced is very striking (see Figure 30); the obliquity of the eyebrows adding the appearance of great mental distress. The original [Fig. 31] was shown to fifteen persons; twelve answered terror or horror, and three agony or great suffering. From these cases, and from an examination of the other photographs given by Dr Duchenne, together with his remarks thereon, I think there can be little doubt that the contraction of the platysma does add greatly to the expression of fear. Nevertheless this muscle ought hardly to be called that of fright, for its contraction is certainly not a necessary concomitant of this state of mind.

A man may exhibit extreme terror in the plainest manner by death-like pallor, by drops of perspiration on his skin, and by utter prostration, with all the muscles of his body, including the platysma, completely relaxed. Although Dr Browne has often seen this muscle quivering and contracting in the insane, he has not been able to connect its action with any emotional condition in them, though he carefully attended to patients suffering from great fear. Mr Nicol, on the other hand, has observed three cases in which this muscle appeared to be more or less permanently contracted under the influence of melancholia, associated with much dread; but in one of these cases, various other muscles about the neck and head were subject to spasmodic contractions.

Dr W. Ogle observed for me in one of the London hospitals about twenty patients, just before they were put under the influence of chloroform for operations. They exhibited some trepidation, but no great terror. In only four of the cases was the platysma visibly contracted; and it did not begin to contract until the patients began to cry. The muscle seemed to contract at the moment of each deep-drawn inspiration; so that it is very doubtful whether the contraction depended at all on the emotion of fear. In a fifth case, the patient, who was not chloroformed, was much terrified; and his platysma was more forcibly and persistently contracted than in the other cases. But even here there is room for doubt, for the muscle which appeared to be unusually developed, was seen by Dr Ogle to contract as the man moved his head from the pillow, after the operation was over.

As I felt much perplexed why, in any case, a superficial muscle on the neck should be especially affected by fear, I applied to my many obliging correspondents for information about the contraction of this muscle under other circumstances. It would be superfluous to give all the answers which I have received. They show that this muscle acts, often in a variable manner and degree, under many different conditions. It is violently contracted in hydrophobia, and in a somewhat less degree in lockjaw; sometimes in a marked manner during the insensibility from chloroform. Dr W. Ogle observed two male patients, suffering from such difficulty in breathing, that the trachea had to be opened, and in both the platysma was strongly contracted. One of these men overheard the conversation of the surgeons surrounding him, and when he was able to speak, declared that he had not been frightened. In some other cases of extreme difficulty of

Fig. 28. Terror. From a photograph by Dr Duchenne. [Ekman comments: Our research suggests some problems with this description of the fearful face. Darwin and Duchenne leave out the importance of raising the upper eyelid strongly, and tensing the lower eyelid. Also, the brows are not just raised but drawn together as shown in Fig. 28. Although the appearance of the lips is correct, the description of what produces it is partly erroneous. The *risorious* muscle, which is a strand of muscle running off the *platysma*, must contract to produce the horizontal stretching of the lips. Typically, this also involves some of the *platysma*, but it is possible to contract the *platysma* without contracting the *risorious*.]

301

Fig. 29. [Ekman comments: I have included the original photograph (Fig. 29) from which the drawing was made. Darwin had the engraver remove the electrodes in Fig. 28 which are very evident in Fig. 29. His instructions were: 'Omit galvanic instruments and hands of operator'. He gave the same instructions to the engraver for Fig. 31. I don't know why he left them in Fig. 30. Perhaps he thought it would be less distracting, and when he could eliminate them (when woodcuts were made) he did so, but they remained in the photograph from which he could not easily delete them.]

respiration, though not requiring tracheotomy, observed by Drs Ogle and Langstaff, the platysma was not contracted.

Mr J. Wood, who has studied with such care the muscles of the human body, as shown by his various publications, has often seen the platysma contracted in vomiting, nausea, and disgust; also in children and adults under the influence of rage – for instance, in Irishwomen, quarrelling and brawling together with angry gesticulations. This may possibly have been due to their high and angry tones; for I know a lady, an excellent musician,

Fig. 30. [Ekman comments: Prodger said of Duchenne: 'Photography, combined with his electrical stimulation techniques to produce expressive postures, afforded Duchenne unprecedented control in the study of expression. In effect, he had devised a means to "activate" expression with electricity, then "fix" it with photography.'[C65] See Prodger's Appendix 3.]

who, in singing certain high notes, always contracts her platysma. So does a young man, as I have observed, in sounding certain notes on the flute. Mr J. Wood informs me that he has found the platysma best developed in persons with thick necks and broad shoulders; and that in families inheriting these peculiarities, its development is usually associated with much voluntary power over the homologous occipito-frontalis muscle, by which the scalp can be moved.

Darwin was right to be troubled by Duchenne's claim that the *platysma* muscle must act to produce the fearful face. Darwin correctly noted that the *platysma* contracts under many circumstances; it can appear in fear, anger, pain, or distress, but it is not a necessary action in any of those expressions. What Darwin failed to note is the importance of the *risorious* muscle in producing the fear mouth (mentioned in my commentary on page 301).

None of the foregoing cases appear to throw any light on the contraction of the platysma from fear; but it is different, I think, with the following cases. The gentleman before referred to, who can voluntarily act on this muscle only on one side of his neck, is positive that it contracts on both sides whenever he is startled. Evidence has already been given showing that this muscle sometimes contracts, perhaps for the sake of opening the mouth widely, when the breathing is rendered difficult by disease, and during the deep inspirations of crying-fits before an operation. Now, whenever a person starts at any sudden sight or sound, he instantaneously draws a deep breath; and thus the contraction of the platysma may possibly have become associated with the sense of fear. But there is, I believe, a more efficient relation. The first sensation of fear, or the imagination of something dreadful, commonly excites a shudder. I have caught myself giving a little involuntary shudder at a painful thought, and I distinctly perceived that my platysma contracted; so it does if I simulate a shudder. I have asked others to act in this manner; and in some the muscle contracted, but not in others. One of my sons, whilst getting out of bed, shuddered from the cold, and, as he happened to have his hand on his neck, he plainly felt that this muscle strongly contracted. He then voluntarily shuddered, as he had done on former occasions, but the platysma was not then affected. Mr J. Wood has also several times observed this muscle contracting in patients, when stripped for examination, and who were not frightened, but shivered slightly from the cold. Unfortunately I have not been able to ascertain whether, when the whole body shakes, as in the cold stage of an ague fit, the platysma contracts.

But as it certainly often contracts during a shudder; and as a shudder or shiver often accompanies the first sensation of fear, we have, I think, a clue to its action in this latter case.* Its contraction, however, is not an invariable concomitant of fear; for it probably never acts under the influence of extreme, prostrating terror.

Dilatation of the pupils. Gratiolet repeatedly insists[23] that the pupils are enormously dilated whenever terror is felt. I have no reason to doubt the accuracy of this statement, but have failed to obtain confirmatory evidence,† excepting in the one instance before given of an insane woman suffering from great fear. When writers of fiction speak of the eyes being widely dilated, I presume that they refer to the eyelids. Munro's statement,[24] that with parrots the iris is affected by the passions, independently of the amount of light, seems to bear on this question; but Professor Donders informs me, that he has often seen movements in the pupils of these birds which he thinks may be related to their power of accommodation to distance, in nearly the same manner as our own pupils contract when our eyes converge for near vision. Gratiolet remarks that the dilated pupils appear as if they were gazing into profound darkness. No doubt the fears of man have often been excited in the dark; but hardly so often or so exclusively, as to account for a fixed and associated habit having thus arisen. It seems more probable, assuming that Gratiolet's statement is correct, that the brain is directly affected by the powerful emotion of fear and reacts on the pupils; but Professor Donders informs me that this is an extremely complicated subject. I may add, as possibly throwing light on the subject, that Dr Fyffe, of Netley Hospital, has observed in two patients that the pupils were distinctly dilated during the

---

* Duchenne takes, in fact, this view (ibid., p. 45), as he attributes the contraction of the platysma to the shivering of fear (*frisson de la peur*); but he elsewhere compares the action with that which causes the hair of frightened quadrupeds to stand erect; and this can hardly be considered as quite correct.

† [Mr T. W. Clark, of Southampton, describes (letters, 25 June, 16 September, 1875) dilatation of the pupil produced by fear in a water-spaniel, a retriever, a fox-terrier, and a cat. Mosso (*La Peur*, p. 95) states, on the authority of Schiff, that pain causes dilatation of the pupil.]

cold stage of an ague fit. Professor Donders has also often seen dilatation of the pupils in incipient faintness.

Horror. The state of mind expressed by this term implies terror, and is in some cases almost synonymous with it. Many a man must have felt, before the blessed discovery of chloroform, great horror at the thought of an impending surgical operation. He who dreads, as well as hates a man, will feel, as Milton uses the word, a horror of him. We feel horror if we see any one, for instance a child, exposed to some instant and crushing danger. Almost every one would experience the same feeling in the highest degree in witnessing a man being tortured or going to be tortured. In these cases there is no danger to ourselves; but from the power of the imagination and of sympathy we put ourselves in the position of the sufferer, and feel something akin to fear.

Sir C. Bell remarks,[25] that 'horror is full of energy; the body is in the utmost tension, not unnerved by fear'. It is, therefore, probable that horror would generally be accompanied by the strong contraction of the brows; but as fear is one of the elements, the eyes and mouth would be opened, and the eyebrows would be raised, as far as the antagonistic action of the corrugators permitted this movement. Duchenne has given a photograph[26] (Fig. 31) of the same old man as before, with his eyes somewhat staring, the eyebrows partially raised, and at the same time strongly contracted, the mouth opened, and the platysma in action, all effected by the means of galvanism. He considers that the expression thus produced shows extreme terror with horrible pain or torture. A tortured man, as long as his sufferings allowed him to feel any dread for the future, would probably exhibit horror in an extreme degree. I have shown the original of this photograph [Fig. 32] to twenty-three persons of both sexes and various ages; and thirteen immediately answered horror, great pain, torture, or agony; three answered extreme fright; so that sixteen answered nearly in accordance with Duchenne's belief. Six, however, said anger, guided no doubt by the strongly contracted brows, and overlooking the peculiarly opened mouth. One said disgust. On the whole, the evidence indicates that we have

Horror and Agony. [The engraving on the left (Fig. 31) was copied from the photograph by Dr Duchenne shown above (Fig. 32, right). Note the absence of electrodes.]

here a fairly good representation of horror and agony. The photograph before referred to (Fig. 30) likewise exhibits horror; but in this the oblique eyebrows indicate great mental distress in place of energy.

The *Oxford English Dictionary* confirms Darwin's use of the term 'horror' as a combination of intense fear and disgust. However, my data suggest that Fig. 31 shows extreme terror, as Duchenne claimed, not horror.

Horror is generally accompanied by various gestures, which differ in different individuals. Judging from pictures, the whole body is often turned away or shrinks; or the arms are violently protruded as if to push away some dreadful object. The most frequent gesture, as far as can be inferred from the acting of persons who endeavour to express a vividly-imagined scene of horror, is the raising of both shoulders, with the bent arms pressed closely against the sides or chest. These movements are nearly the same as those commonly made when we feel very cold;* and they are generally accompanied by a shudder, as well as by a deep expiration or inspiration, according as the chest happens at the time to be expanded or contracted. The sounds thus made are expressed by words like *uh* or *ugh*.[27] It is not, however, obvious why, when we feel cold or express a sense of horror, we press our bent arms against our bodies, raise our shoulders, and shudder.†

Conclusion. I have now endeavoured to describe the diversified expressions of fear, in its gradations from mere attention to a start of surprise, into extreme terror and horror. Some of the signs may be accounted for through the principles of habit, association, and inheritance – such as the wide opening of the mouth and eyes, with upraised eyebrows, so as to see as quickly as possible all around us, and to hear distinctly whatever sound may reach our ears. For we have thus habitually prepared ourselves to discover and encounter any danger. Some of the other signs of fear may likewise be accounted for, at least in part, through these same principles. Men, during numberless generations, have endeavoured to escape from their enemies or danger by headlong flight, or by violently struggling with them; and such great exertions will have caused the heart to beat rapidly, the breathing to be hurried, the chest to heave, and the nostrils to be dilated. As these exertions have often been prolonged to the last extremity, the final result will have been utter prostration, pallor, perspir-

---

* [This attitude is not peculiar to man. The author noted that monkeys when cold huddle together, contract their necks, and raise their shoulders.]
† [Professor Gomperz, of Vienna, suggested, in a letter (25 August 1873), that the gesture of pressing the folded arms to the sides may have been originally associated serviceably with the sensation of cold. This gesture would, therefore, become associated with the shuddering caused by cold. Thus, when a shudder is caused by the feeling of horror, the above gesture might accompany it simply because it had become 'adherent' to it in the frequently recurring sensation of cold. This view necessarily leaves out of account the cause of the shudder – but given this as part of the expression of horror, it helps to account for the occurrence of the above gesture. It is not difficult to guess why the gesture with the arms should be associated with cold, since by flexing the arms and pressing them to the sides, the exposed surface is diminished.]

ation, trembling of all the muscles, or their complete relaxation. And now, whenever the emotion of fear is strongly felt, though it may not lead to any exertion, the same results tend to reappear, through the force of inheritance and association.

Nevertheless, it is probable that many or most of the above symptoms of terror, such as the beating of the heart, the trembling of the muscles, cold perspiration, etc., are in large part directly due to the disturbed or interrupted transmission of nerve-force from the cerebro-spinal system to various parts of the body, owing to the mind being so powerfully affected. We may confidently look to this cause, independently of habit and association, in such cases as the modified secretions of the intestinal canal, and the failure of certain glands to act. With respect to the involuntary bristling of the hair, we have good reason to believe that in the case of animals this action, however it may have originated, serves, together with certain voluntary movements, to make them appear terrible to their enemies; and as the same involuntary and voluntary actions are performed by animals nearly related to man, we are led to believe that man has retained through inheritance a relic of them, now become useless. It is certainly a remarkable fact, that the minute unstriped muscles, by which the hairs thinly scattered over man's almost naked body are erected, should have been preserved to the present day; and that they should still contract under the same emotions, namely, terror and rage, which cause the hairs to stand on end in the lower members of the Order to which man belongs.

CHAPTER XIII

Self-attention – Shame – Shyness – Modesty: Blushing

Nature of a blush – Inheritance – The parts of the body most affected – Blushing in the various races of man – Accompanying gestures – Confusion of mind – Causes of blushing – Self-attention, the fundamental element – Shyness – Shame, from broken moral laws and conventional rules – Modesty – Theory of blushing – Recapitulation.

Blushing is the most peculiar and the most human of all expressions. Monkeys redden from passion, but it would require an overwhelming amount of evidence to make us believe that any animal could blush. The reddening of the face from a blush is due to the relaxation of the muscular coats of the small arteries, by which the capillaries become filled with blood; and this depends on the proper vaso-motor centre being affected. No doubt if there be at the same time much mental agitation, the general circulation will be affected; but it is not due to the action of the heart that the network of minute vessels covering the face becomes under a sense of shame gorged with blood. We can cause laughing by tickling the skin, weeping or frowning by a blow, trembling from the fear of pain, and so forth; but we cannot cause a blush, as Dr Burgess remarks,[1] by any physical means – that is by any action on the body. It is the mind which must be affected. Blushing is not only involuntary; but the wish to restrain it, by leading to self-attention, actually increases the tendency.

The young blush much more freely than the old, but not during infancy,* which is remarkable, as we know that infants at a very

* Dr Burgess, ibid., p. 56. At p. 33 he also remarks on women blushing more freely than men, as stated below.

early age redden from passion. I have received authentic accounts of two little girls blushing at the ages of between two and three years; and of another sensitive child, a year older, blushing, when reproved for a fault. Many children, at a somewhat more advanced age, blush in a strongly marked manner. It appears that the mental powers of infants are not as yet sufficiently developed to allow of their blushing. Hence, also, it is that idiots rarely blush. Dr Crichton Browne observed for me those under his care, but never saw a genuine blush, though he has seen their faces flush, apparently from joy, when food was placed before them, and from anger. Nevertheless some, if not utterly degraded, are capable of blushing. A microcephalous idiot, for instance thirteen years old, whose eyes brightened a little when he was pleased or amused, has been described by Dr Behn,[2] as blushing and turning to one side, when undressed for medical examination.

The American developmental psychologist Michael Lewis[C66] confirms Darwin's observation about how early blushing appears. Lewis suggests that embarrassment is first seen between the ages of two and two and a half. There is also confirmation that in Western cultures blushing occurs more often in women than in men.

Women blush much more than men. It is rare to see an old man, but not nearly so rare to see an old woman blushing. The blind do not escape. Laura Bridgman, born in this condition, as well as completely deaf, blushes.[3] The Rev. R. H. Blair, Principal of the Worcester College, informs me that three children born blind, out of seven or eight then in the Asylum, are great blushers. The blind are not at first conscious that they are observed, and it is a most important part of their education, as Mr Blair informs me, to impress this knowledge on their minds; and the impression thus gained would greatly strengthen the tendency to blush, by increasing the habit of self-attention.

The tendency to blush is inherited. Dr Burgess gives the case[4] of a family consisting of a father, mother, and ten children, all of whom, without exception, were prone to blush to a most painful degree. The children were grown up; 'and some of them were sent to travel in order to wear away this diseased sensibility, but nothing was of the slightest avail'. Even peculiarities in blushing seem to be inherited. Sir James Paget, whilst examining the spine of a girl, was struck at her singular manner of blushing; a big splash of red appeared first on one cheek, and then other splashes, various scattered over the face and neck. He subsequently asked the mother whether her daughter always blushed in this peculiar manner; and was answered, 'Yes, she takes after me.' Sir J. Paget then perceived that by asking this question he had caused the mother to blush; and she exhibited the same peculiarity as her daughter.

In most cases the face, ears and neck are the sole parts which redden; but many persons, whilst blushing intensely, feel that their whole bodies grow hot and tingle: and this shows that the entire surface must be in some manner affected. Blushes are said sometimes to commence on the forehead, but more commonly on the cheeks, afterwards spreading to the ears and neck.[5] In two Albinos examined by Dr Burgess, the blushes commenced by a small circumscribed spot on the cheeks, over the parotidean plexus of nerves, and then increased into a circle; between this blushing circle and the blush on the neck there was an evident line of demarcation; although both arose simultaneously. The retina, which is naturally red in the Albino, invariably increased at the same time in redness.[6] Every one must have noticed how easily after one blush fresh blushes chase each other over the face. Blushing is preceded by a peculiar sensation in the skin. According to Dr Burgess, the reddening of the skin is generally succeeded by a slight pallor, which shows that the capillary vessels contract after dilating. In some rare cases paleness instead of redness is caused under conditions which would naturally induce a blush. For instance, a young lady told me that in a large and crowded party she caught her hair so firmly on the button of a passing servant, that it took some time before she could be extricated; from her sensations she imagined that she had blushed crimson; but was assured by a friend that she had turned extremely pale.

I was desirous to learn how far down the body blushes extend; and Sir J. Paget, who necessarily has frequent opportunities for observation, has kindly attended to this point for me during two or three years. He finds that with women who blush intensely on the face, ears, and nape of the neck, the blush does not commonly extend any lower down the body. It is rare to see it as low down as the collar-bones and shoulder-blades; and he has never himself seen a single instance in which it extended below the upper part of the chest. He has also noticed that blushes sometimes die away downwards, not gradually and insensibly, but by irregular ruddy blotches. Dr Langstaff has likewise observed for me several women whose bodies did not in the least redden while their faces were crimsoned with blushes. With the insane, some of whom appear to be particularly liable to blushing, Dr J. Crichton Browne has several times seen the blush extend as far down as the collar-bones, and in two instances to the breasts. He gives me the case of a married woman, aged twenty-seven, who suffered from epilepsy. On the morning after her arrival in the Asylum, Dr Browne, together with his assistants, visited her whilst she was in bed. The moment that he approached, she blushed deeply over her cheeks and temples; and the blush spread quickly to her ears. She was much agitated and tremulous. He unfastened the collar of her chemise in order to examine the state of her lungs; and then a brilliant blush rushed over her chest, in an arched line over the upper third of each breast, and extended downwards between the breasts nearly to the ensiform cartilage of the sternum. This case is interesting, as the blush did not thus extend downwards until it became intense by her attention being drawn to this part of her person. As the examination proceeded she became composed, and the blush disappeared; but on several subsequent occasions the same phenomena were observed.

The foregoing facts show that, as a general rule, with English women, blushing does not extend beneath the neck and upper part of the chest. Nevertheless Sir J. Paget informs me that he has lately heard of a case, on which he can fully rely, in which a little girl, shocked by what she imagined to be an act of indelicacy, blushed all over her abdomen and the upper parts of her legs.

Moreau also[7] relates, on the authority of a celebrated painter, that the chest, shoulders, arms, and whole body of a girl, who unwillingly consented to serve as a model, reddened when she was first divested of her clothes.

It is a rather curious question why, in most cases the face, ears, and neck alone redden, inasmuch as the whole surface of the body often tingles and grows hot. This seems to depend, chiefly, on the face and adjoining parts of the skin having been habitually exposed to the air, light, and alternations of temperature, by which the small arteries not only have acquired the habit of readily dilating and contracting, but appear to have become unusually developed in comparison with other parts of the surface.[8] It is probably owing to this same cause, as M. Moreau and Dr Burgess have remarked, that the face is so liable to redden under various circumstances, such as a fever-fit, ordinary heat, violent exertion, anger, a slight blow, etc.; and on the other hand that it is liable to grow pale from cold and fear, and to be discoloured during pregnancy. The face is also particularly liable to be affected by cutaneous complaints, by small-pox, erysipelas, etc. This view is likewise supported by the fact that the men of certain races, who habitually go nearly naked, often blush over their arms and chests and even down to their waists. A lady, who is a great blusher, informs Dr Crichton Browne, that when she feels ashamed or is agitated, she blushes over her face, neck, wrists, and hands* – that is, over all the exposed portions of her skin. Nevertheless it may be doubted whether the habitual exposure of the skin of the face and neck, and its consequent power of reaction under stimulants of all kinds, is by itself sufficient to account for the much greater tendency in English women of these parts than of others to blush; for the hands are well supplied with nerves and small vessels, and have been as much exposed to the

---

* [A young lady writes, 'When I am playing on the piano, and any one comes and looks over me, I am afraid they will look at my hands, and I am so afraid of their being red that they blush, though they were not red before. When my governess spoke of my hands being long or able to stretch, or drew attention to them, they blushed.']

air as the face or neck, and yet the hands rarely blush. We shall presently see that the attention of the mind having been directed much more frequently and earnestly to the face than to any other part of the body, probably affords a sufficient explanation.

Blushing in the various races of man. The small vessels of the face become filled with blood, from the emotion of shame, in almost all the races of man, though in the very dark races no distinct change of colour can be perceived. Blushing is evident in all the Aryan nations of Europe, and to a certain extent with those of India. But Mr Erskine has never noticed that the necks of the Hindoos are decidedly affected. With the Lepchas of Sikhim, Mr Scott has often observed a faint blush on the cheeks, base of the ears, and sides of the neck, accompanied by sunken eyes and lowered head. This has occurred when he has detected them in a falsehood, or has accused them of ingratitude. The pale, sallow complexions of these men render a blush much more conspicuous than in most of the other natives of India. With the latter, shame, or it may be in part fear, is expressed, according to Mr Scott, much more plainly by the head being averted or bent down, with the eyes wavering or turned askant, than by any change of colour in the skin.

The Semitic races blush freely, as might have been expected, from their general similitude to the Aryans. Thus with the Jews, it is said in the Book of Jeremiah (vi, 15), 'Nay, they were not at all ashamed, neither could they blush'.* Mrs Asa Gray saw an Arab managing his boat clumsily on the Nile, and when laughed at by his companions, 'he blushed quite to the back of his neck'. Lady Duff Gordon remarks that a young Arab blushed on coming into her presence.†

Mr Swinhoe has seen the Chinese blushing, but he thinks it is

---

* [According to Professor Robertson Smith, these words do not imply blushing. It seems possible that pallor is meant. There is, however, a word *haphar* occurring in Psalm xxxiv, 5, which probably means to blush.]

† *Letters from Egypt*, 1865, p. 66. Lady Gordon is mistaken when she says Malays and mulattoes never blush.

rare;* yet they have the expression 'to redden with shame'. Mr Geach informs me that the Chinese settled in Malacca and the native Malays of the interior both blush. Some of these people go nearly naked, and he particularly attended to the downward extension of the blush. Omitting the cases in which the face alone was seen to blush, Mr Geach observed that the face, arms, and breast of a Chinaman, aged 24 years, reddened from shame; and with another Chinese, when asked why he had not done his work in better style, the whole body was similarly affected. In two Malays† he saw the face, neck, breast, and arms blushing; and in a third Malay (a Bugis) the blush extended down to the waist.

The Polynesians blush freely. The Rev. Mr Stack has seen hundreds of instances with the New Zealanders. The following case is worth giving, as it relates to an old man who was unusually dark-coloured and partly tattooed. After having let his land to an Englishman for a small yearly rental, a strong passion seized him to buy a gig, which had lately become the fashion with the Maoris. He consequently wished to draw all the rent for four years from his tenant, and consulted Mr Stack whether he could do so. The man was old, clumsy, poor, and ragged, and the idea of his driving himself about in his carriage for display amused Mr Stack so much that he could not help bursting out into a laugh; and then 'the old man blushed up to the roots of his hair'. Forster says that 'you may easily distinguish a spreading blush' on the cheeks of the fairest women in Tahiti.‡ The natives also of several of

* [Mr H. P. Lee (letter, 17 January 1873) has observed that the intelligent Chinese brought up from boyhood as servants of Europeans blush readily and profusely, e.g. on being bantered by their masters on their personal appearance.]
† Captain Osborn (*Quedah*, p. 199), in speaking of a Malay, whom he reproached for cruelty, says he was glad to see that the man blushed.
‡ J. R. Forster, *Observations during a Voyage round the World*, 410, 1778, p. 229. Waitz gives (*Introduction to Anthropology*, Eng. translat. 1863, vol. i, p. 135) references for other islands in the Pacific. See, also, Dampier, *On the Blushing of the Tunquinese* (vol. ii, p. 40); but I have not consulted this work. Waitz quotes Bergmann, that the Kalmucks do not blush, but this may be doubted after what we have seen with respect to the Chinese. He also quotes Roth, who denies that the Abyssinians are capable of blushing. Unfortunately, Captain Speedy, who lived so long with the Abyssinians, has not answered my enquiry on this head.

the other archipelagoes in the Pacific have been seen to blush.

Mr Washington Matthews has often seen a blush on the faces of the young squaws belonging to various wild Indian tribes of North America. At the opposite extremity of the continent in Tierra del Fuego, the natives, according to Mr Bridges, 'blush much, but chiefly in regard to women; but they certainly blush also at their own personal appearance'. This latter statement agrees with what I remember of the Fuegian, Jemmy Button, who blushed when he was quizzed about the care which he took in polishing his shoes, and in otherwise adorning himself. With respect to the Aymara Indians on the lofty plateaus of Bolivia, Mr Forbes says,[9] that from the colour of their skins it is impossible that their blushes should be as clearly visible as in the white races; still under such circumstances as would raise a blush in us, 'there can always be seen the same expression of modesty or confusion; and even in the dark, a rise in temperature of the skin of the face can be felt, exactly as occurs in the European'. With the Indians who inhabit the hot, equable, and damp parts of South America, the skin apparently does not answer to mental excitement so readily as with the natives of the northern and southern parts of the continent, who have long been exposed to great vicissitudes of climate; for Humboldt quotes without a protest the sneer of the Spaniard, 'How can those be trusted, who know not how to blush?'[10] Von Spix and Martius, in speaking of the aborigines of Brazil, assert that they cannot properly be said to blush; 'it was only after long intercourse with the whites, and after receiving some education, that we perceived in the Indians a change of colour expressive of the emotions of their minds'.[11] It is, however, incredible that the power of blushing could have thus originated; but the habit of self-attention, consequent on their education and new course of life, would have much increased any innate tendency to blush.

Lastly, I must add that the Rajah Brooke has never observed the least sign of a blush with the Dyaks of Borneo; on the contrary, under circumstances which would excite a blush in us, they assert 'that they feel the blood drawn from their faces'.

Several trustworthy observers have assured me that they have seen on the faces of negroes an appearance resembling a blush, under circumstances which would have excited one in us, though their skins were of an ebony-black tint. Some describe it as blushing brown, but most say that the blackness becomes more intense. An increased supply of blood in the skin seems in some manner to increase its blackness; thus certain exanthematous diseases cause the affected places in the negro to appear blacker, instead of, as with us, redder.* The skin, perhaps, from being rendered more tense by the filling of the capillaries, would reflect a somewhat different tint to what it did before. That the capillaries of the face of the negro become filled with blood, under the emotion of shame, we may feel confident; because a perfectly characterized albino negress, described by Buffon,[12] showed a faint tinge of crimson on her cheeks when she exhibited herself naked. Cicatrices of the skin remain for a long time white in the negro, and Dr Burgess, who had frequent opportunities of observing a scar of this kind on the face of a negress, distinctly saw that it 'invariably became red whenever she was abruptly spoken to, or charged with any trivial offence'.† The blush could be seen proceeding from the circumference of the scar towards the middle, but it did not reach the centre. Mulattoes are often great blushers, blush succeeding blush over their faces. From these facts there can be no doubt that negroes blush, although no redness is visible on the skin.

I am assured by Gaika and by Mrs Barber that the Kafirs of South Africa never blush; but this may only mean that no change of colour is distinguishable. Gaika adds that under the circumstances which would make a European blush, his countrymen 'look ashamed to keep their heads up'.

It is asserted by four of my informants that the Australians,

* See, on this head, Burgess, ibid., p. 32. Also Waitz, *Introduction to Anthropology*, Eng. edit., vol. i, p. 135. Moreau gives a detailed account (Lavater, 1820, vol. iv, p. 302) of the blushing of a Madagascar negress-slave when forced by her brutal master to exhibit her naked bosom.

† Burgess, ibid., p. 31. On mulattoes blushing, see p. 33. I have received similar accounts with respect to mulattoes.

who are almost as black as negroes, never blush. A fifth answers doubtfully, remarking that only a very strong blush could be seen, on account of the dirty state of their skins. Three observers state that they do blush;[*] Mr S. Wilson adding that this is noticeable only under a strong emotion, and when the skin is not too dark from long exposure and want of cleanliness. Mr Lang answers, 'I have noticed that shame almost always excites a blush, which frequently extends as low as the neck.' Shame is also shown, as he adds, 'by the eyes being turned from side to side'. As Mr Lang was a teacher in a native school, it is probably that he chiefly observed children; and we know that they blush more than adults. Mr G. Taplin has seen half-castes blushing, and he says that the aborigines have a word expressive of shame. Mr Hagenauer, who is one of those who has never observed the Australians to blush, says that he has 'seen them looking down to the ground on account of shame'; and the missionary, Mr Bulmer, remarks that though 'I have not been able to detect anything like shame in the adult aborigines, I have noticed that the eyes of the children, when ashamed, present a restless, watery appearance, as if they did not know where to look.'

The facts now given are sufficient to show that blushing, whether or not there is any change of colour, is common to most, probably to all, of the races of man.

Movements and gestures which accompany blushing. Under a keen sense of shame there is a strong desire for concealment.[†] We turn away the whole body, more especially the face, which we endeavour in some manner to hide. An ashamed person can hardly endure to meet the gaze of those present, so that he almost

---

[*] Barrington also says that the Australians of New South Wales blush, as quoted by Waitz, ibid., p. 135.

[†] Mr Wedgwood says (*Dict. of English Etymology*, vol. iii, 1865, p. 155) that the word shame 'may well originate in the idea of shade or concealment, and may be illustrated by the Low German *scheme*, shade or shadow'. Gratiolet (*De la Phys.*, pp. 357–62) has a good discussion on the gestures accompanying shame; but some of his remarks seem to me rather fanciful. See, also, Burgess (ibid., pp. 69, 134) on the same subject.

invariably casts down his eyes or looks askant. As there generally exists at the same time a strong wish to avoid the appearance of shame, a vain attempt is made to look direct at the person who causes this feeling; and the antagonism between these opposite tendencies leads to various restless movements in the eyes. I have noticed two ladies who, whilst blushing, to which they are very liable, have thus acquired, as it appears, the oddest trick of incessantly blinking their eyelids with extraordinary rapidity. An intense blush is sometimes accompanied by a slight effusion of tears,* and this, I presume, is due to the lacrymal glands partaking of the increased supply of blood, which we know rushes into the capillaries of the adjoining parts, including the retina.

Many writers, ancient and modern, have noticed the foregoing movements; and it has already been shown that the aborigines in various parts of the world often exhibit their shame by looking downwards or askant, or by restless movements of their eyes. Ezra cries out (ix, 6), 'O my God I am ashamed, and blush† to lift up my face to thee, my God.' In Isaiah (16) we meet with the words, 'I hid not my face from shame.' Seneca remarks (Epist. xi, 5) 'that the Roman players hang down their heads, fix their eyes on the ground and keep them lowered, but are unable to blush in acting shame'. According to Macrobius, who lived in the fifth century (*Saturnalia*, vii, 11), 'Natural philosophers assert that nature being moved by shame spreads the blood before herself as a veil, as we see any one blushing often puts his hands before his face.' Shakespeare makes Marcus (*Titus Andronicus*, ii, 5) say to his niece, 'Ah! how thou turn'st away thy face for shame.' A lady informs me that she found in the Lock Hospital a girl whom she had formerly known, and who had become a wretched castaway, and the poor creature, when approached, hid her face under the bedclothes, and could not be persuaded to uncover it. We often see little children, when shy or ashamed, turn away, and

---

* Burgess, ibid., pp. 181, 182. Boerhaave also noticed (as quoted by Gratiolet, ibid., p. 361) the tendency to the secretion of tears during intense blushing. Mr Bulmer, as we have seen, speaks of the 'watery eyes' of the children of the Australian aborigines when ashamed.

† [See Professor Robertson Smith's comment, footnote, p. 315.]

still standing up, bury their faces in their mother's gown; or they throw themselves face downwards on her lap.

Darwin does not distinguish embarrassment from shame, but I comment on that distinction at the end of this chapter. Many of my remarks about blushing draw on research on embarrassment, not on shame.

Confusion of mind. Most persons, whilst blushing intensely, have their mental powers confused. This is recognized in such common expressions as 'she was covered with confusion'. Persons in this condition lose their presence of mind, and utter singularly inappropriate remarks. They are often much distressed, stammer, and make awkward movements or strange grimaces. In certain cases involuntary twitchings of some of the facial muscles may be observed. I have been informed by a young lady, who blushes excessively, that at such times she does not even know what she is saying. When it was suggested to her that this might be due to her distress from the consciousness that her blushing was noticed, she answered that this could not be the case, 'as she had sometimes felt quite as stupid when blushing at a thought in her own room'.

I will give an instance of the extreme disturbance of mind to which some sensitive men are liable. A gentleman, on whom I can rely, assured me that he had been an eye-witness of the following scene: A small dinner-party was given in honour of an extremely shy man, who, when he rose to return thanks, rehearsed the speech, which he had evidently learnt by heart, in absolute silence, and did not utter a single word; but he acted as if he were speaking with much emphasis. His friends, perceiving how the case stood, loudly applauded the imaginary bursts of eloquence, whenever his gestures indicated a pause, and the man never discovered that he had remained the whole time completely silent. On the contrary, he afterwards remarked to my friend, with much satisfaction, that he thought he had succeeded uncommonly well.

When a person is much ashamed or very shy, and blushes intensely, his heart beats rapidly and his breathing is disturbed. This can hardly fail to affect the circulation of the blood within the brain, and perhaps the mental powers. It seems however doubtful, judging from the still more powerful influence of anger and fear on the circulation, whether we can thus satisfactorily account for the confused state of mind in persons whilst blushing intensely.

Robert Levenson commented that Darwin's explanation of the confusion does not '. . . make sense physiologically. The amount of blood diverted to the face is quite modest compared to the total blood supply to the head. All the local and central control mechanisms in the cardiovascular system are set up to insure adequate blood flow to the brain above all else. It would be much wiser to look elsewhere for the source of the confusion (e.g., thoughts focused on self rather than on task at hand).'

The true explanation apparently lies in the intimate sympathy which exists between the capillary circulation of the surface of the head and face, and that of the brain. On applying to Dr J. Crichton Browne for information, he has given me various facts bearing on this subject. When the sympathetic nerve is divided on one side of the head, the capillaries on this side are relaxed and become filled with blood, causing the skin to redden and to grow hot, and at the same time the temperature within the cranium on the same side rises. Inflammation of the membranes of the brain leads to the engagement of the face, ears, and eyes with blood. The first stage of an epileptic fit appears to be the contraction of the vessels of the brain, and the first outward manifestation is an extreme pallor of countenance. Erysipelas of the head commonly induces delirium. Even the relief given to a severe headache by burning the skin with strong lotion, depends, I presume, on the same principle.

Dr Browne has often administered to his patients the vapour of the nitrite of amyl,[13] which has the singular property of causing vivid redness of the face in from thirty to sixty seconds. This flushing resembles blushing in almost every detail:* it begins at several distinct points on the face, and spreads till it involves the whole surface of the head, neck, and front of the chest; but has been observed to extend only in one case to the abdomen. The arteries in the retina become enlarged; the eyes glisten, and in one instance there was a slight effusion of tears. The patients are at first pleasantly stimulated, but, as the flushing increases, they become confused and bewildered. One woman to whom the vapour had often been administered asserted that, as soon as she grew hot, she grew *muddled*. With persons just commencing to blush it appears, judging from their bright eyes and lively behaviour, that their mental powers are somewhat stimulated. It is only when the blushing is excessive that the mind grows confused. Therefore it would seem that the capillaries of the face are affected, both during the inhalation of the nitrite of amyl and during blushing, before that part of the brain is affected on which the mental powers depend.

Conversely when the brain is primarily affected, the circulation of the skin is so in a secondary manner. Dr Browne has frequently observed, as he informs me, scattered red blotches and mottlings on the chests of epileptic patients. In these cases, when the skin on the thorax or abdomen is gently rubbed with a pencil or other object, or, in strongly marked cases, is merely touched by the finger, the surface becomes suffused in less than half a minute with bright red marks, which spread to some distance on each side of the touched point, and persist for several minutes. These are the *cerebral maculae* of Trousseau; and they indicate, as Dr Browne remarks, a highly modified condition of the cutaneous vascular system. If, then, there exists, as cannot be doubted, an intimate sympathy between the capillary circulation in that part of the brain on which our mental powers depend, and in the skin

---

* [Professor W. Filehne (quoted in *Kosmos*, Jahrg. iii, 1879–80, p. 480) believes that a complete analogy exists between the action of nitrite of amyl and the mechanism of the natural blush. See also his paper in *Pflüger's Archiv.* (vol. ix, 1874, p. 491), in which he concludes that 'It is perhaps not too rash to assume that the amyl-nitrite and the psychical cause attack the same point in the nervous system and produce the same effects.']

of the face, it is not surprising that the moral causes which induce intense blushing should likewise induce, independently of their own disturbing influence, much confusion of mind.

The nature of the mental states which induce blushing. These consist of shyness, shame, and modesty; the essential element in all being self-attention. Many reasons can be assigned for believing that originally self-attention directed to personal appearance, in relation to the opinion of others, was the exciting cause; the same effect being subsequently produced, through the force of association, by self-attention in relation to moral conduct. It is not the simple act of reflecting on our own appearance, but the thinking what others think of us, which excites a blush. In absolute solitude the most sensitive person would be quite indifferent about his appearance. We feel blame or disapprobation more acutely than approbation; and consequently depreciatory remarks or ridicule, whether of our appearance or conduct, cause us to blush much more readily than does praise. But undoubtedly praise and admiration are highly efficient: a pretty girl blushes when a man gazes intently at her, though she may know perfectly well that he is not depreciating her. Many children, as well as old and sensitive persons blush, when they are much praised. Hereafter the question will be discussed, how it has arisen that the consciousness that others are attending to our personal appearance should have led to the capillaries, especially those of the face, instantly becoming filled with blood.

There is general agreement among contemporary researchers that attention to the self is the cause of blushing. There is disagreement about whether it is aversive social attention,[C67] overpraise,[C68] or an attempt to appease.[C69] (I am indebted to Dacher Keltner for his help on the literature dealing with embarrassment and shame.)

My reasons for believing that attention directed to personal appearance, and not to moral conduct, has been the fundamental element in the acquirement of the habit of blushing, will now be given. They are separately light, but combined possess, as it appears to me, considerable weight. It is notorious that nothing makes a shy person blush so much as any remark, however slight, on his personal appearance. One cannot notice even the dress of a woman much given to blushing, without causing her face to crimson. It is sufficient to stare hard at some persons to make them, as Coleridge remarks, blush – 'account for that he who can'.[14]

With the two albinos observed by Dr Burgess,[15] 'the slightest attempt to examine their peculiarities invariably' caused them to blush deeply. Women are much more sensitive about their personal appearance than men are, especially elderly women in comparison with elderly men, and they blush much more freely. The young of both sexes are much more sensitive on this same head than the old, and they also blush much more freely than the old. Children at a very early age do not blush; nor do they show those other signs of self-consciousness which generally accompany blushing; and it is one of their chief charms that they think nothing about what others think of them. At this early age they will stare at a stranger with a fixed gaze and unblinking eyes, as on an inanimate object, in a manner which we elders cannot imitate.

It is plain to every one that young men and women are highly sensitive to the opinion of each other with reference to their personal appearance; and they blush incomparably more in the presence of the opposite sex than in that of their own.* A young man, not very liable to blush, will blush intensely at any slight ridicule of his appearance from a girl whose judgement on any important subject he would disregard. No happy pair of young lovers, valuing each other's admiration and love more than anything else in the world, probably ever courted each other without many a blush. Even the barbarians of Tierra del Fuego, according to Mr Bridges, blush 'chiefly in regard to women, but certainly also at their own personal appearance'.

* Mr Bain (*The Emotions and the Will*, 1865, p. 65) remarks on 'the shyness of manners which is induced between the sexes ... from the influence of mutual regard, by the apprehension on either side of not standing well with the other'.

Of all parts of the body, the face is most considered and regarded, as is natural from its being the chief seat of expression and the source of the voice. It is also the chief seat of beauty and of ugliness, and throughout the world is the most ornamented.[16] The face, therefore, will have been subjected during many generations to much closer and more earnest self-attention than any other part of the body; and in accordance with the principle here advanced we can understand why it should be the most liable to blush. Although exposure to alternations of temperature, etc., has probably much increased the power of dilatation and contraction in the capillaries of the face and adjoining parts, yet this by itself will hardly account for these parts blushing much more than the rest of the body; for it does not explain the fact of the hands rarely blushing. With Europeans the whole body tingles slightly when the face blushes intensely: and with the races of men who habitually go nearly naked, the blushes extend over a much larger surface than with us. These facts are, to a certain extend, intelligible, as the self-attention of primeval man, as well as of the existing races which still go naked, will not have been so exclusively confined to their faces, as is the case with the people who now go clothed.

Consistent with Darwin's reasoning, but curiously overlooked by him, is that the face is the chief badge of our identity. It is facial appearance that allows us most readily to distinguish one person from another, although we can do so from the voice, and perhaps the posture. That our face *is* the badge of our identity adds to the reasons why it should be the focus of our attention when we are embarrassed or ashamed.

We have seen that in all parts of the world persons who feel shame for some moral delinquency, are apt to avert, bend down, or hide their faces, independently of any thought about their personal appearance. The object can hardly be to conceal their blushes, for the face is thus averted or hidden under circumstances which exclude any desire to conceal shame, as when guilt is fully confessed and repented of. It is, however, probable that primeval man before he had acquired much moral sensitiveness would have been highly sensitive about his personal appearance, at least in reference to the other sex, and he would consequently have felt distress at any depreciatory remarks about his appearance; and this is one form of shame. And as the face is the part of the body which is most regarded, it is intelligible that any one ashamed of his personal appearance would desire to conceal this part of his body. The habit having been thus acquired, would naturally be carried on when shame from strictly moral causes was felt; and it is not easy otherwise to see why under these circumstances there should be a desire to hide the face more than any other part of the body.

The habit, so general with every one who feels ashamed, of turning away, or lowering his eyes, or restlessly moving them from side to side, probably follows from each glance directed towards those present, bringing home the conviction that he is intently regarded; and he endeavours, by not looking at those present, and especially not at their eyes, momentarily to escape from this painful conviction.

Shyness. This odd state of mind, often called shamefacedness, or false shame, or *mauvaise honte*, appears to be one of the most efficient of all the causes of blushing. Shyness is, indeed, chiefly recognized by the face reddening, by the eyes being averted or cast down, and by awkward, nervous movements of the body. Many a woman blushes from this cause, a hundred, perhaps a thousand times, to once that she blushes from having done any-thing deserving blame, and of which she is truly ashamed. Shyness seems to depend on sensitiveness to the opinion, whether good or bad, of others, more especially with respect to external appear-ance. Strangers neither know nor care anything about our conduct or character, but they may, and often do, criticize our appearance; hence shy persons are particularly apt to be shy and to blush in the presence of strangers. The consciousness of anything peculiar, or even new, in the dress, or any slight blemish on the person, and more especially on the face – points which are likely to attract the attention of strangers – makes the shy intolerably shy. On the other hand, in those cases in which conduct and not personal appearance is concerned, we are much more apt to be shy in the presence of acquaintances, whose judgement we in some degree value, than in that of strangers. A physician told me that a young man, a wealthy duke, with whom he had travelled as medical attendant, blushed like a girl, when he paid him his fee; yet this young man probably would not have blushed and been shy, had he been paying a bill to a tradesman. Some persons, however, are so sensitive, that the mere act of speaking to almost any one is sufficient to rouse their self-consciousness, and a slight blush is the result.

Disapprobation or ridicule, from our sensitiveness on this head, causes shyness and blushing much more readily than does approbation, though the latter with some persons is highly efficient. The conceited are rarely shy; for they value themselves much too highly to expect depreciation. Why a proud man is often shy, as appears to be the case, is not so obvious, unless it be that, with all his self-reliance, he really thinks much about the opinion of others, although in a disdainful spirit. Persons who are exceedingly shy are rarely shy in the presence of those with whom they are quite familiar, and of whose good opinion and sympathy they are perfectly assured; for instance, a girl in the presence of her mother. I neglected to enquire in my printed paper whether shyness can be detected in the different races of man; but a Hindoo gentleman assured Mr Erskine that it is recognizable in his countrymen.

The American developmental psychologist Jerome Kagan commented: 'I found myself in strong agreement with Darwin's statement, in the next paragraph, that fear and shyness are different although related. Once again, Darwin is prescient. We are finding that inhibited children classified at age two turn out to be shy as thirteen-year-olds but are not more fearful of specific incentives like lightning storms and animals compared with other children. Thus, the distinction between shyness or social phobia and punctate fears is a wise one. Darwin is also correct in noting that shy people are shy only with unfamiliar adults not with adults or children whom they know well.'

Shyness, as the derivation of the word indicates in several languages,[17] is closely related to fear; yet it is distinct from fear in the ordinary sense. A shy man no doubt dreads the notice of strangers, but can hardly be said to be afraid of them; he may be as bold as a hero in battle, and yet have no self-confidence about trifles in the presence of strangers. Almost every one is extremely nervous when first addressing a public assembly, and most men remain so throughout their lives; but this appears to depend on the consciousness of a great coming exertion [especially one which is in some way strange to us],* with its associated effects on the system, rather than on shyness;† although a timid or shy man no doubt suffers on such occasions infinitely more than another. With very young children it is difficult to distinguish between fear and shyness; but this latter feeling with them has often seemed to me to partake of the character of the wildness of an untamed animal. Shyness comes on at a very early age. In one of my own children, when two years and three months old, I saw a trace of what certainly appeared to be shyness, directed towards myself after an absence from home of only a week. This was shown not by a blush, but by the eyes being for a few minutes slightly averted from me. I have noticed on other occasions that shyness

---

* [The above addition was adopted by the author on the suggestion of a correspondent, who adds: 'The worst fit of nervousness I ever had was in a case which afforded no room for shyness. It was in the Classical Tripos during the first paper. I finished my rough copy in an hour and a half, spent an hour in making corrections, and then found that my hand shook so much that I could not write out my work. In fact, I looked at it for nearly half an hour, swearing meantime and biting my hands, and it was only at the very end of the time that I could scrawl my name.']

† Mr Bain (*The Emotions and the Will*, p. 64) has discussed the 'abashed' feelings experienced on these occasions, as well as the *stage-fright* of actors unused to the stage. Mr Bain apparently attributes these feelings to simple apprehension or dread.

or shamefacedness and real shame are exhibited in the eyes of young children before they have acquired the power of blushing.

As shyness apparently depends on self-attention, we can perceive how right are those who maintain that reprehending children for shyness, instead of doing them any good, does much harm, as it calls their attention still more closely to themselves. It has been well urged that 'nothing hurts young people more than to be watched continually about their feelings, to have their countenances scrutinized, and the degrees of their sensibility measured by the surveying eye of the unmerciful spectator. Under the constraint of such examinations they can think of nothing but that they are looked at, and feel nothing but shame or apprehension.'*

The American psychologist Philip Zimbardo, an expert on shyness, commented: 'Signs of [shyness] inhibition and timidity are evident in about 10–15 percent of newborns, which Jerome Kagan [see preceding commentary] characterizes as "a push from nature". But my research and that of others indicates that about 40 percent of adults (both males and females) consider themselves shy, some having become so after childhood, while others who were shy earlier have overcome it. Thus shyness has both inherited and learned determinants. Darwin links it with fear, shame and self-attention. There are data to support these associations. However, it is more appropriate to base shyness on social anxiety about excessive concerns for rejection by others, a sense of shame over being detected as unworthy or as harboring unacceptable thoughts, and extreme self-focused consciousness. In pointing to public speaking as a general shyness-inducing setting, Darwin identifies what has come to be known as a brand of "situational shyness" that affects most people when in situations where they must perform publicly; blind dates or forced group introductions are others. Shyness can indeed be detected among different races as

---

* *Essays on Practical Education*, by Maria and R. L. Edgeworth, new edit., vol. ii, 1822, p. 38. Dr Burgess (ibid., p. 187) insists strongly to the same effect.

Darwin assumes. Our research in nine countries suggests that it may be a universal reaction to socially arousing situations and people. The lowest level of self-reported shyness was still a high 30 percent (in Israel), and soared to 60 percent in Japan and Taiwan. Shyness may have any or all of the following components: cognitive (negative self statements); affective (feelings of shame, anxiety, tension); behavioral (oral reticence, no eye contact, no smiling); and physical, physiological (blushing, arousal, tremors).'

Moral causes: guilt. With respect to blushing from strictly moral causes, we meet with the same fundamental principle as before, namely, regard for the opinion of others. It is not the conscience which raises a blush, for a man may sincerely regret some slight fault committed in solitude, or he may suffer the deepest remorse for an undetected crime, but he will not blush. 'I blush,' says Dr Burgess,[18] 'in the presence of my accusers'. It is not the sense of guilt, but the thought that others think or know us to be guilty which crimsons the face. A man may feel thoroughly ashamed at having told a small falsehood, without blushing; but if he even suspects that he is detected he will instantly blush, especially if detected by one whom he reveres.

On the other hand, a man may be convinced that God witnesses all his actions, and he may feel deeply conscious of some fault and pray for forgiveness; but this will not, as a lady who is a great blusher believes, ever excite a blush. The explanation of this difference between the knowledge by God and man of our actions lies, I presume, in man's disapprobation of immoral conduct being somewhat akin in nature to his depreciation of our personal appearance, so that through association both lead to similar results; whereas the disapprobation of God brings up no such association.

Many a person has blushed intensely when accused of some crime, though completely innocent of it. Even the thought, as the lady before referred to has observed to me, that others think that we have made an unkind or stupid remark, is amply sufficient to cause a blush, although we know all the time that we have been completely misunderstood. An action may be meritorious or of an indifferent nature, but a sensitive person, if he suspects that others take a different view of it, will blush. For instance, a lady by herself may give money to a beggar without a trace of a blush, but if others are present, and she doubts whether they approve, or suspects that they think her influenced by display, she will blush. So it will be, if she offers to relieve the distress of a decayed gentlewoman, more particularly of one whom she had previously known under better circumstances, as she cannot then feel sure how her conduct will be viewed. But such cases as these blend into shyness.

Breaches of etiquette. The rules of *etiquette* always refer to conduct in the presence of, or towards others. They have no necessary connection with the moral sense, and are often meaningless. Nevertheless as they depend on the fixed custom of our equals and superiors, whose opinion we highly regard, they are considered almost as binding as are the laws of honour to a gentleman. Consequently the breach of the laws of etiquette, that is, any impoliteness or *gaucherie*, any impropriety, or an inappropriate remark, though quite accidental, will cause the most intense blushing of which a man is capable. Even the recollection of such an act, after an interval of many years, will make the whole body to tingle. So strong, also, is the power of sympathy that a sensitive person, as a lady has assured me, will sometimes blush at a flagrant breach of etiquette by a perfect stranger, though the act may in no way concern her.

Modesty. This is another powerful agent in exciting blushes; but the word modesty includes very different states of the mind. It implies humility, and we often judge of this by persons being greatly pleased and blushing at slight praise, or by being annoyed at praise which seems to them too high according to their own humble standard of themselves. Blushing here has the usual signification of regard for the opinion of others. But modesty frequently relates to acts of indelicacy; and indelicacy is an affair of etiquette, as we clearly see with the nations that go altogether or nearly naked. He who is modest, and blushes easily at acts of this nature, does so because they are breaches of a firmly and wisely established etiquette. This is indeed shown by the derivation of the word *modest* from *modus*, a measure or standard of behaviour. A blush due to this form of modesty is, moreover, apt to be intense, because it generally relates to the opposite sex; and we have seen how in all cases our liability to blush is thus increased. We apply the term 'modest', as it would appear, to those who have a humble opinion of themselves, and to those who are extremely sensitive about an indelicate word or deed, simply because in both cases blushes are readily excited, for these two frames of mind have nothing else in common. Shyness also, from this same cause, is often mistaken for modesty in the sense of humility.

Some persons flush up, as I have observed and have been assured, at any sudden and disagreeable recollection. The commonest cause seems to be the sudden remembrance of not having done something for another person which had been promised. In this case it may be that the thought passes half unconsciously through the mind, 'What will he think of me?' and then the flush would partake of the nature of a true blush. But whether such flushes are in most cases due to the capillary circulation being affected, is very doubtful; for we must remember that almost every strong emotion, such as anger or great joy, acts on the heart, and causes the face to redden.

The fact that blushes may be excited in absolute solitude seems opposed to the view here taken, namely, that the habit originally arose from thinking about what others think of us. Several ladies, who are great blushers, are unanimous in regard to solitude; and some of them believe that they have blushed in the dark.* From what Mr Forbes has stated with respect to the Aymaras, and from

* [F. W. Hagen (*Psychologische Untersuchungen*, Brunswick, 1847), who seems a good observer, takes the opposite opinion. He says: 'Many observations on myself have convinced me that this sensation [i.e. of blushing] never arises if the room is dark but does so at once if it is lighted up.']

my own sensations, I have no doubt that this latter statement is correct. Shakespeare, therefore, erred* when he made Juliet, who was not even by herself, say to Romeo (ii, 2):

> 'Thou know'st the mask of night is on my face;
> Else would a maiden blush bepaint my cheek,
> For that which thou hast heard me speak to-night.'

But when a blush is excited in solitude, the cause almost always relates to the thoughts of others about us – to acts done in their presence, or suspected by them; or again when we reflect what others would have thought of us had they known of the act. Nevertheless one or two of my informants believe that they have blushed from shame at acts in no way relating to others. If this be so, we must attribute the result to the force of inveterate habit and association, under a state of mind closely analogous to that which ordinarily excites a blush; nor need we feel surprise at this, as even sympathy with another person who commits a flagrant breach of etiquette is believed, as we have just seen, sometimes to cause a blush.

Finally, then, I conclude that blushing – whether due to shyness – to shame for a real crime – to shame from a breach of the laws of etiquette – to modesty from humility – to modesty from an indelicacy – depends in all cases on the same principle; this principle being a sensitive regard for the opinion, more particularly for the depreciation of others, primarily in relation to our personal appearance, especially of our faces; and secondarily, through the force of association and habit, in relation to the opinion of others on our conduct.

Darwin remains consistent in not considering the communicative value of the blush, although he tells us it is caused by people paying attention to our appearance, especially our faces. Research on the physiology of blushing suggests that the change in facial coloration occurs

---

* [Mr Topham suggests (letter 5 December 1872) that Shakespeare meant that the blush was unseen, not that it was absent.]

before the increase in the temperature of the skin. Since it is the temperature change which makes us aware that we are blushing, it is likely that '. . . our blushing will be seen by others before we detect it'.[C70]

Theory of blushing. We have now to consider, why should the thought that others are thinking about us affect our capillary circulation? Sir C. Bell insists[19] that blushing 'is a provision for expression, as may be inferred from the colour extending only to the surface of the face, neck, and breast, the parts most exposed. It is not acquired; it is from the beginning.' Dr Burgess believes that it was designed by the Creator in 'order that the soul might have sovereign power of displaying in the cheeks the various internal emotions of the moral feelings'; so as to serve as a check on ourselves, and as a sign to others, that we were violating rules which ought to be held sacred. Gratiolet merely remarks – 'Or, comme il est dans l'ordre de la nature que l'être social le plus intelligent soit le plus intelligible, cette faculté de rougeur et de pâleur qui distingue l'homme, est un signe naturel de sa haute perfection.' ['Now, as it is in the nature of things that the most intelligent social beings will also be the most expressive, the capacity to blush and grow pale which distinguishes man is a natural sign of his high perfection.']

The belief that blushing was *specially* designed by the Creator is opposed to the general theory of evolution, which is now so largely accepted; but it forms no part of my duty here to argue on the general question. Those who believe in design, will find it difficult to account for shyness being the most frequent and efficient of all the causes of blushing, as it makes the blusher to suffer and the beholder uncomfortable, without being of the least service to either of them. They will also find it difficult to account for negroes and other dark-coloured races blushing, in whom a change of colour in the skin is scarcely or not at all visible.

No doubt a slight blush adds to the beauty of a maiden's face; and the Circassian women who are capable of blushing, invariably fetch a higher price in the seraglio of the Sultan than less

335

susceptible women.[20] But the firmest believer in the efficacy of Sexual Selection will hardly suppose that blushing was acquired as a sexual ornament. This view would also be opposed to what has just been said about the dark-coloured races blushing in an invisible manner.

The hypothesis which appears to me the most probable, though it may at first seem rash, is that attention closely directed to any part of the body tends to interfere with the ordinary and tonic contraction of the small arteries of that part. These vessels, in consequence, become at such times more or less relaxed, and are instantly filled with arterial blood. This tendency will have been much strengthened, if frequent attention has been paid during many generations to the same part, owing to nerve-force readily flowing along accustomed channels, and by the power of inherit-ance. Whenever we believe that others are depreciating or even considering our personal appearance, our attention is vividly directed to the outer and visible parts of our bodies; and of all such parts we are most sensitive about our faces, as no doubt has been the case during many past generations. Therefore, assuming for the moment that the capillary vessels can be acted on by close attention, those of the face will have become eminently susceptible. Through the force of association, the same effects will tend to follow whenever we think that others are considering or censuring our actions or character.*

As the basis of this theory rests on mental attention having some power to influence the capillary circulation, it will be necess-ary to give a considerable body of details, bearing more or less

---

* [Hagen (*Psychologische Untersuchungen*, Brunswick, 1847, pp. 54–5) upholds an almost identical theory. When our attention is directed to our face, he writes, 'it is naturally directed towards the sensory nerves, because it is by means of these that we are aware of the condition of our face. Now it is certain from many other facts (and is probably explicable as a reflex effect on the nerves of the vessels) that stimulation of a sensory nerve is followed by an increased flow of blood to the part. And this, moreover, is especially the case in the face, where a slight pain easily produces a reddening of the eyelids, forehead, and cheeks.' He thus makes the assumption that thinking intently about the face acts as a stimulus to the nerves of sensation.]

directly on this subject. Several observers,* who from their wide experience and knowledge are eminently capable of forming a sound judgement, are convinced that attention or consciousness (which latter term Sir H. Holland thinks the more explicit) concentrated on almost any part of the body produces some direct physical effect on it. This applies to the movements of the involuntary muscles, and of the voluntary muscles when acting involuntarily – to the secretion of the glands – to the activity of the senses and sensations – and even to the nutrition of parts.

It is known that the involuntary movements of the heart are affected if close attention be paid to them. Gratiolet[21] gives the case of a man, who by continually watching and counting his own pulse, at last caused one beat out of every six to intermit. On the other hand, my father told me of a careful observer, who certainly had heart-disease and died from it, and who positively stated that his pulse was habitually irregular to an extreme degree; yet to his great disappointment it invariably became regular as soon as my father entered the room. Sir H. Holland remarks,[22] that the 'effect upon the circulation of a part from the consciousness suddenly directed and fixed upon it, is often obvious and immediate'. Professor Laycock, who has particularly attended to phenomena of this nature,[23] insists that 'when the attention is directed to any portion of the body, innervation and circulation

* In England, Sir H. Holland was, I believe, the first to consider the influence of mental attention on various parts of the body, in his *Medical Notes and Reflections*, 1839, p. 64. This essay, much enlarged, was reprinted by Sir H. Holland in his *Chapters on Mental Physiology*, 1858, p. 79, from which work I always quote. At nearly the same time, as well as subsequently, Professor Laycock discussed the same subject: see *Edinburgh Medical and Surgical Journal*, July, 1839, pp. 17–22. Also his *Treatise on the Nervous Diseases of Women*, 1840, p. 110; and *Mind and Brain*, vol. ii, 1860, p. 327. Dr Carpenter's views on mesmerism have a nearly similar bearing. The great physiologist Müller treated (*Elements of Physiology*, Engl. translat., vol. ii, pp. 937, 1085) of the influence of the attention on the senses. Sir J. Paget discusses the influence of the mind on the nutrition of parts, in his *Lectures on Surgical Pathology*, 1853, vol. i, p. 39: I quote from the 3rd edit. revised by Professor Turner, 1870, p. 28. See, also, Gratiolet, *De la Phys.*, pp. 283–7. [Dr Tuke (*Journal of Mental Science*, October 1872) quotes a saying of John Hunter's: 'I am confident that I can fix my attention to any part until I have a sensation in that part.']

are excited locally, and the functional activity of that portion developed.'*

Robert Levenson commented: 'The increased blood flow is probably not a *direct* effect of the cognitive activity. Rather, thinking or focusing on an area is likely to increase muscle tonus in that area (such as would be the case in the preparation for action). Then blood flow will increase to serve the needs of the activated muscles.'

It is generally believed that the peristaltic movements of the intestines are influenced by attention being paid to them at fixed recurrent periods; and these movements depend on the contraction of unstriped and involuntary muscles. The abnormal action of the voluntary muscles in epilepsy, chorea, and hysteria is known to be influenced by the expectation of an attack, and by the sight of other patients similarly affected.[24] So it is with the involuntary acts of yawning and laughing.

Certain glands are much influenced by thinking of them, or of the conditions under which they have been habitually excited. This is familiar to every one in the increased flow of saliva, when the thought, for instance, of intensely acid fruit is kept before the mind.[25] It was shown in our sixth chapter, that an earnest and long-continued desire either to repress, or to increase, the action of the lacrymal glands is effectual. Some curious cases have been recorded in the case of women, of the power of the mind on the mammary glands; and still more remarkable ones in relation to the uterine functions.†

* [Professor Victor Carus describes (letter, 20 January 1877) how, when engaged in 1843 with a friend in working for a prize set by the Medical Faculty, in which it was necessary to determine the average rate of the pulse, he found it impossible to get correct results when either observer felt his own pulse, because the rate materially increased when attention was directed to the pulse.]

† Dr J. Crichton Browne, from his observations on the insane, is convinced that attention directed for a prolonged period on any part or organ may ultimately influence its capillary circulation and nutrition. He has given me some extraordinary cases; one of these, which cannot here be related in full, refers to a married woman fifty years of age, who laboured under the firm and long-continued delusion that she was pregnant. When the expected period arrived, she acted

What Darwin describes here is relevant to the effects of meditation. Richard Davidson, an American psychophysiologist who has been studying meditative practices, remarked: 'Some meditation practices involve attention to specific parts of the body, such as the point just at the tip of the nostrils. The notion that when attention is focused in this way, we notice odd sensations [as Darwin observed] is consistent with reports in the meditation literature.[C71] For example, when practitioners have pain in a particular bodily location and then train their attention on this location, a frequent report is they notice a variety of different sensations, including heat, tingling, etc. The monolithic concept of pain is thereby questioned in these accounts.'

When we direct our whole attention to any one sense, its acuteness is increased;* and the continued habit of close attention, as with blind people to that of hearing, and with the blind and deaf to that of touch, appears to improve the sense in question permanently. There is, also, some reason to believe, judging from the capacities of different races of man, that the effects are inherited. Turning to ordinary sensations, it is well known that pain is increased by attending to it; and Sir B. Brodie goes so far as to believe that pain may be felt in any part of the body to which attention is closely drawn.[26] Sir H. Holland also remarks that we become not only conscious of the existence of a part subjected to concentrated attention, but we experience in it various

---

precisely as if she had been really delivered of a child, and seemed to suffer extreme pain, so that the perspiration broke out on her forehead. The result was that a state of things returned, continuing for three days, which had ceased during the six previous years. Mr Braid gives, in his *Magic, Hypnotism*, etc., 1852, p. 95, and in his other works, analogous cases, as well as other facts showing the great influence of the will on the mammary glands, even on one breast alone.

* Dr Maudsley has given (*The Physiology and Pathology of Mind*, 2nd edit., 1868, p. 105), on good authority, some curious statements with respect to the improvement of the sense of touch by practice and attention. It is remarkable that when this sense has thus been rendered more acute at any point of the body, for instance, in a finger, it is likewise improved at the corresponding point on the opposite side of the body.

odd sensations, as of weight, heat, cold, tingling, or itching.[27]

Lastly, some physiologists maintain that the mind can influence the nutrition of parts. Sir J. Paget has given a curious instance of the power, not indeed of the mind, but of the nervous system, on the hair. A lady 'who is subject to attacks of what is called nervous headache, always finds in the morning after such an one, that some patches of her hair are white, as if powdered with starch. The change is effected in a night, and in a few days after, the hairs gradually regain their dark brownish colour.'*

We thus see that close attention certainly affects various parts and organs, which are not properly under the control of the will. By what means attention – perhaps the most wonderful of all the wondrous powers of the mind – is effected, is an extremely obscure subject. According to Müller,[28] the process by which the sensory cells of the brain are rendered, through the will, susceptible of receiving more intense and distinct impressions, is closely analogous to that by which the motor cells are excited to send nerve-force to the voluntary muscles. There are many points of analogy in the action of the sensory and motor nerve-cells; for instance, the familiar fact that close attention to any one sense causes fatigue, like the prolonged exertion of any one muscle.[29] When therefore we voluntarily concentrate our attention on any part of the body, the cells of the brain which receive impressions, or sensations from that part are, it is probable, in some unknown manner stimulated into activity. This may account, without any local change in the part to which our attention is earnestly directed, for pain or odd sensations being there felt or increased.

Davidson commented: 'Darwin was astoundingly prescient here and anticipated much research. The idea that attention to a specific bodily location has discernible local physiological effects is one that has received experimental confirmation over the past decade. Darwin also indicates

---

* *Lectures on Surgical Pathology*, 3rd edit., revised by Professor Turner, 1870, pp. 28, 31. [Dr W. Ogle contributes a similar instance of a London physician who suffers from neuralgia over the eyebrow; and with each attack a patch of hair in the brow whitens, to recover its colour again when the attack is past.]

that those parts of the brain related to the location of attention are, in some unknown manner, stimulated into activity. There is contemporary work on the neural sub-strates of attention which is consistent with this idea.[C72] Moreover, some of the anatomical circuitry by which such local neural changes can be produced are beginning to be characterized.'

If, however, the part is furnished with muscles, we cannot feel sure, as Dr Michael Foster has remarked to me, that some slight impulse may not be unconsciously sent to such muscles; and this would probably cause an obscure sensation in the part.

In a large number of cases, as with the salivary and lacrymal glands, intestinal canal, etc., the power of attention seems to rest, either chiefly, or as some physiologists think, exclusively, on the vaso-motor system being affected in such a manner that more blood is allowed to flow into the capillaries of the part in question. This increased action of the capillaries may in some cases be combined with the simultaneously increased activity of the sensorium.

The manner in which the mind affects the vaso-motor system may be conceived in the following manner. When we actually taste sour fruit, an impression is sent through the gustatory nerves to a certain part of the sensorium; this transmits nerve-force to the vaso-motor centre, which consequently allows the muscular coats of the small arteries that permeate the salivary glands to relax. Hence more blood flows into these glands, and they secrete a copious supply of saliva. Now it does not seem an improbable assumption, that, when we reflect intently on a sensation, the same part of the sensorium, or a closely connected part of it, is brought into a state of activity, in the same manner as when we actually perceive the sensation. If so, the same cells in the brain will be excited, though, perhaps, in a less degree, by vividly think-ing about a sour taste, as by perceiving it; and they will transmit in the one case, as in the other, nerve-force to the vaso-motor centre with the same results.

To give another, and, in some respects, more appropriate

illustration. If a man stands before a hot fire, his face reddens. This appears to be due, as Dr Michael Foster informs me, in part to the local action of the heat, and in part to a reflex action from the vaso-motor centres.[30] In this latter case, the heat affects the nerves of the face; these transmit an impression to the sensory cells of the brain, which act on the vaso-motor centre, and this reacts on the small arteries of the face, relaxing them and allowing them to become filled with blood. Here, again, it seems not improbable that if we were repeatedly to concentrate with great earnestness our attention on the recollection of our heated faces, the same part of the sensorium which gives us the consciousness of actual heat would be in some slight degree stimulated, and would in consequence tend to transmit some nerve-force to the vaso-motor centres, so as to relax the capillaries of the face. Now as men during endless generations have had their attention often and earnestly directed to their personal appearance, and especially to their faces, any incipient tendency in the facial capillaries to be thus affected will have become in the course of time greatly strengthened through the principles just referred to, namely, nerve-force passing readily along accustomed channels, and inherited habit. Thus, as it appears to me, a plausible explanation is afforded of the leading phenomena connected with the act of blushing.

Recapitulation. Men and women, and especially the young, have always valued, in a high degree, their personal appearance; and have likewise regarded the appearance of others. The face has been the chief object of attention, though, when man aboriginally went naked, the whole surface of his body would have been attended to. Our self-attention is excited almost exclusively by the opinion of others, for no person living in absolute solitude would care about his appearance. Every one feels blame more acutely than praise. Now, whenever we know, or suppose, that others are depreciating our personal appearance, our attention is strongly drawn towards ourselves, more especially to our faces. The probable effect of this will be, as has just been explained, to excite into activity that part of the sensorium which receives the sensory nerves of the face; and this will react through the vaso-motor system on the facial capillaries. By frequent reiteration during numberless generations, the process will have become so habitual, in association with the belief that others are thinking of us, that even a suspicion of their depreciation suffices to relax the capillaries, without any conscious thought about our faces. With some sensitive persons it is enough even to notice their dress to produce the same effect. Through the force, also, of association and inheritance our capillaries are relaxed, whenever we know, or imagine, that any one is blaming, though in silence, our actions, thoughts, or character; and, again, when we are highly praised.

On this hypothesis we can understand how it is that the face blushes much more than any other part of the body, though the whole surface is somewhat affected, more especially with the races which still go nearly naked. It is not at all surprising that the dark-coloured races should blush, though no change of colour is visible in their skins. From the principle of inheritance it is not surprising that persons born blind should blush. We can understand why the young are much more affected than the old, and women more than men; and why the opposite sexes especially excite each other's blushes. It becomes obvious why personal remarks should be particularly liable to cause blushing, and why the most powerful of all the causes is shyness; for shyness relates to the presence and opinion of others, and the shy are always more or less self-conscious. With respect to real shame from moral delinquencies, we can perceive why it is not guilt, but the thought that others think us guilty, which raises a blush. A man reflecting on a crime committed in solitude, and stung by his conscience, does not blush; yet he will blush under the vivid recollection of a detected fault, or of one committed in the presence of others, the degree of blushing being closely related to the feeling of regard for those who have detected, witnessed, or suspected his fault. Breaches of conventional rules of conduct, if they are rigidly insisted on by our equals or superiors, often cause more intense blushes even than a detected crime; and an act which is really criminal, if not blamed by our equals, hardly raises

343

a tinge of colour on our cheeks. Modesty from humility, or from an indelicacy, excites a vivid blush, as both relate to the judgement or fixed customs of others.

From the intimate sympathy which exists between the capillary circulation of the surface of the head and of the brain, whenever there is intense blushing, there will be some, and often great, confusion of mind. This is frequently accompanied by awkward movements, and sometimes by the involuntary twitching of certain muscles.

As blushing, according to this hypothesis, is an indirect result of attention, originally directed to our personal appearance, that is to the surface of the body, and more especially to the face, we can understand the meaning of the gestures which accompany blushing throughout the world. These consist in hiding the face, or turning it towards the ground, or to one side. The eyes are generally averted or are restless, for to look at the man who causes us to feel shame or shyness, immediately brings home in an intolerable manner the consciousness that his gaze is directed on us. Through the principle of associated habit, the same movements of the face and eyes are practised, and can, indeed, hardly be avoided, whenever we know or believe that others are blaming, or too strongly praising, our moral conduct.

It is surprising that Darwin did not mention embarrassment, for the word was in use in his time.[C73] Embarrassment is the emotion that current researchers mention most often with regard to blushing. Many of those who now study embarrassment have adopted Darwin's view that it is attention to the appearance of the person which most often is the cause of blushing. Shyness, like modesty, is not considered an emotion but a personality trait. Some writers and researchers treat embarrassment and shame as variations on the same fundamental emotion,[C74] while others[C75] argue that they are very different emotions.

CHAPTER XIV

Concluding Remarks and Summary

The three leading principles which have determined the chief movements of expression – Their inheritance – On the part which the will and intention have played in the acquirement of various expressions – The instinctive recognition of expression – The bearing of our subject on the specific unity of the races of man – On the successive acquirement of various expressions by the progenitors of man – The importance of expression – Conclusion.

I have now described, to the best of my ability, the chief expressive actions in man, and in some few of the lower animals. I have also attempted to explain the origin or development of these actions through the three principles given in the first chapter. The first of these principles is, that movements which are serviceable in gratifying some desire, or in relieving some sensation, if often repeated, become so habitual that they are performed, whether or not of any service, whenever the same desire or sensation is felt, even in a very weak degree.

Our second principle is that of antithesis. The habit of voluntarily performing opposite movements under opposite impulses has become firmly established in us by the practice of our whole lives. Hence, if certain actions have been regularly performed, in accordance with our first principle, under a certain frame of mind, there will be a strong and involuntary tendency to the performance of directly opposite actions, whether or not these are of any use, under the excitement of an opposite frame of mind.

Our third principle is the direct action of the excited nervous system on the body, independently of the will, and independently, in large part, of habit. Experience shows that nerve-force is generated and set free whenever the cerebro-spinal system is excited. The direction which the nerve-force follows is necessarily determined by the lines of connection between the nerve-cells, with each other and with various parts of the body. But the direction is likewise much influenced by habit; inasmuch as nerve-force passes readily along accustomed channels.

The frantic and senseless actions of an enraged man may be attributed in part to the undirected flow of nerve-force, and in part to the effects of habit, for these actions often vaguely represent the act of striking. They thus pass into gestures included under our first principle; as when an indignant man unconsciously throws himself into a fitting attitude for attacking his opponent, though without any intention of making an actual attack. We see also the influence of habit in all the emotions and sensations which are called exciting; for they have assumed this character from having habitually led to energetic action; and action affects, in an indirect manner, the respiratory and circulatory system; and the latter reacts on the brain. Whenever these emotions or sensations are even slightly felt by us, though they may not at the time lead to any exertion, our whole system is nevertheless disturbed through the force of habit and association. Other emotions and sensations are called depressing, because they have not habitually led to energetic action, excepting just at first, as in the case of extreme pain, fear, and grief, and they have ultimately caused complete exhaustion; they are consequently expressed chiefly by negative signs and by prostration. Again, there are other emotions, such as that of affection, which do not commonly lead to action of any kind, and consequently are not exhibited by any strongly marked outward signs. Affection indeed, in as far as it is a pleasurable sensation, excites the ordinary signs of pleasure.

On the other hand, many of the effects due to the excitement of the nervous system seem to be quite independent of the flow of nerve-force along the channels which have been rendered habitual by former exertions of the will. Such effects, which often reveal the state of mind of the person thus affected, cannot at present be explained; for instance, the change of colour in the hair from extreme terror or grief – the cold sweat and the trembling of the muscles from fear – the modified secretions of the intestinal canal – and the failure of certain glands to act.

Notwithstanding that much remains unintelligible in our present subject, so many expressive movements and actions can be explained to a certain extent through the above three principles, that we may hope hereafter to see all explained by these or by closely analogous principles.

Actions of all kinds, if regularly accompanying any state of the mind, are at once recognized as expressive. These may consist of movements of any part of the body, as the wagging of a dog's tail, the shrugging of a man's shoulders, the erection of the hair, the exudation of perspiration, the state of the capillary circulation, laboured breathing, and the use of the vocal or other sound-producing instruments. Even insects express anger, terror, jealousy, and love by their stridulation. With man the respiratory organs are of especial importance in expression, not only in a direct, but in a still higher degree in an indirect manner.

Few points are more interesting in our present subject than the extraordinarily complex chain of events which lead to certain expressive movements. Take, for instance, the oblique eyebrows of a man suffering from grief or anxiety. When infants scream loudly from hunger or pain, the circulation is affected, and the eyes tend to become gorged with blood: consequently the muscles surrounding the eyes are strongly contracted as a protection: this action, in the course of many generations, has become firmly fixed and inherited: but when, with advancing years and culture, the habit of screaming is partially repressed, the muscles round the eyes still tend to contract, whenever even slight distress is felt: of these muscles, the pyramidals of the nose are less under the control of the will than are the others, and their contraction can be checked only by that of the central fasciae of the front muscle: these latter fasciae draw up the inner ends of the eyebrows, and wrinkle the forehead in a peculiar manner, which we instantly recognize as the expression of grief or anxiety. Slight movements, such as these just described, or the scarcely perceptible drawing down of the corners of the mouth, are the last remnants or rudiments of strongly marked and intelligible movements. They are as full of significance to us in regard to expression, as are ordinary rudiments to the naturalist in the classification and genealogy of organic beings.

That the chief expressive actions, exhibited by man and by the lower animals, are now innate or inherited – that is, have not been learnt by the individual – is admitted by every one. So little has learning or imitation to do with several of them that they are from the earliest days and throughout life quite beyond our control; for instance, the relaxation of the arteries of the skin in blushing, and the increased action of the heart in anger. We may see children, only two or three years old, and even those born blind, blushing from shame; and the naked scalp of a very young infant reddens from passion. Infants scream from pain directly after birth, and all their features then assume the same form as during subsequent years. These facts alone suffice to show that many of our most important expressions have not been learnt; but it is remarkable that some, which are certainly innate, require practice in the individual, before they are performed in a full and perfect manner; for instance, weeping and laughing. The inheritance of most of our expressive actions explains the fact that those born blind display them, as I hear from the Rev. R. H. Blair, equally well with those gifted with eyesight. We can thus also understand the fact that the young and the old of widely different races, both with man and animals, express the same state of mind by the same movements.

We are so familiar with the fact of young and old animals displaying their feelings in the same manner, that we hardly perceive how remarkable it is that a young puppy should wag its tail when pleased, depress its ears and uncover its canine teeth when pretending to be savage, just like an old dog; or that a kitten should arch its little back and erect its hair when frightened and angry, like an old cat. When, however, we turn to less common gestures in ourselves, which we are accustomed to look at as artificial or conventional – such as shrugging the shoulders, as a sign of impotence, or the raising the arms with open hands and extended fingers, as a sign of wonder – we feel perhaps too much surprise at finding that they are innate. That these and some other gestures are inherited, we may infer from their being performed by very young children, by those born blind, and by the most widely distinct races of man. We should also bear in mind that new and highly peculiar tricks, in association with certain states of the mind, are known to have arisen in certain individuals, and to have been afterwards transmitted to their offspring, in some cases, for more than one generation.

Certain other gestures which seem to us so natural that we might easily imagine that they were innate, apparently have been learnt like the words of a language. This seems to be the case with the joining of the uplifted hands, and the turning up of the eyes, in prayer. So it is with kissing as a mark of affection; but this is innate, in so far as it depends on the pleasure derived from contact with a beloved person. The evidence with respect to the inheritance of nodding and shaking the head, as signs of affirmation and negation, is doubtful; for they are not universal, yet seem too general to have been independently acquired by all the individuals of so many races.

We will now consider how far the will and consciousness have come into play in the development of the various movements of expression. As far as we can judge, only a few expressive movements, such as those just referred to, are learnt by each individual; that is, were consciously and voluntarily performed during the early years of life for some definite object, or in imitation of others, and then became habitual. The far greater number of the movements of expression, and all the more important ones, are, as we have seen, innate or inherited; and such cannot be said to depend on the will of the individual. Nevertheless, all those included under our first principle were at first voluntarily performed for a definite object – namely, to escape some danger, to relieve some distress, or to gratify some desire. For instance, there can hardly be a doubt that the animals which fight with their teeth, have acquired the habit of drawing back their ears closely to their heads, when feeling savage, from their progenitors having voluntarily acted in this manner in order to protect their ears from being torn by their antagonists; for those animals which do not fight with their teeth do not thus express a savage state of mind. We may infer as highly probable that we ourselves have acquired the habit of contracting the muscles round the eyes, whilst crying gently, that is, without the utterance of any loud sound, from our progenitors, especially during infancy, having experienced, during the act of screaming, an uncomfortable sensation in their eyeballs. Again, some highly expressive movements result from the endeavour to check or prevent other expressive movements; thus the obliquity of the eyebrows and the drawing down of the corners of the mouth follow from the endeavour to prevent a screaming-fit from coming on, or to check it after it has come on. Here it is obvious that the consciousness and will must at first have come into play; not that we are conscious in these or in other such cases what muscles are brought into action, any more than when we perform the most ordinary voluntary movements.

With respect to the expressive movements due to the principle of antithesis, it is clear that the will has intervened, though in a remote and indirect manner. So again with the movements coming under our third principle; these, in as far as they are influenced by nerve-force readily passing along habitual channels, have been determined by former and repeated exertions of the will. The effects indirectly due to this latter agency are often combined in a complex manner, through the force of habit and association, with those directly resulting from the excitement of the cerebro-spinal system. This seems to be the case with the increased action of the heart under the influence of any strong emotion. When an animal erects its hair, assumes a threatening attitude, and utters fierce sounds, in order to terrify an enemy, we see a curious combination of movements which were originally voluntary with those that are involuntary. It is, however, possible that even strictly involuntary actions, such as the erection of the hair, may have been affected by the mysterious power of the will.

Some expressive movements may have arisen spontaneously, in association with certain states of the mind, like the tricks lately referred to, and afterwards been inherited. But I know of no evidence rendering this view probable.

The power of communication between the members of the same tribe by means of language has been of paramount importance in the development of man; and the force of language is much aided by the expressive movements of the face and body. We perceive this at once when we converse on an important subject with any person whose face is concealed. Nevertheless there are no grounds, as far as I can discover, for believing that any muscle has been developed or even modified exclusively for the sake of expression. The vocal and other sound-producing organs, by which various expressive noises are produced, seem to form a partial exception; but I have elsewhere attempted to show that these organs were first developed for sexual purposes, in order that one sex might call or charm the other. Nor can I discover grounds for believing that any inherited movement, which now serves as a means of expression, was at first voluntarily and consciously performed for this special purpose – like some of the gestures and the finger-language used by the deaf and dumb. On the contrary, every true or inherited movement of expression seems to have had some natural and independent origin. But when once acquired, such movements may be voluntarily and consciously employed as a means of communication. Even infants, if carefully attended to, find out at a very early age that their screaming brings relief, and they soon voluntarily practise it. We may frequently see a person voluntarily raising his eyebrows to express surprise, or smiling to express pretended satisfaction and acquiescence. A man often wishes to make certain gestures conspicuous or demonstrative, and will raise his extended arms with widely opened fingers above his head, to show astonishment, or lift his shoulders to his ears, to show that he cannot or will not do something. The tendency to such movements will be strengthened or increased by their being thus voluntarily and repeatedly performed; and the effects may be inherited.

It is perhaps worth consideration whether movements at first used only by one or a few individuals to express a certain state of mind may not sometimes have spread to others, and ultimately have become universal, through the powers of conscious and unconscious imitation. That there exists in man a strong tendency to imitation, independently of the conscious will, is certain. This is exhibited in the most extraordinary manner in certain brain diseases, especially at the commencement of inflammatory soften-ing of the brain, and has been called the 'echo sign'. Patients thus affected imitate, without understanding, every absurd gesture which is made, and every word which is uttered near them, even in a foreign language.[1] In the case of animals, the jackal and wolf have learnt under confinement to imitate the barking of the dog. How the barking of the dog, which serves to express various emotions and desires, and which is so remarkable from having been acquired since the animal was domesticated, and from being inherited in different degrees by different breeds, was first learnt, we do not know; but may we not suspect that imitation has had something to do with its acquisition, owing to dogs having long lived in strict association with so loquacious an animal as man?

In the course of the foregoing remarks and throughout this volume, I have often felt much difficulty about the proper applica-tion of the terms, will, consciousness, and intention. Actions, which were at first voluntary, soon become habitual, and at last hereditary, and may then be performed even in opposition to the will. Although they often reveal the state of the mind, this result was not at first either intended or expected. Even such words as that 'certain movements serve as a means of expression' are apt to mislead, as they imply that this was their primary purpose or object. This, however, seems rarely or never to have been the case; the movements having been at first either of some direct use, or the indirect effect of the excited state of the sensorium. An infant may scream either intentionally or instinctively to show that it wants food; but it has no wish or intention to draw its features into the peculiar form which so plainly indicates misery; yet some of the most characteristic expressions exhibited by man are derived from the act of screaming, as has been explained.

Although most of our expressive actions are innate or instinc-tive, as is admitted by everyone, it is a different question whether we have any instinctive power of recognizing them. This has generally been assumed to be the case; but the assumption has been strongly controverted by M. Lemoine.[2] Monkeys soon learn to distinguish, not only the tones of voice of their masters, but the expression of their faces, as is asserted by a careful observer.[3] Dogs well know the difference between caressing and threatening gestures or tones; and they seem to recognize a compassionate tone. But as far as I can make out, after repeated trials, they do not understand any movement confined to the features, excepting a smile or laugh; and this they appear, at least in some cases, to recognize. This limited amount of knowledge has probably been gained, both by monkeys and dogs, through their associating harsh or kind treatment with our actions; and the knowledge certainly is not instinctive. Children, no doubt, would soon learn the movements of expression in their elders in the same manner as animals learn those of man. Moreover, when a child cries or laughs, he knows in a general manner what he is doing and what he feels; so that a very small exertion of reason would tell him what crying or laughing meant in others. But the question is, do our children acquire their knowledge of expression solely by experience through the power of association and reason?

As most of the movements of expression must have been gradually acquired, afterwards becoming instinctive, there seems to be some degree of *a priori* probability that their recognition would likewise have become instinctive. There is, at least, no greater difficulty in believing this than in admitting that, when a female quadruped first bears young, she knows the cry of distress of her offspring, or than in admitting that many animals instinctively recognize and fear their enemies; and of both these statements there can be no reasonable doubt. It is however extremely difficult to prove that our children instinctively recognize any expression. I attended to this point in my first-born infant, who could not have learnt any thing by associating with other children, and I was convinced that he understood a smile and received pleasure from seeing one, answering it by another, at much too early an age to have learnt anything by experience. When this child was about four months old, I made in his presence many odd noises and strange grimaces, and tried to look savage; but the noises, if not too loud, as well as the grimaces, were all taken as good jokes; and I attributed this at the time to their being preceded or accompanied by smiles. When five months old, he seemed to understand a compassionate expression and tone of voice. When a few days over six months old, his nurse pretended to cry, and I saw that his face instantly assumed a melancholy expression, with the corners of the mouth strongly depressed; now this child could rarely have seen any other child crying, and never a grown-up person crying, and I should doubt whether at so early an age he could have reasoned on the subject. Therefore it seems to me that an innate feeling must have told him that the pretended crying of his nurse expressed grief: and this, through the instinct of sympathy, excited grief in him.*

Oster comments that it is well known that infants pay attention to face-like stimuli from birth. The question is whether it is because of something special about faces or because of more general features, such as high contrast. Infants prefer smiling to non-smiling faces, but whether it is because they have an innate smile detector or because of more general stimulus characteristics such as 'toothiness', is not clear.[C76]

M. Lemoine argues that, if man possessed an innate knowledge of expression, authors and artists would not have found it so difficult, as is notoriously the case, to describe and depict the characteristic signs of each particular state of mind. But this does not seem to me a valid argument. We may actually behold the expression changing in an unmistakable manner in a man or animal, and yet be quite unable, as I know from experience, to analyse the nature of the change. In the two photographs given by Duchenne of the same old man (Plate III, Figs 5 and 6), almost every one recognized that the one represented a true, and the other a false smile; but I have found it very difficult to decide in

---

* [Mr Wallace (*Quarterly Journal of Science*, January, 1873) makes the ingenious objection that the strange expression on the nurse's face may have simply frightened the child and thus made it cry.

Compare the case of Chad Cranage, the blacksmith, in *Adam Bede*, at whom, when he had his clean Sunday face, his little granddaughter used to cry as at a stranger.]

what the whole amount of difference consists. It has often struck me as a curious fact that so many shades of expression are instantly recognized without any conscious process of analysis on our part. No one, I believe, can clearly describe a sullen or sly expression; yet many observers are unanimous that these expressions can be recognized in the various races of man. Almost every one to whom I showed Duchenne's photograph of the young man with oblique eyebrows (Plate II, Fig. 2), at once declared that it expressed grief or some such feeling; yet probably not one of these persons, or one out of a thousand persons, could beforehand have told anything precise about the obliquity of the eyebrows with their inner ends puckered, or about the rectangular furrows on the forehead. So it is with many other expressions, of which I have had practical experience in the trouble requisite in instructing others what points to observe. If, then, great ignorance of details does not prevent our recognizing with certainty and promptitude various expressions, I do not see how this ignorance can be advanced as an argument that our knowledge, though vague and general, is not innate.

I have endeavoured to show in considerable detail that all the chief expressions exhibited by man are the same throughout the world. This fact is interesting, as it affords a new argument in favour of the several races being descended from a single parent-stock, which must have been almost completely human in structure, and to a large extent in mind, before the period at which the races diverged from each other. No doubt similar structures, adapted for the same purpose, have often been independently acquired through variation and Natural Selection by distinct species; but this view will not explain close similarity between distinct species in a multitude of unimportant details. Now if we bear in mind the numerous points of structure having no relation to expression, in which all the races of man closely agree, and then add to them the numerous points, some of the highest importance and many of the most trifling value, on which the movements of expression directly or indirectly depend, it seems to me improbable in the highest degree that so much similarity, or rather identity of structure, could have been acquired by independent means. Yet this must have been the case if the races of man are descended from several aboriginally distinct species. It is far more probable that the many points of close similarity in the various races are due to inheritance from a single parent-form, which had already assumed a human character.

It is a curious, though perhaps an idle speculation, how early in the long line of our progenitors the various expressive movements, now exhibited by man, were successively acquired. The following remarks will at least serve to recall some of the chief points discussed in this volume. We may confidently believe that laughter, as a sign of pleasure or enjoyment, was practised by our progenitors long before they deserved to be called human; for very many kinds of monkeys, when pleased, utter a reiterated sound, clearly analogous to our laughter, often accompanied by vibratory movements of their jaws or lips, with the corners of the mouth drawn backwards and upwards, by the wrinkling of the cheeks, and even by the brightening of the eyes.

We may likewise infer that fear was expressed from an extremely remote period, in almost the same manner as it now is by man; namely, by trembling, the erection of the hair, cold perspiration, pallor, widely opened eyes, the relaxation of most of the muscles, and by the whole body cowering downwards or held motionless.

Suffering, if great, will from the first have caused screams or groans to be uttered, the body to be contorted, and the teeth to be ground together. But our progenitors will not have exhibited those highly expressive movements of the features which accompany screaming and crying until their circulatory and respiratory organs, and the muscles surrounding the eyes, had acquired their present structure. The shedding of tears appears to have originated through reflex action from the spasmodic contraction of the eyelids, together perhaps with the eyeballs becoming gorged with blood during the act of screaming. Therefore weeping probably came on rather late in the line of our descent; and this conclusion agrees with the fact that our nearest allies, the anthropomorphous apes, do not weep. But we must here exercise some caution, for as certain monkeys, which are not closely related to man, weep, this habit might have been developed long ago in a sub-branch of the group from which man is derived. Our early progenitors, when suffering from grief or anxiety, would not have made their eyebrows oblique, or have drawn down the corners of their mouths, until they had acquired the habit of endeavouring to restrain their screams. The expression, therefore, of grief and anxiety is eminently human.

Rage will have been expressed at a very early period by threatening or frantic gestures, by the reddening of the skin, and by glaring eyes, but not by frowning. For the habit of frowning seems to have been acquired chiefly from the corrugators being the first muscles to contract round the eyes, whenever during infancy pain, anger, or distress is felt, and there consequently is a near approach to screaming; and partly from a frown serving as a shade in difficult and intent vision. It seems probable that this shading action would not have become habitual until man had assumed a completely upright position, for monkeys do not frown when exposed to a glaring light. Our early progenitors, when enraged, would probably have exposed their teeth more freely than does man, even when giving full vent to his rage, as with the insane. We may, also, feel almost certain that they would have protruded their lips, when sulky or disappointed, in a greater degree than is the case with our own children, or even with the children of existing savage races.

Our early progenitors, when indignant or moderately angry, would not have held their heads erect, opened their chests, squared their shoulders, and clenched their fists, until they had acquired the ordinary carriage and upright attitude of man, and had learnt to fight with their fists or clubs. Until this period had arrived the antithetical gesture of shrugging the shoulders, as a sign of impotence or of patience, would not have been developed. From the same reason astonishment would not then have been expressed by raising the arms with open hands and extended fingers. Nor, judging from the actions of monkeys, would astonishment have been exhibited by a widely open mouth; but the eyes would have been opened and the eyebrows arched. Disgust would have been shown at a very early period by movements round the mouth, like those of vomiting – that is, if the view which I have suggested respecting the source of the expression is correct, namely, that our progenitors had the power, and used it, of voluntarily and quickly rejecting any food from their stomachs which they disliked. But the more refined manner of showing contempt or disdain, by lowering the eyelids, or turning away the eyes and face, as if the despised person were not worth looking at, would not probably have been acquired until a much later period.

Of all expressions, blushing seems to be the most strictly human; yet it is common to all or nearly all the races of man, whether or not any change of colour is visible in their skin. The relaxation of the small arteries of the surface, on which blushing depends, seems to have primarily resulted from earnest attention directed to the appearance of our own persons, especially of our faces, aided by habit, inheritance, and the ready flow of nerve-force along accustomed channels; and afterwards to have been extended by the power of association to self-attention directed to moral conduct. It can hardly be doubted that many animals are capable of appreciating beautiful colours and even forms, as is shown by the pains which the individuals of one sex take in displaying their beauty before those of the opposite sex. But it does not seem possible that any animal, until its mental powers had been developed to an equal or nearly equal degree with those of man, would have closely considered and been sensitive about its own personal appearance. Therefore we may conclude that blushing originated at a very late period in the long line of our descent.

From the various facts just alluded to, and given in the course of this volume, it follows that, if the structure of our organs of respiration and circulation had differed in only a slight degree from the state in which they now exist, most of our expressions would have been wonderfully different. A very slight change in the course of the arteries and veins which run to the head, would probably have prevented the blood from accumulating in our eyeballs during violent expiration; for this occurs in extremely few quadrupeds. In this case we should not have displayed some of our most characteristic expressions. If man had breathed water by the aid of external brachiae (though the idea is hardly conceivable), instead of air through his mouth and nostrils, his features would not have expressed his feelings much more efficiently than now do his hands or limbs. Rage and disgust, however, would still have been shown by movements about the lips and mouth, and the eyes would have become brighter or duller according to the state of the circulation. If our ears had remained movable, their movements would have been highly expressive, as is the case with all the animals which fight with their teeth; and we may infer that our early progenitors thus fought, as we still uncover the canine tooth on one side when we sneer at or defy any one, and we uncover all our teeth when furiously enraged.

The movements of expression in the face and body, whatever their origin may have been, are in themselves of much importance for our welfare. They serve as the first means of communication between the mother and her infant; she smiles approval, and thus encourages her child on the right path, or frowns disapproval. We readily perceive sympathy in others by their expression; our sufferings are thus mitigated and our pleasures increased; and mutual good feeling is thus strengthened. The movements of expression give vividness and energy to our spoken words. They reveal the thoughts and intentions of others more truly than do words, which may be falsified. Whatever amount of truth the so-called science of physiognomy may contain, appears to depend, as Haller long ago remarked,[4] on different persons bringing into frequent use different facial muscles, according to their dispositions; the development of these muscles being perhaps thus increased, and the lines or furrows on the face, due to the habitual contraction, being thus rendered deep and more conspicuous. The free expression by outward signs of an emotion intensifies it.* On the other hand, the repression, as far as this is possible,

* [In speaking of the effect of acting, Maudsley (*The Physiology of Mind*, 1876, pp. 387, 388) says that the emotion is intensified and made definite by the bodily action. Other writers have made similar remarks, e.g., Wundt, *Essays*, 1885, p. 235. Braid found that passions can be produced by putting hypnotized people in appropriate attitudes.]

of all outward signs softens our emotions.* He who gives way to violent gestures will increase his rage; he who does not control the signs of fear will experience fear in a greater degree; and he who remains passive when overwhelmed with grief loses his best chance of recovering elasticity of mind. These results follow partly from the intimate relation which exists between almost all the emotions and their outward manifestations; and partly from the direct influence of exertion on the heart, and consequently on the brain. Even the simulation of an emotion tends to arouse it in our minds. Shakespeare, who from his wonderful knowledge of the human mind ought to be an excellent judge, says:

> 'Is it not monstrous that this player here,
> But in a fiction, in a dream of passion,
> Could force his soul so to his own conceit,
> That, from her working, all his visage wann'd;
> Tears in his eyes, distraction in 's aspect,
> A broken voice, and his whole function suiting
> With forms to his conceit? And all for nothing!'
>
> *Hamlet*, ii, 2

We have seen that the study of the theory of expression confirms to a certain limited extent the conclusion that man is derived from some lower animal form, and supports the belief of the specific or sub-specific unity of the several races; but as far as my judgement serves, such confirmation was hardly needed. We have also seen that expression in itself, or the language of the emotions, as it has sometimes been called, is certainly of importance for the welfare of mankind. To understand, as far as is possible, the source or origin of the various expressions which may be hourly seen on the faces of the men around us, not to mention our domesticated animals, ought to possess much interest for us. From these several causes, we may conclude that the philosophy of our subject has well deserved the attention which it has already received from several excellent observers, and that it deserves still further attention, especially from any able physiologist.

* Gratiolet (*De la Physionomie*, 1865, p. 66) insists on the truth of this conclusion.

AFTERWORD

Universality of Emotional Expression?
A Personal History of the Dispute

BY PAUL EKMAN

There is a story to be told. Not just the scientific story of how Darwin's views on expression were confirmed (or not) by research in the hundred years after his death. There is a story about how the clash of strong personalities, world politics, and the role of friendship and loyalty influenced the judgments of key figures in the scientific community. It is a drama that involves strong feelings and concealment, a drama not entirely over as I write, with the actors struggling over the ownership and interpretation of Charles Darwin's legacy about facial expressions of emotion.

Darwin's work on expression was published near the end of the nineteenth century, in 1872. The struggle about how to interpret *Expression* was fought in the twentieth century when many scientists were reacting against the 'Social Darwinists' who argued that there was no need to change society, to make working conditions better, or offer equal access to education. Let the fittest survive!* It was a time when eugenics, the selective breeding of a 'better' race seemed possible. When the Nazis came to power, a biological basis for the superiority of one group of humans, the 'Aryan race', became a powerful nation's policy, imposed by force on many conquered nations.

Controversy about Darwin is not new. His *Origin of Species*, published in 1859 (thirteen years before *Expression*) challenged

---

* The well-known phrase ('survival of the fittest') comes from Herbert Spencer, not Darwin, although Darwin did cite it and agreed with what it implies in terms of natural selection.

the creationist view of man, which resulted in fierce exchanges in the scientific community and in the press. Religious commitments and personality played an enormous role then. Darwin was careful not to speak out directly against those who attacked *Origin*. But he did not stop his colleagues from doing so for him.

I play that role now, speaking out against his opponents for Darwin's claims about the nature of emotional expression. I considered limiting myself to the scientific evidence, but if I had, readers might not understand what all the furor is about. The story involves more than Darwin's evidence, or evidence found since then. For readers to understand the controversy and make their own judgments, they need to know what is not in the scientific reports; they need to know the motives, history and social factors which influenced the principal antagonists. It was only a small group of actors. I was one of them, and I knew all the others, and am the only one still alive to tell this story. The key members of the cast were:

MARGARET MEAD, a famous anthropologist and the most outspoken cultural relativist of this century. In her early years Mead argued persuasively that social behavior was malleable, determined by culture. Darwin could not be correct about universals; expressions must be culture specific, to be consistent with her claims about the absolute power of culture. Later in life she brought in the role of biology, but (for reasons I explain later) still denied that expressions are universal. Although Mead never studied expressions, she is the central character, re-entering again and again, with her former husband Gregory Bateson, her protégé Ray Birdwhistell (the strongest voice against universal facial expressions), and her denunciation of an earlier book[1] I had edited supporting Darwin's views.

GREGORY BATESON, another world-famous anthropologist, who later became a major communication theorist. He was the first to use a camera to record non-verbal behavior when studying another culture, in his famous book[2] with Mead on Balinese character. Gregory tried to convince me that Darwin was wrong in thinking of facial expressions as signs of emotion. They were more usefully considered solely as communicative signals, he said, not signs of internal physiological changes. This view is still common among some of the ethologists who study the biological basis of social behavior in animals and man. I understand now that there is no contradiction between Gregory's view and the traditional view of emotional expression, but I only sensed it then and could not explain it to him. Despite our disagreement, it was typical of Gregory that he lent me the camera he had used in Bali and encouraged me to go to New Guinea to pursue my research on expression, being host to me in his home for a few days when I began that journey.

RAY BIRDWHISTELL, an anthropologist-linguist, initially thought Darwin was right, but when he examined people in different cultures he saw no universal expressions.[3] Ray was a spectacular performer, able to mimic instantly and accurately the posture, expression and mannerisms of anyone. But he had little beyond his personal observations and skill as an observer to prove that emotional expressions were culture-specific.

SILVAN TOMKINS, a philosopher and a psychologist, in mid-life wrote[4] a theory about emotion and the face, which incorporated Darwin's ideas that facial expressions of emotion are innate and universal. Silvan amazed people by his ability to interpret emotions and personality from facial expression, but he too had little scientific evidence for his theory.

I AM THE LAST ACTOR, entering this fray as an unknown scientist, half the age of each of these luminaries when I began my research on expression in 1965. I came to know each of them, fought with some, loved and admired others. I will try to tell the story fairly, but I am not an impartial observer. I am a protagonist. I believe the facts I report speak for themselves, but they did not convince all the other actors. I am convinced by the evidence; but evidence does not always overcome loyalties, rivalries or political commitments, and not all of us agree about what constitutes evidence. I try to present each protagonist in the most sympathetic light I can manage. As I describe in more detail later, when I began to study facial expression I did not have a strong commitment about whether or not they were universal. My goal was to settle the matter decisively. Margaret Mead later wrote that it was outrageous for me to have such a goal.

I begin with what Darwin said and the evidence he provided about facial expressions of emotion. Their universality is one of his central themes in *Expression*. It is the one idea in it for which he gathered data himself, asking those who had lived or traveled in foreign countries about the expressions they had observed. For the two other central themes – that expressions are not unique to humans, and the three principles which explain why particular expressions occur – he relied upon argument, example and the work of others.

Universality mattered to Darwin because it provided support for his theory of evolution. Universality would make more plausible his claim that emotional expressions are not unique to humans but are shared with other primates. Consider the reverse: what if our expressions were found to be constructed from what we learn from our parents, school or magazines, if a 'frown'* meant enjoyment in some part of the world and was never visible at all in some other culture? If we do not share these expressions, then how can they be the product of our evolutionary history, how can they be shared with other primates? Although evolutionary theory can survive a discontinuity between species – some argue that language is unique to humans – evidence for continuity on something as fundamental as emotion and expression certainly buttresses an evolutionary view.

Proof of the universality of facial expressions was relevant to a second of Darwin's concerns: it would support his belief that human beings had descended from a common progenitor. Evidence for universal facial expressions would challenge the claims by racists and others of his time that Europeans had descended from more advanced progenitors than those of Africans.

Ironically, Darwin's insight that facial expressions of emotion are universal has stood the test of time, but his evidence has not. Recall please from my Introduction that Darwin's evidence was

---

* I have put the 'frown' in quotes because it is not clear exactly what it refers to. Is the frown in the forehead or the mouth? A number of words which refer to expression are vague in this way. This is one of the reasons we had to develop a new 'language' – The Facial Action Coding System[5] – to describe facial movements precisely.

the replies he received to questions sent to British colonials asking them about expressions they observed in foreign lands.* There are three problems with this evidence. First, Darwin did not ask a sufficient number of people in each country for answers; for most countries he had just one informant, who could have been mistaken or biased. Second, he relied upon what these English-men living or traveling abroad told him; it would have been better if he had been able to ask the natives of each country instead (or asked his English correspondents to ask the natives).

Third, Darwin's wording suggested the answer he wanted. For example, he asked, 'Is astonishment expressed by the eyes and mouth being opened wide, and by the eyebrows being raised?' He should have asked, 'What emotion is being expressed when people you observe have their eyes and mouth open wide and their eyebrows raised?' Even better than describing the expres-sions would have been to send photographs of them to his inform-ants in the various countries, who could have asked the natives what emotion the person in the photograph was feeling. Darwin did show photographs, but only to people in England. I assume he did not send photographs abroad because it would have been costly, and because he did not have adequate photographs depicting all the emotions he was studying.[7]

Most of those who challenged the universality of facial expressions of emotion in the century after Darwin (and there were many) were not bothered by the flaws in his evidence or by his evolutionary theory. Their attack was on the relevance of evolutionary theory to the personal, intimate, and complex emo-tions we feel. Such feelings are distinctly human, they argued; our environment – what we learn, our experience in the world – not our biology constructs our emotions and their expressions. And because experiences are different from one culture to another, so too must be emotions and their expression.

---

* Stephen Jay Gould reports that: 'Darwin shamelessly made requests upon friends, colleagues and acquaintances in all modes of life. He would ask for anything he needed, no matter how peculiar, and no matter how extensive the effort required. He always asked politely, and with profound apology in advance for requesting so much effort – but ask he did.'[6]

Through the first half of this century, the behaviorists in psychology claimed that learning was responsible for all that we do and all that we are, including our attitudes and personalities. Individual differences could be wiped out if everyone had the same environment. There would be no differences between men and women if they were only brought up in the same way. Parents were held responsible by psychiatrists for the neuroses and psychoses of their children. If they had acted differently, their offspring would be healthy, creative and productive. In education, differences in cognitive skills were attributed solely to poor schooling and impoverished home environments, with no acknowledgment that there might be inborn differences in kinds of intelligence. In anthropology, the cultural relativists triumphantly produced accounts of exotic cultures where people lived, mated and raised their offspring in ways so different from ours. The first half of the twentieth century was a time of optimism about the perfectibility of man. There was no acknowledged limit to how much human nature could be reconstructed by changing the environment. Change the state, educate the parents, modify child-rearing practices and we would have a nation of renaissance men and women. Nothing was innate. Our genes played no role in any of the differences in talent, ability or personality. Everything about our social lives was thought to be created by experience, and experiences could be changed and improved. As Margaret Mead put it in her book *Sex and Temperament in Three Primitive Societies* (published in 1935), 'We are forced to conclude that human nature is almost unbelievably malleable, responding accurately and contrastingly to contrasting cultural conditions.'[8] This one-sided view developed in part as a backlash against Social Darwinism, eugenics and the threat of Nazism. Looking back on her life in 1972, Mead explained how she and other anthropologists explicitly decided *not* to consider the biological aspects of behavior because of the political problems it would cause. This extract from her autobiography describes the time when she was developing her views about temperament:

[W]e also recognized that there were dangers in such a formulation because of the very human tendency to associate particular traits with sex or age or race, physique or skin color, or with membership in one or another society, and then to make invidious comparisons based on such arbitrary associations. We knew how politically loaded discussions of inborn differences could become; we knew that the Russians had abandoned their experiment in rearing identical twins when it was found that, even reared under different circumstances, they displayed astonishing likenesses. By then [spring 1935] it seemed clear to us [Gregory Bateson and herself] that the further study of inborn differences would have to wait upon less troubled times.[9]

I sympathize with Mead's political concerns, but she had more than postponed the study of inborn differences. She had argued forcefully that biology played no role in human nature, '. . . that human nature is almost unbelievably malleable . . .' While I credit her foresight in anticipating the dangers ahead for anyone who studied the genetic basis of individual differences in behavior, she over-generalized. Biology plays a role not only in individual differences (her worry) but in producing common features shared among members of a species. Her concern that racists would misuse evidence of biologically based individual differences led her to attack any claim for the biological basis of social behavior, even when biology is responsible for what unites us as a species, as in the case of universal expressions of emotions.

For decades any scientist who emphasized the biological contributions to social behavior, who believed in an innate contribution to individual differences in personality, learning, or intelligence, was suspected of being racist. Finding individual differences is a far cry, however, from the racist assertion that one sub-group of mankind is biologically superior to other sub-groups. But this concern about the racist use of biologically based individual differences is irrelevant to Darwin's argument in *Expression*. He focused on the innate basis of similarities – universals – not differences. That his claims for universality challenged the racist theories of his time was forgotten in the zeal to yield no ground to racists. In that political climate the claim that facial expressions are the product of culture was accepted without evidence, but no one looked for evidence. It was obvious, it fitted so well with the reigning dogma.

The most influential spokesman for this view was the anthropologist Birdwhistell, a protégé of Mead's. Birdwhistell wrote about *kinesics*, a term he coined to describe his approach to body movement, facial expression and posture: 'When I first became interested in studying body motion I was confident that it would be possible to isolate a series of expressions, postures and movements that were denotative of primary emotional states. As research proceeded . . . it became clear that this search for universals was culture bound . . . there are probably no universal symbols of emotional states.'[10]

Birdwhistell convinced a generation or more of social scientists.* In a 1955 edition of *Expression* (now out of print) prepared by Margaret Mead, she included pictures from a conference on kinesics, showing Birdwhistell, herself and others who were drawn to this approach. In her introduction to this edition, Mead did not say anything of Darwin's proposal that expressions are universal, nor did she mention the word 'emotion'. Instead she praised Birdwhistell's new science of kinesics, and recommended substituting the term 'communication' for Darwin's term 'expression'. I wonder how Darwin would have felt had he known that his book was introduced by a cultural relativist who had included in his book pictures of those most opposed to his theory of emotional expressions.

I entered this argument in the late 1950s. As a freshly trained clinical psychologist, my therapeutic orientation was psychoanalytic, but as a researcher I had been trained as a behaviorist, a radical Skinnerian. Skinner[14] said that psychology should examine only observable behavior; there were to be no theories or infer-

---

* Nearly as influential was the anthropologist Weston La Barre[11] who provided many examples of how expressions differed from one culture to another. The distinguished social psychologist Otto Klineberg[12] also argued that expressions were culture-specific, although he did acknowledge there might be a few universals. Elsewhere[13] I have explained and rebutted their views.

ences about what might be going on inside the head. He would deal only with what could be directly observed about how we learned and what we learned.

I was dissatisfied with the evidence for the effectiveness of psychoanalytic therapy, which rested on what the patient and a therapist said. I wanted to examine not words but real behavior (from a Skinnerian viewpoint) – body movements and facial expressions. Examining the non-verbal behaviors of patient and therapist might reveal evidence of clinical improvement not shown in their words, and perhaps would suggest ways to improve therapeutic techniques. After a few years studying hand and leg movements[15] I approached the face. I had not read *Expression*, but had heard about it and thought Darwin was probably wrong. As a Skinnerian, I thought it unlikely that expressions would be universal, and I was sure that inheritance could *not* play a role in emotional behavior. But it didn't really matter what I thought; as a Skinnerian, it was better not to have any forethought about what you were going to study. I would just get the facts. I was excited that I might be able to settle a 100-year-old dispute, about such a fundamental issue. An agnostic about universality, I was a zealot about using quantitative methods to measure observable behavior.

Before starting my research on the face, I visited Birdwhistell. I expected to find file cabinets full of data, notebooks crammed with detailed observations, or racks of film documenting his position. Birdwhistell was surprised at my request to see his documentation, for what he had seen and observed was all in his head. We did not get along. He could not understand what I thought I might be able to prove by re-opening the question of whether facial expressions are universal, when he had found the answer was 'no'. He could not comprehend why I was dissatisfied with his conclusions with no documentation or data others could inspect or attempt to repeat.

I also talked about my plans with Gregory Bateson, for we had become friendly a few years earlier when we were both working at the Palo Alto Veterans Administration Hospital. Gregory was charming, inspiring, and often mystifying. I could not always follow what he was saying, but I enjoyed his warmth, his challenging ideas and his generosity. While he had been interested in my study of how gestures relate to the flow of conversation, he was not sympathetic to my new plan to study emotional expression. Like Margaret Mead, he did not think facial expressions were universal. I told him I didn't think they were either, but I wanted to settle the argument about universality one way or the other. Gregory, like Margaret, objected to the word expression. I was being misled by Darwin. Use of the word expression directed attention away from the role of facial movements as communicative signals. It was a mistake to consider expressions as tied to internal sensations and physiological activity; they were tied to the back-and-forth flow of conversation.

As I explain in my Introduction, Darwin had not given much attention to how expressions communicate information to others. There is no question in my mind that providing information to others is important, not only in understanding the function of expressions in our daily life but in understanding how expressions have been shaped and preserved through evolution. Recognizing that does not mean, however, that we have to throw out the idea that these are expressions of *emotion*. When I talked to Bateson thirty years ago I could not explain why that was so; now I know. Here is what I would say to him if he were alive today. This is part of my own theory of emotion and expression; it goes beyond what Darwin wrote about, in a Darwinian framework:

> I think we can resolve our disagreement because we are both right, each emphasizing different sides of the same coin. Emotions are not like thoughts, which need no external sign; most emotions have expressions which communicate to others. They inform us that something important is happening inside the person who shows the emotion. Those internal changes are preparing the person to deal quickly with an important event, most often some interpersonal encounter, in a way that has been adaptive in the past. The past refers to our past as individuals, and what has been adaptive in the history of our species.
>
> We should not focus just on the signal and ignore the emotion. When we see an angry expression on someone's face, we know

that person is likely to attack. The internal changes in that person's physiology are preparing them to attack, their thinking is changing in a way which makes attacking seem to be a more useful response than if the person were not angry. (Of course the person may not attack, and perhaps that may also be detectable from his or her expression.) One of the most distinctive features of an emotion is that it is typically not hidden: we hear and see signs of it in the expression. An emotional expression tells others something about how the person showing the expression is going to behave. That is usually useful information to the one who gets the information and the one who shows the expression.

Here the argument may get harder. Not all signals are the same; emotional expressions are special, and we should not lose sight of that. They are special because they are involuntary, not intentional. Unlike the 'A-OK' or 'good luck' hand gestures, emotional expressions occur without choice. Most of those who study communication, like you Gregory, and some ethologists, have not wanted to consider intent. I believe it is crucial. The communicative value of a signal differs if it is intended or unintended. Emotional expressions have such an impact; we trust them precisely because they are unintended. We don't make an emotional expression to send a deliberate message, although a message is received. Of course there are occasions when we use expressions deliberately for social purposes, to show agreement or disagreement, or even to lie about how we feel. My research has shown that the signal doesn't look exactly the same in these deliberate, social uses of facial expressions. We may also try to conceal our emotions, but what I have called *leakage* occurs.[16] Our emotional expressions have been shaped and preserved by evolution because they are informative, but that does not mean that we deliberately make emotional expressions to signal information to others.[17]

Bateson arranged for me to meet Margaret Mead. I clearly remember that meeting, the appearance of her office, and her unfriendly, gruff manner. She had little patience for the quest I was about to begin. She knew I had been to see Birdwhistell and that I had disagreed with Birdwhistell's view that the question of universality was settled. I did not anticipate how angrily she would react later when my findings challenged Birdwhistell's claims.

I could not share with Bateson, Mead or Birdwhistell my worries that their theoretical commitments might have biased what they noticed and how they interpreted it. I may well have seemed presumptuous, for each was more than thirty years my senior and quite famous, while I was unknown. They believed in the value of the lone anthropologist and his or her fieldwork, trusting in his or her own intuitions and judgments.* The idea of using multiple observers, of gathering quantitative data, of building in safeguards against the influence of the scientist's commitments, which are standard in experimental psychology, were foreign to them. Admittedly, such safeguards are easier to achieve in the laboratory than in field research.

The last expert I met was Silvan Tomkins,[21] who had just published a complex theory of personality and emotion, in which facial expression played a central role. Silvan believed that emotions were innate and their expressions universal. Although he did not emphasize Darwin, I later found when I studied Darwin that Tomkins's ideas about expression were consistent with what Darwin had written, although he had developed his own complex theory of emotion. Tomkins dazzled me with his ability to 'read' facial expressions, seeing things which I missed. But so had Birdwhistell – also an extraordinarily keen observer. The two totally disagreed about whether facial expressions are universal.

Unlike Mead and Birdwhistell, Tomkins was eager to have me put his ideas to the test. He was keen that I should do the cross-cultural research, which he was certain would prove him

---

* The American anthropologist Marvin Harris[18] criticized Mead's methods and result in Samoa, citing other findings which suggest that Mead's claims were exaggerated. Harris points out that Mead '. . . was twenty-three years old when she left for Samoa and that she had to form her impressions of personality differences through the muffling effect of an imperfectly learned second language . . .' Harris criticized Mead for not recognizing sufficient individual variability in the traits she said characterized a culture. The Australian anthropologist Derek Freeman[19] has interviewed many of Mead's Samoan informants; he reported that they deliberately misled Mead, telling her outrageous stories because it was clear that she wanted to hear such accounts. There are now a number of analyses of the Mead–Freeman controversy.[20]

right, and willing to take the risk that it might show him to be wrong. He gave me his own photographs of facial expression which I used in my initial studies (Fig. 1), and helped me plan how I would do my first experiment.

This experiment – and most of the other studies that I and other scientists have conducted – incorporated different elements of what Darwin had done. Like Darwin, I showed to people photographs of facial expressions (the ones Tomkins provided) and asked them what emotion they recognized. Darwin did this, but only in England. As Darwin did, I obtained data from different countries. Instead of relying upon what travelers or outsiders observed, I asked the people of each country to judge the photographs. Unlike Darwin, I did not tell people the answers I expected. Instead I gave them a list of emotion words, and it was up to them to choose which word they thought described the emotion shown by each facial expression.

In the first study, in 1966, I showed the pictures to people in Chile, Argentina, Brazil, the USA and Japan. There was no way I could influence the way people in each of these countries would judge each expression. If the relativists were right, the person in Fig. 1A, for example, might be judged as feeling angry by people in one culture, happy by those in another, and sad by a third group. Perhaps the expression might mean nothing to people in yet another culture. I found just the opposite, and the evidence was overwhelming.

Within a few years I had studied other countries, as did the American psychologist Carroll Izard,[22] whom Tomkins had also advised. Different photographs of expressions were shown to people in twenty-one countries: Africa,* Argentina, Brazil, Chile, China, England, Estonia, Ethiopia, France, Germany, Greece, Indonesia, Italy, Japan, Kirghizistan, Malaysia, Scotland, Sweden, Switzerland, Turkey, and the USA.[23] This includes two studies I led,[24] and separate independent studies by five other investigators or groups of investigators.[25] With individuals in 21 countries

---

* This included subjects from more than one country in Africa, and is the only group who were not tested in their own languages but in English.

Fig. 1c is of Frois-Wittman, who wrote on facial expression in the 1930s; the rest are from those made by Tomkins. These and other similar expressions were shown one at a time for 10–15 seconds. Each observer had to choose from the list: anger, fear, sadness, disgust, surprise, happiness – the word which best fitted the picture.

The results across cultures were that A was judged to be showing happiness, B disgust, C surprise, D sadness, E anger and F fear.

seeing photographs representing fear, anger, sadness, disgust, happiness, and surprise expressions, there were many opportunities for people in these different places to disagree about the emotions they saw. Instead, there was an extraordinary amount of agreement about which emotion was shown in which photographs across each of the countries. In *every* case, the majority in each country agreed about the pictures that showed happiness, those that showed sadness, and those that showed disgust. For expressions of surprise there was agreement by the majority in 20 out of the 21 countries, for fear in 19 out of 21, and for anger in 18 out of 21. In the six cases where the *majority* did not choose the same emotion as was chosen in every other country, the *most frequent* response (although not the majority) was the same as that given by the majority in the other countries. In my own studies, in which we exercised a great deal more care than other investigators in selecting photographs which clearly depict each emotion, *all* the expressions were judged as showing the same emotion by the majority in *every* country we studied. I also found agreement across cultures in which expressions showing a particular emotion were judged as most and least intense.[26]

Contrary evidence, against Darwin's claim of universality, would have been to find that the expressions the majority of people in one country judged as showing – let us say anger – were judged as showing another emotion – say fear – by the majority in a different culture. This never happened.

When Birdwhistell learned what I had found, he came up with an ingenious way to discount our findings of universality. He argued that people had learned their 'universal' expressions from watching John Wayne or Charlie Chaplin on television, not from our common evolutionary heritage. Admittedly, all the people who saw the photographs of expression could have learned these expressions from one another or from a common source. If I were to study people who were visually isolated, his argument went, people who had seen no magazines, cinema or television, I would find that they did not agree with the judgments of expressions obtained from people who had all learned to interpret expression in the same way.

To deal with this challenge I went to Papua New Guinea in 1967 to study the South Fore culture. These people were visually isolated; most had seen few outsiders or none at all. They were still using stone implements, and very few had seen a photograph, magazine, film or television. Since they had no written language,

FEAR   HAPPY   ANGER

Fig. 2. In presenting this to a person, all three photographs were shown. Only one of the stories would be read and the individual asked to select the photograph to fit the story.

Fear – She is sitting in her house all alone and there is no one else in the village; and there is no knife, ax or bow and arrow in the house. A wild pig is standing in the door of the house and the woman is looking at the pig and is very afraid of it. The pig has been standing in the doorway for a few minutes and the person is looking at it very afraid and the pig won't move away from the door and she is afraid the pig will bite her.

Happy – Her friends have come and she is happy.

Anger – She is angry and is about to fight.

I could not do what I and others had done in the 21 literate cultures: give them a list of emotion words and ask them to choose the one to fit the expression. Instead, a translator read them the list of emotion words each time they saw a photograph. Even then it was not easy for them to keep the list in mind. And it became tedious to read the list again and again. I needed a procedure by which the people could make their judgments without having to speak.

The procedure I adopted had been used many years earlier for studying young children who could not read.[27] My translator read out a brief story, and asked the person to point to the picture that fitted the story. Fig. 2 shows a set of photographs I used with a few of the stories read to the people in the New Guinea

Highlands. I took every precaution to prevent the translator or me from influencing the choices made: the translator did not know what emotion I expected to be chosen, and I did not look at the person choosing until each choice had been made. Usually the pictures were held so that I could not see them, and I would have to bend over to learn afterward which picture had been selected.

These stone-age people, who could not have learned expressions from the media, chose the same expressions for each emotion as had the people in the 21 literate cultures.[28] The only exception was that they failed to differentiate between the fear and surprise faces, although both were distinguished from anger, happy, sad and disgust expressions.

In another study I asked some of them to show me what their face would look like if they were the person in one of the stories. I videotaped or photographed them as they enacted the emotions, and then showed these videotapes to Americans. Fig. 3 shows some frames of their poses. If expressions are universal, Americans who have never seen any people from the New Guinea culture should have no trouble judging the emotion they are showing. That is just what happened except, once again, fear and surprise were not distinguishable from each other.[29]

In addition to these experiments I did more informal studies, in which I arranged for something to happen and filmed how people reacted. For example, I tape-recorded two men while they played jew's harp and talked to each other. Then when I had my motion-picture camera running, I played back the audio tape, filming how they acted when they heard their voices coming out of the audio machine. They showed extreme happiness mixed with surprise, just as would be the reaction to an enjoyable novel occurrence anywhere. On another occasion, I waited by the side of a road for people to meet who had not seen one another for some time. Again I saw expressions of happiness. I inadvertently made a woman angry by looking directly at her in public. No one should have difficulty determining which woman in Fig. 4 is angry. I also inadvertently frightened a child. I wasn't fast enough to catch the fear, but Fig. 5 shows the distress which quickly

Fig. 3. The instructions were to show how your face would look if you were the person in the story.

    A = your friend has come and you are happy.

    B = your child has died.

    C = you are angry and about to fight.

    D = you see a dead pig that has been lying there a long time.

followed. It is the same facial configuration for distress as is found anywhere else in the world.*

I also examined in slow motion nearly 100,000 feet of motion-picture film which had been taken by Carleton Gaedjusek and Richard Sörenson[31] of the South Fore people and of another different, isolated culture (the Agape) in Papua New Guinea. Most of these films had been made in the years previous to my visit. It took me and my colleague Wallace Friesen nearly six months to view these films. *We did not see any expression that was unfamiliar to us – there were no new expressions.* Whenever the scenes were sufficiently complete for us to check whether our interpretation of an expression was correct, our judgments, it seemed, were accurate; we had no trouble understanding the expressions of these people. Our New Guinea studies were published in a series of papers from 1969 to 1972, and have been considered crucial evidence for universality by many social scientists who commented on them. Despite the care we took to prevent any personal preconceptions from influencing the findings we obtained, I cannot prove that we succeeded. Cultural relativists were later to seize on that possibility in an attempt to discredit our findings. The only answer to such doubters is to have someone who totally disagrees with you and intends to prove you wrong, repeat your research, and find exactly what you found. And that is just what happened.

In 1969, soon after the first report of our findings was published I met Karl Heider, an anthropologist who had been working in a very remote area of West New Guinea (what is now called Irian Jaya, and is part of Indonesia), studying a group called the Dani. Heider was in the United States preparing for another trip to

---

* Eibl-Eibesfeldt did many similar studies in remote and preliterate cultures,[30] finding many examples of what he interpreted as universals. A human ethologist, he did not do any quantitative research or conduct experiments, but his large collection of films on expression and gesture are valuable. Like most ethologists, he avoided using the term emotion, focusing on describing the signals. In my earlier monologue with Gregory Bateson, I explained this view and gave my answer to it.

Fig. 4.

Fig. 5.

the Dani. He was certain I was wrong, for the Dani do not have words for most of the emotions I was claiming had a universal expression. Heider had read our first study, in which we had asked the New Guineans to look at a picture and choose the one word, from a list of emotion terms we read to them, that fitted what the person's face was showing. The emotion words had been translated into their own language.

I told Heider that we had abandoned the emotion word method, because it was hard for the subjects to keep in mind all the choices from the list. I described the new procedure we had developed in which a translator told a story and the New Guinean picked the expression which fitted the story. We had not yet published those findings, but I told Heider that they were very strong. Before he left for his next trip, I showed him how to use this method, and gave him the materials so he could try it out among the Dani, and see if he could prove me wrong. If unwitting influence was a factor in our work, it would work in the opposite direction for Heider, and his collaborator, psychologist Eleanor Rosch. Instead they found nearly the same results as we did.[32] The one exception was that the Dani did not differentiate between anger and disgust expressions, although they did distinguish these from all the other emotions. Heider had predicted this finding, as he had observed that the Dani avoid expression of anger and often mask it with disgust.

We did one more study, and it is as important as the New Guinea work because it helps to explain why others had thought there were no universals.[33] We studied the spontaneous facial expressions shown by Japanese and American college students. We selected Japan as the comparison culture because of the popular notion of 'Oriental inscrutability'. We hoped to show that this was due to what we termed *display rules* about masking negative emotions in the presence of an authority. Students in Tokyo and in California watched a neutral travelogue and stress-inducing films (i.e., surgery, accidents, etc.) while a hidden camera recorded their facial expressions. We did two different studies: in the first, the videotapes were shown to people in the US and Japan who were asked to guess whether the people they saw had been watching the stressful or neutral film. In the second study we measured the videotaped facial expressions shown by the Japanese and American students when they had been watching the stressful and travelogue films.

Our first study of spontaneous facial expressions strongly supported universals. It didn't matter whether a Japanese or an American was judging someone from their own culture or not; they made virtually the same judgments. If the Japanese observers were correct in deciding whether a Japanese student was watching a stressful or non-stressful film, so were the Americans. And so it was when Americans were judged by Americans and Japanese. We repeated this study a second time, with a new set of students in Japan and in California, who watched the stressful and non-stressful films, and a new group of observers in Japan and in California who were asked to judge the spontaneous facial expressions. The results were the same – neither the culture of the observer nor the culture of the facial expresser mattered in the accurate judgment of whether facial expressions were reactions to the stressful or the neutral film.

As strong as this evidence is, a critic could argue that it does not prove that the same facial expressions occurred in the two cultures. Remember the observers were not asked what emotion they saw, but only when that expression was shown – during the stressful or neutral film. Suppose the Americans and Japanese had shown entirely different expressions when watching the surgical film: let us say the Americans showed sadness and the Japanese showed disgust. Our results would have been found as long as both Japanese and American observers decided that the Americans' sadness occurred during the stressful not the neutral film, and the Japanese disgust similarly occurred during the stressful film. To rule this out – to show that the *same* facial expressions were shown – a different type of study had to be done in which the facial expressions themselves were measured.

We videotaped a third group of American and Japanese subjects, when they sat alone watching the stress-inducing and neutral films. But this time we added a second condition in which a scientist dressed in a white coat entered the room and sat with the subject while he or she watched a stressful film. We expected that display rules for managing facial expressions in the presence of an authority figure would be operative, more so in the Japanese subjects than in the Americans. The videotapes were measured by people who did not know which film was being seen when the facial expressions occurred. A very high correlation was found between the particular facial movements shown by the American and Japanese students *when they were alone*. Virtually the same repertoire of facial movements occurred at the same points during the film. But when there was another person present the Japanese and Americans, as predicted, showed entirely different facial expressions. The Japanese showed more smiling than the Americans to mask their negative emotional expressions. No wonder that foreigners, travelers and anthropologists who visited or lived among the Japanese thought their expressions different from Americans. They would have seen the result of the display rules masking and modifying the underlying universal expressions of emotion.

I brought all these studies of facial expression together in a book, entitled *Darwin and Facial Expression*, to celebrate 100 years since the publication of *Expression*.[34] In addition to my chapter on expression, I had asked other authors to write chapters reviewing the evidence on non-human primates, on infants and children, and a historical chapter on Darwin's influence in psychology. Two years later Margaret Mead wrote a scathing five-page review:

> The narrowness and discipline-centric nature of the book is a continuing example of the appalling state of the human sciences, when members of each discipline treat their specialized approach as the only approach. . . . Ekman's single-minded research goal – to resolve with absolute certainty (an attitude which we usually do not associate with science, which proceeds by a succession of discarded paradigms) that the expression of some, if not all, of the emotions of which the human face is capable, is innate and universal – is outlined in full detail.[35]

It isn't obvious why Mead was so offended by the evidence I had marshaled in support of Darwin's early evidence of universals.

Although she was the best-known cultural relativist from the 1920s through most of the 1940s, at that time she had privately acknowledged the role of biology. With Nazism on the rise she had decided that '. . . the study of inborn differences would have to wait upon less troubled times' (see note 9). After the war she recognized the role of biology publicly, at least regarding the differences in the roles of men and women. 'It is important to take into consideration the possibility that the biological bases of aggression in the two sexes – in human beings as in other mammals – may differ significantly.'[36]

Perhaps Mead thought I was claiming that emotions operate like instincts, uninfluenced by social experience. That was not my position; finding universals in expressions does not mean that expressions are not socially influenced. Our findings on how socially learned display rules produced a cultural difference in the public behavior of Japanese and Americans should have made that clear. But the terminology I adopted to account for the finding of universals may have been confusing. I had used Silvan Tomkins's concept of an 'affect program' to describe the innate basis of universal expressions, although I had emphasized that facial expressions '. . . are embedded in a context; they may be elicited by different stimuli, be operated upon by different display rules, be blended with other affects, and be followed by different behavioral consequences. We do not mean to belittle these factors; in actuality we want to focus attention on these factors as the major sources of cultural differences in affect displays.'[37]

Despite this attempt to emphasize the role of culture, my use of the term 'program' may have seemed to imply that everything about emotion and expression was fixed. A few years after I wrote the passage I have just quoted the noted American zoologist Ernst Mayr clarified this matter by distinguishing between an 'open program' and a 'closed program'.[38] In a closed program nothing can be inserted by experience, while an open genetic program '. . . allows for additional input during the lifespan of its owner'. Mayr pointed out that in creatures which have a long period of parental care, when there is time for learning, there will be a selective advantage in an open rather than a closed genetic program. It is important to remember that '. . . an open program is by no means a *tabula rasa*; certain types of information are more easily incorporated than others.'

Mead may have thought I was proposing a closed program, whereas it is clearly an open program. Social experience influences attitudes about emotions, creates display and feeling rules, develops and tunes the particular occasions which will most rapidly call forth an emotion. The expressions of our emotions, the particular configurations of muscular movements, however, appear to be fixed, enabling understanding across generations, across cultures, and within cultures between strangers as well as intimates. I believe that much of the initial emotion-specific physiological activity in the first few milliseconds of an emotional experience is also not penetrable by social experience, but that takes us beyond the scope of Darwin's book. Mead made it clear that she was offended by my attack on her colleague Birdwhistell. Citing my report that Birdwhistell had no evidence for his claims other than his personal observations, Mead wrote, 'This is the type of canard which disgraces scientific controversy. . . . By repeating the clichéd criticism that Birdwhistell has become a "captive of his own linguistic model" Ekman is guilty of the most gross misrepresentation, a misrepresentation which has been popularized among psychologists who are more interested in validity and reliability than in what they are actually studying.'[39]

I was and am concerned with the validity and reliability of evidence, but that is essential, not an interference, to knowing what one is studying. Our disagreement, at least in part, is due to the different rules of evidence in academic psychology on the one hand, and parts of anthropology and the clinical areas of psychology on the other hand. Birdwhistell had not published, nor had he any material, qualitative or quantitative, to substantiate his claims. They were his personal judgments, illustrated by examples. That was sufficient for Mead, and perhaps for some anthropologists, clinical psychologists and psychiatrists, but not for experimental psychologists. My admittedly single-minded purpose was to gather evidence independent of my own observations, evidence which others could examine, using methods which others could repeat, so that a person like Heider could try to prove me wrong.

Although she criticized me severely in her review, Mead never came right out and said there are no universals in facial expressions. Her dilemma was how to acknowledge universals in facial expressions and not disavow Ray Birdwhistell's conclusion that there were no universals. She came up with a far-fetched idea.

> These findings, dramatic and significant as they are, must be placed beside Birdwhistell's analysis of culturally patterned expressive movement ... there is no need to reject the presence of possible innate and evolutionarily and potentially neurologically explicable facial expressions, in order to recognize that in all the individuals Birdwhistell has studied in such detail he did not find them. . . . The fact that those who have studied facial expressions in many cultures [she is referring to Birdwhistell] find patterning from birth, and possibly before birth, does not necessarily conflict with the possibility that human beings may share a core of innate behaviors which are usually highly modified but which are available for simulation [she is referring to *my work*].[40]

What Mead proposed makes no sense. She allowed for universal, innate expressions; but they are never manifest in actual life. These innate expressions are, she said, culturally patterned from birth or before (presumably in the uterus), and that is why Birdwhistell never saw them. I found that people in different cultures agree about the emotion shown in posed expressions because, according to Mead, they base their judgments upon their knowledge of the innate universal expressions never seen in social life.

There are two problems with Mead's formulation. First, why would people know how to interpret and adopt posed facial expressions if they never saw them in real life. She said it was innate, but she wisely never attempted to explain how it would have been adaptive to have this knowledge. What benefit would result from knowing about poses which are never shown in real encounters? Second, my evidence was not limited to posed expressions. In my study of Japanese and American students, we had measured spontaneous facial expressions, and found universals when the subjects were alone. I had reported that study in detail in the book Mead reviewed; she ignored it. For the next fifteen years, despite Mead, the findings on universality were generally accepted in psychology. (Perhaps her review had little impact because it was published in a small circulation journal, catering to specialists in communication, not one of the major journals in either psychology or anthropology.) Emotion became a subject of renewed interest, and a Darwinian perspective seemed increasingly viable to a growing number of behavioral scientists.

In the last five years, however, the argument against Darwin's *Expression* has been renewed. The American psychologist Alan Fridlund attacked Darwin for not emphasizing that expressions were selected because of their communicative value.[41] This is an overstatement, for Darwin did recognize the importance of communication, explaining its role in the origin of some expressions in animals. His principle of antithesis – some expressions have the form they do because their appearance is the opposite of other expressions – implies communication. In my Introduction I explained why Darwin did not emphasize natural selection in explaining the origin of expressions. Fridlund has echoed the position of Bateson and some ethologists who claim that it is not useful to think of expressions in terms of *emotion*, but only as communicative signals; in my monologue with Bateson (pp. 372– 3) I have explained why this is a false dichotomy. Fridlund also raises technical questions which I have answered elsewhere.[42]

A quite different attack on the evidence for universals that I and others have published has focused on the words used to describe emotion. The Australian linguist Anna Wierzbicka said we have been misled by relying on Western words for emotions.[43] These words, she claimed, do not exist in many non-Western cultures. But the evidence for universals does not rely simply on studies in which people use words to label the emotion shown in a photograph. Neither we nor Heider and Rosch used emotion words in our studies in New Guinea, and our Japanese–American study found evidence of universals by measuring the spontaneous facial movements, with no use of emotion words. The Canadian psychologist James Russell imagined we would not have found universals if we had let the people in each country choose their own word to describe each emotion, rather than giving them lists of emotion words from which they had to choose the word which best fit each expression.[44] But Izard (*The Face of Emotion*) did just what Russell claimed was required and found evidence of universality. Besides, as I have pointed out, the evidence for universals does not rest solely on studies in which words are linked to faces.

Despite these criticisms, I believe most scientists consider the universality of facial expressions of emotion to be well established. The American anthropologist Donald Brown used the evidence on facial expressions as one of six cases which form the cornerstone for understanding human universals.[45] While robust, the evidence is limited to just a handful of emotions: anger, disgust, sadness, enjoyment, and fear/surprise. I agree with Darwin in believing that fear and surprise do have separate distinct expressions, but the evidence for it comes only from literate cultures. In the preliterate cultures fear and surprise were not differentiated although each was distinguished from the other emotions. I do not know why I was unable to obtain evidence for that in New Guinea.

We have also found evidence that contempt, the emotion when you feel morally superior to another, has a universal expression,[46] but this is also from literate cultures, as the research was done in the 1980s when I no longer could find any visually isolated preliterate cultures to study. One of my former students, Dacher Keltner, has evidence that there is a universal expression for embarrassment, but he has not yet studied sufficient literate cultures.[47] The group of emotions for which there is some evidence of universality includes most, but not all, of the emotions Darwin studied: surprise, sadness, anger, enjoyment, contempt, disgust, shame, and fear.* Darwin also asked his informants whether there

---

* Darwin did not use the words surprise, sadness, anger, enjoyment or contempt in the questions he sent to his English informants, but it is clear that he considered the words he did use either to be synonymous or to vary only in intensity from the words I have listed.

are expressions for guilt, slyness, and jealousy, although he told them he did not know how to describe those expressions. I have not studied the expression of those emotions, nor have others. I think that guilt and shame expressions do not differ from each other, and that they differ from sadness only in the attempt to hide the face. Jealousy seems to have no distinctive expression, perhaps because it is an emotion where the person feels a number of other emotions: angry with the one whose attention is lost or with the rival; sadness at the loss; fear in anticipation of further loss; or disgust at himself or herself for feeling jealous. Envy, a term often confused with jealousy, also does not have a unique expression.[48]

Darwin also included questions about obstinacy, which no one has since studied, and about puzzlement, which most scientists today consider a form of thinking, not an emotion. Darwin recognized that most symbolic gestures are learned and therefore differ from one culture to another, but he did ask his informants about three symbolic gestures: the head nod and head shake as signs of affirmation and negation; and the shrug as a sign of being unable to do something. His informants reported that the head nod and shake for affirmation and negation are not universal, although the negation head shake is widespread.[49] He believed on the basis of his evidence that the shrug is universal, but I did not find it among the people I studied in New Guinea. But these are minor quibbles. Darwin's central point is well established: a number of emotions have a universal expression. This would have pleased Darwin, for he acknowledged that not *every* emotion has an expression, let alone a universal one. But to find evidence of universals for six to eight emotions is consistent with an evolutionary view.

To have shown that there are universals in facial expressions of emotion does not mean that expressions are universal in every regard. Our evidence, and that of others, shows only that when people are experiencing certain strong emotions, and are not making any attempt to mask their expressions (display rules), the expression will be the same regardless of age, race, culture, sex, or education. That is a powerful finding.

There are a number of ways in which cultures do differ in their emotional expressions. I have already mentioned one – the display rules which specify who can show which emotion to whom and when. Cultures differ also in some of the specific events which are likely to call forth an emotion. For example, some of the foods which people in one culture find a delicacy, people in another culture find revolting, but differences are also found within a culture. Although the specific event varies – the type of food, the general theme – ingesting something repulsive as a cause for disgust, or ingesting something attractive as a cause of enjoyment – is universal. I think this is a good model for all the emotions. The event which makes me angry may be different from what makes a Samoan angry, or my wife angry, but the theme will be the same. Anger can be brought forth by something that is provocative, insulting, or frustrating, to name just a few of the anger themes, although what you find provocative, insulting or frustrating may not be the same across or within cultures.

I will mention only one more way in which cultures differ in emotional expression, because to go further would take us too far from Darwin. I expect that languages differ in the words they have for emotions, not only in terms of the numbers of words for each emotion, but the extent to which a word gives subtle nuances or combines emotions or tells us what caused the emotion. The Germans have the evocative word *Schadenfreude*, for that distinctive pleasure when you learn of a misfortune which has befallen an enemy. English-speakers have no single word for that feeling, although we do feel the emotion. Not having a word for an emotional state may well influence emotional experience. Without being able to name feelings, it may be harder to distinguish them, think about them, and so on.

An extreme example of how lack of emotion words can change emotional experience was reported by the American psychiatrist and anthropologist Robert Levy.[50] He said that the Tahitians had no word or concept for sadness in their culture. They acted in a sad way – loss of appetite, inactivity and sad expressions – when rejected by a lover, but not only could they not name the feeling but they did not relate their experience to the rejection. They explained their feelings as due to sickness.*

If true, this is a dramatic example of how cultural differences influence emotional experience. Even though the expressions are universal (present when the emotion of sadness is felt), culture determines whether the person even knows that the feelings are related to the event. Less dramatically perhaps, the other differences between cultures and within any culture which I have outlined – in the words for emotions, in what is learned about an event which calls forth an emotion, in display rules, in attitudes about emotions – all these shape our emotional experience. Our evolution gives us these universal expressions, which tell others some important information about us, but *exactly* what an expression tells us is not the same in every culture.

Universals in facial expressions of emotion can serve as a model for understanding other aspects of our social behavior. In part our social behavior is constructed by experience, in part it is constructed as a result of our evolution as a species. What has been adaptive to us in our lives is malleable, and may vary from one family setting to another, among different social classes and ethnic groups within a culture and across cultures. What has been adaptive to our species, to our history on this planet, may not always be adaptive to our current life circumstance. How much we are influenced by individual experience and how much by our evolutionary history varies, depending upon what aspect of our behavior we are considering. It is never a question only of nature or only of nurture. We are biosocial creatures, our minds are embodied, reflecting our lives and the lives of our ancestors. Darwin led the way not only in the biological sciences but in the social sciences as well.

San Francisco,
September, 1996

---

* This is such an important example, it is a shame that no one else has tried to verify it in Tahiti, or observe something similar elsewhere.

THAT TROUBLES OUR MONKEY AGAIN.

Female descendant of Marine Ascidian:—"REALLY, MR. DARWIN, SAY WHAT YOU LIKE ABOUT MAN; BUT I WISH YOU WOULD LEAVE MY EMOTIONS ALONE!"

APPENDIX I

Charles Darwin's Obituary

T. H. HUXLEY

Very few, even among those who have taken the keenest interest in the progress of the revolution in natural knowledge set afoot by the publication of the 'Origin of Species'; and who have watched, not without astonishment, the rapid and complete change which has been effected both inside and outside the boundaries of the scientific world in the attitude of men's minds towards the doctrines which are expounded in that great work, can have been prepared for the extra-ordinary manifestation of affectionate regard for the man, and of profound reverence for the philosopher, which followed the announce-ment, on Thursday last, of the death of Mr Darwin.

Not only in these islands, where so many have felt the fascination of personal contact with an intellect which had no superior, and with a character which was even nobler than the intellect; but, in all parts of the civilized world, it would seem that those whose business it is to feel the pulse of nations and to know what interests the masses of mankind, were well aware that thousands of their readers would think the world the poorer for Darwin's death, and would dwell with eager interest upon every incident of his history. In France, in Germany, in Austro-Hungary, in Italy, in the United States, writers of all shades of opinion, for once unanimous, have paid a willing tribute to the worth of our great countryman, ignored in life by the official represen-tatives of the kingdom, but laid in death among his peers in West-minster Abbey by the will of the intelligence of the nation.

It is not for us to allude to the sacred sorrows of the bereaved home at Down [sic]; but it is no secret that, outside that domestic group, there are many to whom Mr Darwin's death is a wholly irreparable loss. And this not merely because of his wonderfully genial, simple, and generous nature; his cheerful and animated conversation, and the infinite variety and accuracy of his information; but because the more one knew of him, the more he seemed the incorporated ideal of a man of science. Acute as were his reasoning powers, vast as was his knowledge, marvellous as was his tenacious industry, under physical difficulties which would have converted nine men out of ten into aimless invalids; it was not these qualities, great as they were, which impressed those who were admitted to his intimacy with involuntary veneration, but a certain intense and almost passionate honesty by which all his thoughts and actions were irradiated, as by a central fire.

It was this rarest and greatest of endowments which kept his vivid imagination and great speculative powers within due bounds; which compelled him to undertake the prodigious labours of original investigation and of reading, upon which his published works are based; which made him accept criticisms and suggestions from any body and every body, not only without impatience, but with expressions of gratitude sometimes almost comically in excess of their value; which led him to allow neither himself nor others to be deceived by phrases, and to spare neither time nor pains in order to obtain clear and distinct ideas upon every topic with which he occupied himself.

One could not converse with Darwin without being reminded of Socrates. There was the same desire to find some one wiser than himself; the same belief in the sovereignty of reason; the same ready humour; the same sympathetic interest in all the ways and works of men. But instead of turning away from the problems of nature as hopelessly insoluble, our modern philosopher devoted his whole life to attacking them in the spirit of Heraclitus and of Democritus, with results which are as the substance of which their speculations were anticipatory shadows.

The due appreciation or even enumeration of these results is neither practicable nor desirable at this moment. There is a time for all things – a time for glorying in our ever-extending conquests over the realm of nature, and a time for mourning over the heroes who have led us to victory.

None have fought better, and none have been more fortunate than Charles Darwin. He found a great truth, trodden under foot, reviled by bigots, and ridiculed by all the world; he lived long enough to see it, chiefly by his own efforts, irrefragably established in science, inseparably incorporated with the common thoughts of men, and only hated and feared by those who would revile, but dare not. What shall a man desire more than this? Once more the image of Socrates rises unbidden, and the noble peroration of the 'Apology' rings in our ears as if it were Charles Darwin's farewell:–

'The hour of departure has arrived, and we go our ways – I to die and you to live. Which is the better, God only knows.'

T. H. HUXLEY, Nature,
Thursday, April 27, 1882

Changes to the Text

PAUL EKMAN

CHAPTER I

Page 50: In the first edition, after the sentence ending '. . . any more than do dogs', the following sentence appears: 'All these animals, however, bury superfluous food.' The last sentence in this paragraph, which begins 'The burying of superfluous . . .' did not appear in the first edition.

CHAPTER II

Page 56: The sentence 'Not one of the above movements, so clearly expressive of affection are of the least direct service to the animal.' In the first edition the verb 'is' was used; Darwin changed this to 'are' in his copy.

CHAPTER IV

Page 107: In Darwin's copy of *Expression*, the word 'all' is crossed out in the sentence '. . . the word *toad* expresses in all the languages . . .', and the phrase 'in some of' is pencilled in its place. In the second edition the phrase 'in several of' was inserted.

Page 111: In Darwin's copy, the phrase 'or bead like' was pencilled into the sentence which begins 'The Trigonocephalus . . .', but it was not included in the second edition.

Page 113: In the first (and second) edition the sentence 'Although their ears are thus to a large extent protected, yet they often get much torn in old male cats during their battles', originally read, '. . . during their mutual battles'. In Darwin's copy the word 'mutual' was crossed out.

CHAPTER XI

Page 272: I split Plate VI into two, so that the two indignation illustrations could appear earlier where indignation is discussed, leaving the shrugs in place where shrugs are discussed. Since Darwin contrasts the indignation expressions with the shrug on p. 272, I have used the indignation expressions again in Plate VII. All that had to be changed in Darwin's words is the reference to Plate VII instead of Plate VI.

Photography and *The Expression of the Emotions*

PHILLIP PRODGER

Lying on his deathbed in December of 1874, the photographer Oscar Rejlander (1813–1875) scrawled a final message to his friend and colleague, Charles Darwin. Anticipating his demise, Rejlander informed Darwin that he had arranged to have a taxidermist prepare a tableau of stuffed birds for him. 'I dare say I shall not see you again,' he wrote, 'but I have a good thing to give you: A group of sparrows, i.e. a hen with a little one on either side – with fluttering wings – feeding – one at a time. I saw it 15 years ago. I sketched it then, but have this year got it represented like nature.'[1] One month after writing this letter, Rejlander died of Bright's Disease, a kidney disorder which plagued him throughout the last years of his life. The birds he had sent were intended as an affectionate farewell. This simple gift marked the end of one of the most extraordinary collaborations of the nineteenth century.

The two men had met in 1871, just one year before *Expression* was published. In the course of that year, Rejlander presented Darwin with more than seventy photographs of human expression. For Darwin, who had long struggled to find photographs suitable for inclusion in *Expression*, Rejlander provided a wealth of useful photographic images. The enthusiasm and imagination with which he embraced Darwin's project transformed the content of the book, and in turn revolutionized the way in which scientists study human behaviour. As one reviewer declared, the partnership of Darwin and Rejlander had 'scattered to the winds' all previous attempts at portraying the passions.[2]

Rejlander is the most famous of the photographers who contributed to *Expression*, and the one who had the greatest impact on its visual content. For this reason, he is sometimes mistakenly assumed to have produced all the photographs published in the book. In fact, he is one of five photographers represented. Of the thirty photographs used as illustrations, nineteen were produced by Rejlander. The remainder were produced by James Crichton Browne (1840–1938), Guillaume-

Benjamin Duchenne de Boulogne (1806–1875), Adolph Diedrich Kindermann (1823–1892), and George Charles Wallich (1815–1899). These photographers are less frequently recognized for their contributions, although each played an important part in the production of the book.

Expression also contains illustrations by the draughtsmen Joseph Wolf (1820–1899), Briton Riviere (1840–1920), and Thomas W. Wood (fl. 1855–1872). Each was renowned for his zoological illustrations; Riviere's work was particularly highly prized. The drawings they produced were made into the wood engravings which illustrate the first and last sections of the book. These engravings were made by James Davis Cooper (1823–1904), a printmaker who had developed a system for copying drawings on to printing plates using a photographic transfer process.

Although Darwin wrote in his Introduction that Cooper's photographic engraving process ensured 'almost complete fidelity' in reproduction,[3] there is little evidence to suggest that this process was actually used. Photographic reproduction was just one of the services Cooper offered his clients, for which he charged an extra fee. Most of the transcription from drawings to engravings was probably done freehand. Many of the original drawings from which Cooper's plates were made are preserved in the Manuscripts Room at Cambridge University Library; these frequently bear little resemblance to the final plates published in *Expression*.[4] Surprisingly, in view of Darwin's remark on the fidelity of these images, a number even include handwritten notes from Darwin, instructing Cooper to change or correct his renditions of the drawings.

It may seem curious that engravings are confined to the first and last parts of the book, the sections which focus on the expressions of animals and the human expressions of fear, terror and insanity. No doubt this helped to reduce production costs, as engravings were much less expensive to publish than photographs. The visual distinction between the two types of illustration may also have been intended to add dramatic emphasis to the sections on 'normal' human expression. The engravings provide a visual counterbalance to the photographs which succeed them, and help to integrate photography into the book in a visually exciting way.[5] The relationship between engravings and photographs in *Expression* is itself a subject of considerable interest, yet it is the unique composition of the photographs in particular which makes the illustrations in *Expression* so important.

The Expression of the Emotions in Man and Animals was one of the first scientific books ever published with photographic illustrations.

Produced at a time when technical limitations hindered the application of photography to scientific research, the book played a major role in bringing photographic evidence into the scientific world. The photographs constitute one of the first public attempts to use photography to freeze motion for analysis and study, predating the pioneering motion studies of the Anglo-American photographer Eadweard Muybridge (1830–1904) and the French physiologist Etienne-Jules Marey (1830–1904).[6] Darwin's photographs have proved inspirational to generations of artists, and may even have fuelled the invention of motion pictures.[7] Yet they were produced despite great adversity, and very nearly not included at all.

Darwin's English publisher, John Murray, was at first opposed to the idea of using photographs to illustrate the book. He advised Darwin that the inclusion of photographs would make *Expression* a money-losing proposition, costing an additional £75 per 1000 sets.[8] At the time, it was usually necessary for photographic illustrations to be glued, or 'tipped' into the pages of books. This was extremely labour-intensive, and the quality of the finished product was difficult to control. Darwin canvassed photographic printers in London for suggestions on alternative ways of reproducing photographs. He happened upon a new, photomechanical method of reproduction called heliotype, a process invented by the photographer Ernest Edwards (1837–1903), for whom Darwin had sat for a portrait in 1868.[9]

The use of heliotype for photomechanical reproduction was one of the many important innovations employed in the production of the book. Unlike ordinary photographic prints, which must be made individually, heliotypes are made using printing plates, and may be mass produced. The heliotype process involves coating a printing plate with light-sensitive gelatin emulsion, which is exposed photographically using an ordinary negative. The gelatin emulsion reticulates, or develops tiny fissures, in a pattern corresponding to the negative used. These fissures form a relief copy of the photographic image on the plate, which can be inked and run through a printing press using ordinary paper stocks. The resulting prints may be bound together directly with pages of text, eliminating the need for expensive, tipped-in photographs. Although low in detail and high in contrast compared with alternatives such as the rival Woodbury-type process, the use of heliotype reduced the costs of production considerably, enabling Darwin to afford the unprecedented number of photographic plates included in *Expression*. Using heliotype, it was possible to publish photographic images without relying on skilled artists to copy photographs on to printing plates by hand. This allowed Darwin to claim

that the subtle details of his photographic originals had been reproduced with absolute precision. Nevertheless, an example of the manual
method of reproducing photographs appears in Figure 4 of *Expression*
itself: an engraving after an original photograph by Rejlander.

The mixture of illustration types in the book reflects profound
changes which occurred in the visual culture of Britain in the late
Victorian era. In 1869, when Darwin was just beginning to compile
illustrations for inclusion in *Expression*, the practice of using photography for scientific purposes was still in its infancy. Thirty years earlier,
in 1839, William Henry Fox Talbot (1800–1877) had introduced photography to Britain, predicting that it would prove of value to the
'inductive methods of modern science'.[10] By capturing chance natural
events for scientific study, then 'following them up with experiments,
and varying the conditions of these until the true law of nature which
they express is apprehended',[11] Talbot believed photography would
change the face of scientific research. Unfortunately, it was several
decades before photographic technology advanced to the point where
it could be applied easily in scientific research.

The earliest photographic materials were extremely complicated and
awkward to use. To produce even a simple photograph in 1869, it was
necessary to make negatives by hand, using a sticky, noxious solution
of photo-sensitive silver nitrate mixed with potassium iodide and collodion (guncotton dissolved in ether).[12] This was a tricky procedure,
requiring considerable patience and manual dexterity. The solution
had to be painted on a glass plate immediately before exposure, otherwise the collodion in the solution would dry and become impervious
to the chemicals needed to develop it. Consequently, the preparation
and development of negatives had to be performed at roughly the
same time that the photographer was taking pictures. In addition to
their work as cameramen, photographers had to act as skilled chemists,
planners and manufacturers, as they shuttled from darkroom to studio
and back. Evidence of this problem is visible in *Expression*, for example
in Plate VII, Fig. 4, and Fig. 25. On close inspection, one can see that
the hands of Oscar Rejlander, who posed for these pictures, were
stained with the chemicals he used to prepare his negatives.

To make matters worse, normal exposure times ranged from several
seconds to a minute or two depending on conditions, so that subjects
had to remain absolutely still while their photographs were taken.
True action, or 'instantaneous' photographs, as they were popularly
called, were not possible. Nevertheless, many photographers attempted
to produce images which appeared to have been taken instantaneously;
that is, which presented the illusion of movement frozen in time. By

the late 1860s and early 1870s 'instantaneous' photography had become a preoccupation in photographic circles. Prizes were granted in competitions to the most successful and a wide range of photographic paraphernalia, including lenses, light reflectors, and even whole studios were developed with the express purpose of shortening exposure times.[13]

For Darwin, who was not a photographer, the problem of producing photographs of rapidly occurring action was critical. To illustrate *Expression* convincingly, he required images which captured the subtle, momentary actions of the muscles involved in emotional expression. As Darwin explained in his Introduction:

> The study of Expression is difficult, owing to the movements being often extremely slight, and of a fleeting nature. A difference may be clearly perceived, and yet it may be impossible, at least I have found it so, to state in what the difference consists. When we witness any deep emotion, our sympathy is so strongly excited, that close observation is forgotten or rendered almost impossible ... Our imagination is another and still more serious source of error; for if from the nature of the circumstances we expect to see any expression, we readily imagine its presence.[14]

If Darwin could capture the ephemeral movements of facial muscles for analysis and study, each of the problems highlighted in this passage would be solved. Moreover, the potential objectivity of photography suggested a vantage from which to view discrete moments in the occurrence of expression with both accuracy and detachment. The naked eye was incapable of recording the kind of detail Darwin wished to study. Furthermore, objective images of the emotions could not be produced through the conventional methods of drawing or printmaking, as these relied on the observations of an artist who would be subject to the same limitations and biases as any other person. To overcome these difficulties, Darwin required photographs which had been produced in a fraction of a second: the same sort of 'instantaneous' imagery which had up to that time eluded the photographic community.

There was no obvious single source for the material he needed. As a result, when he began his search for photographs to include in *Expression*, he approached a variety of suppliers, including a number of London shops and studios. He started collecting photographs, many of which are preserved in the Darwin Manuscripts Collection at Cambridge. The Collection includes some forty-one photographs which appear to have been purchased specifically for their expressive content, including images by The London Stereoscopic Company (1854–1898), the Leicester firm of John Burton & Sons (fl. 1860s), the Italian photographer Giacomo Brogi (1822–1881), the French firm of Fernand Vadon & Cie, and James Landy (1838–1887), an American photographer who worked for the Library of Congress.[15]

Initially, Darwin approached the problem of finding photographs in the same way that he approached the acquisition of natural history specimens. By sifting through the volumes of photographs available commercially, he hoped to discover evidence relevant to his research. Any photograph which revealed aspects of the physiology of expression was of interest, regardless of how and why it had been created. Although photography was not yet capable of producing truly instantaneous images, Darwin surveyed as many photographs as he could for clues to the mechanisms of expression. At the same time, he studied prints and paintings with action scenes from sources as divers as William Hogarth's 'Rake's Progress' (c. 1735) and John James Audubon's 'Birds of America' (1827–38).[16] Together, these pictures provided a broad overview of how expressions were popularly portrayed and perceived. Ultimately, Darwin deemed them inappropriate for inclusion in *Expression*, but they helped him to formulate his views.

The first photographs which he considered suitable had already been published in another pioneering scientific treatise. In 1862, the French physiologist Guillaume-Benjamin Duchenne de Boulogne had published a book on electrically induced expression called *Mécanisme de la Physionomie Humaine* (*The Mechanism of Human Facial Expression*). Produced with the assistance of the photographer Adrien Tournachon (1825–1903), brother of the great French photographer Félix Nadar (1820–1910), the book included eighty-four large-format photographs depicting human subjects in various expressive poses.[17] This work proved extremely influential to Darwin's project to portray expression. With Duchenne's permission, eight of the illustrations which appear in *Expression* (Plate II, Figs 1 and 2, Plate III, Figs 4, 5 and 6, Plate VII, Fig. 2, and the engraved Figs 20 and 21) were copied directly from original photographs first published in *The Mechanism of Human Facial Expression*.

Duchenne was a resident clinician at La Salpêtrière, a hospital for the poor on the outskirts of Paris. The hospital was entrusted with the care of a large number of patients with neurological problems, including cases of epilepsy, palsy, paralysis and insanity. Believing each of these conditions to be related to electrical dysfunction in the nervous system, Duchenne began to experiment with electrical current as a means to induce neural action. He soon learned that, with the right equipment, it was possible to galvanize isolated groups of muscles to contract. By applying this electrical technique to groups of muscles in the face, he found that he could artificially stimulate his subjects to produce a variety of facial expressions. By applying a constant flow of electricity, he was able to hold the expressions induced long enough to produce photographs of several seconds' exposure. Instead of acce-lerating the photographic process to produce instantaneous images, as others had tried to do, Duchenne devised a system to freeze the activity of his subjects long enough to accommodate the lengthy exposure times necessitated by photographic technology.

Most of the Duchenne plates published in *Expression* were taken of a single subject, 'an old, toothless man, with a thin face, whose features, without being absolutely ugly, approached ordinary triviality and whose facial expression was in perfect agreement with his inoffensive character and his restricted intelligence'.[18] The subject, who appears in Plate III, Figs 4, 5 and 6, and Figs 19, 20, 24, and 28–31 of this edition, was originally chosen by Duchenne for practical reasons. He suffered from an anaesthetic condition of the face, which made it possible to stimulate individual groups of his facial muscles without causing involuntary response among others. It was as if, as Duchenne remarked, he were 'working with a still irritable cadaver'.[19]

The grotesqueness of this metaphor may help to explain changes Darwin made to some of the plates prior to publication. Duchenne's toothless man has the distinction of being the only subject portrayed in the book in both photographs and engravings. Although the photo-graphs which appear in Plates III and VII are faithful, reduced copies of the original, the engraved reproductions in Figs 28 and 31 were substantially altered before publication. In both, Darwin instructed the engraver, James Cooper, to 'Attend to the wrinkles on neck & forehead – form of mouth. Omit galvanic instruments and hands of operator.'[20] These instructions were probably designed to clarify detail in the original, and make the figures appear more natural. While Duchenne's experiments had been performed with the consent of his subjects and with minimal discomfort to them, the photographic results were chilling, horrific images. The subjects had been stimulated to assume false expressions with an arrangement of wires and probes clearly visible in Duchenne's photographs. Darwin, while accepting these images for inclusion in *Expression*, felt compelled to remove the disturbing apparatus before publishing them.

References to *The Mechanism of Human Facial Expression* first appear in correspondence between Darwin and the psychiatrist James

Crichton Browne in 1869. As a physician, and director of the West Riding Lunatic Asylum in Yorkshire, Browne had adopted photography as a tool in the treatment of patients in his care. Psychiatry was one of the few scientific disciplines in which the use of photography had become established at this time. In the 1850s, a psychiatrist named Hugh Welch Diamond (1809–1886) had reported success in using photographs of patients as a therapeutic tool. Diamond claimed that he had been able to cure some of his patients by showing them their photographic portraits. Although not widely reproduced, these findings attracted considerable publicity, and the usefulness of photography in cataloguing behavioural disorders was immediately recognized. As a result, Browne was one of a number of Victorian psychiatrists who began to use photography to record and analyse the physiognomy of the mentally ill.

Darwin and Browne corresponded regularly between 1869 and the publication of *Expression* in 1872. Nearly every letter Browne sent to Darwin was accompanied by portraits of patients in the asylum, who suffered from conditions ranging from 'erotomania' to 'homicidal impulses'.[21] In total, he sent Darwin at least thirty-seven photographs of his patients, many accompanied by lengthy descriptions of their symptoms. Although these interested Darwin, only one of these, an engraved head of a lunatic woman with erect hair (Figs 26 and 27) was reproduced.[22] As Browne concentrated on the depiction of 'abnormal' expression, his photographs were of limited value to Darwin.

Browne's main contribution to *Expression* was conceptual. Darwin asked his opinion on a number of matters relating to expression, including his interpretation of Duchenne's *Mechanism of Human Facial Expression*. Darwin incorporated so many of Browne's observations in *Expression* that in March 1871 he wrote suggesting that Browne should be credited as a co-author of the book.[23] Although Browne politely declined, his influence on the theoretical content was nevertheless extensive.

Having failed to secure all the images he needed from stocks of existing photographs, Darwin decided to adopt a new approach to procuring photographic illustrations. In a letter to Browne dated June 1870, Darwin revealed that he had begun to commission new photographs. Writing that he had been trying to get a London photographer to make a picture of a 'young baby screaming or crying badly', at the same time Darwin commented that he feared 'he will not succeed'.[24] The photographer in question was almost certainly George Charles Wallich, a medical doctor by training, best known for oceanographic discoveries he made while serving as a marine biologist on the voyage of the *Bulldog* in 1860. Not content with his careers in medicine and oceanography, Wallich opened a professional photographic studio at 2 Warwick Gardens in Kensington around 1870. Darwin, who must have known Wallich from his work as a naturalist, was one of his first customers.

Darwin included only a single plate by Wallich in *Expression*, a relatively conventional portrait of Wallich's daughter Beatrice smiling while wearing a fancy bonnet (Plate III, Fig. 2). In the text Darwin noted merely that her expression had been a 'genuine one',[25] and, indeed, this picture does exhibit some of the unaffected intimacy one might expect from a successful family snapshot. Unfortunately, it was one of only a handful of photographs Wallich completed for Darwin. Although he had accepted Darwin's commission for a 'screaming or crying baby', he was unable to deliver this or any other particular expressive image. It seems the majority of Darwin's requirements were beyond the abilities of Wallich's studio.

In a further attempt to satisfy his need for 'screaming baby' photographs, Darwin approached the ironically named Adolph Diedrich Kindermann, a Hamburg-based painter and photographer who specialized in pictures of children. Unlike Wallich, Kindermann had abundant experience in the photography of crying children, and sent Darwin a group of photographs selected from negatives in his studio. Ultimately, Darwin decided to include three of them (Plate I, Figs 2 and 5, and Plate IV, Fig. 1). While Darwin valued Kindermann's work, his narrow specialization and geographical remoteness prevented all but a modest contribution to the illustrations in the book.

After almost three frustrating years of both collecting and commissioning photographs to illustrate human facial expression, Darwin had acquired only eleven of the thirty photographs eventually published in *The Expression of the Emotions*. Although he had built a promising collection of photographs of children and the mentally ill, and despite his discovery of Duchenne's *Mechanism* photographs, Darwin had still found nothing suitable to illustrate the ordinary expressions of adults. None of the photographers he had approached seemed capable of producing the range of photographs he needed to complete his project. It was at this desperate stage that Darwin met Oscar Rejlander. In April 1871 Darwin declared, 'I am now rich in photographs for I have found in London, Rejlander, who for years has had a passion for photographing all sorts of chance expressions exhibited on various occasions.'[26] How the two met is not known, although it is possible they were introduced by a mutual acquaintance, the photographer Julia Margaret Cameron (1815–1879).[27] It is also possible that Darwin simply encountered Rejlander on one of his numerous London expeditions, as Rejlander's Albert Mansions studio stood (and still stands) conspicuously adjacent to Victoria Station, the terminus for trains from Downe, Kent, where Darwin lived.

Rejlander was one of the pioneers of Victorian photography, and a vocal advocate for photography's role as a fine art. Trained as a painter in Rome and his native Sweden, he first took up photography in 1853 as an adjunct to his artistic work. At first, he believed photography should serve as a 'handmaid' to art by providing studies which artists could copy in their paintings. Later, he claimed that photography was an art in its own right, and could be used to create pictures with as much beauty and meaning as any other artistic medium. Arguing that control in photography is crucial to its artistic merit, Rejlander devised a sophisticated system for manipulating the printing of photographic negatives. By combining details from several negatives in a single photographic print, he tried to create elaborate compositions comparable in quality to the traditional fine arts. His ideas about the artistic value of photography were controversial, and brought him as much criticism as praise. In particular, he was frequently berated for a picture called 'The Two Ways of Life', which he had exhibited at the Manchester Art Treasures Exhibition in 1857. It was Rejlander's most ambitious composite photograph; a large, fresco-like composition produced from approximately thirty separate negatives. Critics disliked its fine art pretensions, and denounced the complex manipulations involved in its production as mere photographic trickery.

In this context, it may seem strange that Darwin turned to Rejlander to produce photographic illustrations for *Expression*. Darwin aspired to produce an objective study of expression, using photography as evidence for the minutiae of expressive behaviour. By contrast, Rejlander was known as a master of photographic manipulation. There is evidence of some of this manipulation in the book, most notably in Plate 1, Fig. 1, the so-called 'Ginx's Baby',[28] a photograph ostensibly depicting infant distress. Widely celebrated for its precocious spontaneity, it is now clear that this figure was not produced by photography alone. Although it was based on a photograph in Rejlander's possession, the illustration published in *Expression* is actually a drawing, carefully rendered by Rejlander to resemble an original photograph.

While the photographs in *Expression* were widely perceived as setting new standards in the field of scientific photography, they were produced at the expense of true photographic objectivity. In an attempt to overcome the inadequacy of available photographic materials, Rejlander posed for many of the photographs himself: 'It is very difficult to get, at will – those expressions you wish – Few have the command or imagination to appear real. In time I might catch some – So I have tried *in propria persona* – even cut my moustache shorter to try to please you . . ."[29] As this comment indicates, Rejlander believed manipulation was needed to produce convincing illustrations for the book. By posing for some of the illustrations, he was able to control the behaviour he sought to depict. His approach was not unlike that of Duchenne to the production of his *Mechanism* photographs, in which electrical stimulation had been used to induce expression artificially.

The photographs Rejlander produced contain a mixture of contrived and genuine expressions. Although Darwin advised his readers that the photographs in the book were 'faithful copies', which were 'much superior for my purposes to any drawing, however carefully executed',[30] each reflects sometimes arbitrary decisions made by Darwin and his photographers. Darwin was concerned that his photographs should contain as much factual information as possible, but the difficulties inherent in early photographic materials prevented the production of completely authentic documents. Given these constraints, Rejlander was the ideal choice to produce the photographs: his mastery of photographic technique bridged the gap between the desire for empirical imagery and the need for convincing illustrations.

Darwin and Rejlander have been widely criticized for the compromises they made in preparing the illustrations. Although much of this criticism may be justified by contemporary standards, it is wise to remember the historical context in which the book was produced. The distinction between *evidence* and *illustration* is blurred because there was little precedent for the acceptance of photographs as scientific data. Rules about photographic objectivity did not yet exist, in part because photographers frequently found it necessary to manipulate their work to enhance the visual appeal and clarity of their images. In many ways publication of *Expression* marked the birth of empirical photography. It could not conform to rules about scientific photography, because it was part of the creation of those rules. Before it was published, photographs were judged on how real they looked, not on how scrupulously they had been produced. Later, as scientists began to use photography as evidence of events invisible to the unassisted eye, viewers began to demand proof that photographs were accurate. As a result, scientists began to look more carefully at the circumstances in which photographic information had been produced, and devised systems for collecting reliable photographic data. *Expression* was produced on the cusp of this change in attitude.

Leafing through the photographs Rejlander sent Darwin between

1871 and 1872, now housed at Cambridge, one is overwhelmed by the exuberance and sense of fun with which Rejlander accepted Darwin's commission. He was an eccentric man, full of wit and humour, who had made his career out of producing photographic entertainment. The application of his craft to an audience of scientists was a final challenge in his artistic career. Although the photographs Darwin commissioned were meant to be sober, objective examples, one can occasionally glimpse the ebullient personality of Rejlander, peering through the thin veneer of his illustrations. He would have been delighted to know that even after 125 years, his photographs continue to beguile readers.

Note on the Orientation of the Plates

PHILLIP PRODGER AND PAUL EKMAN

This edition of *Expression* includes all the photographic plates from the original edition, together with a number of illustrations described in the text but not previously published. In arranging these illustrations, the editor tried to preserve Darwin's intentions for the look and feel of the book, while taking advantage of modern printing methods to integrate pictures with text in a convenient way. In this Appendix we discuss the left–right orientation of the photographs of facial expressions.

It may seem that the orientation of photographs is a trivial matter, but in the last fifty years anthropometric research has reported differences in emotion shown in the two sides of the face (Borod and Cannon, 1980; Chaurasia and Goswami, 1975; Moscovitch and Olds, 1979; Sackeim, Gur and Saucy, 1978). These asymmetries were usually stronger on the left than on the right side. Because many of the pathways from the motor cortex cross over before reaching the facial nucleus, stronger left asymmetries suggest greater involvement of the right than of the left cerebral hemisphere. This is consistent with the accepted view that the right hemisphere has a special role in emotion.

Questioning the findings that expressions are stronger on the left side, Ekman (1980) raised the possibility that those who had studied this matter may have examined more deliberate, posed expressions, rather than spontaneous emotional ones. Ekman, Hager and Friesen (1981) examined both kinds of facial movements in children and adults and found that asymmetries were more frequent in deliberate than emotional expressions. In another study Hager and Ekman (1985) found that among deliberate facial actions, some were more intense on the left side while others were stronger on the right side. Spontaneous facial actions were more symmetrical than deliberate facial actions.

Given this current interest in whether the left or right side of the

Original sketch for Plate 1 of *The Expression of the Emotions in Man and Animals*, showing Darwin's understanding of the left–right orientation of the Figures. The layout of this sketch was later altered to accommodate the vertical format reproduced in this edition. Photo: Cambridge University Library, Darwin Manuscripts Collection, volume 53.1, folio 72, item 142.

face shows emotion more intensely, it seems important to present correctly in this edition of *Expression* the left–right orientation of the facial photographs. To understand how it might have been confused it is necessary to explain how the illustrations were made in earlier editions.

The photographs published in the first and second editions of *Expression* varied in quality, layout, and orientation. R. B. Freeman (1975) has noted at least three separate states of plates in the first edition, as well as an additional state in the posthumous second edition of 1890. There may be many more. The photographs in the book were originally printed by the Heliotype Company, a London firm, who supplied the principal publishers with sheets of plates which were hand-collated and inserted into the book. Corrections to the plates were made separately to corrections to the text. As a result, runs of plates were not necessarily consistent within each issue. In some versions of *Expression* for example, the first, second and sixth plates were folded, in others they were not. In addition, the plate and figure numbers, which were lithographed and printed on to the photographic plates, appear alternately in both Roman and Arabic numerals.

Particularly puzzling is the apparently arbitrary reversal of some photographic figures in different issues of the book. Mirror-image reversals of some plates occur; for example, in some versions, Plate I, Figs 4 and 6 face towards each other. In others, they face away from each other, and in some, they both face the same way. Figs 1, 2, 3 and 5 on Plate I also varied in orientation in different printings, but not in any predictable way. Although it is possible these variations may have been instigated by Darwin to alter the appearance of the plates, it is more likely the changes were the result of misunderstandings by the Heliotype Company. The first edition was released in Britain by John Murray on 26 November 1872 in a run of 7000 copies, of which 5267 were sold immediately. Foreign editions, including those published simultaneously by D. Appleton & Co. in New York, Schwiezerbart in Germany, C. Reinwald in France, and F. S. Suchinskiĭ in Russia, also required a substantial number of photographs. This put immense pressure on the Heliotype Company to produce a large number of plates in an extremely short time. The heliotype process was new, and the company had little experience in large-scale commercial production. To make matters worse, just days before the book was due to be published, workers in the company's factory went on strike. Concerned about their ability to cope, Darwin wrote to John Murray, his publisher, six days before publication:

> It is a very bad job about the Heliotype Plates and will I fear cause us loss; but it is obvious that the Coy. [Company] must be at least as anxious as we are, and therefore I honestly hope the difficulty will soon be overcome. It will be necessary to have a look at the Plates, to see that they do not palm off poor copies owing to the employment of incompetent workmen.*

Darwin wrote again about two weeks later, to express his concern about the quality of the finished product:

> One of my sons saw a copy of Expressions the other day with very poor heliotypes. Would it not be well to caution

---

* Unpublished letter from Charles Darwin to Robert Cooke (of John Murray Publishers), 20 November 1872, Darwin Manuscripts Collection, Cambridge University Library, volume 143, folio 288.

the Coy. that they will lose credit if they distribute poor copies?*

Darwin's concern at this stage was primarily with the clarity of the photographs, and not their orientation. Any correspondence he may have had with the publishers regarding orientation has not been preserved. However, given the extraordinary difficulty involved in preparing the plates for publication, it is reasonable to assume that the Heliotype Company became confused about the precise arrangement of plates.

Heliotype printing involves the coating of a metal plate with bichromated gelatin, which is put in contact with a photographic negative and exposed to light. The light passes through the negative and creates small cracks in the emulsion (known as reticulation) in proportion to the light transmitted. These cracks form an intaglio copy of the photographic image on the plate, which can then be inked, and printed on paper. Unlike conventional printing plates which may be strengthened by electroplating, heliotype plates are fragile and must be replaced often. To produce them requires the creation of a complicated series of negatives and prints, each one a reversal of the previous state. Without careful attention, it would be easy to lose track of the proper left–right orientation of each image. This appears to have happened in the various editions of *Expression*.

In this (the third) edition the left–right orientation of a number of the photographs has been reversed, to correct printing mistakes made in earlier versions of the book. These corrections are based, when possible, on original photographs and sketches Darwin made in his manuscript (see figure, p. 412), now preserved in the Darwin Archive. Photographs and sketches do not exist for all of the plates, and in those instances the layout in the second edition, edited by Francis Darwin (1890) was adopted. (The University of Chicago Press edition (1965), which was the most common version of *Expression* available previously, is consistent with the left–right orientation as it appeared in the second edition.)

We relied upon the second edition when there were no originals because it corresponded more closely to the known sketches and photographs. The orientation of plates in the second edition is generally accurate, although it does contain a few small errors, including the reversal of each of the figures reproduced from Duchenne de

---

* Unpublished letter from Charles Darwin to Robert Cooke, 7 December 1872, Darwin Manuscripts Collection, Cambridge University Library, volume 143, item 289.

Boulogne's *Mécanisme de la Physionomie Humaine* (1862/1990). By correcting these errors, we believe this edition is most likely to have the correct left–right orientation. The concordance of plates (Appendix 5) lists each of the changes in orientation made in the production of this edition.

REFERENCES TO APPENDIX IV

J. C. Borod and H. S. Caron, 'Facedness and emotion related to lateral dominance, sex, and expression type', *Neuropsychologia*, 1908, *18*, 237–42.

B. D. Chaurasia and H. K. Goswami, 'Functional asymmetry in the face', *Acta Anatomica*, 1975, *91*, 154–60.

B. Duchenne, *Mécanisme de la physionomie humaine ou analyse électrophysiologique de l'expression des passions*. Paris: Baillière, 1862; B. Duchenne, *The mechanism of human facial expression or an electro-physiological analysis of the expression of the emotions* (A. Cuthbertson, trans.). New York: Cambridge University Press, 1990.

P. Ekman, 'Asymmetry in facial expression', *Science*, 1980, *209*, 833–4.

P. Ekman, J. C. Hager and W. V. Friesen, 'Symmetry and the nature of facial action'. *Psychophysiology*, 1981, *18*, 101–106.

R. B. Freeman, *The Works of Charles Darwin: An Annotated Bibliographical Handlist*, second edition. Folkestone: Wm. Dawson & Sons, 1975, 143.

J. C. Hager and P. Ekman, 'The asymmetry of facial actions is inconsistent with models of hemispheric specialization', *Psychophysiology*, 1985, *22*, 307–18.

M. Moscovitch and J. Olds, 'Asymmetries in spontaneous facial expressions and their possible relation to hemispheric specialization', *Neuropsychologia*, 1982, *10*, 71–81.

H. A. Sackeim, R. C. Gur and M. C. Saucy, 'Emotions are expressed more intensely on the left side of the face', *Science*, 1978, *202*, 434–6.

Concordance of Illustrations

PHILLIP PRODGER

This concordance will help readers with earlier editions of *Expression* to compare the plates of the current edition with its predecessors. It also contains previously unpublished information about the artists and authors who prepared illustrations for the book. Complete descriptions of the new illustrations in this edition are included at the end of the concordance.

Original Figure refers to the plate and figure numbers given to the illustrations in previous editions of *Expression*. **New Figure** refers to the plate and figure numbers used in the current edition. **Orientation** refers to the left–right orientation of the illustration compared to the second edition of the book (see Appendix IV). The second edition was used as it is the most common early printing of the book, and is widely available in facsimile form (University of Chicago Press, 1965). 'Same' means that the illustration in this edition is oriented exactly as the second edition, 'Reversed' means that the current illustration is the mirror reverse of the second edition.

The titles listed were taken from the text wherever possible. Those capitalized in title case are proper titles given to the illustration in a caption. Other titles, which are based on descriptions given in the text, appear with ordinary capitalization.

All the wood engravings in the book were prepared by the London-based artist James Davis Cooper (1823–1904), who sometimes used a photographic transfer process to prepare the plates.

The photographs in early editions were reproduced using the heliotype technique. Later editions used photogravure. In both cases, these reproductions were created from albumen print originals.

Original Figure	New Figure	Orientation	Illustration	Produced by	Medium
Fig. 1	Same	Same	Diagram of the muscles of the face	Sir Charles Bell (1774–1842)	Wood engraving, after Plate 2 of *The Anatomy of Expression as Connected with the Fine Arts* (1806)
Fig. 2	Same	Same	Diagram (of muscles of the face)	Jacob Henle (1809–1885)	Wood engraving, after Figure 67 of *Handbuch der Systematischen Anatomie des Menschen*, Volume 1, Part 3 (1858)
Fig. 3	Same	Same	Diagram (of muscles of the face)	Jacob Henle	Wood engraving, after Figure 63 of *Handbuch der Systematischen Anatomie des Menschen*, Volume 1, Part 3 (1858)
Fig. 4	Same	Same	Small Dog Watching a Cat on a Table	Oscar Rejlander (c. 1813–1875)	Wood engraving after a photograph by Rejlander
Fig. 5	Same	Same	Dog Approaching Another Dog with Hostile Intentions	Briton Riviere (1840–1920)	Wood engraving
Fig. 6	Same	Same	The Same in a Humble and Affectionate Frame of Mind	Briton Riviere	Wood engraving
Fig. 7	Same	Same	Half-bred Shepherd Dog in the Same State as in Fig. 5	Arthur Dampier May (fl. 1872–1900)	Wood engraving
Fig. 8	Same	Same	The Same Caressing His Master	Arthur Dampier May	Wood engraving
Fig. 9	Same	Same	Cat, Savage and Prepared to Fight, from life	Thomas William Wood (fl. 1855–1872)	Wood engraving

Fig. 10	Same	Same	Cat in an Affectionate Frame of Mind	Thomas William Wood	Wood engraving
Fig. 11	Same	Same	Sound-Producing Quills from the Tail of the Porcupine	Thomas William Wood	Wood engraving
Fig. 12	Same	Same	Hen Driving away a Dog from Her Chickens. Drawn from life	Thomas William Wood	Wood engraving
Fig. 13	Same	Same	Swan Driving away an Intruder. Drawn from life	Thomas William Wood	Wood engraving
Fig. 14	Same	Same	Head of a Snarling Dog. Drawn from life	Thomas William Wood	Wood engraving
Fig. 15	Same	Same	Cat Terrified at a Dog. Drawn from life	Thomas William Wood	Wood engraving
Fig. 16	Same	Same	*Cynopithecus niger* in a Placid Condition. Drawn from life	Joseph Wolf (1820–1899)	Wood engraving
Fig. 17	Same	Same	The Same, when Pleased by being Caressed	Joseph Wolf	Wood engraving
Fig. 18	Same	Same	Chimpanzee Disappointed and Sulky. Drawn from life	Thomas William Wood	Wood engraving
Plate 1, Fig. 1	Same	Same	Crying child ('Ginx's Baby')	Oscar Rejlander	Photograph, after a drawing by Rejlander
Plate 1, Fig. 2	Same	Same	Crying child	Adolph Diedrich Kindermann (1823–1892)	Photograph
Plate 1, Fig. 3	Same	Same	Crying child	Oscar Rejlander	Photograph
Plate 1, Fig. 4	Same	Same	Crying child	Oscar Rejlander	Photograph
Plate 1, Fig. 5	Same	Same	Crying child	Adolph Diedrich Kindermann	Photograph

Plate 1, Fig. 6	Same	Reversed	Moderate crying in an older child	Oscar Rejlander	Photograph
Plate II, Fig. 1	Same	Reversed	Face of an actor (the sculptor Jules Talrich) in its natural state	G. B. Duchenne de Boulogne (1806–1875)	Photograph, after Plate 4 of *Mécanisme de la Physionomie Humaine* (1862)
Plate II, Fig. 2	Same	Reversed	Face of an actor (the sculptor Jules Talrich) in its natural state	G. B. Duchenne de Boulogne	Photograph, after Plate 24 of *Mécanisme de la Physionomie Humaine* (1862)
Plate II, Fig. 3	Same	Same	Furrowed brow of a woman (possibly Darwin's niece, Katherine Wedgwood)	Maker unknown	Photograph
Plate II, Fig. 4	Same	Same	Boy in a placid state	Oscar Rejlander	Photograph
Plate II, Fig. 5	Same	Same	Boy with a pathetic expression	Oscar Rejlander	Photograph
Plate II, Fig. 6	Same	Same	Boy with depression of the corners of the mouth (profile)	Oscar Rejlander	Photograph
Plate II, Fig. 7	Same	Same	Boy with depression of the corners of the mouth	Oscar Rejlander	Photograph
Plate III, Fig. 1	Same	Same	Girl smiling	Oscar Rejlander	Photograph
Plate III, Fig. 2	Same	Reversed	Girl (the photographer's daughter, Beatrice) smiling	George Charles Wallich (1815–1899)	Photograph
Plate III, Fig. 3	Same	Same	Girl smiling	Oscar Rejlander	Photograph
Plate III, Fig. 4	Same	Reversed	Old man in his usual passive condition	G. B. Duchenne de Boulogne	Photograph, after Plate 3 of *Mécanisme de la Physionomie Humaine* (1862)

Plate III, Fig. 5	Same	Reversed	Old man smiling naturally	G. B. Duchenne de Boulogne	Photograph, after Plate 32 of *Mécanisme de la Physionomie Humaine* (1862)
Plate III, Fig. 6	Same	Reversed	Old man with corners of his mouth strongly retracted by electrical stimulation	G. B. Duchenne de Boulogne	Photograph, after Plate 31 of *Mécanisme de la Physionomie Humaine* (1862)
Plate IV, Fig. 1	Figure 22	Same	Lady (the photographer's wife, Mary) displaying the canine on one side	Oscar Rejlander	Photograph
Plate IV, Fig. 2	Plate IV, Fig. 1	Reversed	Angry girl	Adolph Diedrich Kindermann	Photograph
Plate V, Fig. 1	Plate VI, Fig. 1	Same	Young lady tearing up the photograph of a despised lover	Oscar Rejlander	Photograph
Plate V, Fig. 2	Plate VI, Fig. 2	Same	Disgusted man (Oscar Rejlander)	Oscar Rejlander	Photograph
Plate V, Fig. 3	Plate VI, Fig. 3	Same	Disgusted man (Oscar Rejlander)	Oscar Rejlander	Photograph
Plate VI, Fig. 1	Plates V and VII, Fig. 1	Same	Indignant man with clenched fists	Oscar Rejlander	Photograph
Plate VI, Fig. 2	Plates V and VII, Fig. 2	Same	Indignant man (Oscar Rejlander) with clenched fists	Oscar Rejlander	Photograph
Plate VI, Fig. 3	Plate VII, Fig. 3	Same	Man (Oscar Rejlander) shrugging his shoulders	Oscar Rejlander	Photograph
Plate VI, Fig. 4	Plate VII, Fig. 4	Same	Man (Oscar Rejlander) shrugging his shoulders	Oscar Rejlander	Photograph

Fig. 19	Same	From a Photograph of an Insane Woman, to Show the Condition of Her Hair	Maker unknown (possibly F. W. Grierson)	Wood engraving, after a photograph given to Darwin by James Crichton Browne
Fig. 20	Same	Terror	G. B. Duchenne de Boulogne	Wood engraving, after a photograph, Plate 61 of *Mécanisme de la Physionomie Humaine* (1862)
Plate VII, Fig. 1	Same	Surprised man (Oscar Rejlander) with hands open and raised above his head	Oscar Rejlander	Photograph
Plate VII, Fig. 2	Reversed	Old man with the platysma contracted by means of galvanism	G. B. Duchenne de Boulogne	Photograph, after Plate 64 of *Mécanisme de la Physionomie Humaine* (1862)
Fig. 21	Same	Horror and Agony	G. B. Duchenne de Boulogne	Wood engraving, after a photograph, Plate 65 of *Mécanisme de la Physionomie Humaine* (1862)
Plate IV, Fig. 2		Lowered brow (to study the lines that characterize weeping)	G. B. Duchenne de Boulogne	Photograph, from Plate 46 of *Mécanisme de la Physionomie Humaine* (1862)
Fig. 19		Half-smile (to study the differential expressive lines of m. zygomaticus minor and m. zygomaticus major)	G. B. Duchenne de Boulogne	Photograph, from Plate 48 of *Mécanisme de la Physionomie Humaine* (1862)
Fig. 20		Half-cry (to study the association of m. zygomaticus major and m. levator labii superioris)	G. B. Duchenne de Boulogne	Photograph, from Plate 49 of *Mécanisme de la Physionomie Humaine* (1862)

List of Head Words from the Index to the First Edition

A

Abstraction.

Actions, reflex; coughing, sneezing, &c.; muscular action of decapitated frog; closing the eyelids; starting; contraction of the iris.

Admiration.

Affirmation, signs of.

Albinos, blushing in.

Alison, Professor.

Ambition.

Anatomical drawings by Henle.

Anatomy and Philosophy of expression.

Anderson, Dr.

Anger; in monkeys.

Animals, special expressions of. *See* Expression.

——, habitual associated movements in the lower; wolves and jackals; horses; cats; chickens; sheldrakes; flamingo, kagu, and kingfisher.

Annesley, Lieut., R.A.

Antithesis, the principles of; dogs; cats; conventional signs.

Anxiety.

Ape, the Gibbon, produces musical sounds.

Arrectores pili, the.

Association, the power of; instances of.

Astonishment; in monkeys.

Audubon.

Avarice.

Azara.

B

Baboon, the Anubis.

Bain, Mr.

Baker, Sir Samuel.

Barber, Mrs.

Bartlett, Mr.

Behn, Dr.

Bell, Mr.

——, Sir Charles.

Bennett, G.

Bergeon.

Bernard, Claude.

Billiard-player, gestures of the.

Birds ruffle their feathers when angry, when frightened adpress them.

Blair, the Rev. R. H.

Blind, tendency of the, to blush.

Blush, the tendency to, inherited.

Blushing, inheritance of, in the various races of man, movements and gestures which accompany, confusion of mind, the nature of the mental states which induce, shyness, moral causes: guilt, breaches of etiquette, modesty, theory of.

——, the physiology or mechanism of.

Blyth, Mr.

Bowman, Mr.

Brehm.

Bridges, Mr.

Bridgman, Laura.

Brinton, Dr.

Brodie, Sir B.

NOTES

PREFACE TO THE THIRD EDITION

1. Charles Darwin, *The Descent of Man*. New York: D. Appleton and Company, 1871.
2. Richard Broke Freeman, *The Works of Charles Darwin. An Annotated Bibliographical Handlist*, Second Edition; revised and enlarged. Kent, England: Dawson/Archon Books, 1977. While Freeman lists the second edition as 1880, a copy in the home of Milo Keynes, a Darwin descendant, was dated 1879.
3. This information is contained in *A Concordance To Darwin's* The Expression of the Emotions in Man and Animals, edited by Paul H. Barrett, Donald J. Weinshank, Paul Ruhlen, Stehan J. Ozminski and Barbara N. Berghage, and published by Cornell University Press in 1986.
4. Some of these typographical errors were reported in the *Concordance*. The Pickering and Chatto reprint of the second edition also noted this problem and corrected it.
5. A briefer account of this incident was published in Darwin's 'Biographical Sketch of an Infant', *Mind*, 7 July 1877, 285–94. I am indebted to Michael Ghiselin for the information.
6. I am also grateful to Phillip Prodger for his help in obtaining some of the illustrations.
7. The correspondence on this point was not with John Murray himself, but with Robert Cooke. Jon Topham, a historian at Cambridge University who specializes in nineteenth-century publishing in England, agrees that this is a likely explanation. Murray Archives 1875, document 9219, letter 10 May 1871; 28 May 1871. I am grateful to Joy Harvey who made this information available to me.

INTRODUCTION TO THE THIRD EDITION

1. Klaus R. Scherer, 'Vocal Affect Signaling: a comparative approach', in *Advances in the Study of Behavior*, edited by J. Rosenblatt, C. Beer, M. C. Busnell and P. J. B. Slater. New York: Academic Press, 1985; and 'Vocal Affect Expression: a Review and a Model for Future Research', *Psychological Bulletin*, 99, 1986, 143–65.

2. Margaret Mead review of my Darwin book (*Journal of Communication*, 25, 1975, 205–13).

3. The quote is in C. Swisher, 'Charles Darwin on the Origins of Behavior', *Bulletin of Historical Medicine, 41*, 1967, p. 40.

4. J. Browne, 'Darwin and the Expression of the Emotions', in *The Darwinian Heritage*, edited by David Kohn. Princeton University Press, 1985, 313.

5. J. Bowlby makes this specific point, in *Charles Darwin: A New Life*. W. W. Norton, 1991, 402.

6. Sandra Herbert, 'Man in the Development of Darwin's Theory of Transmutation: Part II', *Journal of the History of Biology, 10*, 1977, 155–227. The quote is from p. 206.

7. Gallup Organization, 21–23 November 1991.

8. See Bowlby's interesting discussion of Darwin's reaction to the response to *Origin*, in Chapter 23 of *Charles Darwin*.

9. *Autobiography of Charles Darwin*. W. W. Norton, 1969, 131–2.

10. H. E. Gruber, *Darwin on Man*. New York: E. P. Dutton & Co., 1974, 122; Swisher agrees. See Gruber for M and N notebook transcriptions.

11. Herbert, loc. cit., p. 164.

12. See C. Le Brun, 1974, *A Method to Learn to Design the Passions*, 1980. Facsimile edition introduced by Q. T. McKenzie. Los Angeles: William Andrews Clark Memorial Library, University of California, Augustan Reprint Society; J. C. Lavater, *Physiognomische Fragmente, zur Beförderung der Menschenkenntnis und Menschenliebe*. Leipzig and Winterthur: 1775–8.

13. J. Lefas, *Physiognomy: the Art of Reading Faces* (trans. D. Macrae). Spain: Delta Editrice, 1975; R. L. Whiteside, *Face Language*. New York: Pocket Books, 1975; T. T. Mar, *Face Reading: The Chinese Art of Physiognomy*. New York: Dodd, Mead & Co., 1974.

14. P. Ekman, 'Facial Signs: Facts, Fantasies, and Possibilities', in *Sight, Sound and Sense*, T. Sebeok (ed.). Bloomington: Indiana University Press, 1978.

15. Duchenne's masterful book was out of print for more than one hundred years, not translated into English until a few years ago. *The Mechanism of Human Facial Expression* by G.-B. Duchenne de Boulogne, translated and edited by R. A. Cuthbertson. New York: Cambridge University Press, 1990.

16. Ernst Mayr, 'Darwin's Five Theories of Evolution', in *The Darwinian Heritage*, op. cit., p. 771.

17. M. T. Ghiselin, *The Triumph of the Darwinian Method*. Berkeley: University of California Press, 1969.

18. Ghiselin, op. cit., p. 188.

19. S. Chevalier-Skolnikoff, 'Facial Expression of Emotion in Nonhuman Primates', in *Darwin and Facial Expression*, P. Ekman (editor). New York: Academic Press, 1973, p. 23.

20. For the argument that many other animals do experience emotion see D. R. Griffin, *The Question of Animal Awareness: Evolutionary Continuity of Mental Experience*. New York: Rockefeller Press, 1976; *Animal Thinking*. Cambridge, MA: Harvard University Press, 1984. Although there is no definitive research on this question, lesion areas of the brain likely to be associated with such mental functioning, and observing changes in emotional behavior could be informative.

21. R. W. Burkhardt, 'Darwin on Animal Behavior and Evolution', in *The Darwinian Heritage*, 328; D. R. Oldroyd, *Darwinian Impacts*. Atlantic Highlands, N.J.: Humanities Press, 1983, 29; Gruber, op. cit., 193; M. Ruse, *Darwinism Defended*. Reading, Mass.: Addison Wesley, 1982, 32; Bowlby, op. cit.

22. These quotes are from Degler's excellent book *In Search of Human Nature*. Oxford University Press, 1991, 20.

23. Quoted by Ruse, op. cit., 233.

24. 'The Development of an Evolutionary Ethology', in *Evolution from Molecules to Men*, D. S. Bendall (ed.). Cambridge University Press, 1983, p. 433. In this section I have relied also on the excellent article by the American historian William Montgomery, 'Charles Darwin's Thought on Expressive Mechanisms in Evolution', in the book, *The Development of Expressive Behavior*, and also on Ghiselin.

25. Ghiselin, op. cit., 191–2.

26. An exception is the marvellous book, *Human Universals*, by D. E. Brown. Philadelphia: Temple University Press, 1991.

INTRODUCTION TO THE FIRST EDITION

1. [John Bulwer, in his *Pathomyotomia*, 1649, gives a fairly good description of a variety of expressions, and discusses at length the muscles involved in each. Dr D. Hack Tuke (*Influence of the Mind upon the Body*, 2nd edit., 1884, vol. i, p. 232) quotes the 'Chirologia' of John Bulwer as containing admirable remarks on gesture. Lord Bacon recommended, among the works to be supplied by posterity, 'The Doctrine of Gesture; or, the Motions of the Body with a view to their interpretation'.]

2. J. Parsons, in his paper in the Appendix to the *Philosophical Transactions* for 1746, p. 41, gives a list of forty-one old authors who have written on expression. [Mantegazza has given an 'Esquisse historique de la science de la physionomie et de la mimique humaine' in chapter i of his *La Physionomie et l'Expression des Sentiments* (International Series), 1885.]

3. *Conférences sur l'expression des différentes Caractères des Passions*, Paris, 4to, 1667. I always quote from the republication of the *Conférences* in the edition of Lavater, by Moreau, which appeared in 1820, as given in vol. ix, p. 257.

4. *Discours par Pierre Camper sur le Moyen de représenter les diverses Passions,* etc. 1792.

5. I always quote from the third edition, 1844, which was published after the death of Sir C. Bell, and contains his latest corrections. The first edition of 1806 is much inferior in merit, and does not include some of his more important views.

6. *De la Physionomie et de la Parole,* by Albert Lemoine, 1865, p. 101.

7. *Handbuch der systematischen Anatomie des Menschen,* vol. 1, dritte Abtheilung, 1858.

8. *The Senses and the Intellect,* 2nd edit., 1864, pp. 96 and 288. The preface to the first edition of this work is dated June, 1855. See also the 2nd edition of Mr Bain's work on the *Emotions and Will.*

9. *The Anatomy of Expression,* 3rd edit., p. 121.

10. *Anatomy of Expression,* 3rd edit., pp. 98, 121, 131.

11. *Anatomy of Expression,* pp. 121, 138.

12. *De la Physionomie,* pp. 12, 73.

13. *Mécanisme de la Physionomie Humaine,* 8vo edit., p. 31.

14. *Elements of Physiology,* English translation, vol. ii, p. 934.

15. *Anatomy of Expression,* 3rd edit., p. 198.

16. See remarks to this effect in Lessing's *Laocoon,* translated by W. Ross, 1836, p. 19.

17. Mr Partridge in Todd's *Cyclopaedia of Anatomy and Physiology,* vol. ii, p. 227.

18. *La Physionomie,* by J. C. Lavater, vol. iv, 1820, p. 274. On the number of the facial muscles, see vol. iv, pp. 209–11.

19. *Mimik und Physiognomik,* 1867, p. 91.

CHAPTER I · GENERAL PRINCIPLES OF EXPRESSION

1. Müller, *Elements of Physiology,* Eng. translat., vol. ii, p. 939. See also Mr H. Spencer's interesting speculations on the same subject, and on the genesis of nerves, in his *Principles of Biology,* vol. ii, p. 346; and in his *Principles of Psychology,* 2nd edit., pp. 511–57.

2. See for my authorities, and for various analogous facts, *The Variation of Animals and Plants under Domestication,* 1868, vol. ii, p. 304.

3. *Mécanisme de la Physionomie Humaine,* 1862, p. 17.

4. Dr Maudsley, *Body and Mind,* 1870, p. 8.

5. See the very interesting discussion on the whole subject by Claude Bernard, *Tissus Vivants,* 1866, pp. 353–6.

6. *Chapters on Mental Physiology,* 1858, p. 85.

7. See Mr F. H. Salvin's account of a tame jackal in *Land and Water,* October, 1869.

8. Carpenter, *Principles of Comparative Physiology,* 1854, p. 690; and Müller's *Elements of Physiology,* Eng. translat., vol. ii, p. 936.

9. Mowbray, *Poultry,* 6th edit. 1830, p. 54.

10. See the account given by this excellent observer in *Wild Sports of the Highlands*, 1846, p. 142.
11. *Philosophical Transactions*, 1823, p. 182.

CHAPTER II · GENERAL PRINCIPLES OF EXPRESSION – CONTINUED

1. *Naturgeschichte der Säugethiere von Paraguay*, 1830, p. 55.
2. Mr Tylor gives an account of the Cistercian gesture-language in his *Early History of Mankind* (2nd edit., 1870, p. 40), and makes some remarks on the principle of opposition in gestures.

CHAPTER III · GENERAL PRINCIPLES OF EXPRESSION – CONCLUDED

1. *Leçons sur les Prop. des Tissus Vivants*, 1866, pp. 457–66.
2. Mr Bartlett, 'Notes on the Birth of a Hippopotamus', *Proc. Zoolog. Soc.*, 1871, p. 255.
3. See, on this subject, Claude Bernard, *Tissus Vivants*, 1866, pp. 316, 337, 358. Virchow expresses himself to almost exactly the same effect in his essay *Ueber das Rückenmark* (Sammlung/Wissenschaft, *Vorträge*, 1871, p. 28).
4. H. Spencer, *Essays, Scientific, Political*, etc., second series. 1863, pp. 109, 111.
5. [A somewhat similar view is given by Henle, *Anthropologische Vorträge*, 1876, vol. i, p. 66.] [1890]
6. Dr Darwin, *Zoonomia*, 1794, vol. i, p. 148.
7. Mrs Oliphant, in her novel of *Miss Marjoribanks*, p. 362.

CHAPTER IV · MEANS OF EXPRESSION IN ANIMALS

1. See the evidence on this head in my *Variation of Animals and Plants under Domestication*, vol. i, p. 27. On the cooing of pigeons, vol. i, pp. 154, 155.
2. *Essays, Scientific, Political, and Speculative*, 1858, 'The Origin and Function of Music', p. 359.
3. Mr Tylor (*Primitive Culture*, 1871, vol. i, p. 166), in his discussion on this subject, alludes to the whining of the dog.
4. *Naturgeschichte der Säugethiere von Paraguay*, 1830, p. 46.
5. Quoted by Gratiolet, *De la Physionomie*, 1865, p. 115.
6. As quoted in Huxley's *Evidence as to Man's Place in Nature*, 1863, p. 52.
7. *Illust. Thierleben*, 1864, vol. i, p 130.
8. The Hon. J. Caton, Ottawa, *Acad. of Nat. Sciences*, May, 1868, pp. 36, 40. For the *Capra Aegagrus, Land and Water*, 1867, p. 37.

9. *Land and Water*, 20 July, 1867, p. 659.
10. *Phaeton rubricauda: Ibis*, vol. iii, 1861, p. 180.
11. *Melopsittacus undulatus*. See an account of its habits by Gould, *Handbook of Birds in Australia*, 1865, vol. ii, p. 82.
12. *Lehrbuch der Histologie des Menschen*, 1857, p. 82. I owe to Professor W. Turner's kindness an extract from this work.
13. *Quarterly Journal of Microscopical Science*, 1853, vol. i, p. 262.
14. *Lehrbuch der Histologie*, 1857, p. 82.
15. *Dictionary of English Etymology*, p. 403.
16. See the account of the habits of this animal by Dr Cooper, as quoted in *Nature*, 27 April 1871, p. 512.
17. Dr Günther, *Reptiles of British India*, p. 262.
18. Mr J. Mansel Weale, *Nature*, 27 April 1871, p. 508.
19. See the account by Dr Anderson, *Proc. Zool. Soc.*, 1871, p. 196.
20. Mr des Voeux, in *Proc. Zool. Soc.*, 1871, p. 3.
21. *The Sportsman and Naturalist in Canada*, 1866, p. 53.
22. Mr H. Reeks (letter, 8 March, 1873) has made a similar observation.
23. *The Nile Tributaries of Abyssinia*, 1867, p. 443.

CHAPTER V · SPECIAL EXPRESSIONS OF ANIMALS

1. *The Anatomy of Expression*, 1844, p. 190
2. *De la Physionomie*, 1865, pp. 187, 218.
3. *The Anatomy of Expression*, 1844, p. 140.
4. *Land and Water*, 6 November, 1869.
5. Azara, *Quadrupèdes de Paraguay*, 1801, vol. i, p. 136.
6. *Land and Water*, 1867, p. 657. See also Azara on the puma, in the work above quoted.
7. *Land and Water*, 1869, p. 152.
8. On this subject see *Descent of Man*, Supplemental Note, reprinted from *Nature*, 1876, p. 18.
9. *Natural History of Mammalia*, 1841, vol. i, pp. 383, 410.
10. Rengger, ibid. p. 46; Humboldt, *Personal Narrative*, Eng. trans. vol. iv, p. 527.
11. *Nat. Hist. of Mamm.*, 1841, p. 351.
12. Brehm, *Thierleben*, vol. i, p. 84. On baboons striking the ground, p. 61.
13. G. Bennett, *Wanderings in New South Wales*, etc., vol. ii, 1834, p. 153.
14. W. L. Martin, *Nat. Hist. of Mamm. Animals*, 1841, p. 405.
15. *Boston Journal of Nat. Hist.*, 1845–7, vol. v, p. 423. On the chimpanzee, ibid., 1843–4, vol. iv, p. 365.
16. See on this subject, *Descent of Man*, 2nd edit., vol. i, p. 18.
17. *Descent of Man*, 2nd edit., vol. i, p. 108.
18. *The Anatomy of Expression*, 3rd edit., 1844, pp. 121, 138.

CHAPTER VI · SOCIAL EXPRESSIONS OF MAN:
SUFFERING AND WEEPING

1. Mrs Gaskell, *Mary Barton*, new edit., p. 84.
2. *Mimik und Physiognomik*, 1867, p. 102. Duchenne, *Mécanisme de la Phys. Humaine*, Album, p. 34.
3. Dr Duchenne makes this remark, ibid. p. 39.
4. *The Origin of Civilisation*, 1870, p. 355.
5. See, for instance, Mr Marshall's account of an idiot in *Philosoph. Transact.*, 1864, p. 526. With respect to the cretins, see Dr Piderit, *Mimik und Physiognomik*, 1867, p. 61.
6. *New Zealand and its Inhabitants*, 1855, p. 175.
7. *De la Physionomie*, 1865, p. 126.
8. *The Anatomy of Expression*, 1844, p. 106. See also his paper in the *Philosophical Transactions*, 1822, p. 284, ibid., 1823, pp. 166 and 289. Also *The Nervous System of the Human Body*, 3rd edit., 1836, p. 175.
9. See Dr Brinton's account of the act of vomiting, in *Todd's Cyclop. of Anatomy and Physiology*, 1859, vol. v. Supplement, p. 318.
10. This memoir first appeared in the *Nederlandsch Archief voor Genees en Natuurkunde*, Deel 5, 1870. It has been translated by Dr W. D. Moore, under the title of 'On the Action of the Eyelids in determination of Blood from expiratory effort', in *Archive of Medicine*, edited by Dr L. S. Beale, 1870, vol. v, p. 20.
11. Donders, ibid., p. 36.
12. *De la Physionomie*, 1865, p. 217.
13. Bergeon, as quoted in the *Journal of Anatomy and Physiology*, November 1871, p. 235.
14. See, for instance, a case given by Sir Charles Bell, *Philosophical Transactions*, 1823, p. 177.
15. See, on these several points, Professor Donders, *On the Anomalies of Accommodation and Refraction of the Eye*, 1864, p. 573.
16. Quoted by Sir J. Lubbock, *Prehistoric Times*, 1865, p. 458.

CHAPTER VII · LOW SPIRITS, ANXIETY, GRIEF, DEJECTION,
DESPAIR

1. Professor Victor Carus called the attention of the author to a paper by Nasse in Meckel's *Deutsches Archiv für Physiologie*, vol. ii, 1816, p. 1, in which this characteristic form of sighing is described. [1890]
2. The above descriptive remarks are taken in part from my own observations, but chiefly from Gratiolet (*De la Physionomie*, pp. 53, 337; on Sighing, 232), who has well treated this whole subject. See, also Huschke, *Mimices et Physionomices, Fragmentum Physiologicum*, 1821, p. 21. On the dullness of the eyes, Dr Piderit, *Mimik und Physiognomik*, 1867, p. 65.

3. On the action of grief on the organs of respiration, see more especially Sir C. Bell, *Anatomy of Expression*, 3rd edit., 1844, p. 151.
4. *Mécanisme de la Phys. Humaine*, Album, p. 15.
5. See W. W. Keen, *Transactions of the College of Physicians of Philadelphia*, 1875, p. 104. [1890]
6. Henle, *Handbuch der Anat. des Menschen*, 1858, vol. i, p. 148, Figs 68 and 69.
7. See the account of the action of this muscle by Dr Duchenne, *Mécanisme de la Physionomie Humaine*, Album (1862), viii, p. 34.

CHAPTER VIII · JOY, HIGH SPIRITS, LOVE, TENDER FEELINGS, DEVOTION

1. Herbert Spencer, *Essays Scientific*, etc., 1858, p. 360.
2. F. Lieber on the vocal sounds of L. Bridgman, *Smithsonian Contributions*, 1851, vol. ii, p. 6.
3. See, also, Mr Marshall, in *Phil. Transact.*, 1864, p. 526.
4. Mr Bain (*The Emotions and the Will*, 1865, p. 247) has a long and interesting discussion on the ludicrous. The quotation above given about the laughter of the gods is taken from this work. See, also, Mandeville, *The Fable of the Bees*, vol. ii, p. 168.
5. *The Physiology of Laughter*, Essays, second series, 1863, p. 114.
6. J. Lister in *Quarterly Journal of Microscopical Science*, 1853, vol. i, p. 266.
7. *De la Physionomie*, p. 186.
8. Sir C. Bell (*Anat. of Expression*, p. 147) makes some remarks on the movement of the diaphragm during laughter.
9. *Mécanisme de la Physionomie Humaine*, Album, légende vi.
10. *Handbuch der System. Anat. des Menschen*, 1858, vol. i, p. 144. See my woodcut (H, Fig. 2 [p.ooo]).
11. See, also, remarks to the same effect by Dr J. Crichton Browne in *Journal of Mental Science*, April, 1871, p. 149.
12. C. Vogt, *Mémoire sur les Microcéphales*, 1867, p. 21.
13. Sir C. Bell, *Anatomy of Expression*, p. 133.
14. *Mimik und Physiognomik*, 1867, pp. 63–7.
15. *La Physionomie*, by G. Lavater, edit. of 1820, vol. iv, p. 224. See, also, Sir C. Bell, *Anatomy of Expression*, p. 172, for the quotation given below.
16. A *Dictionary of English Etymology*, 2nd edit., 1872, Introduction, p. xliv.
17. Crantz, quoted by Tylor, *Primitive Culture*, 1871, vol. i, p. 169.
18. F. Lieber, *Smithsonian Contributions*, 1851, vol. ii, p. 7.
19. See a full account, with references, by E. B. Tylor, *Researches into the Early History of Mankind*, 2nd edit., 1870, p. 51.
20. *The Descent of Man*, edit. ii, vol. ii, p. 364.
21. Dr Maudsley has a discussion to this effect in his *Body and Mind*, 1870, p. 85.

22. *The Anatomy of Expression*, p. 103, and *Philosophical Transactions*, 1823, p. 182.

CHAPTER IX · REFLECTION — MEDITATION — ILL-TEMPER — SULKINESS — DETERMINATION

1. *Mécanisme de la Physionomie Humaine*, Album, légende iii.
2. *Mimik und Physiognomik*, p. 46.
3. *History of the Abipones*, Eng. translat, vol. ii, p. 59, as quoted by Lubbock, *Origin of Civilisation*, 1870, p. 355.
4. *Miles Gloriosus*, act ii, sc. 2.
5. *Mécanisme de la Physionomie Humaine*, Album, légende iv, Figs 16–18.
6. Hensleigh Wedgwood on *The Origin of Language*, 1866, p. 78.
7. Müller, as quoted by Huxley, *Man's Place in Nature*, 1863, p. 38.
8. *Anatomy of Expression*, p. 190.
9. *De la Physionomie*, pp. 118–21.
10. *Mimik und Physiognomik*, p. 79.

CHAPTER X · HATRED AND ANGER

1. See some remarks to this effect by Mr Bain, *The Emotions and the Will*, 2nd edit., 1865, p. 127.
2. Rengger, *Naturgesch. der Säugethiere von Paraguay*, 1830, p. 3. Also in the dark chocolate-coloured Papuans of New Guinea: see N. von Miklucho-Maclay in *Natuurkundig Tijdschrift voor Nederlandsch Indie*, xxxiii, 1873.
3. Moreau and Gratiolet have discussed the colour of the face under the influence of intense passion: see the edit. of 1820 of Lavater, vol. iv, pp. 282 and 300; and Gratiolet, *De la Physionomie*, p. 345.
4. *Iliad*, i, 104.
5. *De la Physionomie*, 1865, p. 346.
6. *Oliver Twist*, vol. iii, p. 245.
7. *The Spectator*, 11 July, 1868, p. 819.
8. *Body and Mind*, 1870, pp. 51–3.
9. *Transact. Philosoph. Soc.*, Appendix, 1746, p. 65.
10. Hensleigh Wedgwood, *Dictionary of English Etymology*, 1865, vol. iii, pp. 240, 243.
11. *The Descent of Man*, 2nd edit., vol. i, p. 60.

CHAPTER XI · DISDAIN — CONTEMPT — DISGUST — GUILT — PRIDE ETC. — HELPLESSNESS — PATIENCE — AFFIRMATION AND NEGATION

1. *De la Physionomie et la Parole*, 1865, p. 89.
2. *Early History of Mankind*, 2nd edit., 1870, p. 45.
3. See, to this effect, Mr Hensleigh Wedgwood's Introduction to the *Dictionary of English Etymology*, 2nd edit., 1872, p. xxxvii.
4. As quoted by Tylor, *Primitive Culture*, 1871, vol. i, p. 169.
5. Both these quotations are given by Mr H. Wedgwood, *On the Origin of Language*, 1866, p. 75.
6. *Principles of Psychology*, 2nd edit., 1872, p. 552.
7. Gratiolet (*De la Phys.*, p. 351) makes this remark, and has some good observations on the expression of pride. See Sir C. Bell (*Anatomy of Expression*, p. 111) on the action of the *musculus superbus*.
8. *Anatomy of Expression*, p. 166.
9. *Journey Through Texas*, p. 352.
10. Mrs Oliphant, *The Brownlows*, vol. ii, p. 206.
11. *Essai sur le Langage*, 2nd edit., 1846. I am much indebted to Miss Wedgwood for having given me this information, with an extract from the work.
12. *On the Origin of Language*, 1866, p. 91.
13. 'On the Vocal Sounds of Laura Bridgman', *Smithsonian Contributions*, 1851, vol. ii, p. 11.
14. *Mémoire sur les Microcéphales*, 1867, p. 27.
15. Quoted by Tylor, *Early History of Mankind*, 2nd edit., 1870, p. 38.
16. Mr J. B. Jukes, *Letters and Extracts*, etc., 1871, p. 248.
17. Dr King, *Edinburgh Phil. Journal*, 1845, p. 313.
18. Tylor, *Early History of Mankind*, p. 53.

CHAPTER XII · SURPRISE — ASTONISHMENT — FEAR — HORROR

1. *Mécanisme de la Physionomie*, Album, 1862, p. 42.
2. *The Polyglot News Letter*, Melbourne, December 1858, p. 2.
3. *The Anatomy of Expression*, p. 106.
4. *Mécanisme de la Physionomie*, Album, p. 6.
5. See, for instance, Dr Piderit (*Mimik und Physiognomik*, p. 88), who has a good discussion on the expression of surprise.
6. Dr Murie has also given me information leading to the same conclusion, derived in part from comparative anatomy.
7. *De la Physionomie*, 1865, p. 234.
8. See, on this subject, Gratiolet, ibid., p. 254.
9. Lieber, 'On the Vocal Sounds of Laura Bridgman', *Smithsonian Contributions*, 1851, vol. ii, p. 7.

10. *Wenderholme*, vol. ii, p. 91.
11. Lieber, 'On the Vocal Sounds, etc.', ibid., p. 7.
12. Huschke, *Mimices et Physiognomices*, 1821, p. 18. Gratiolet (*De la Phys.*, p. 255) gives a figure of a man in this attitude, which, however, seems to me expressive of fear combined with astonishment. Le Brun also refers (Lavater, vol. ix, p. 299) to the hands of an astonished man being opened.
13. Huschke, ibid., p. 18.
14. *North American Indians*, 3rd edit., 1842, vol. i, p. 105.
15. H. Wedgwood, *Dict. of English Etymology*, vol. ii, 1862, p. 35. See, also, Gratiolet (*De la Physionomie*, p. 135) on the sources of such words as 'terror, horror, rigidus, frigidus', etc.
16. Sir C. Bell, *Transactions of Royal Phil. Soc.*, 1822, p. 308. *Anatomy of Expression*, p. 88 and pp. 164–9.
17. See Moreau on the rolling of the eyes, in the edit. of 1820 of Lavater, vol. iv, p. 263. Also, Gratiolet, *De la Phys.*, p. 17.
18. *Observations on Italy*, 1825, p. 48, as quoted in *The Anatomy of Expression*, p. 168.
19. [Hindoos change colour from fear, according to Dr Stanley Haynes, 1890.]
20. Quoted by Dr Maudsley, *Body and Mind*, 1870, p. 41.
21. *Anatomy of Expression*, p. 168.
22. *Mécanisme de la Phys. Humaine*, Album, légende xi.
23. *De la Physionomie*, pp. 51, 256, 346.
24. As quoted in White's *Gradation in Man*, p. 57.
25. *Anatomy of Expression*, p. 169.
26. *Mécanisme de la Physionomie*, Album, pl. 65, pp. 44, 45.
27. See remarks to this effect by Mr Wedgwood, in the Introduction to his *Dictionary of English Etymology*, 2nd edit., 1872, p. xxxvii.

CHAPTER XIII · SELF-ATTENTION – SHAME – SHYNESS – MODESTY: BLUSHING

1. *The Physiology or Mechanism of Blushing*, 1839, p. 156. I shall have occasion often to quote this work in the present chapter.
2. Quoted by Vogt, *Mémoire sur les Microcéphales*, 1867, p. 20. Dr Burgess: ibid., p. 56, doubts whether idiots ever blush.
3. Lieber, 'On the Vocal Sounds, etc.', *Smithsonian Contributions*, 1851, vol. ii, p. 6.
4. Ibid., p. 182.
5. *Moreau*, in edit. of 1820 of Lavater, vol. iv, p. 303.
6. Burgess, ibid., p. 38, on paleness after blushing, p. 177.
7. See Lavater, edit. of 1820, vol. iv, p. 303.
8. Burgess, ibid., pp. 114, 122. Moreau in Lavater, ibid., vol. iv, p. 293.

9. *Transact. of the Ethnological Soc.*, 1870, vol. ii, p. 16.

10. Humboldt, *Personal Narrative*, Eng. translat., vol. iii, p. 229.

11. Quoted by Prichard, *Phys. Hist. of Mankind*, 4th edit., 1851, vol. i, p. 271.

12. Quoted by Prichard, *Phys. Hist. of Mankind*, 4th edit., 1851, vol. i, p. 225.

13. See also Dr J. Crichton Browne's memoir on this subject in the *West Riding Lunatic Asylum Medical Report*, 1871, pp. 95–8.

14. In a discussion on so-called animal magnetism in *Table Talk*, vol. i.

15. Ibid., p. 40.

16. See, for evidence on this subject, *The Descent of Man*, 2nd edit., vol. ii, pp. 78, 370.

17. H. Wedgwood, *Dict. English Etymology*, vol. iii, 1865, p. 184. So with the Latin word *verecundus*.

18. Ibid., p. 50.

19. Bell, *Anatomy of Expression*, p. 95. Burgess, as quoted below, ibid., p. 49. Gratiolet, *De la Phys.*, p. 94.

20. On the authority of Lady Mary Wortley Montagu; see Burgess, ibid., p. 43.

21. *De la Phys.*, p. 283.

22. *Chapters on Mental Physiology*, 1858, p. 111.

23. *Mind and Brain*, vol. ii, 1860, p. 327.

24. *Chapters on Mental Physiology*, pp. 104–6.

25. See Gratiolet on this subject, *De la Phys.*, p. 287.

26. *The Lancet*, 1838, pp. 39–40, as quoted by Professor Laycock, *Nervous Diseases of Women*, 1840, p. 110.

27. *Chapters on Mental Physiology*, 1858, pp. 91–3.

28. *Elements of Physiology*, Eng. translat., vol. ii, p. 938.

29. Professor Laycock has discussed this point in a very interesting manner. See his *Nervous Diseases of Women*, 1840, p. 110.

30. See, also, Dr Michael Foster on the action of the vaso-motor system, in his interesting lecture before the Royal Institution, as translated in the *Revue des Cours Scientifiques*, 25 September 1869, p. 683.

CHAPTER XIV · CONCLUDING REMARKS AND SUMMARY

1. See the interesting facts given by Dr Bateman on *Aphasia*, 1870, p. 110.

2. *La Physionomie et la Parole*, 1865, pp. 103, 118.

3. Rengger, *Naturgeschichte der Säugethiere von Paraguay*, 1830, p. 55.

4. Quoted by Moreau, in his edition of Lavater, 1820, vol. iv, p. 211.

AFTERWORD

1. P. Ekman, *Darwin and Facial Expression: A Century of Research in Review*. New York: Academic Press, 1973.

2. G. Bateson and M. Mead, *Balinese Character: A Photographic Analysis*. New York Academy of Sciences, 1942.

3. R. Birdwhistell, *Kinesics and Context*. Philadelphia: University of Pennsylvania Press, 1970.

4. S. Tomkins, *Affect, Imagery and Consciousness, vol. 1, The Positive Affect*. New York: Springer, 1962; *vol. II, The Negative Affects*. New York: Springer, 1963.

5. P. Ekman and W. V. Friesen, *The Facial Action Coding System*. Palo Alto, CA: Consulting Psychologists Press, 1978.

6. *Charles Darwin's Letters, A Selection* (ed. Frederick Burkhardt), Cambridge: Cambridge University Press, 1996. Stephen Jay Gould's foreword, pp. ix–xx; quote from p. xviii. I am grateful to Nancy Etcoff for bringing this to my attention.

7. Phillip Prodger pointed this out.

8. The quotation, from *Sex and Temperament*, is cited by Carl Degler in *In Search of Human Nature*. Oxford University Press, 1991, p. 134.

9. M. Mead, *Blackberry Winter*. Kodansa International, 1995, pp. 220, 222. I am grateful to Professor Dale F. Lott, a wildlife biologist at the University of California, Davis, for bringing this passage to my attention.

10. Birdwhistell, op. cit., 29–30.

11. W. LaBarre, 'The Cultural Basis of Emotions and Gestures', *Journal of Personality*, *16*, 1947, 49–68.

12. O. Klineberg, *Social Psychology*. New York: Holt, 1940.

13. P. Ekman, 'Cross Cultural Studies of Facial Expression', in *Darwin and Facial Expression*, 169–222.

14. B. F. Skinner, *The Behavior of Organisms*. New York: Appleton-Century-Crofts, 1938.

15. P. Ekman and W. V. Friesen, 'Hand Movements', *Journal of Communication*, *22*, 1972, 353–74.

16. P. Ekman and W. V. Friesen, 'Nonverbal Leakage and Clues to Deception', *Psychiatry*, *32*, 1969, 88–105; P. Ekman, *Telling Lies: Clues to Deceit in the Market Place, Marriage, and Politics*. New York: W. W. Norton, 1985; second edition, 1992.

17. For a full treatment of these issues see my article, 'Expression or Communication about Emotion', in *Genetic, Ethnological and Evolutionary Perspectives on Human Development: Essays in Honor of Dr Daniel G. Freedman* (eds N. Segal, G. E. Weisfeld and C. C. Weisfeld). Washington, DC: American Psychological Association (1997).

18. Marvin Harris, *The Rise of Anthropological Theory*. Columbia University Press, 1968. The quote is from page 413.

19. Derek Freeman, *Margaret Mead and Samoa: the Making and Unmaking*

of an Anthropological Myth. Canberra: Australian National University Press, 1983.

20. Martin Orans, *Not Even Wrong. Margaret Mead, Derek Freeman and the Samoans.* Novato, CA: Chandler and Sharp Publishers, 1996; Hiram Caton, *The Samoan Reader: Anthropologists Take Stock.* Lanham, MD: The University Press of America, 1990; Lowell D. Holmes, *Quest for the Real Samoa. The Mead/Freeman Controversy and Beyond.* South Hadley, Mass: Bergin and Garvey Publishers, 1987.

21. See note 4.

22. C. Izard, *The Face of Emotion.* New York: Appleton-Century-Crofts, 1971.

23. I have chosen as the data set the findings listed and discussed by James Russell (see p. 389) ('Is There Universal Recognition of Emotion From Facial Expression? A Review of the Cross-Cultural Studies', *Psychological Bulletin, 115,* 1994, 102–41) in his attack on universality. A fuller account of how Russell misunderstood, misinterpreted and misrepresented the research findings is contained in my reply ('Strong Evidence for Universals in Facial Expressions: A Reply to Russell's Mistaken Critique', *Psychological Bulletin, 115,* 1994, 268–87). Usually only one group of people was studied in each country, but in some instances there were two or three; the total number of groups was thirty-one. I grouped together the different samples from the same countries, even though they had been gathered at different times, sometimes by different scientists.

24. P. Ekman, E. R. Sorenson and W. V. Friesen, 'Pan-Cultural Elements in Facial Displays of Emotions', *Science, 164,* 1969, 86–8; P. Ekman, W. V. Friesen, M. O'Sullivan, A. Chan, I Diacoyanni-Tarlatzis, K. Heider, R. Krause, W. A. LeCompte, T. Pitcairn, P. E. Ricci-Bitti, K. R. Scherer, M. Tomita and A. Tzavaras, 'Universals and Cultural Differences in the Judgments of Facial Expressions of Emotion', *Journal of Personality and Social Psychology, 53,* 1987, 712–17.

25. The other investigators were: C. Izard (see Note 22); T. Niit and J. Valsiner, 'Recognition of Facial Expressions: An Experimental Investigation of Ekman's Model', *Acta et Commentationes Universitatis Tarvensis, 429,* 1977, 85–107; J. D. Boucher and G. E. Carlson, 'Recognition of Facial Expression in Three Cultures', *Journal of Cross-Cultural Psychology, 11,* 1980, 263–80; L. Ducci, L. Arcuri, T. Georgis and T. Sineshaw, 'Emotion Recognition in Ethiopia', *Journal of Cross-Cultural Psychology, 13,* 1982, 340–51; F. T. McAndrew, 'A Cross-Cultural Study of Recognition Thresholds for Facial Expression of Emotion', *Journal of Cross-Cultural Psychology, 17,* 1986, 211–24.

26. Ekman, *et al.*, 'Universals and Cultural Differences in the Judgments of Facial Expressions of Emotion', loc. cit., 712–17.

27. J. F. Dashiell, 'A New Method of Measuring Reactions to Facial Expression of Emotion', *Psychological Bulletin, 24,* 1927, 174–5.

28. P. Ekman and W. V. Friesen, 'Constants across Cultures in the Face and Emotion', *Journal of Personality and Social Psychology*, 17, 1971, 124–9.

29. P. Ekman, 'Universals and Cultural Differences in Facial Expressions of Emotion', in J. Cole (ed.), *Nebraska Symposium on Motivation*, 1971. Lincoln, Neb.: University of Nebraska Press, 1972, 207–83. See also note 1.

30. See his book, *Ethology* (Holt Rinehart & Winston, 1970), and his article 'Human Ethology: Concepts and Implications for the Sciences of Man', *Brain and Behavioral Sciences*, 1979, 2, 1–57.

31. I am grateful to Gaedjusek and Sörenson for lending me this film and for providing facilities for my first trip to New Guinea in 1967. For my second trip in 1968 I was helped by Dr Neville Hoffman, an Australian public health doctor in the South Fore area during my first trip.

32. Presented in P. Ekman, 1972, see note 29.

33. ibid.

34. Published by Academic Press in 1973, 101 years rather than 100 years after Darwin's book, because Silvan Tomkins was so slow in writing his manuscript. Finally we went to press without him.

35. M. Mead, review of *Darwin and Facial Expression*, *Journal of Communication*, 25, 210.

36. Quoted by Degler, *In Search of Human Nature*, 137.

37. P. Ekman and W. V. Friesen, 'The Repertoire of Nonverbal Behavior: Categories, Origins, Usage, and Coding', *Semiotica*, 1, 1969, 76.

38. Both quotes are from 'Behavior Programs and Evolutionary Strategies', in *American Scientist*, 1974, vol. 62, 650–9. The quotes are from pp. 651, and 652 respectively.

39. Mead (see note 35), p. 211.

40. ibid.

41. A. Fridlund, *Human Facial Expression: An Evolutionary View*. San Diego, CA: Academic Press, 1994.

42. See note 17.

43. A Wierzbicka, *Semantics, Culture and Cognition*. New York: Oxford University Press, 1992.

44. See note 23.

45. D. E. Brown, *Human Universals*. Philadelphia: Temple University Press, 1991.

46. P. Ekman and W. V. Friesen, 'A New Pan Cultural Expression of Emotion', *Motivation and Emotion*, 10, 1986, 159–68; P. Ekman and K. G. Heider, 'The Universality of a Contempt Expression: A Replication', *Motivation and Emotion*, 12, 1988, 303–8.

47. D. Keltner, 'Signs of Appeasement: Evidence for the Distinct Displays of Embarrassment, Amusement, and Shame', *Journal of Personality and Social Psychology*, 68, 1995, 441–54.

48. For a fuller discussion see my article, 'An Argument for Basic Emotions', *Cognition and Emotion*, 6, 1992, 169–200.

49. A fascinating discussion of the head nod and head shake can be found in Roman Jakobson's *Language in Literature*, Harvard University Press, 1987, Chapter 28. I am indebted to Nancy Etcoff for bringing this to my attention.

50. R. I. Levy, *Tahitians: Mind and Experience in the Society Islands*. Chicago: University of Chicago Press, 1973. Also, Levy, 'The Emotions in Comparative Perspective', in *Approaches to Emotion* (eds K. Scherer and P. Ekman). Hillsdale, NJ: Lawrence Erlbaum Associates, 1984.

APPENDIX III

1. Oscar Rejlander, Letter to Charles Darwin, 15 December 1874. Darwin Manuscripts Collection, Cambridge University Library, Volume 176, Item 118. The punctuation of this passage has been altered slightly to make it easier to read.

2. *Photographic News*, 2 July 1875, cited in Edgar Yoxall Jones, *Oscar Rejlander: Father of Art Photography*. Newton Abbot: David & Charles, 1973, p. 38.

3. *Expression*, p. 32.

4. Darwin Manuscripts Collection, Cambridge University Library, Volume 53.1, especially Items 169–190.

5. Elsewhere I have argued that the layout of *Expression* helped to make it more palatable to Darwin's intended audience. See Phillip Prodger, 'Illustration as Strategy in Charles Darwin's *Expression of the Emotions in Man and Animals*', in *Inscribing Science: Scientific Texts and the Materiality of Communication* (T. Lenoir, ed.). Stanford: Stanford University Press, 1998.

6. Eadweard Muybridge (1830–1904) was certainly aware of Darwin's work, and began his experiments with animal motion the year after *Expression* was published. It seems likely Etienne-Jules Marey (1830–1904) also read it. Both are widely considered to have been instrumental in the invention of cinema. Muybridge may even have been guided in his study by a short article on the subject published by Oscar Rejlander following his work with Darwin. See Oscar Rejlander, 'On Photographing Horses', in *The British Journal Photographic Almanac*, 1873, 115.

7. For more on the role of Rejlander, Muybridge and Marey in the invention of cinema, see Phillip Prodger, 'The Romance and Reality of the Horse in Motion', in *Marey/Muybridge, Pionniers du Cinéma*. Dijon: Conseil Régional de Bourgogne, 1996, 44–71.

8. Adrian Desmond and James Moore, *Darwin: The Life of a Tormented Evolutionist*. New York: Warner Books, 1991, 594.

9. The portrait is in Ernest Walford's *Representative Men in Literature, Science and Art*, 1868.

10. William Henry Fox Talbot, 'The Art of Photogenic Drawing', 1839, reprinted in Vicki Goldberg (ed.), *Photography in Print*, Albuquerque: University of New Mexico Press, 1981, 41.

11. ibid.

12. Dry-plate collodion negatives were available from 1856, but would not have been used, as they required much longer exposure times. There were of course other processes which did not require the use of collodion, but these were also slow and even less suited to motion photography.

13. Rejlander published details of his own specially designed light-enhancing studio in 1863. See 'Mr Rejlander's Glass Room', *The British Journal of Photography*, 2 March 1863, 96–97.

14. *Expression*, p. 19.

15. For the whole of Darwin's collection, see Phillip Prodger, *Illustrations of Human and Animal Expression from the Collection of Charles Darwin*. Lampeter: Edwin Mellen Press, 1998.

16. Darwin refers indirectly to both these works in *Expression*. The footnote on p. 102 refers to Audubon, the first footnote on p. 238 refers to Hogarth.

17. Strictly speaking, *Mécanisme* contained an astonishing 228 photographic images, as it included 9 'synoptic' plates, each containing 16 miniature photographs which had been masked to point up various aspects of expression unclear in the large-format plates. An octavo version of the album was also published, which contained only the synoptic plates. Darwin had both versions of the book in his possession.

18. G. B. Duchenne de Boulogne, *The Mechanism of Human Facial Expression* (R. Andrew Cuthbertson trans.). Cambridge: Cambridge University Press, 1990, 42.

19. ibid., 43.

20. G. B. Duchenne de Boulogne, *Mécanisme de la Physionomie Humaine*. Paris: Jules Renouard, 1862. Marginalia from Darwin's copy in the Cambridge University Library.

21. For 'Erotomania', see Darwin Manuscripts Collection, Cambridge University Library, Volume 53.1, Items 20 and 30. For 'Homicidal Impulses', see Item 25.

22. Even this was probably not produced by Browne himself. A copy of this photograph in the collections of the University of Edinburgh is annotated 'F. W. Grierson'.

23. Charles Darwin, Letter to James Crichton Browne, 26 March 1871, Darwin Manuscripts Collection, Cambridge University Library, Volume 143.

24. Charles Darwin, Letter to James Crichton Browne, 8 June 1870.

25. *Expression*, p. 199.

26. Charles Darwin, Letter to James Crichton Browne, 1 April 1871, Darwin Manuscripts Collection, Cambridge University Library, DAR 143.

27. Darwin and Cameron were acquainted socially; Rejlander had taught Cameron the basics of photography some years earlier.

28. Named after Edward Jenkins's satirical novel. For more on the history of this particular piece, see Phillip Prodger, 'Darwin, Rejlander, and the Evolution of Ginx's Baby', *Journal of the History of Photography*.

29. Oscar Rejlander, Letter to Charles Darwin, 30 April 1871, Darwin Manuscripts Collection, Cambridge University Library, Volume 176, Item 115.

30. 'List of Illustrations', *Expression*, p. xii.

NOTES TO THE COMMENTARIES

c1. I am indebted for this quote and for his many insights to Richard W. Burkhardt Jr. The quote appears in Burkhardt's chapter, 'Darwin on Animal Behavior and Evolution', in *The Darwinian Heritage*, edited by David Kohn, Princeton University Press, 1985.

c1b. *The Autobiography of Charles Darwin*, W. W. Norton, 1969, p. 131.

c2. This quote is from page 313 of Darwin biographer Janet Browne's chapter 'Darwin and the Expression of the Emotions', in *The Darwinian Heritage*. I am grateful to Browne for her ideas about this and other matters and for very helpful conversations about *Expression*.

c3. *The Autobiography of Charles Darwin*, p. 72.

c4. *The Voyage of the Beagle*, Doubleday Anchor, 1962, p. ix.

c5. For a current and much more appreciative appraisal of Le Brun, see *The Expression of the Passions* by Jennifer Montagu, Yale University Press, 1994.

c6. P. Ekman, 'Felt, False and Miserable Smiles', *Journal of Nonverbal Behavior*, 4, 1982, 238–52.

c7. *The Mechanism of Human Facial Expression* by G.-B. Duchenne de Boulogne (A. Cuthbertson, editor and translator). New York: Cambridge University Press, 1990.

c8. P. Ekman and W. V. Friesen, *The Facial Action Coding System: a Technique for the Measurement of Facial Movement*. Palo Alto, CA: Consulting Psychologists Press, 1978.

c9. P. Ekman, W. V. Friesen, and M. O'Sullivan, 'Smiles When Lying', *Journal of Personality and Social Psychology*, 54, 1984, 414–20.

c10. C. Izard, C. Fantauzzo, J. Castle, O. Haynes, M. Rayias and P. Putnam, 'The Ontogeny and Significance of Infants' Facial Expressions in the First Nine Months of Life', *Developmental Psychology 31*, 1995, 997–1013; H. Oster, D. Hegley and L. Nagel, 'Adult Judgments and Fine-Grained Analysis of Infant Facial Expressions: Testing the Validity of a priori Coding Formulas', *Developmental Psychology*, 28, 1992, 115–31; H. Oster, 'Facial Expression as a Window on Sensory Experience and Affect in Newborn Infants', in P. Ekman and E. Rosenberg (eds), *What the Face Reveals: Basic and Applied Studies of Spontaneous Expression Using the Facial Action Coding System (FACS)*. New York: Oxford University Press (1997); L. Camras, 'Basic Emotions and Expressive

Development', *Cognition and Emotion*, 6, 1992, 269–84; L. Camras, 'Early Development of Emotional Expression', in K. Strongman (ed.), *International Review of Studies on Emotion*, vol. I, pp. 16–28, 33–6. New York: John Wiley & Sons, 1991.

C11. See R. B. Freeman and P. J. Gautrey, 'Charles Darwin's Queries About Expression', *The Bulletin of the British Museum*, 24, 1972, 207–19.

C12. M. Merzenich, 'Development and Maintenance of Cortical Somatosensory Representations: Functional "maps" and Neuroanatomical Repertoires', in K. E. Barnard and T. B. Brazelton (eds), *Touch; The Foundation of Experience*; Full Revised and Expanded Proceedings of the Johnson & Johnson Pediatric Round Table X. Clinical Infant Reports. Madison, CT: International Universities Press, 1990.

C13. A. Karni, G. Meyer, P. Jezzard, M. M. Adams, R. Turner and L. G. Ungerlelder, 'Functional MRI Evidence for Adult Motor Cortex Plasticity During Motor Skill Learning', *Nature*, 377, 1995, 115–58.

C14. C. Izard, *The Face of Emotion*. New York: Appleton Century-Crofts, 1971; D. Keltner and L. Harker, 'The Nonverbal Signal of Shame', in P. Gilbert and B. Andrews (eds), *Shame, Interpersonal Behaviour and Culture*. Oxford: Oxford University Press (in press).

C15. I have not published my findings on shame, but they are very well documented in my work among the South Fore of Papua New Guinea.

C16. S. Mineka, M. Davidson, M. Cook, and R. Keir, 'Observational Conditioning of Snake Fear in Rhesus Monkeys', *Journal of Abnormal Psychology*, 93, 1984, 355–72.

C17. C. Landis and W. A. Hunt, *The Startle Pattern*. New York: Farrar, 1939; P. Ekman, W. V. Friesen and R. C. Simons, 'Is the Startle Reaction an Emotion?' *Journal of Personality and Social Psychology*, 49, 1985, 1416–26.

C18. Burkhardt (see note C1).

C19. For an excellent modern discussion of signaling see W. John Smith, 'Consistency and Change in Communication', in G. Zivin (ed.), *The Development of Expressive Behavior*, San Diego, CA: Academic Press, 1985, pp. 51–75.

C20. J. C. Hager and P. Ekman, 'Long Distance Transmission of Facial Affect Signals', *Ethology and Sociobiology*, 1, 1979, 77–82.

C21. N. Frijda, *The Emotions*, Cambridge University Press, 1986.

C22. P. Ekman, R. W. Levenson and W. V. Friesen, 'Autonomic nervous system activity distinguishes between emotions', *Science*, 221, 1983, 1208–10; R. W. Levenson, P. Ekman and W. V. Friesen, 'Voluntary Facial Action Generates Emotion-Specific Autonomic Nervous System Activity', *Psychophysiology*, 27, 1990, 363–84.

C23. P. Ekman, 'An argument for basic emotions', *Cognition and Emotion*, 6, 1992, 169–200.

C24. K. R. Scherer, 'Vocal Affect Signaling: A Comparative Approach', in

J. Rosenblatt, C. Beer, M.-C. Busnel and P. J. B. Slater (eds), *Advances in the Study of Behavior*, vol. 15, pp. 189–244. New York: Academic Press, 1985.

c25. K. R. Scherer, 'Emotional Expression in Speech and Music', in J. Sundberg, L. Nord and R. Carlson (eds), *Music Language, Speech and Brain*. Wenner-Gren International Symposium Series, 1991, pp. 146–56, London: Macmillan.

c26. P. Ekman, W. V. Friesen and K. Scherer, 'Body Movement and Voice Pitch in Deceptive Interaction', *Semiotica, 16*, 1976, 23–7.

c27. P. Ekman, W. V. Friesen, M. O'Sullivan and K. Scherer, 'Relative Importance of Face, Body, and Speech in Judgments of Personality and Affect', *Journal of Personality and Social Psychology, 38*, 1980, 270–7.

c28. Amotz Zahavi, 'The theory of signal selection and some of its implications' in Vittorio Pesce Delfino (ed.), *International Symposium Biological Evolution*, Adriatica Editrice, 1987, 305–27. My quote is from page 314.

c29. T. H. Clutton-Brock and S. D. Albon, 'The Roaring of the Red Deer and the Evolution of Honest Advertisement', *Behavior, 69*, 1979, 145–70.

c30. E. S. Morton, 'On the Occurrence and Significance of Motivation-Structural Rules in Some Bird and Mammal Sound', *American Naturalist, 11*, 1977, 855–68.

c31. N. B. Davies and T. R. Halliday, 'Deep Croaks and Fighting Assessment in Toads Bufo Bufo', *Nature, 391*, 1978, 56–8.

c32. S. Chevalier-Skolnikoff, 'Facial Expression of Emotion in Nonhuman Primates', in P. Ekman (ed.), *Darwin and Facial Expression: a Century of Research in Review*. New York: Academic Press, 1973; W. K. Redican, 'An Evolutionary Perspective on Human Facial Displays', in P. Ekman (ed.), *Emotion in the Human Face*, 2nd edition. Cambridge: Cambridge University Press, 1982; S. Preuschoft, *'Laughter' and 'Smiling' in Macaques – an Evolutionary Perspective*, 1995.

c33. P. Prodger, 'Illustration as Strategy in Charles Darwin's *The Expression of the Emotions in Man and Animals*', in T. Lenoir (ed.), *Inscribing Science: Scientific Texts and the Materiality of Communication*. Palo Alto, CA: Stanford University Press (in press).

c34. P. Ekman, G. Roper and J. Hager, 'Deliberate Facial Movement', *Child Development, 51*, 1980, 886–91.

c35. P. Lersch, *Gesicht und Seele*. Munich: Ernst Reinhardt Verlag, 1932, republished 1971; A. Peiper, *Cerebral Function in Infancy and Childhood*, New York: Consultants Bureau, 1963.

c36. P. Ekman and W. V. Friesen, *Unmasking the Face: A Guide to Recognizing Emotions from Facial Clues*. New Jersey: Prentice Hall, 1975.

c37. J. C. Hager and P. Ekman, 'The Asymmetry of Facial Actions is Inconsistent with Models of Hemispheric Specialization', *Psychophysiology*, 22, 1985, 307–18.

c38. M. Frank and P. Ekman, 'Not All Smiles are Created Equal: The Differentiation Between Enjoyment and Nonenjoyment Smiles', *Humor*, 6, 1993, 9–26; M. Frank, P. Ekman and W. V. Friesen, 'Behavioral Markers and Recognizability of the Smile of Enjoyment', *Journal of Personality and Social Psychology*, 64, 1993, 83–93.

c39. See note c33.

c40. E. Hecker, *Die Physiologie und Psychologie des Lachens und des Komischen*. Berlin: Duemmler, 1973.

c41. W. Wundt, *Grundzüge der Physiologischen Psychologie (vol. 2)*. Leipzig: Engelmann, 1903 (originally published 1874).

c42. G. S. Hall and A. Allin, 'The Psychology of Tickling, Laughing, and the Comic', *American Journal of Psychology*, 9, 1897, 1–41.

c43. *The Mechanism of Human Facial Expression*, pp. 41–2 (see note c6).

c44. N. A. Fox and R. J. Davidson, 'Electroencephalogram Asymmetry in Response to the Approach of a Stranger and Maternal Separation in 10-Month-Old Children', *Developmental Psychology*, 23, 1987, 233–40; N. A. Fox and R. J. Davidson, 'Patterns of Brain Electrical Activity During Facial Signs of Emotion in 10-Month-Old Infants', *Developmental Psychology*, 24, 1988, 230–6.

c45. P. Ekman, R. J. Davidson and W. V. Friesen, 'The Duchenne Smile: Emotional Expression and Brain Physiology II', *Journal of Personality and Social Psychology*, 58, 1990, 342–53.

c46. John Gottman, personal communication, 1995.

c47. P. Ekman, 'The Argument and Evidence about Universals in Facial Expressions of Emotion', in H. Wagner and A. Manstead (eds), *Handbook of Social Psychophysiology*. Chichester: John Wiley Ltd., 1989, 143–64.

c48. See note 44 and note 45.

c49. P. Ekman, 'Expression and the Nature of Emotion', in K. Scherer and P. Ekman (eds), *Approaches to Emotion*. Hillsdale, NJ: Lawrence Erlbaum, 1984, 319–44; P. Ekman, 'An Argument For Basic Emotions', *Cognition and Emotion*, 6, 1992, 169–200.

c50. E. Rosenberg, P. Ekman and J. Blumenthal, 'Facial Expressions of Emotion Predict Transient Myocardial Ischemia in Coronary Patients' (manuscript under review).

c51. See Phillip Prodger, note c33.

c52. P. Ekman and Heider, K G., 'The Universality of a Contempt Expression: A Replication', *Motivation and Emotion*, 1988, *12*(4), 303–08.

c53. R. Plutchik, *The Emotions: Facts, Theories, and a New Model*. New York: Random House, 1962.

c54. S. Tomkins, *Affect, Imagery, Consciousness, vol. II, The Negative Affects*. New York: Springer, 1963; S. Tomkins, 'Affect Theory', in P. Ekman (ed.), *Emotion in the Human Face*, 2nd edition, Cambridge: Cambridge University Press, 1982.

c55. D. Symons, *The Evolution of Human Sexuality*. New York: Oxford University Press, 1979; D. M. Buss, 'Mate Preference Mechanisms: Consequences for the Partner Choice and Intrasexual Competition', in J. J. Barkow, L. Cosmides and J. Tooby (eds), *The Adapted Mind: Evolutionary Psychology and the Generation of Culture*, New York: Oxford University Press.

c56. P. Ekman, *Telling Lies: Clues to Deceit in the Marketplace, Marriage, and Politics*, second edition. New York: W. W. Norton, 1992.

c57. P. Ekman, 'About Brows: Emotional and Conversational Signals', in M. von Cranach, K. Foppa, W. Lepenies and D. Ploog (eds), *Human Ethology*. Cambridge: Cambridge University Press, 1979, 169–248.

c58. N. B. Blurton Jones and M. J. Konner, 'An Experiment on Eyebrow-Raising and Visual Searching in Children'. *Journal of Child Psychology and Psychiatry*, *11*, 233–40.

c59. A. Peiper, *Cerebral Function in Infancy and Childhood*. New York: Consultants Bureau, 1963.

c60. H. Oster, 'Facial Expression and Affect Development', in M. Lewis and L. Rosenblum (eds), *The Development of Affect*. New York: Plenum, 1978.

c61. I am grateful for the help of Ed Engle, University of Kentucky, for his advice on how muscle actions influence vision and for directing me to literature on this topic.

c62. P. Ekman, W. V. Friesen and R. C. Simons, 'Is the Startle Reaction an Emotion?' *Journal of Personality and Social Psychology, 49*, 1985, 1416–26.

c63. S. Tomkins, *Affect, Imagery, Consciousness: vol. 1: The Positive Affects*. New York: Springer, 1962, Chapter 13.

c64 P. Ekman, R. W. Levenson and W. V. Friesen, 'Autonomic Nervous System Activity Distinguishes Between Emotions', *Science, 221*, 1983, 1208–10; R. W. Levenson, P. Ekman and W. V. Friesen, 'Voluntary Facial Action Generates Emotion-Specific Autonomic Nervous System Activity', *Psychophysiology, 27*, 1990, 363–84; R. W. Levenson, P. Ekman, K. Heider and W. V. Friesen, 'Emotion and Autonomic Nervous System Activity in the Minangkabau of West Sumatra', *Journal of Personality and Social Psychology, 62*, 1992, 972–88.

c65. See note c33.

c66. M. Lewis, 'Self-conscious emotions: embarrassment, pride, shame and guilt', in M. Lewis and J. M. Haviland (eds), *Handbook of Emotions*. New York: Guilford Publications, 1993, 353–64. I am grateful to the American social psychologist Darwin Keltner for providing me with information about blushing and embarrassment, and for reference to much of the literature I cite.

c67. R. S. Miller and M. R. Leary, 'Social sources and interactive functions of embarrassment', in M. Clark (ed.), *Emotion and Social Behavior*. New York: Sage, 1992.

c68. See M. R. Leary and S. Meadows, 'Predictors, elicitors and concomitants of social blushing', *Journal of Personality and Social Psychology*, 60, 254–62.

c69. R. S. Miller, 'The nature and severity of self-reported embarrassing circumstances', *Personality and Social Psychology Bulletin*, 1992, *18*, 190–8.

c70. D. Shearn, E. Bergman, K. Hill, A. Abel and L. Hinds, 'Facial coloration and temperature response in blushing', *Psychophysiology*, 27, 6, 687–93. The quote is from page 691.

c71. B. H. Cohen, 'The motor theory of voluntary thinking', in R. J. Davidson, G. E. Schwartz and D. Shapiro (eds), *Consciousness and Self Regulation: Advances in Research and Theory*. New York: Plenum Press, 1986.

c72. For a review see M. I. Posner, 'Attention in Cognitive Neuroscience: An Overview', in M. S. Gazzaniga (ed.), *The Cognitive Neurosciences*. Cambridge, MA: MIT Press, 1995, 615–24.

c73. *Oxford English Dictionary*, Compact Edition, vol. 1, New York: Oxford University Press, 1971.

c74. S. Tomkins, *Affect, Imagery, Consciousness, vol. II, The Negative Affects*. New York: Springer, 1963; I. Borg, T. Staufenbiel and K. R. Scherer, 'On the Symbolic Basis of Shame', in K. R. Scherer (ed.), *Facets of Emotion; Recent Research*. Hillsdale, NJ: Erlbaum, 1988, 79–98; E. Goffman, *Interaction Rituals: Essays on Face-to-Face Behavior*. Garden City, NY: Anchor; G. Kaufman, *The Psychology of Shame; Theory and Treatment of Shame-Based Syndromes*. New York: Springer, 1989; E. Nathanson, *Shame and Pride; Affect, Sex, and The Birth of the Self*. New York: W. W. Norton, 1992.

c75. D. Keltner and B. Buswell, 'Evidence for the Distinctness of Embarrassment, Shame and Guilt: A Study of Recalled Antecedents and Facial Expressions of Emotion', *Cognition and Emotion*, *10*, 1996, 155–72; B. R. Schlenker and M. R. Leary, 'Social Psychology and Self-Presentation: A Conceptualization and Model', *Psychological Bulletin*, *92*, 1982, 641–69; C. Castelfranchi and I. Poggi, 'Blushing as Discourse: Was Darwin wrong?', in W. R. Crozier (ed.), *Shyness and Embarrassment: Perspectives from Social Psychology*. Cambridge: Cambridge University Press, 1990, 230–54; J. M. Sattler, 'Embarrassment and Blushing: A Theoretical Review', *The Journal of Social Psychology*, *69*, 1966, 117–33; J. P. Tangney, R. S. Miller, L. Flicker and D. H. Barlow, 'Are Shame, Guilt and Embarrassment Distinct Emotions?', *Journal of Personality and Social Psychology*, 70, 1996, 1256–69; J. Haidt and D. Keltner, 'Culture and Emotion: New Methods and New Emotions' (manuscript in preparation).

c76. L. R. Sherrod, 'Issues in Cognitive – Perceptual Development: The Special Case of Social Stimuli', in M. E. Lamb and L. R. Sherrod (eds), *Infant Social Cognition: Empirical and Theoretical Considerations*. Hillsdale, NJ: Lawrence Erlbaum Associates, 1981, 11–36; H. Oster, 'Recognition of Emotional Expression in Infancy?', in Lamb and Sherrod (eds), op. cit., 85–125; H. Oster, L. Daily and G. Goldenthal, 'Processing Facial Affect', in A. Young and H. Ellis (eds), *Handbook of Research on Face Processing*. Amsterdam: North Holland Press, 1989, 107–61.

INDEX

Page numbers in **bold** refer to Paul Ekman's Introduction, Commentaries and Afterword.

459

Hecker, E. **198**
Heiden, David **163**
Heider, Karl **381-3**
Heliotype Company **412-14**
Helmholtz **91**, 93, 95, 96, 97, 285
helplessness, shrug of 264-72
Henle, Jacob 85n, 150n, 256n; diagrams of facial muscles 179n, 201, **418**, Figs. 2-3; on physical effects of emotions 164-5n
Herbert, Sandra **xxvi**, **xxviii**
heredity: of acquired characteristics **xxxii-xxxiii**, 35, 45, 349, 351; of blushing 311-12, 343; and control of grief muscles 182-3; of habitual movements 14, 35-6, 39-40, 45, 48, 54, 60, 63, 212, 266-7, 308-9, 347-9; of opposite movements 60, 63, 67; and social behaviour **xxxiv**; use-inheritance **xxxii-xxxiii**, **xxxvn**, **36**
herpestes 100, 110, 111
hierarchies, social **58**
high spirits 210-12
Hindoos 38, 192, 207, 211, 220, 228, 229, 236, 238, 258, 275, 295, 315, 328
Hippocrates 36n, 76
hippopotamus 73, 77, 113
Hogarth, William **xvi**, 238n, 281, **404**, **422**, Fig. 21
Holbeach, H. 251n
Holland, Sir Henry 42, 43, 75n, 337, 339
Homer 195, 237; *Odyssey* 214
horror 146, 306-8, Fig. 31
horses: associated habitual movements 51; dilating of nostrils 129; drawing back of ears 113; fear 82; erection of hair 101; fighting 113; frisking 80, 81; galloping 118; nibbling 51; pain 77; pawing ground 51, 129; pleasure 129; savage 128-9; special expressions 128-9; starting 44, 129; tail position 117-18, 123-4; terror 129; vocal expression 88-9
Human Genome Project **xxxvi**
Humboldt, Alexander von 136, 317
humility 260, 264, 332-3, 344
humor 196-9
Huschke 288

Huxley, Thomas **xv**, 36n, 41n, **395-6**
hyaena 101, 123
hypochondria 184
hysteria 207

idiots, *see* insane
ill-temper 226-31, 234
illness 136, **393**
illustrations **xiv**, **xvi-xvii**, **xxixn**, 180-2, **400**;
concordance **417-23**; *see also* photography
imagination 258n; in horror 306; misleading nature of 18, 20, 24-5; and reflex actions 43-4; in terror 290
imitation 40, 348, 349, 351-2
impatience 129
impotence, shrug of 264-72
India 27, 186, 192, 244-6, 261n, 267-8, 280, 289, 315
indignation 22, 234, 242-5, 272, 288, 357, Plate 5
infants: absence of furrows 180; absence of tears 155-6, 165; blushing 310-11, 325; cold shouldering 231; crying 15, 146-56, 159, 174-5, 188, 222, Plate 1; denial 273; disgust 259; expression 20; frowning 221-2, 226; grief-muscles in **190**; guilt 261; laughter 195, 207; pain 146; pouting 228-9, 230; rage 236; recognition of expressions 353-4; screaming 146-7, 192, 221, 347, 348, 351; shrug 266; shyness 329-30; smiling and laughing 209-10; sobbing in 158; surprise in 284; upturned eyes during sucking 217
inflation of body 107-12
inheritance, *see* heredity
innate expressions **xxii**, 22, 348, 349; in animals 60-2, 124; astonishment/amazement 280, 287; and behaviorism **xxxiv-xxxv**; cultural relativism and **368-9**, **388**; nodding and shaking of head 273; shrug 267; Tomkins on **374**; *see also* instinctive behaviour
insane/idiots 20; blushing in 311, 313; brutal nature of 241; depression of mouth in 191; fear/terror in 293, 300; general paralysis of 204-5; grief-